COMPLETE HANDBOOK ON FROZEN FOOD PROCESSING AND FREEZE DRYING TECHNOLOGY

LIST OF PUBLICATIONS/BOOKS PUBLISHED BY

ENGINEERS INDIA RESEARCH INSTITUTE 4449, NAI SARAK, MAIN ROAD, DELHI - 6 (INDIA)

DAIRY FARMING & MILK PROCESSING & ICE CREAM

Name of Books	₹	US$
* Dairy Formulations Processes & Milk Processing Industries	750/-	75
* Milk Processing and Dairy Products Industries	750/-	75
* Hand Book of Dairy Farming	375/-	50
* Hand Book of Ice Cream Technology and Formulae	525/-	75
* H.B.Milk Processing, Dairy Products and Packaging Technology	975/-	100

HERBS CULTIVATION/MEDICINES

Name of Books	₹	US$
* Herbs, Medicinal & Aromatic Plants Cultivation	650/-	65
* औषधीयए वंस गन्धितप धोंक I व्यवसायिकक षिकरण(हिन्दी)	800/-	80
* Hand Book of Medicinal & Aromatic Plants	875/-	90
* Hand Book of Aromatic & Plants and Biodiesel (Jatropha)	1100/-	110

FOOD PROCESSING, PRESERVATION, FOOD DEHYDRATION, SNACK FOOD, MEAT PROCESSING

Name of Books	₹	US$
* Fruits & Vegetables Processing Hand Book	750/-	75
* Food Processing & Agro Based Industries	975/-	100
* Manufacture of Snacks Food, Namkeen,Pappad & Potato Products	750/-	75
* Agro Based and Food Processing with E.O.U	1300/-	130
* Preservation & Canning of Fruits and Vegetables	900/-	90
* Hand Book of Food Dehydration and Drying	650/-	65
* Meat Processing & Meat Products Hand Book	900/-	90
* Technology of Food Preservation and Processing	950/-	100
* Agro Based & Processed Food Products	1100/-	110
* Hand Book of Mushroom Cultivation, Processing & Packaging	550/-	60
* Potato & Potato Processing Technology	750/-	75
* Technology of Maize & Allied & Allied Corn Products	650/-	65
* Fruit Beverage & Processing with Mango Products	750/-	75
* Technology of Food Processing Indu.	975/-	100
* Technology of Sweets (Mithai) with Formulae	1050/-	105
* Citrus Fruits Cultivation and Processing Technology	1000/-	100

HOSIERY/TEXTILES/GARMENTS

Name of Books	₹	US$
* Hosiery, Ready-Made Garments & Textile Projects	1300/-	130
* Technology of Textiles (Spinning & Weaving, Dyeing, Scouring, Drying, Printing and Bleaching)	900/-	90
* Hand Book of Garments Manufacturing Technology	900/-	90

PRODUCT FROM WASTE

Name of Books	₹	US$
* Technology of Products From Waste	900/-	90

SOAP & DETERGENTS ACID SLURRY

Name of Books	₹	US$
* Household Soaps, Toilet Soaps & Other Soaps	750/-	75
* Profitable Small Scale Manufacture of Soaps & Detergents	375/-	40
* Hand Book of Synthetic Detergents with Formulations	900/-	90
* Modern Technology of Acid Slurry, Surfactants, Soap and Detergents with Formulae	900/-	90

COSMETIC (SYNTHETIC & HERBAL)

Name of Books	₹	US$
* Cosmetics Processes & Formulations Hand Book	900/-	90
* Herbal Cosmetics & Beauty Products with Formulations	750/-	75
* Profitable Small Scale Manufacture of Cosmetics (Synthetic & Herbal)	950/-	95
* Hand Book of Synthetic and Herbal Cosmetics	575/-	60
* Technology of Herbals Cosmetics & Toiletries Products with Formulae	1100/-	110

ESSENTIAL OILS & AROMATIC PLANTS

Name of Books	₹	US$
* Hand Book of Essential Oils Mfg. & Aromatic Plants	650/-	65
* Essential Oils Processes and Formulations Hand Book	650/-	65
* Modern Technology of Essential Oils	850/-	85
* Technology of Perfumes, Flavours & Essentials Oil	1175/-	120

PERFUMES AND FLAVOURS

Name of Books	₹	US$
* Hand Book of Perfumes & Flavours	600/-	60
* Technology of Perfumes & Flavours and Essential Oils	1175/-	120
* Hand Book of Perfumes with Formulations	750/-	75
* Hand Book of Flavour Technology	750/-	75
* Hand Book of Flavour & Food Colourants Technology	1400/-	140

OIL AND FATS

Name of Books	₹	US$
* Oils, Fats and Derivatives with Refining & Packaging Technology	950/-	95

BUILDING MATERIALS & CHEMICALS

Name of Books	₹	US$
* Technology of Building Materials & Chemicals with Processes	950/-	95

AGRO CULTIVATION, ANIMAL FARMING, AGRO PLANTATION & AGRO CHEMICAL/PESTICIDES

Name of Books	₹	US$
* Hand Book of Tree Farming	800/-	80
* Hand Book of Poultry Farming and Feed Formulations	450/-	45
* Hand Book of Pig Farming	400/-	40
* Agro Based H.B. of Plantation, Cultivation & Farming	500/-	50
* Agro-Based Plantation Cultivation & Farming	475/-	50
* Agro Based Industries (Plantation & Farming)	1300/-	130
* Technology of Modern Rice Milling and Basmati Rice	600/-	60
* Floriculture Hand Book (Flowers Growing Technology)	1000/-	100
* Hand Book of Goat Farming	450/-	45
* Modern Bee Keeping & Honey Processing	375/-	45

COMPLETE HANDBOOK ON FROZEN FOOD PROCESSING AND FREEZE DRYING TECHNOLOGY

Written By

Dr. Himadri Panda, Ph.D., F.I.C., F.I.C.S.

Industrial Consultant

Fellow of the Essential Association of India

Fellow of the Indian Pulp & Paper Technical Association of India

Fellow of the Indian National Science Congress

Fellow of the Oil & Colour Chemist's Association, U.K.

Member of Chinese Academy of Forests

Former Chemist, I.T.R. Co. Ltd., Bareilly (U.P.)

Former Chief Chemist (Q.C. & R & D) Tarpina Pvt. Ltd., Ramnagar, Uttrakhand

ENGINEERS INDIA RESEARCH INSTITUTE

4449, Nai Sarak, Main Road, Delhi - 110006 (India)

Ph: +91-11-23918117, 23916431, 23947058, 45120361

*** E-Mail: eiribooks@yahoo.com; eiriprojects@gmail.com**

***Website: www.eiriindia.org; www.eiribooksandprojectreports.com**

www.industrialprojectreports.com

PRINTED & PUBLISHED BY

ENGINEERS INDIA RESEARCH INSTITUTE

4449, Nai Sarak, Main Road, Delhi - 110006 (India)
Ph: +91-11-23918117, 23916431, 23947058, 45120361
* E-Mail: eiribooks@yahoo.com
*Website: www.eiriindia.org,
www.eiribooksandprojectreports.com
www.industrialprojectreports.com

Sole Distributors:

EIRI PROJECT CONSULTANTS AND PUBLISHERS
4/54 Roop Nagar, Delhi-110007

ISBN: 9789380772158

Printed in New Delhi (INDIA)

₹ 1000/-

Printed & Published by Sudhir Gupta for "Engineers India Research Institute", 4449 Nai Sarak, Main Road, New Delhi -110006

Preface

Frozen food has revolutionized the way people are able to receive and store foods like fruit, vegetables, convenience foods and meats. Based on freezing techniques from arctic communities, meats and fish were frozen in ice to last through the winter and was adopted to prevent spoilage in the 1700s and 1800s in the United States. While freezing and packaging technology has changed through the years, frozen food as we know it today was invented and popularized in the 1920s and 1930s.

Birdseye took the technique home to New York in 1922 and began experimenting with freezing food at a local refrigeration company. His result was quick freezing of packaged foods but consumer interest waned. In 1925 Birdseye patented a new invention, which froze food under pressure between belts pumped with a brine solution to freeze vegetables and meats in their packaging. This procedure allowed the frozen foods to be easily sold to consumers. The invention took off, and he sold his company, the General Seafood Co., and patents to Goldman Sachs and the Postum Co. The resulting corporation was food giant General Foods.

Commercial freezing is based on well established modern technologies and there can be no comparison of freezing with any other technology in keeping the original quality of food in tact. If most of the foods available in the western markets belong to the frozen category, the reason is that consumers have come to recognize that these products meet with their expectations fully. Further fillip to the frozen food industry was received when microwave heating system became omnipotent in almost all kitchens making it easier to thaw and reheat for consumption. The extraordinary success of frozen food industry in many rich countries is also attributable to the high per capita income, excellent transportation facilities, efficient nation-wide infrastructure, adequate storage facilities at homes and above all the predominance of animal based diet that cannot be preserved by other processes as efficiently as the freezing process.

Freeze drying is the process of dehydrating frozen foods under a vacuum so the moisture content changes directly from a solid to a gaseous form without having to undergo the intermediate liquid state through sublimation. In this process, the product maintains its original size and shape with a minimum of cell rupture. Removing moisture prevents a product from deteriorating at room temperature. The process is used for drying and preserving a number of food products, including meats, vegetables, fruits, and instant coffee products. The dried product will be the same size and shape as the original frozen material and will be found to have excellent stability and convenient reconstitution when placed in water.

Freeze dried products will maintain nutrients, colour, flavour, and texture often indistinguishable from the original product. Depending on the product and the packaging environment, freeze dried foods are shelf-stable at room temperature for up to twenty-five years or more, if canned, and between 6 months to 3 years if stored in a poly-bag container.

Benefits of Freeze-Drying

- Retains original characteristics of the product, including: colour, form, size, taste, texture and nutrients
- Reconstitutes to original state when placed in water
- Shelf stable at room temperature - cold storage not required
- The weight of the freeze-dried products is reduced by 70 to 90 percent, with no change in volume
- The product is light weight and easy to handle
- Shipping costs are reduced because of the light weight and lack of refrigeration

- Low water activity virtually eliminates microbiological concerns
- Offers highest quality in a dry product compared to other drying methods
- Virtually any type of food or ingredient, whether solid or liquid, can be freeze-dried

This book describes the current frozen food processing and freeze drying technologies to preserve food and the best practices to ensure production of safe, high-quality frozen food and it's transportation including colour, form, size, taste, texture and nutrients etc.. It also points to some new technologies that are already making waves and are likely to cast an even greater impact on the frozen food industry in the future.

Author

Contents-cum-Index

LIST OF PUBLICATIONS/BOOKS PUBLISHED BY

ENGINEERS INDIA RESEARCH INSTITUTE 4449, NAI SARAK, MAIN ROAD, DELHI - 6 (INDIA)

Name of Books	₹	US$
EXPORT ORIENTED INDUSTRIES/PROCEDURES		
* Hand Book of Export Oriented Industries	1300/-	130
SPICES & COLD STORAGE		
* Hand Book of Spices & Packaging with Formulaes	750/-	75
* Start Your Own Cold Storage Unit	750/-	75
TEXTILE AUXILIARIES & CHEMICALS		
* Textile Auxiliaries and Chemicals with Processes and Formulations	950/-	95
* Modern Technology of Bleaching Dyeing Printing and Finishing of Textiles	750/-	75
PHARMACEUTICALS & DRUGS		
* Pharmaceuticals and Drugs Technology with Formulations	950/-	95
LEATHER & LEATHER PRODUCTS		
* Hand Book of Leather & Leather Products Technology	850/-	85
BIOTECHNOLOGY/BIOFERTILIZERS		
* Hand Book of Biotechnology	900/	90
* Hand Book of Biofertilizers and Vermiculture	900/-	90
AYURVEDIC MEDICINES		
* Ayurvedic & Herbal Medicines with Formulaes	750/-	75
* Hand book of Ayurvedic Medicines with Formulation	900/-	90
RUBBER & RUBBER INDUSTRIES		
* Rubber Chemicals & Processing Industries	400/-	40
* Technology of Rubber & Rubber Goods Industries	900/-	90
* Modern Rubber Chemicals Compounds and Rubber Goods Technology	1500/-	150
MINERAL & MINERALS		
* Hand book of Minerals and Minerals based Industries	975/-	100
FISH FARMING		
* Hand Book of Fish Farming and Fishery Products	650/-	65
ORGANIC FARMING/FOOD		
* Hand Book of Organic Farming & Organic Foods with Vermi-Composting and Neem Products	1100/-	110
PULP & PAPER BASED TECHNOLOGY		
* Hand book of Pulp & Paper, Paper Board and Paper Based Technology	1150/-	115
STEEL / S.S./ NON FERROUS METALS		
* Modern Technology of Non Ferrous Metals and Metal Extraction	1100/-	100
* Processing Technology of Steels and Stainless Steels	1900/-	190

MULTIPLE PROJECT REPORTS IN CD-ROM AT ECONOMY COSTS

Title	₹
* 92 New Lucrative Project Reports in Cd	25,000/-
* 45 Infotech/IT, Hospitality, Hospital, College, School & Clubs	16,000/-
* 23 Profitable Construction Projects	16,000/-
* 56 Agro Based & Food Process Projects	16,000/-
* 52 Food, Dairy, Bakery, Confectionery & Snacks Foods	16,000/-
* 100 Profitable Plastic, Polymers & Allied Projects (100 Project Reports)	25,000/-
* 45 New Chemicals & Allied Reports	18,000/-
* 44 Textile, Garments, Hosiery & Allied	16,000/-
* 23 Dairy Farming (Buffaloe & Jersey Cows), Dairy Products and other Milk Processing Industries	16,000/-
* 42 Paper & Pulp, Paper Board and Paper Converting Industries	18,000/-
* 31 Essential Oils, Perfumes, Flavours & Aromatic Compounds	16,000/-
* 63 Profitable Packaging & Allied Projects	16,000/-
* 36 Profitable Printing & Allied Projects	16,000/-
* 28 Surgical & Disposable Medical Projects	16,000/-
* 99 Profitable Printing & Packaging Projects	25,000/-
* 42 Electroplating, Anodizing & Allied Proj.	16,000/-
* 31 Profitable Plantation, Cultivation & Farm	18,000/-
* 55 Profitable Projects from Agro and other Industrial Wastes	18,000/-
* 35 Gums, Adhesives, Sealants & Resins	18,000/-
* 43 Iron, Steel, Casting, Fabrication, Wire Drawing & Rolling Mills Projects	18,000/-
* 54 Paint, Varnish, Solvents, Lacquers, Enamels, Thinner & Powder Coating Proj.	18,000/-
* 26 Educational Projects (Schools, Colleges, Management/Training Institutes etc.)	16,000/-
* 12 Mosquitoes Preventive Projects (Coils, Mat, Liquids, Agarbatti, Nets, Spray etc.)	12,000/-
* 52 Cosmetics (Herbal & Synthetics) Technology Projects (52 Proj. Reports)	18,000/-
* 67 Rubber & Rubber Goods Industries	18,000/-
* 21 Bakery & Allied Project Reports	12,000/-
* 37 Aluminium & Aluminium Based Ind.	16,000/-
* 14 Potato & Potato Based Industries	12,000/-
* 50 Electrical, Electronic & Computer/IT Based Industries (50 Project Reports)	18,000/-
* 5 Power Plant Projects (Thermal, Hydro, Solar, Wind Energy & Lignite Coal Based)	16,000/-
* 35 New Profitable Industries (35 Reports)	16,000/-
* 10 Molasses Based Lucrative Projects	16,000/-
* 24 Fruits/Veg. & Allied Food Dehydration Proj.	16,000/-
* 24 Soap and Detergents	18,000/-
* 30 Chemicals, Mechanicals, Packaging and other Profitable Projects	16,000/-
* 43 Automobile and Automobile Based Projects	18,000/-
* 160 New Export Oriented Units & Most Profitable Projects (160 Project Reports)	30,000/-
* 5 Ginger and Ginger Based Industries	12,000/-
* 13 Fish Farming & Fishery Projects	16,000/-
* 9 Tea Plantation & Processing Industries	15,000/-
* 14 Roasted/Salted, Cashewnuts, Almonds, Namkeens and Spice Projects	15,000/-
* 28 Fruit Juice, Food Dehydration & Allied	16,000/-
* 6 Agarbatti and Allied Projects	15,000/-
* 23 Injection Moulded Plastic Projects	15,000/-
* 38 Biofertilizer, Biofuel, Enzyme, Organic Farming, Protein & Allied Projects	18,000/-
* 11 Infotech/IT Lucrative Projects	16,000/-
* 11 Solar & Solar Based Projects	15,000/-
* 42 Hospitality, Building Materials, Power, Steels, Alcohol & Other Food Products	18,000/-
* 10 Coconut & Coconut Bye Products	16,000/-
* 22 Alcohol, Beer, IMFL, Country Liquor, Wine & Other Related Projects	22,000/-
* Food Processing & Agro Proj.	30,000/-

1

Freezing of Fruits and Vegetables

The benefits of eating fruits and vegetables are well recognised by the general consumers. Fruits and vegetables are key parts of a proper daily diet, resulting from being great sources of vitamins, mineral salts and dietary fibres with health-promoting or disease-preventing properties.

Fruits and vegetables are perishable foods with extremely rapid deterioration; this means that their stability after harvesting and during sub-sequent storage is critical. Preservation of foods usually involves technologies that prevent microbial growth as well as retard quality degradation reactions. Among such processes, freezing is a proven and efficient method. For vegetables, freezing is widely recognised as the most satisfactory method for long-term preservation, and it is an important segment of the frozen food market. The market for frozen fruits is rising slowly. They may suffer from the image of being second best, when compared to fresh or chilled produces. However, the growing consumer demand for healthy products that ease busy lifestyles, with little meal preparation and shopping, makes frozen fruits a fashionable market.

Raw fruits and vegetables contain large quantities of water in proportion to their weight and, consequently, the water phase change occurring in freezing makes these products more susceptible to ice crystal formation and thawing than other types of food. Due to their cellular structural characteristics, fruits are less resistant to the freezing process than vegetables. Adding to these characteristics, the fact that frozen vegetables are most often consumed cooked, with thawing and cooking operations occurring simultaneously, make quality aspects less relevant for frozen vegetables than for frozen fruits. Consumers expect more from a frozen fruit. The attractive aroma, colour, texture and freshness are strong characteristics that are difficult to dissociate from the raw product, and hence the negative impact of freezing on fruit quality is huge.

Some novel methods for rapid freezing and thawing of foods, aiming at improving quality, have been applied in frozen food technology. In the particular case of fruits and vegetables, dehydrofreezing has been successfully used, since part of thewater is removed before freezing, thus being an advantage for plant texture preservation. Other techniques, yet expensive and challenging, such as addition of antifreeze proteins, may be applied aiming at controlling the growth of ice crystals and recrystallisation, and thus improving textural properties.

The impact of the freezing process on product quality is enormous. However, a large number of other factors may also contribute to the final frozen product characteristics. Factors such as product type and variety, degree of ripening, raw product quality, harvesting methods, elapsed time between harvesting and processing and pre-freezing treatments are some examples. All these factors, and/or their combinations, combined with packaging and storage conditions during the distribution chain, lead to difficulties in accurate prediction of frozen fruit and horticultural product quality.

In terms of safety, consumers have confidence in frozen products. Obviously, those safety records depend directly on the quality of the raw products prior to the freezing process, and on hygiene practices and standards along all process steps, storage and distribution. Food industries want to diversify and to innovate whilst maintaining high quality and safety levels. Currently, the challenge for the frozen food industry is to maintain a role for frozen products in a market where the consumer prefers fresh food. Frozen food fits well with changing consumer trends. This type of product allows great flexibility in meal preparation, and enables consumers to select healthy foods. Consumers have not only expected frozen food suppliers to meet their needs, for convenient and healthy food, but also to expand variety and improve its quality. Quality and safety aspects and traditional and innovative freezing technologies applied to fruits and vegetables will be examined further in the following sections.

QUALITY AND SAFETY OF FROZEN FRUITS AND VEGETABLES

Quality and safety are two major food issues. Quality is a broad concept, which embraces both sensory attributes readily perceived by the human senses (such as general appearance, texture, taste and aroma), and hidden attributes (such as nutritional value, chemical constituents, and mechanical and functional properties) that may involve quantification and instrumental measurements. Safety is related to chemical and microbiological characteristics of the product. Obviously, more than characteristics, quality and safety are requirements and standards of product excellence.

A huge variety of products are commonly named as 'vegetables'. This is not a botanical term and refers to the most diverse plant parts, such as roots (carrots), stems (asparagus), leaves (lettuce), flowers (broccoli), seeds (peas) and also fruits such as cucumbers and pumpkins. This great diversity of plant tissues and structures is one important influencing factor for the final frozen fruit and vegetable quality. Most vegetables, however, have fibrous structures that allow structural retention when they are thawed after freezing. On the other hand, fruits present softer structures, being physically much more susceptible to firmness loss. Quality and stability of frozen fruits and vegetables is influenced markedly by the Product itself, by the applied freezing Process and by Packaging. These factors are commonly referred to as PPP factors. These aspects are well documented in several handbooks of frozen foods.

Product influence

The raw material used in the preparation of frozen fruits and vegetables is an important influencing factor, affecting both physical characteristics and nutritive value of the final product. The suitability for freezing varies greatly with agronomic practices and conditions, the involved species and varieties, the degree of ripening, and the time elapsed between harvesting and processing.

It is also obvious that only raw material that is clean and sound should be selected for freezing, but this is not enough. The agronomic factors, including soil type, climatic conditions, irrigation, methods of cultivation, fertiliser composition and application, can and do have significant effect on the nutrient content and texture of the frozen product. It should be pointed out that most fruits and some vegetables intended for freezing are harvested at the same stage of maturity as for fresh consumption. However, the determination of the optimum maturity stage is very important for maximum quality retention of some species and varieties during frozen storage, particularly for fruits.

Another obvious quality loss source is the time elapsed between harvesting and freezing. Raw materials change with time and, unless careful handling, transportation, and storage procedures are used, the initial quality of the raw materials fed into a process may be lost. Products that undergo some rapid changes in chemical composition, sensory attributes and nutritional value and the ones with intense metabolism, directly related to high respiration heat, should be processed as quickly as possible. Sweet corn, green peas and asparagus are some of the most susceptible vegetable products, since a severe decrease in quality may occur if the time between harvesting and processing is long. Vegetables such as peas and lima beans, which are vined mechanically and badly bruised during the threshing process, may suffer rapid deterioration. Bruising during the vining operation brings about abnormal respiration, which is responsible for off-flavour production, just as if these vegetables had been under a low-oxygen atmosphere. Holding under refrigeration temperatures retards spoilage but, even so, they will not keep longer than 5 or 6 hours in good conditions, unless they are blanched.

In spite of the above-mentioned studies, little has been done to relate the structure and chemical composition of the rawtissue, to the organoleptic properties of the frozen fruit or vegetable products. Research into the specific mechanisms that produce these quality losses in individual products is required, as well as in the selection and breeding of varieties more adapted to the freezing process. Research workers should turn greater attention to these aspects, with the aim of expanding the number of available varieties suitable for the freezing process.

Process influence

Processing often results in a marked influence on the finished product. The following subtopics consider the stages of preparatory or pre-freezing treatments, where blanching is included, and the freezing process itself.

Pre-freezing treatments

Preparatory or pre-freezing treatments are usually necessary to obtain ready-to-use products and to provide the best preservation conditions. Grading, cleaning, sorting, removal of defective produce and inspecting, and in some cases peeling, shelling, trimming, chopping and slicing are the main common operations for fruits and vegetables. These operations reduce microbial load, remove foreign material and minimize product variation, but may also destroy the protective barrier provided by cellular compartmentation and allow oxygen access. The resulting effects include leaching of nutrients, browning, desiccation and interaction of enzymes, which can lead to loss of nutrients, and texture and colour changes.

Some endogenous enzymes are responsible for undesirable changes, such as off-flavours and odours, and colour and nutritive alterations, during frozen storage. The enzymes can be separated into four groups, related to changes in flavour, colour, texture/consistency and nutritional value. However, which are the enzymes responsible for quality deterioration in frozen vegetables, still remains a question. The amount of research work carried out trying to find a correlation between frozen vegetable's quality losses and its enzyme content is large. These deteriorative enzymes may have to be inactivated by applying particular treatments before the freezing step. Therefore, blanching is the most important pre-freezing treatment for vegetable tissues stabilisation. Blanching is a thermal treatment designed to inactivate a target enzyme to a given extent. Normally, peroxidase, followed by catalase, and in some cases polygalacturonase or lipoxygenase, are used as criteria, due to their higher resistance to thermal treatment. However, as mentioned above, there is no evidence that these enzymes are the main factors responsible for quality deterioration.

Blanching also affords a series of secondary benefits, which result from the complementary functions of washing, destroying vegetative cells of micro-organisms present on the surface, eliminating any remaining insecticide residues, enhancing the colour of green vegetables and eliminating off-flavours produced by gases and other volatile substances, that may have formed during the time between harvesting and processing. However, since blanching is a thermal treatment, detrimental effects exist, like alteration of plant tissue and consequent texture change, solubilisation and destruction of nutrients and vitamins in the blanching medium, loss of weight and colour changes, resulting in quality loss.

Due to these changes, research has also been carried out into possible alternatives that can replace blanching, without producing adverse effects on product quality. As a result of such research, some vegetables, with a high natural flavour, low enzymatic activity or when shorter frozen storage periods are envisaged, can be preserved without blanching. This is the case for onions, green peppers, parsley, leeks and cucumbers. Except for these few products, blanching remains an essential step in the freezing process for vegetables, and consequently research in this area should be continued, in order to optimize procedures and reduce the adverse effects on the final product quality.

In general terms, the optimisation of the blanching process implies:

- a careful characterisation of the raw material, since enzyme level depends on variety, maturity, and other factors;
- product analysis prior to blanching, to identify the enzyme levels within the tissue and estimate the required heat treatment to inactivate those enzymes responsible for deleterious changes in freezing and frozen storage;

- the selection of the most adequate blanching system, and;
- the understanding and quantification of the degree to which the physico-chemical and sensorial enzymatic changes occur during the process.

Fruits cannot be subjected to a blanching treatment, due to their tissue sensitivity. Therefore, alternative pre-treatments have to used, such as chemical treatments or use of additives, to inactivate deteriorative enzymes. Barbosa-C´anovas *et al.* (2005) compiled a freezing guide for fruits, but there is still a great need for research in this field, in order to obtain better quality products.

Freezing process

The process of freezing requires the controlled removal of heat from the product, at a steady uniform rate, until the heat remaining in the product is equal to its equilibrium after stabilisation. Besides the great number of species and varieties included in the category of fruits and vegetables, these products have in common a considerable amount of water in their constitution. This characteristic makes them very sensitive to water phase changes and, consequently, to quality deterioration.

The ice crystal formation that occurs during the freezing processes tends to disrupt cellular structure. Ice crystals begin to form in the extracellular medium and progress towards the cytoplasm, after the cell membrane has lost its permeability. The ice crystals' growth causes cells to decompartmentalise, which does not allow the return of the water to the intracellular medium during thawing. Consequently, the turgidity of the cells is affected and texture may suffer pronounced damage. These alterations may also promote drip loss while thawing. Fruit tissues, being more delicate, are particularly susceptible, and the impact of freezing on cell turgidity and firmness can be disastrous.

In conclusion, the colour, flavour, taste, texture and aroma *bouquet* of fresh fruits and vegetables is affected strongly by the freezing technology, and these characteristics determine the product quality excellence and therefore they should be preserved. The freezing process involves several stages (Fig. 1.1).

The first stage – pre-freezing stage:

(a) corresponds to the removal of heat from the food during the cooling period, when the temperature is reduced to the freezing point. This initial freezing temperature varies with product, depending on the moisture content. During this initial period sensible heat is removed from the product.

The second stage – super-cooling

(b) when the temperature falls below the freezing point, is essentially transitory and not always observed.

The third stage – freezing stage

(c) is the period of transformation of water into ice, throughout the whole mass of food. During this stage, the temperature remains constant in an ideal system, but in real situations falls slowly and continually while latent heat is extracted. The transformation of water into ice is an example of crystallisation. Crystallisation is the formation of a systematically organised phase from a solution. The crystallisation process consists of nucleation and crystal growth. Nucleation is the association of molecules into

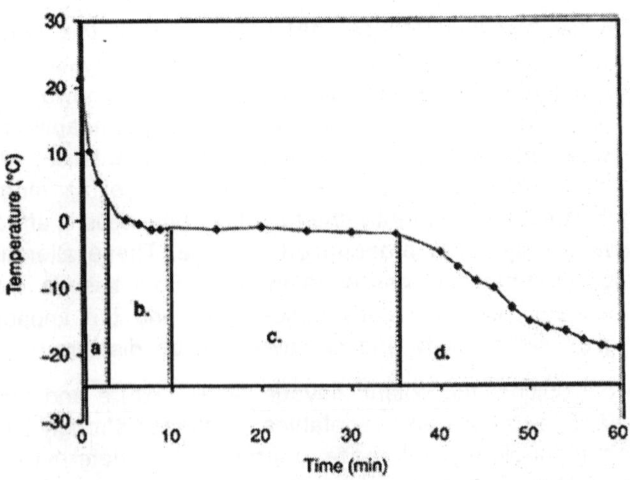

Fig. 1.1. Typical temperature of a product throughout the freezing process.

a tiny ordered particle of a size sufficient to survive and serves as a site for crystal growth. Crystal growth is simply the enlargement of the nucleus by the orderly addition of molecules.

The last stage – sub-freezing stage

(d) is the period where the product temperature is lowered to the end temperature, which should be the intended storage temperature. In this part of the process, mostly sensible heat is removed. The freezing time is affected by the product size (particularly thickness) and shape, composition of the fruit or vegetable, and by the parameters of the heat transfer process and the temperature of the cooling medium. Many attempts have been made to mathematically model the freezing process, therefore the freezing time can be theoretically predicted from the system physical parameters.

From a physical point of view, foods may be considered as dilute aqueous solutions, with a freezing point below 0°C. The freezing point depression is 1.86°C mol^{-1} L^{-1}, which means that the freezing point depends on the concentration of dissolved molecules in the water phase, and not only on the water content. In general, the temperature range which causes most irreversible changes is from about 1°C to –5°C. Therefore, during freezing, foods should pass this temperature range reasonably quickly. Tressler and Evers (1957) suggested that the solidification, the zone of the maximum crystal formation between 0°C and –3.9°C, must be passed in less than 30 minutes. It is a characteristic of frozen foods that a high proportion of the water content is ice, and it is also well-known that the quicker the cooling process is, the smaller the ice crystals will be. During the freezing of foods, ice crystals begin to form in the liquid between the cells, and the main reason is assumed to be the higher freezing point of this extracellular liquid, compared with the intracellular liquid. During slowfreezing, ice crystals grow between the cells making the extracellular liquid more concentrated. The cells will lose water by osmosis, and this leads to an extensive dehydration and contraction of the cells. The result is, relatively few large ice crystals in between shrunken cells. On the other hand, during rapid freezing, heat is removed so quickly that there is little time for dehydration of the cells, and ice crystals will also be formed in the cells. The distribution and size of frozen food's ice crystals has been the subject of many investigations. It is easy to imagine that a slowly frozen product will lose a certain amount of water during thawing, simply because the water may be unable to return to its original position. It is equally easy to conclude that no such problems arise in a rapidly frozen product. Therefore, quick freezing leads to small ice crystals and superior quality of the frozen foods, specially frozen plant materials.

During the freezing process,water is converted into ice crystals with a high degree of purity, leading to a concentrated solution of salts, minerals, and other substances. The concentration extent depends on the product, the end temperature, and also on the freezing rate. This increased solutes concentration often causes a pH change, usually towards the acid side, that can influence product quality.

Freezing may also cause physico-chemical changes, such as loss ofwater-binding capacity, resulting in drip loss; protein changes, leading to toughening or dryness; and loss of turgour. Many of these changes increase with increasing water-phase solute concentration, but may at the same time decrease with colder freezing temperature.

Different kinds of cell damage can occur in the freezing processes, depending on the rate of heat removal and the water permeability. The pre-freezing stage brings an increase in the permeability of the tissue membranes, with a final loss of intracellular pressure, but the irreversible adverse effects of freezing on quality are the result of crystallisation. Researcher stated that these changes are due to ice formation, rather than to the decrease in temperature *per se*.

The water volume increase, caused by the change of state of water into ice, depends mainly on the free water content in tissues and the amount of gas in their intercellular spaces. Through the expansion, caused by freezing of water, cell tissues will be exposed to strong mechanical forces. Due to the volume increase, intercellular ice development forces the cells apart, rupturing the middle lamellae and tearing the cell wall. Therefore, freezing causes disruption of the cell membranes, considerable cell disorganisation, the major result being usually a loss in tissue firmness.

Related to the freezing rate, as an example, researchers concluded that for potato low freezing rates promoted more mechanical damage than fast freezing. But confusion exists about the real influence of freezing rate on quality of frozen foods. It seems that for many products the effects, which may be caused by different freezing rates, are not big enough. In most vegetables, where freezing follows blanching, the freezing rate is of minor importance, because blanching induces marked structural changes. The number of studies available in the literature about the effect of freezing *per se,* on the nutrient components and changes in fruits and vegetable pigments is very limited. Lopez and Williams (1985) determined the effect of freezing on the concentration of essential elements, such as cadmium and lead in frozen green beans, and concluded that there were fewer changes. Jansen (1969) reported little or no effect of freezing rate on ascorbic acid and vitamin B in peas and snap beans.

Packaging influence

The packaging has a determinant role on frozen fruits and vegetables quality preservation, by protecting the food from external contamination or deterioration that may occur along the distribution chain from producer to consumer. Therefore, the main packaging function is product preservation. In addition to that, an attractive package with a good design projects an image of quality.

At the same time, the packaging material cannot affect and/or contaminate the food, and the choice of the material has to be in line with the existing legislation. The materials employed in packages for frozen foods should, first of all, possess all the usual features normally required for food packaging, namely: they should be chemically inert and stable; odour-free and not permeable to odour; free of toxic substances, that could be absorbed; impermeable to water vapour, volatile substances, and external odours; mechanically transformable into the appropriate size and shape for display in retail sales; easy to open; attractive; and able to afford protection against microbial contamination. In addition to those requirements, packaging materials should be shaped in such a way as to promote rapid freezing of the product inside, yet resistant to food products expansion during freezing. They should also be: impermeable to liquids; resistant to moisture, weak acids and low temperatures; reflective and as opaque as possible; and permeable and resistant to microwave energy, in those cases in which reheating or cooking may be done in microwave ovens.

Frozen fruits and vegetables have their own special requirements for preparatory treatments and packaging. Certain products are particularly fragile, calling for packages that can withstand the compression and shocks during production. Ultraviolet radiation, to a wavelength of 500 nm, can also catalyse certain chemical reactions that may give rise to significant colour changes, in the case of chlorophyll-containing vegetables, and makes the use of opaque packaging materials essential.

Frozen fruits and vegetables can undergo significant dehydration during storage, as a result of storage temperatures fluctuations, and water permeability of packaging. Such dehydration is irreversible, giving rise to ice formation inside the package and exerting detrimental effects on quality (changes in colour and flavour, freezer burn, increased risk of oxidation and structural deterioration). Consequently, during storage packages should ideally be air-tight, totally impermeable to water vapour, and effective as thermal insulators to limit possible temperatures fluctuations within the product.

There are numerous papers dealing with the mechanical and physical properties of packaging material, but relatively few with the effect of packaging type on the quality and stability of frozen fruits and vegetables.

Safety

Nowadays, due to the global market and consumer behaviour, the occurrence of microbiological outbreaks is common. Nevertheless, frozen foods are generally recognised as safe. The freezing and frozen storage under proper conditions do not affect significantly the microbial level, and the frozen foodstuff's final safety record depends mainly on the quality of the raw materials, thawing conditions and final handling by consumer.

The spoilage of fresh fruits and vegetables can be caused by microbial activity. The rich nutrient composition and high water activity of these products make them attractive substrates for micro-organisms to grow. Soil and improper irrigation waters are prime sources of contamination. If the contaminants are pathogenic bacteria, viruses or parasites, consumers' health will certainly be at risk, since serious foodborne illnesses are associated with those micro-organisms.

In terms of spoilage, from a quality point of view, the genera *Bacillus*, *Clostridium*, *Corynebacterium*, *Cytophaga*, *Erwinia*, *Pseudomonas* and *Xanthomonas* are the most common bacteria. Fungi also adversely affect some produces. *Salmonella*, *Shigella*, *Escherichia coli*, *Listeria monocytogenes* and *Aeromonas* are the major threats to fruits and vegetables safety.

For maximum hazard control and consumer defence, this microbial flora should be inactivated before the freezing stage. Disinfectant washings, thermal (blanching) or alternative non-thermal treatments (such as ozonation, ultrasonication, UV-C radiation) may be applied to reduce the risk of final frozen product contamination.

In most processing plants, conveyer belts and other equipment are the chief source of microbial contamination. Therefore, continuous cleaning of the equipment and environment is a requirement. The freezing process *per se* affects microbial activity in foods as unfavourable conditions for microbial survival are involved (e.g. the low temperatures and the water phase change). However, this impact varies greatly with the type of micro-organisms and its physiological state, the type of fruit and vegetable and its composition, and the rates of freezing and thawing. The level of nitrates in foods has caused concern, because of potential toxicity, and high levels of nitrites may cause methaemoglobinaemia in infants. Several authors have demonstrated that the blanching treatment can reduce plant material nitrate content significantly. Blanching was shown to remove other contaminants, such as DDT (dichlorodiphenyltrichloroethane) and carbonyl residue, di-syston, adrin, heptaclor epoxide, and endrin.

TRADITIONAL FREEZING TECHNOLOGIES

As described before, the freezing process can be divided into two main phases, which are the pre-freezing treatments that include blanching processes, and freezing. The next sub topics summarise the traditional freezing technologies and give indications for innovative techniques, aiming at maximising the final frozen fruits and vegetables products quality.

Traditional preparatory treatments

The most common preparatory procedures for freezing fruits and vegetables are grading, selection, washing, peeling and, in some cases, shelling, trimming, chopping and slicing Washing cleans the product of dirt and impurities and removes pesticide residues. Beuchat (2000) reported that wash-water with about 5 ppm chlorine reduced microbial populations by more than 90%, from an initial population of 104-106 CFU g^{-1}. However, the efficacy of this operation depends on pH, temperature, type of product and diversity of micro-organisms. For example, it observed that dipping lettuce in water containing 300 ppm chlorine, reduced total microbial counts, by about 1000-fold, but had no effect on microbial counts on carrots.

Peeling, one of the most delicate pre-treatments, is performed industrially by abrasion, high-pressure steam or treatment with sodium hydroxide solution. The disadvantage of all these methods is the substantial raw material losses. After washing and peeling, the product may, depending upon the product type and variety, be subjected to other procedures such as shelling, chopping and slicing. All these operations must be carried out with the utmost care, under the most stringent hygienic conditions, in order to prevent product contamination and mechanical damage. The varying degree of complexity, and automation of the preparatory treatments, requires a thorough understanding of the mechanisms according to the product type, and further research studies are desirable, in order to improve quality and optimise procedures. Blanching is a thermal treatment, commonly applied to a variety of vegetables, with different objectives, the most important being to preserve and stabilise the products through enzyme in activation. Blanching may be carried out in boiling water, steam, or in a combination of both. The product is heated typically by brief immersion in water, to a temperature between 85°C and 100°C and for times of about 1–10 minutes, depending on the product requirements, or in steam up to 100°C.

Mechanical arrangements to obtain uniform heating of all pieces, and control of piece size, is important, to shorten the heating time for adequate blanching. The relative merits of steam and water blanching have been widely studied. Although some disagreement exists, the consensus seems to be that retention of soluble nutrients is higher in steam-blanched than in water-blanched vegetables, due to less leaching losses. As described before, being a thermal treatment, blanching always presents a negative impact, and actual research is directed towards innovative technologies that try to maximise final product quality.

Traditional freezing methods

Because it is not very meaningful to compare freezing times for products of vastly different size, the concept of freezing rate has been introduced. Freezing rate can be expressed in several ways. Temperature change per time unit, e.g. °C s^{-1}, is sometimes used, but the temperature change will vary considerably from the surface to the centre, thus making this approach less useful for characterising certain freezing processes. Freezing rate is normally expressed, therefore, as the average velocity at which the ice front advances from the surface to the thermal centre. When depth is measured in centimetres and freezing time in hours, the freezing rate is expressed in cm h^{-1}. The freezing methods may be characterised by the freezing rate (Table 1.1), and the usual categories are:

- Ultra-rapid freezing may be achieved by freezing small-sized products in liquid nitrogen, or carbon dioxide (cryogenic freezing).
- Rapid freezing can take place in fluidised-bed freezers and plate freezers.
- Normal freezing is found in most air-blast freezers.
- Slow freezing is found during air-blast freezing of foods in cartons.

- Very slow freezing can result when the air speed around the product, in a blast freezer, is too low, or when the air temperature is not much low, or a product is frozen in too large units.

Barbosa-C´anovas *et al.* (2005) presented a systematic review on the available equipment for freezing of fruits and vegetables.

Table 1.1 Freezing rate of different freezing methods

Freezing methods	Freezing rate (cm h^{-1})
Ultra rapid freezing	Over 10
Rapid freezing	1-10
Normalfreezing	0.3-1
Slow freezing	1.0–0.3
Very slow freezing	less than 0.1

Air-blast and multi-plate freezers are most widespread, while air fluidising systems are used for IQF (individual quick freezing) of small products. Cryogenic IQF is more restricted, because of the high price of the liquefied gases. However, the need for longer shelf-life and improved product taste and quality has motivated the development of this type of equipment.

Air fluidisation (IQF) was studied extensively and has been increasingly used commercially, during the last 40 years. This freezing process has many attractive features, including:

- High freezing rate due to the small product size and thermal resistance of the IQF products, and high surface heat transfer coefficients;
- Good quality of the frozen products that have an attractive appearance and do not stick together;
- Continuity and possibilities for complete automation of the freezing process. Notwithstanding these advantages, fluidisation freezing by air has some drawbacks as well, such as:
- Lower surface heat transfer coefficients and freezing rates in comparison to immersion methods;

- Need for a high-speed and pressure air flow, that results in high fan energy consumption;
- Some moisture losses from the product surface and a rapid frosting of the air coolers (evaporator), caused by the great temperature differential between the products and the evaporating refrigerant;
- Excessive sensitivity of the process parameters to the product shape, mass and sizes, which requires careful control, specific for each food commodity.

The immersion freezing in non-boiling liquid refrigerating media is a well-known method, having several important advantages: high heat transfer rate, fine ice crystal system in foods, great throughput, low investments and operational costs. The immersion applications have been limited, because of the uncontrolled solute uptake by the refrigerated products and operational problems with the immersion liquids (high viscosity at low temperatures, difficult maintaining the medium at a definite constant concentration and free from organic contaminants). Recent achievements in heat and mass transfer, physical chemistry, fluid dynamics and automatic process control make it possible to solve these problems and to develop advanced innovative immersion IQF systems. The selection of the most adequate system for a given product must be a balance between costs, quality and feasibility.

INNOVATIVE TECHNOLOGIES

Freezing is unquestionably the most satisfactory method currently available for long-term preservation of fruits and vegetables. The nutrient content is largely retained and the product resembles the fresh material more closely than thermally processed foods. However, as it has been described, some changes occur that are mainly textural, and to a smaller extent losses of nutrients, colour and odour. Therefore, there is a strong driving force to develop innovative research mainly dedicated to overcome the drawbacks of the required pre-treatments, specially blanching, and freezing process.

Innovative preparatory treatments

Developments have been mainly on systems that try to minimise thermal pre-treatments, or even avoid it, in order to better retain the original quality of the raw fruits and vegetables. Several patents exist for microwave blanching, both at atmospheric and higher pressures. The use of microwaves may not be generally advantageous in blanching, partly because of its characteristic non-uniform heating. It has been reported that microwaved vegetables were worse in colour than water or steam blanched green vegetables. Moreover, the use of microwave may not reduce significantly the operation time. However, some advantage is seen in the use of this system for vegetables of large cross-section, such as potatoes and brussels sprouts.

It seems that the optimisation of the system can involve the joint use of microwaves and steam, to raise the product temperature rapidly, followed by a holding time controlled by steam alone. However, there is still little information on the consequences of this alternative blanching on quality. The use of new blanching techniques, such as electro-conductive, is still very limited. This may be due to the high capital cost needed to replace current water blanchers, and to the fact that more work is required to show that product quality is higher, compared to conventionally blanched products. The increasing consumer demand for high quality standards has spurred the search for new and gentle processing technologies that prolong shelf-life without the detrimental effects caused by blanching. This fact promoted the search and the development of other methods, as efficient as blanching, to reduce the enzyme activity and microbial load on products. Non-thermal methods have emerged as attractive alternatives to conventional methods of thermal processing, and constitute challenging methods aiming at reducing pernicious effects of thermal methods, by preserving quality and nutritional attributes of fruits and vegetables, and yielding safe and less-perishable products.

The application of ozone, ultrasounds and ultraviolet (UV-C) irradiation are examples of non-thermal technologies that may have potential applications in the food industry. Because they do not use heat, these technologies are commonly designated as non-thermal technologies. Moreover, they consume small amount of energy, and appear much more economical and environment-friendly technologies.

Ozone is a gas molecules of which are formed by three oxygen atoms. In nature, this triatomic molecule is formed by the UV part (185 nm) of sunlight. Commercially, this molecule is obtained by submitting oxygen molecules to electrical discharges. This molecule is very unstable, and it rapidly dissociates, returning to its former oxygen form. Ozone is considered as a potent disinfecting agent, due to its high oxidation power. Studies show that ozone enables a fast inactivation of micro-organisms through the reaction with intracellular enzymes, nucleic material or membrane components, destroying the coating of spores or viral capsules. Disinfection is the most usual and known application of ozone. Some applications of ozone in the food industry include food preservation, surface hygienisation, sanitation, water disinfection andwastewater reutilisation Ozone, applied as a gas or in dissolvedwater, has been tested for the post-harvest treatments of fruits and vegetables, such as apples, oranges, berries, grapes, onions, lettuce and spices.

However, its use still presents some controversies, and its efficacy, concerning its application in foods, still needs to be further studied. Ultraviolet (UV) light occupies a wide band of wavelengths in the non-ionising region of the electromagnetic spectrum, between X-rays (200 nm) and violet part of visible light (400 nm). The germicidal range is in the region of short-wave UV (UV-C), with wavelengths between 200 and 280 nm, with 254 nm being the most lethal. Exposure to low doses of UV-C has been reported to reduce post-harvest decay of fruits and vegetables, with potential applications in the post-harvest industry. Ultrasound is defined as pressure waves with a frequency of 20 kHz or more. Ultrasound may be used at frequencies between 20 kHz and 10 MHz. Higherpower ultrasound, at lower frequencies (20–100 kHz), has the ability to cause cavitation, which has the capacity to inactivate microbes and enzymes.

Ultrasounds technology has been increasingly used in the food industry, either for analysis or for the modification of foods. Low-intensity ultrasound provides information about physical and chemical properties, and high-intensity ultrasound is normally used to physically and chemically change the properties of foods, such as emulsification, cell disruption, chemical reaction promotion, enzyme inhibition, meat softening and modification of crystallisation processes.

The single use of ultrasounds seems not to be effective in inactivating micro-organisms in foods. However, the conjoint application of mild temperatures may enhance the ultrasonication effect (thermosonication), with minor changes in terms of quality parameters, when compared to conventional thermal methods. Other combinations that also seem to be successful in terms of microbial and enzymatic inactivation are the manosonication and thermomanosonication, which combine the use of pressure, and pressure and temperature together with ultrasound, respectively.

Innovative freezing methods

Recent developments in freezing technology have been characterised mainly by improvements in process control to increase freezing rate and reduce costs. As explained, ice crystal nucleation and growth are one of the main causes of degradation of fruits and vegetables quality during freezing. Therefore, a series of strategies for controlling ice crystals in food have been attempted, and are listed below:

- *The inhibition of nucleation.* There is an attempt to reduce freezing temperature, with the benefits of minimising chemical and physical processes, without the deleterious effects of freezing and freeze concentration. This approach has been pursued by the Rich Corporation in a series of patents and products, where the freezing point has been lowered by introducing massive quantities of osmotically active materials.
- *The control of nucleation.* Since ice nucleation and growth are temperature-dependent rate processes, with optima at different temperatures, the relative rates of nucleation and growth of ice crystals maybe exploited, by the appropriate manipulation of the rates of heat transfer. Examples of novel techniques are high-pressure freezing and impingement jet freezing. High-pressure freezing promotes

instantaneous and homogeneous formation of ice throughout the whole volume of the product, and is one promising innovative technology to improve product's quality Impingement jet freezing, characterised by its high turbulence, results in a very rapid freezing process and less expensive method, compared to cryogenic freezing.

- *The control of ice crystal growth.* Crystals are desired, but of the right size. One approach may be to inhibit partially the accretion of water molecules at the ice interface. Alternatively, the presence and accumulation of micro- and macro-molecular additives may modify the diffusion/colligative properties at the ice crystal–water interface and, thereby, limit extensive ice crystal growth. Antifreeze proteins may be directly added to the product to lower the freezing temperature and slowrecrystallisation rate during frozen storage.
- *Exploitation of the glassy state.* This area has been the subject of a number of investigations. Researcher has observed that, depending on the rate of cooling in a system, the fraction of water in the ratio of vitrified to crystalline state will vary in a systematic fashion. Therefore, there is an obvious and exploitable correlation between the kinetics of ice crystallisation and the degree of cell damage, depending on whether the ice crystallises inside or outside the cells. An even more interesting development has been the conclusion of researchers, who have demonstrated that glassy temperature (Tg) is a function of molecular mass, and have discussed how the use of appropriate raw materials, in a formulated food product, allow us to manipulate Tg and, therefore, promote product stability.
- *Bacterial ice nucleation.* Bacterial ice nucleation, by strains of *Pseudomonas*, *Erwinia* and *Xanthomonas*, has been both detected and investigated since the 1970s, and it has been recognised as one of the major causes of frost injury in plants. These micro-organisms are very useful in such processes where ice nucleation is a limiting step. The application of these bacterial ice nucleators to the freezing of some model food systems, elevating nucleation

temperature, may reduce freezing times and improve the quality (e.g. the flavour and textural properties) of frozen foods.

- *Reduction of water content.* By reducing the product's water content, especially of fruits, the negative impact of freezing may be minimised. Dehydrofreezing is a promising new technology to reduce or avoid the negative phenomena that occurs in most frozen fruits and vegetables after storage and thawing.

2

Preservation of Fruits and Vegetables

Loss of weight in fresh fruits and vegetables due to moisture evaporation is an economic problem for both producers and retailers. In addition, the relatively short shelf life of more perishable foods, particularly fruits such as bananas, pears, grapes, pineapples, apricots, avocados, peaches, plums, melons, citrus fruits, berries, tomatoes, peppers and the like, causes economic loss due to spoilage.

Some fruits and vegetables can be somewhat protected from moisture loss and spoilage by the application thereto of wax films. However, this expedient has limited effectiveness and is sometimes objectionable from the consumer standpoint. Too, the application of wax films often adversely affects colour and flavor of foods such as bananas.

It is therefore a major object of this method to provide a new method for preserving fruits and vegetables without adversely affecting colour or flavor thereof.

Another object of the method is to provide a method for extending the shelf life of perishable fruits and vegetables.

A still further object of the method is to provide a method for reducing moisture loss from perishable fruits and vegetables after harvest.

These and other objects are accomplished in accordance with this method by treating fruits and vegetables with a protein precipitate. The protein precipitate is obtained by treating a protein-containing liquid with an anionic surface active agent to cause precipitation of protein. An aqueous solution of this protein precipitate is applied to fruits and vegetables such as by spraying or dipping the fruits and vegetables therein to preserve them. Fruits and vegetables treated with the protein exhibit reduced moisture loss and prolonged shelf life with normal development of colour and flavour.

The protein-containing liquid from which the protein precipitate is obtained is preferably an aqueous extract of a protein source material such as corn steep liquor, soy whey, cheese whey, corn gluten filtrate, wheat steep liquor, brewer's wort and the like. Precipitation of protein from the protein-containing liquid is achieved by adding to said liquid an anionic surface active agent containing not less than 8 carbon atoms. Generally, the anionic precipitant is used in amounts ranging from about 1 to 4 grams per liter of the protein-containing liquid. Examples of anionic precipitants are alkyl aryl sulfonates, in particular alkylbenzene sulfonates in which the alkyl group contains from 8 to 20 carbon atoms, e.g. dodecylbenzene sulfonate, octadecylbenzene sulfonate, higher aliphatic sulfates and sulfonates in which the aliphatic radical comprises from 8 to 20 carbon atoms, such as lauryl sulfate, heptadecyl sulfate, lauryl sulfonate; and higher fatty acid amides in which the acyl group contains from 8 to 20 carbon atoms, such as tallow fatty acid amide, cocoa fatty acid amide and the like. The sulfonates and sulfates referred to above are commonly used in the form of alkali metal sulfonates, in particular sodium sulfonates and sodium sulfates, although the corresponding salts of ammonium or organic bases, such as, e.g. ethanol amine, triethanol amine and the like may also be used.

In a presently preferred but optional embodiment, a plasticizer is incorporated in the aqueous solution of the protein precipitate which is utilized to preserve fruits and vegetables. The plasticizer employed is preferably a di- or polyhydroxyalkane, such as ethylene glycol, propylene glycol, glycerol, polyglycerol and other related di- or polyhydroxy compounds. Plasticizers, such as dimethyl-sulfoxide and ethanolamine, can likewise be employed.

As is known, corn steep liquor which is the aqueous extract obtained when corn is soaked in water containing sulfur dioxide, is a by-product of the corn wet milling industry and contains about 45-50% (dry basis) soluble protein measured as Kjeldahl nitrogen.

According to one specific preferred embodiment of the method, an aqueous extract of corn (corn steep liquor) containing about 7 to 10 grams per liter of a filter aid material is treated with an anionic precipitant such as sodium lauryl sulfate. The pH of the corn steep liquor is maintained preferably between pH 2 and pH 6 and most preferably between pH 3.2 and pH 3.6. The sodium lauryl sulfate is used in amounts of from about 1.0 to 4.0 grams per liter of corn steep liquor. The resulting precipitate is recovered by filtration or centrifugation, washed with water (pH 4) and redissolved in dilute sodium hydroxide at a pH from about 7.0 to 10.0 and preferably between pH 7.5 to 8.5. Other alkali or alkaline salts such as ammonium hydroxide, calcium hydroxide, sodium carbonate and the like can be used in lieu of the sodium hydroxide. The protein content (Kjeldahl nitrogen X 6.25) of the solution after removal of the filter aid is preferably high, such as above about 80%, dry basis, and depends upon the level of sodium lauryl sulfate employed and the effectiveness of the washing of the precipitate. The protein precipitate can be recovered in dry form by known freeze drying or spray drying techniques.

For the preservation of fruits and vegetables in accordance with the method, a 1 to 10% by weight, preferably 3 to 4% by weight, solution of the protein precipitate dissolved in water is utilized. The pH of this preserving solution is preferably maintained at about 7.5 to about 8.0. The preserving solution is applied to the fruits or vegetables such as by spraying or by dipping the fruits or vegetables into the solution for a few seconds and allowing the treated fruits or vegetables to air dry at room temperature. Although the amount of the protein preservative required per ton of fruit or vegetable varies with the size of the food item, texture of its surface and so forth, the generally effective range is between 0.1 and about 1.0 pound of protein product per ton of the fruit or vegetable. By treating fruits and vegetables with the preservative in accordance with this invention, the weight loss of the treated food is significantly reduced and shelf life is extended without adverse effect on the texture, appearance or flavor of the treated food.

The advantages of the method will be further apparent from the following methods.

Method 1

Green bananas were divided into four groups of four bananas in each group. Three of the groups were dipped in 3, 5 and 7% by weight aqueous solutions of protein precipitate resulting from treating corn steep liquor with sodium lauryl sulfate. The precipitate contained 82.3% protein on dry basis. The pH of the aqueous protein solution used to treat the bananas was 7.9. After dipping the bananas into the preserving solution, the bananas were allowed to dry in air and weighed. After treatment, the bananas were allowed to stand at room temperature for five days during which time weight loss and colour development were observed. These results are shown in Table 2.1.

TABLE 2.1

Day	Protein Level (pounds/ton)			
	0	0.3	0.47	0.73
		% weight loss		
2	3.03	2.49	2.50	2.79
3	4.47	3.79	3.98	4.03
4	7.76	5.90	6.67	6.49
5	11.56	8.94	9.58	9.20
Weight loss as % of control (5 days)	100	77	83	80

As the results show, the treated bananas lost weight and developed colour at a slower rate than the control bananas.

The control group was more yellow and had more black spots than any of the treated bananas.

Method 2

Green bananas were given a water wash and divided into three equivalent groups of four bananas each. Two groups were dipped into 3 and 10% by weight aqueous solutions of protein precipitated from corn steep liquor by sodium lauryl sulfate. The precipitate contained 79% protein on dry basis. The aqueous protein solution used to treat the fruit had a pH of 8. The untreated group was employed as a control. Each group was weighed daily and weight loss determined. Observations of colour change were made and scored on a basis of 1 to 8 as explained below:

1. green
2. light green
3. yellow-green
4. yellow
5. yellow with small dark spots
6. yellow with many dark spots
7. yellow with large dark spots
8. mostly dark

The results are given in Table 2.2 below:

Table 2.2

Day	Protein Level (pounds/ton)					
	0	0.3	1.0	0	0.3	1.0
	Color Score			% Weight Loss		
1	4	4	4	1.47	1.39	1.34
2	5	4	4	2.39	2.11	2.06
3	5+	4	4	3.89	3.03	3.20
4	6	4	4	7.66	5.91	6.63
5	7	5	5	8.92	6.97	7.70
6	7	5	5	11.16	8.47	8.76

After six days the following measurements were made.

	Protein Level (pounds/ton)		
	0	0.3	1.0
Banana Pulp, % Dry Solids	18.07	17.59	16.66
Flavor	Normal	Normal	Normal
Texture	Firm	Firm	Slightly soft
DE*	70.8	68.4	65.0

*DE = grams of reducing sugar expressed as dextrose per 100 grams of solids.

Moisture loss in the protein-treated bananas was between 76 to 78% of the control group. Color development was about two days behind that of the controls. Flavor and texture were normal in all cases.

Method 3

The same procedure as described in Methods 1 and 2 was employed except lower levels of the protein were used, the protein levels being 0.1, 0.2 and 0.3 pounds per ton. The results are shown in Table 2.3. In this test the weight loss of the treated bananas at 0.2 and 0.3 pounds protein per ton was approximately 90% of the control bananas. Color development in the treated bananas was about two days behind that of the controls. Flavor appeared normal in all groups after six days but texture of the control bananas and the bananas treated at the 0.1 pound per ton level was softer than the bananas treated at 0.2 and 0.3 pound per ton levels.

Table 2.3

	Protein Level (pounds/ton)		
	0	0.3	1.0
Banana Pulp, % Dry Solids	18.07	17.59	16.66
Flavor	Normal	Normal	Normal
Texture	Firm	Firm	Slightly soft
DE*	70.8	68.4	65.0

*DE = grams of reducing sugar expressed as dextrose per 100 grams of solids.

Method 4

Pears, grapes and pineapples were dipped in a 4% by weight aqueous solution of protein having a pH of 7.8. Corresponding untreated fruit were used as controls. The samples were allowed to stand at room temperature and the weight loss determined daily. The results of these tests are shown in Table 2.4.

TABLE 2.4

Day	Protein Level, pounds/ton					
	Pears		Grapes		Pineapple	
	0	0.6	0	0.8	0	3.3
	% Weight Loss					
1	0.90	0.85	1.80	1.65	2.07	1.93
2	1.76	1.67	3.41	3.10	3.96	3.68
4	3.46	3.17	5.79	5.21	6.86	6.43
5	4.05	3.71	6.89	6.18	8.63	7.84
6	4.99	4.54	8.03	7.21	10.10	9.06

After six days the following determinations were made:

Flavour	Normal	Unripe	Normal	Normal	Slightly tart	Sweet
Colour	Yellow	Green-yellow	Normal	Normal	Normal	Normal
Texture	Soft	Firm	Normal	Normal	Firm	Firm to slightly soft

Method 5

An aqueous extract of corn (corn steep liquor) containing about 7-10 grams per liter of a filter aid material is treated with sodium heptadecyl sulfate. The pH of the corn steep liquor is maintained preferably between 3 and 3.6 and the sodium heptadecyl sulfate is used in an amount of approximately 1.5 grams (dry basis) per liter of corn steep liquor. The resulting precipitate is recovered by filtration or centrifugation, washed with water and redissolved in dilute sodium hydroxide at a pH from about 7.0 to 10.0 and preferably between 7.5 and 8.5. The product obtained contains about 80.4% protein (dry basis) and the solids recovery is about 6.2% based on the original solids in the corn steep liquor. The protein is completely soluble in water above pH 7.5 and forms a clear, tough film on glass.

Method 6

One liter of cheese whey containing 10 grams of filter aid (Celite 505) maintained at a pH of 4.7 is treated with 2 grams of sodium lauryl sulfate. The resulting precipitate is recovered by filtration or centrifugation, washed with water and redissolved in dilute sodium hydroxide at a pH preferably between 7.5 and 8.5. The protein content (Kjeldahl nitrogen × 6.25) of the solution is about 65.4% protein (dry basis) and the solids recovery is about 10.1% based on original cheese whey solids.

Method 7

Forty grams of spray dried concentrate obtained from the ultrafiltration of soy whey is slurried in 800 milliliters of water and filtered to remove haze. Five hundred milliliters of the clear filtrate is adjusted to pH 3.8, five grams of filter aid (Celite 505) added and one gram of sodium lauryl sulfate added. The slurry is filtered, washed with water and redissolved in dilute sodium hydroxide at a pH between 7.5 and 8.5. The protein content of the solution is about 68.3% protein (dry basis) and the solids recovery is about 11.7% based on original spray dried concentrate. This material exhibits excellent film properties when spread on glass plates.

Method 8

Gluten filtrate obtained from the filtration of the corn gluten fraction in the wet milling processing of corn is maintained at a pH of 4 and treated with 10 grams/liter of Celite 505. To the slurry is added sodium lauryl sulfate (2 grams per liter). The resulting precipitate is recovered by filtration or centrifugation, washed with water and redissolved in dilute sodium hydroxide at a pH between 7.5 and 8.5. The protein content (Kjeldahl nigrogen×6.25) of the solution is about 73.1% (dry basis) and the solids recovery is about 7.7% based on original gluten filtrate solids. This material exhibits excellent film properties when spread on glass plates.

Method 9

Protein precipitates were obtained by adding to corn steep liquor, in one case, sodium lauryl sulfate, and in another case, by adding sodium heptadecyl sulfate. The precipitates were recovered and redissolved in an aqueous alkaline solution.

To 10 milliliter aliquots of the aqueous protein solutions were added varying amounts of glycerol. The aqueous solution of the sodium lauryl sulfate precipitate contained 4.4% solids and had a pH of 8.0, while the aqueous solution of the sodium heptadecyl sulfate precipitate contained 4.8% solids and had a pH of 8.4. The 10 milliliter aliquots were placed in aluminum pans and dried at 100° C. The results of observing the resulting films are shown in Table 2.5.

Similar results were obtained by the use of ethylene glycol, polyethylene glycol, erythritol, sorbitol, propylene glycol, ethanolamine and dimethylsulfoxide in place of glycerol. The glycol materials apparently act as a plasticizer to improve film properties.

Method 10

Bananas in a green condition were divided into six groups of six bananas each. The bananas were then dipped into aqueous solutions of protein precipitates, air dried and stored at room temperature. Weight loss and colour changes were recorded daily for seven days, after which texture and flavor were noted. In these tests "Capsul," a modified waxy maize starch product manufactured by National Starch Company was also tested with preserving agents of the invention. The results are shown in Table 2.6.

TABLE 2.5

Glycerol (% Protein Precipitate, Dry Basis)	Film Observations
Sodium lauryl Sulfate precipitate*	
0	Light green, hazy, many cracks
6	Tan-green, hazy, fewer cracks
11	Tan-green, hazy, fewer cracks
17	Tan-green, clear, few cracks
23	Tan-green, clear, no cracks
29	Tan-green, clear, no cracks
34	Brown, clear, no cracks
Sodium heptadecyl sulfate precipitate**	
0	Light tan, clear, many cracks
5	Light tan, clear, fewer cracks
10	Light tan, clear, fewer cracks
16	Light tan, clear, few cracks
21	Light tan, clear, few cracks
26	Light tan, clear, few cracks
31	Light tan, clear, no cracks

*All solutions containing glycerol turned turbid after standing overnight at room temperature.

**All solutions still clear to slightly hazy on standing overnight.

Method 11

Corn steep liquor was treated with sodium lauryl sulfate and a precipitate recovered therefrom. A preserving solution was obtained by dissolving the precipitate in water at pH 7.8 and at a solids level of 3.6%. Twelve tomatoes and seven peppers were dipped into the preserving solution and air dried and permitted to stand at room temperature (23° C.) for six days. Observations and weight loss data are shown below in Table 2.7.

TABLE 22.6

Group Description	1 Control	2 Solution A*	3 Solution B*	4 Capsul	5 Solution C*	6 Solution D*
Solution Solids, % w/v	0	4.09	4.23	25.4	4.00	4.87
pH		8.4	8.4	6	7.8	7.8
Pounds of Protein/ Ton of Bananas	0	0.32	0.33	8.14	0.42	0.38
Days			Weight Loss, %			
1	1.52	1.52	1.42	1.98	1.62	1.55
2	3.36	3.21	2.19	4.11	3.32	3.11
3	4.78	4.57	4.25	5.94	4.79	4.35
4	6.72	6.26	5.66	7.99	6.41	5.91
5	8.44	7.78	7.08	9.97	7.96	7.27
6	9.63	8.91	8.05	11.42	9.04	8.24
7	11.05	10.11	9.17	13.24	10.27	9.41

Group Description	1 Control	2 Solution A*	3 Solution B*	4 Capsul	5 Solution C*	6 Solution D*
				Colour		
0	2	2	2	2	2	2
1	3	2+	2+	3	2+	3
2	4	3	3	3	2+	3
3	5	4	3+	4	3	3+
4	6	4+	4	4	4	4
5	6+	5	5	4	4+	4+
6	7	5+	5	4+	4+	4+
7	7+	6	5	6+	5	5
Texture (7 days)	Soft	Firm	Firm	Soft	Firm	Firm
Flavor (7 days)	Normal (Slightly overripe)	Normal	Normal	Different	Normal	Normal

*Solution A Protein precipitated from cheese whey with sodium lauryl sulfate.
*Solution B Protein precipitated from corn steep liquor with sodium heptadecyl sulfate.
*Solution C Protein precipitated from corn steep liquor with sodium lauryl sulfate.
*Solution D Protein precipitated from corn steep liquor with sodium lauryl sulfate and containing glycerol.

TABLE 2.7

	Tomatoes		Peppers	
	Control	Treated	Control	Treated
Lbs. Protein Precipitate/Ton of Vegetable	0	0.33	0	0.67
Days	Weight Loss, %			
1	0.54	0.60	2.92 Wrinkled Appearance	2.74 Smooth
2	1.19	1.37	7.31 Wrinkled	6.60 Less Wrinkled
3	1.68	1.91	10.61	9.56
4	2.22	2.46	14.48	12.95
6	3.09	3.39	18.33 All Peppers Wrinkled	16.77 Two Still Smooth

Method 12

Corn steep liquor was treated with sodium lauryl sulfate and a precipitate removed therefrom. A preserving solution was prepared by dissolving the precipitate in water at a pH of 7.8 and at a solids level of 3.6%.

A comparative solution was prepared by dissolving zein in 90% isopropanol at a solids level of 3.6%.

Twelve bananas were dipped into each solution, air dried and allowed to stand at 23° C. for seven days. Observations and weight loss data are shown below in Table 2.8.

Method 13

Corn steep liquor was processed with twelve different anionic surfactants in the same manner as previously described for sodium lauryl sulfate. Solids recovery, protein content and film forming properties of the resulting products from each surfactant are recorded in the attached Table 2.9. Of the twelve surfactants examined, the following six gave the best results.

TABLE 2.8

	Control	Zein	SLS Corn Protein
Pounds of Protein Preserving Precipi-tate/Ton	0	0.51	0.32
Days		Weight Loss, %	
1	1.48	1.58	1.48
2	3.31	3.37	3.15
3	4.38	4.49	4.22
5	6.87 Many small, dark spots	6.94 Fewer spots than control	6.51 Had fewest spots
6	8.40	8.37	7.91
7	9.77 Dark	9.60 Less Dark	9.01 Best Looking

Treatment of Corn Steep Liquor with Anionic Surfactants

Trade Name	Manufacturer	Type	Conc. %	Level Used[a] ml/200 ml	Solids Recovery[b] %	Protein % DB	Film Properties On glass[c]	Film Properties Drying @100°C[d]	
W A Specials	Stepan Chemical Co.	Sodium lauryl sulfate	29	1.4	6.6	66.2	Good	Good	R = 12 carbon $R—SO_4Na$
Niaproof 4	Niacet Corp.	Sodium tetradecyl sulfate	27	1.5	6.4	67.2	Good	Good	R = 14 carbon $R—SO_4Na$
Niaproof 7	Niacet Corp.	Sodium heptadecyl sulfate	26	1.6	4.1	54.6	Good	Good	R = 17 carbon $R—SO_4Na$
Niaproof 08	Niacet Corp.	2-ethylhexyl sulfate	39	1.1	3.0	50.0	Good	Gcod	R = 8 carbon $R—SO_4Na$
Avirol 110	Henkel Corp.	Sodium n-decyl sulfate	30	1.4	5.8	68.2	Good	Fair	R = 10 carbon $R—SO_4Na$

Treatment of of Corn Steep Liquor with Anionic Surfactants

Trade Name	Manufacturer	Type	Conc. %	Level Used[a] ml/200 ml	Solids Recovery[b]	Protein % DB	Film Properties On glass[c]	Drying @100°C[d]	
Petrowet R	E.I. Du Pont de Nemours	Sodium alkyl sulfonate	22	1.9	4.3	55.3	Good	Fair	$R-SO_3Na$
Conco Sulfate C	Continental Chemical Co.	Sodium cetyl stearyl sulfate	30	1.4	11.2	14.4	Good	Fair	$R-SO_4Na$
Clindrol 206 CGN	Clintwood Chemical Co.	Coco alkanolamide	100	0.4	3.8	46.8	Good	Fair	$R_1-C(=O)-NR$
Conoco C550	Conoco Chemical Co.	Sodium alkylbenzene sulfonate	52	0.8	4.5	44.17	Good	Good	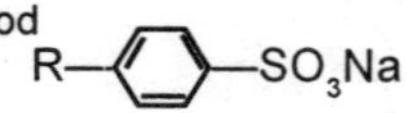
Carboxane TW-100	Henkel Corp.	Alcohol ethoxylate	100	0.4	2.8	43.01	Good	Fair	Reaction of alcohol with ethylene oxide
Calsolene Oil HSA	ICI	Sulfated fatty acid ester	45	0.9	4.5	67.42	Good, Hazy	Fair-good	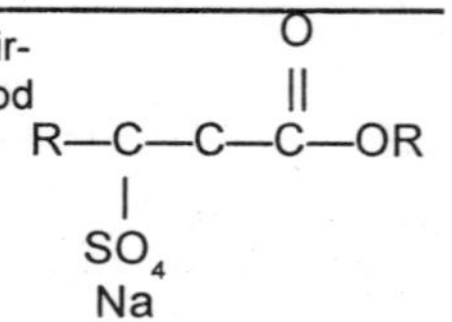

Conco Sulfate 219	Continental Chemical Co.	Sodium lauryl ether sulfate	4.5	53.0	Good, hazy	Good	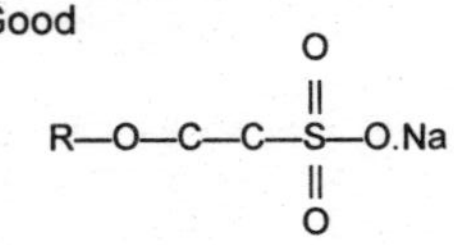
Corn Steep Liquor				46.1		No film	

a: Quantity equivalent to 0.41 g of active ingredient.

b: Based on dry solids in 200 ml of filtered corn steep liquor.

c: 0.1-0.2 ml of 3-5% solution spread on 8" .times. 8" glass plate with 0.001" Bird applicator.

d: Ten ml of 3-5% solution dried down at 100°C. in 2" aluminum pan.

3

Freezing of Vegetables

It is well-known to freeze a broad range of vegetables in freezers having operating temperatures from -25° C. to -50° C., for instance, band freezers, batch-freezers and fluidised bed freezers. The main advantages of such freezers are that the freezing time is very short and that the final product is free flowing.

Some food particles are, however, quite difficult to handle in such freezers. One reason is that the particles are very sticky. Another reason is that the particles absorb a good deal of water which results in poor fluidisation and a lot of frozen lumps. Although small lumps of less than 20 mm diameter are acceptable in most cases, large lumps are either wasted or they have to be thawed and refrozen which increases the processing costs. Typical examples of food products which are difficult or impossible to freeze in such freezers are boiled rice and blanched leafy vegetables such as onions, leek, parsley and spinach. At the present time such food products are preferably frozen in liquid freezants such as freon or nitrogen. However, liquid freezants are expensive and there are unavoidable losses to the atmosphere. In the case of freon, the risks of atmospheric pollution have been the subject of much discussion and there is a strong desire among food processors to avoid the use of freon as a liquid freezant.

We have now found, surprisingly, that boiled rice or blanched leafy vegetables can be frozen in such freezers to give a substantially non-lumpy free-flowing product if a certain amount of already frozen free-flowing product is intimately mixed with the unfrozen product before entering the freezer.

Accordingly, the present method provides a freezing boiled rice or a blanched leafy vegetable in a freezer having an operating temperature from -25° C. to -50° C. characterised in that before entering the freezer the unfrozen product is cooled and intimately mixed with from 20% to 80% by weight based on the weight of the mixture of already frozen free-flowing boiled rice or blanched leafy vegetable.

The freezer may be a band freezer or a batch freezer but the method of this method is most advantageously carried out in a fluidised bed freezer. Before being mixed with the already frozen product, the unfrozen product is preferably cooled in water or air to a temperature from 5° C. to 25° C. and especially from 7.5° C. to 20° C., and then it may advantageously be dewatered, for instance by mild pressing or in a vibrating dewatering screen. By "dewatered" we do not mean the removal of the natural cell-moisture content of the product as by heat-drying techniques. Preferably, the unfrozen blanched leafy vegetable is in the form of small pieces obtained, for instance, by dicing.

Preferably, the amount of already frozen product mixed with the unfrozen product is from 30% to 70% by weight and especially from 40% to 60% by weight based on the weight of the mixture. The mixing is advantageously carried out immediately before entry to the freezer. There are a variety of ways in which the frozen product may be mixed with the unfrozen product. For example, the mixing may be carried out in a mechanical mixing screw. Alternatively, it is possible to use air transport in a tube where the frozen and unfrozen products are fed by screws into the tube and the mixing is achieved during a few seconds transport in air. The temperature of the mixture as it enters the freezer is preferably from -5° C. to +2° C. and preferably from -3° C. to +1° C.

The temperature in the freezer during operation is conveniently from -30° C. to -45° C. and preferably from -32.5° C. to -42.5° C. The duration of the freezing may be from 2 to 10 minutes, preferably from 3 to 7 minutes and especially from 4 to 6 minutes.

After freezing, the temperature of the frozen product is generally from -20° C. to -35° C. and preferably from -25° C. to -30° C. A certain quantity of the frozen product is recirculated to be mixed with fresh unfrozen product and the remainder is collected.

In addition to providing a free-flowing product substantially free of lumps, another advantage of the method of this invention is the lower temperature of the product entering the freezer. Most products enter a fluidised bed freezer after having been cooled by air or water to a temperature of from 5° C. to 25° C. whereas in the method of the present invention the mixture of frozen and unfrozen product enters the freezer at a temperature around 0° C. or just below. A product frozen in a fluidised bed always loses some water by evaporation and this water condenses in the cooling battery which has to be defrosted regularly, resulting in a loss of freezing capacity and energy. The water evaporation is reduced by the method of the present invention and therefore, there is not only less condensation in the cooling battery but also an increased product yield.

The following methods further illustrate the present method.

Method 1

Long grain rice was fed by a screw and pumped into an inclined thermoscrew which was partially filled with water. The rice was blanched in water for 8 minutes and then in steam for 2 minutes. The blanched rice was pumped in cold water until the temperature fell to 15° C. and then pumped to a vibrating screen for dewatering. From the screen the rice fell into a mixing screw. Frozen product was transported by another screw from the outfeed end of a fluidised bed freezer to the mixing screw where it was mixed with the unfrozen rice in a 50:50 ratio for 1 minute. The mixing screw was used to feed the mixture directly into the infeed end of the fluidised bed freezer in which the mixture was frozen for 5 minutes at a temperature from -35° C. to -40° C.

At the start of the process, a certain quantity of prefrozen free-flowing rice was mixed with unfrozen rice to fill up the fluidised bed freezer. After freezing, some of the rice was collected in sacks and the remainder was recirculated via a screw to be mixed with fresh unfrozen product. The temperature of the frozen rice was -28° C.

After 8 hours, 600 kg of frozen rice were obtained and the rice was screened to measure the amount of lumps. The screen was designed to separate lumps having a diameter of 20 mm or more and no such lumps were present in the frozen sample.

Method 2

A similar procedure to that described in Method 1 was followed but in which the ratio of unfrozen to frozen rice was 46:54. No lumps having a diameter of 20 mm or more were present in the final frozen sample.

Method 3

A similar procedure to that described in Method 1 was followed but in which the ratio of unfrozen to frozen rice was 52:48. No lumps having a diameter of 20 mm or more were present in the final frozen sample.

Method 4

A similar procedure to that described in Method 1 was followed but instead of rice, diced onion was used which was blanched in steam for 1 minute in the thermoscrew. Only 1% of lumps having a diameter of 20 mm or more were found to be presentin the final frozen sample.

Comparative Method A

A similar procedure to that described in Method 1 was followed but in which no frozen free-flowing rice was added back and mixed with the blanched unfrozen rice. The amount of lumps having a diameter larger than 20 mm was found to be 14% Byweight Of The Total Weight Produced.

Comparative Method B

A similar procedure to that described in Method 4 was followed but in which no frozen free-flowing onions were added back and mixed with the blanched unfrozen diced onions. The amount of lumps having a diameter larger than 20 mm was found to be10.1% by weight of the total weight produced.

4

Frozen Block Process for Vegetable or Fruit Convenience Foods

A growing segment of the frozen food industry is the preparation of convenience foods and "finger foods". These foods are usually specially prepared so that the purchaser saves much time in final preparation for eating. An illustration of convenience food is frozen french fried potatoes which may be oven heated by the purchaser because the original processor blanched them in oil. Other examples come to mind, like frozen complete dinners, frozen breaded fish portions, and the like.

Finger foods is the term generally given in the related art to battered, breaded bite-sized portions, chunks or elongated sticks which may be prepared by a variety of methods suitable for finger selection by the individual consumer.

Heretofore convenience foods utilizing vegetables or fruit have entered the market within the last decade or so, and have been developed and presented to the consumer in basically two different types of "finger foods". One type of vegetable or fruit finger foods includes individual vegetable or fruit pieces in their natural state which are either battered, breaded and frozen or battered, breaded, deep fat fried to set the coating and impart oil and frozen to be reheated by the purchaser.

The list of such natural food products includes for example onion rings, mushrooms, zucchini slices, cauliflower buds, clarets or heads, eggplant slices and chunks, apple and pineapple slices. However, several problems continue to plague the processor and increase his costs in the processing of this type of finger food product. One is the fact that many vegetables and/or fruit pieces may vary excessively in size, so that the processor must sort and pack into various size ranges to please the consumer. Even when sorting, the processor oftentimes cannot pack by count and rely on accuracy in weight, so he must pack by weight, which means the packer must select various sizes of the food product in an effort to arrive at the desired weight, which is costly in labor because it requires judgment by the workers. Another problem is that individual vegetable pieces are difficult to arrange on high speed processing lines so that the arranging becomes still more labor intensive. Another problem is that a substantial quantity of the vegetable or fruit product in its natural state cannot be used because, even though the food is wholesome and nutritious, it may be unattractive in size, shape, texture, etc.

A second type of vegetable or fruit finger foods is for the processor to take vegetable or fruit pieces which may include scraps which, heretofore have been discarded as waste but which are still wholesome for human consumption, and to thoroughly mix them with a suitable binder, well known in the art, into a porridge-like mixture. This mixture is then extruded into a shape that, in an effort to gain consumer acceptance, is oftentimes made to simulate the shape of the vegetable or fruit in its natural state. As will be appreciated, the taste of such extruded product is not particularly characteristic of the "natural taste" of the food product per se but rather to a significant degree is characteristic of and dependent upon the binder used which the consumer finds unattractive and unacceptable.

Heretofore the assignee of the present method has utilized a process using fish and poultry products in which individual frozen pieces of fish or poultry are placed into a suitable press and compressed under substantial pressure into a frozen block. Because fish and poultry are known to be inherently high in protein, it is believed that during this compression, weeping or protein secretion occurs which enables the individual pieces to adhere to each other to form the frozen food block as well as in subsequent cooking of the food pieces.

To the present time in the food processing industry it has been generally believed that this frozen block process is not adaptable to other products such as vegetables and/or fruits and like products by reason of their lacking the type of protein found in fish or poultry.

As will be hereinafter explained in greater detail, the applicants hereof have discovered a new and novel process heretofore unknown in the related art for making vegetable and fruit finger foods, which process incorporates therein the formation of a frozen block of vegetables and/or fruit and the like and wherein the raw vegetable or fruit food material, in its natural and frozen state, constitutes all or substantially all of the food product that is in the end "finger food" product resulting from this process. The term "raw vegetables" is hereinafter identified to be the products presently available in the frozen food department of a typical market which conventionally may be either raw or blanched, i.e. partially cooked.

Referring to Figs. 4.1 and 4.2, a comparison may be made between a present conventional processing line 100 for vegetable processing for the two types of finger foods as heretofore mentioned and the block processing line of this invention 200, both lines producing convenience type "finger food" pieces which are coated with batter and breading, which may be deep fat fried, and then individually quick frozen before packing. Numerals assigned to the various operating stations are the same in each Figure when the operating stations are identical. Thus it may be seen that the main differences in the two processing lines, 100 and 200, lie in the piece preparation between wash-and-trim 12 and coat-with-batter 30, and piece packaging between freeze 36 and pack-mastercarton 50.

In each processing line 100 or 200, identical facilities for receiving raw vegetables at a station identified at 10 are provided, along with facilities for temporary cold-cool storage at a station 11 to retard spoilage before use. Such facilities at all stations in both processing lines may be interconnected by suitable conveying apparatus, such as a conventional mesh-belt type of conveyor

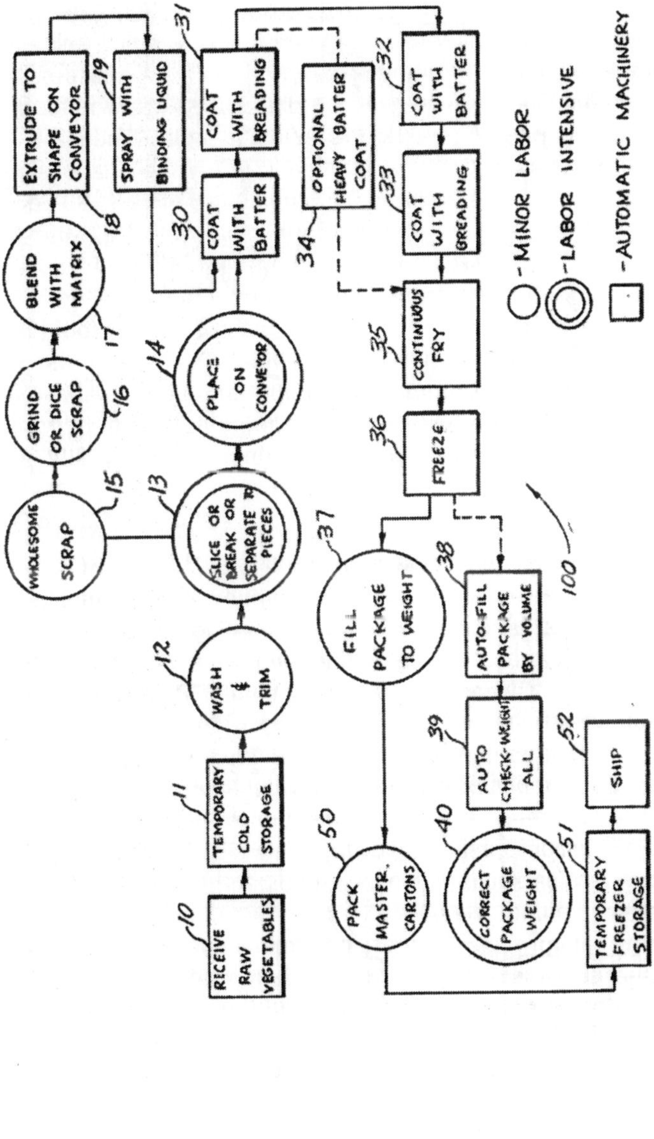

Fig. 4.1. Flow Diagram of a Typical Prior Art Vegetable Processing Line Wherein Natural Shapes of Vegetables are Processed as Convenience Foods;

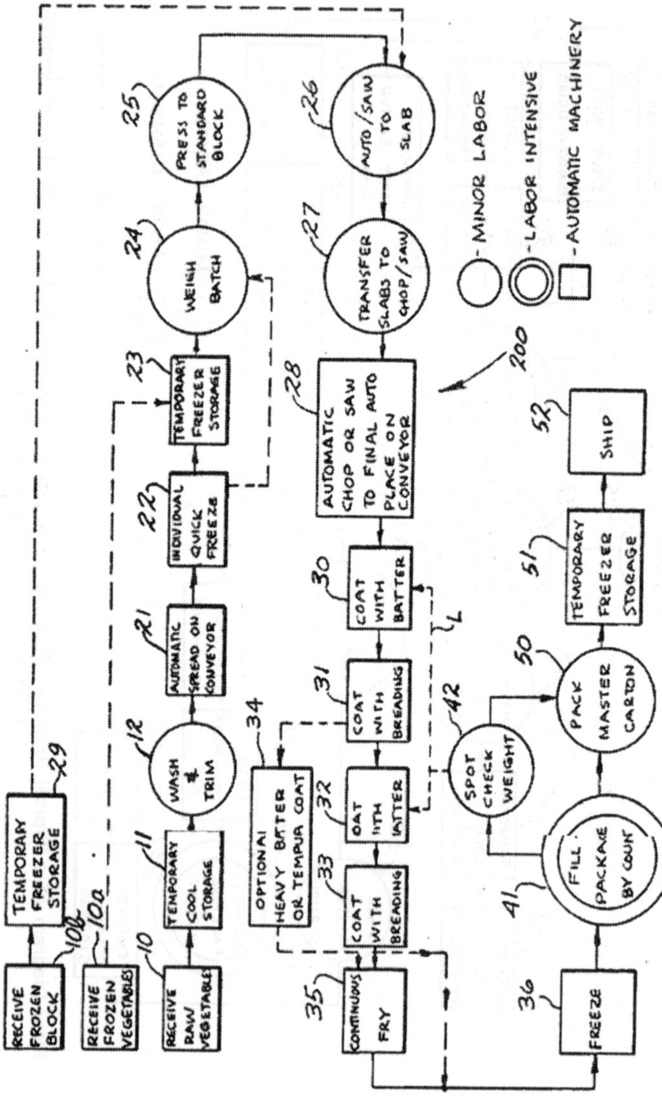

Fig. 4.2.Flow Diagram of a Vegetable Processing Line Utilizing the Method of this Method

or the like now in common use in the food processing industry as identified schematically at C. Unwholesome parts and adhering debris must be removed at station 10 before vegetables are cut up or separated into small pieces. Further, after each separation, either line 100 or line 200 has facilities for coating, possibly frying and freezing the product, such processing being accomplished in a batter machine at station 30, a breading machine at station 31, a second batter machine at station 32, a second breading machine at station 33, a fryer at station 35 and a freezer at station 36. An alternate method common to both processing lines 100 and 200 of coating the food product may involve dipping product pieces into a suitable batter at station 34 rather than using the last set of batter-breading machines 32, 33. Finally, the food product is packaged by weight, and master cartoned at 40, temporarily stored in a freezer at 51 and shipped at station 52. Any variations in the equipment common to both lines, as described in this paragraph, can be identical for both lines 100 and 200. Such equipment for accomplishing these automatic operations are well known in the related art, and will be briefly described hereinafter.

Referring now to Fig. 4.1., the special handling and equipment for a conventional vegetable processing line 100 will now be described. In general, for one type of product previously mentioned, i.e., the natural state, most vegetables cannot be coated in their natural state because they are too large. Exceptions include small mushrooms and some peppers. Consequently, the vegetables selected for this process are taken out of the temporary storage at station 11 and washed and trimmed, and then presented to station 13 for further reduction in size. The equipment at station 13 is adapted to process all the vegetables that the processor wishes to utilize. For instance, zucchini requires slicing, eggplant may require slicing in two or three directions, onions may require slicing and separation into rings, cauliflower requires breaking into useful size buds, and so on. In each case much labor is generally required for handling pieces, especially odd shaped pieces like cauliflower buds. Onion rings are a special case because many of the small diameter rings plus the end pieces do not make satisfactory product. In many cases of vegetable processing, a substantial proportion of the vegetables are scrap at this stage, not utilizable in prime product, but certainly wholesome and worth saving as will be described later. This work station 13 can be very labor intensive as indicated in Fig. 4.1. by the double circle legend. Cauliflower, for instance, can only be broken apart into buds, and the extent of break-apart, being normally manually accomplished, is a matter of judgment for the worker to decide, whereby many tiny buds may be inadvertently produced. Individual mushrooms may be cut in two, in four or allowed to pass whole. Onions are mostly automatically sliced and sorted with human inspection and correction. As a result it becomes necessary that the required equipment and personnel variations at station 13 are almost endless for different vegetables, so that the processor is frequently limited to processing those vegetables which "match" in separation requirements, or in the alternative he must have several different types of processing equipment available as needed.

From work station 13 the food product pieces may be placed onto an interconnecting conveyor C at 14 which, in most cases, is done by hand in order to separate the pieces so that they do not later fry together, yet the pieces should be close enough on the conveyor so that the coating, frying and freezing machinery is well loaded. This operation can be extremely labor intensive as is also similarly identified by the double circle legend. As an illustration, if the product path through processing stations 30 to 36 is thirty inches wide as determined by the selected conveyor C and the conveyor travels at thirty feet per minute and product spacing is two inches one way by three inches the other way, then each square foot of belt should carry twenty-four pieces of food product, while the total belt may carry eighteen hundred pieces per minute. If each worker can place 150 pieces per minute (a very high rate), then twelve workers would be required to keep the conveyor belt loaded at station 14.

As mentioned above, considerable wholesome scrap may be generated at station 13 during separation into small pieces, scrap which should be utilized in the interest of economy. The flow diagram of Fig. 4.1. illustrates one possible prior art method of using this scrap for the second type of product, i.e., extruded, especially in the processing of onions. The scrap is collected at station 15, transported to station 16 where it is chopped, ground, finely diced or otherwise minced. The scrap may then be transferred in batches or by a conveyor C to a mixing station 17 where it is blended into a porridge-like mixture with a matrix well known in the art which binds such scrap pieces together after extrusion at station 18. Transfer to the hopper of the extruder 18 may occur in any of several ways, either by batch or conveyor, but requires some labor. After extrusion onto a conveyor belt C in the pattern desired, the extruded pieces may be sprayed at station 19 with a special liquid known in the art, which creates a skin on the extruded piece so that it can be conveyed and transferred through the subsequent coating, frying and freezing process steps as illustrated at stations 30, 31, 32-36. As aforementioned, this extruded product suffers in consumer acceptance principally by reason that it does not have a natural taste but rather a taste that is characteristic of the binder material used.

When pre-packaging food of almost any kind, individual packages must contain a net weight of product no less than that pre-printed on the label, and as little excess as possible. Any shortages in weight may be interpreted as mis-marking, while any excess weight is a free gift to the consumer. Therefore, packaging closely to net weight is extremely important to the processor. However, when pieces to be placed into a package vary greatly in size and shape, it is difficult to package them automatically. Thus, the finished food product received from the freeze station 36 may be hand packaged in a suitable carton by weight as at packaging station 36 which requires many workers but results in accurate weights, or an alternate method is to auto-fill the packages to a nominal weight as a packaging station 38, and to then check weigh all packages at weighing station 39, and have workers add or subtract pieces as indicated at weight correcting station 40. Fewer people are usually necessary in the latter case because fewer packages must be corrected. As indicated in Fig. 4.1., intensive labor, i.e., double ring legend, is required in at least three places, at stations 13, 14, and 37 or 40. Additional labor, though usually a lesser amount, is required at stations 12, 15, 16, 17. The elimination of some of this labor is one justification and patentable distinction for the block processing line 200 of this invention.

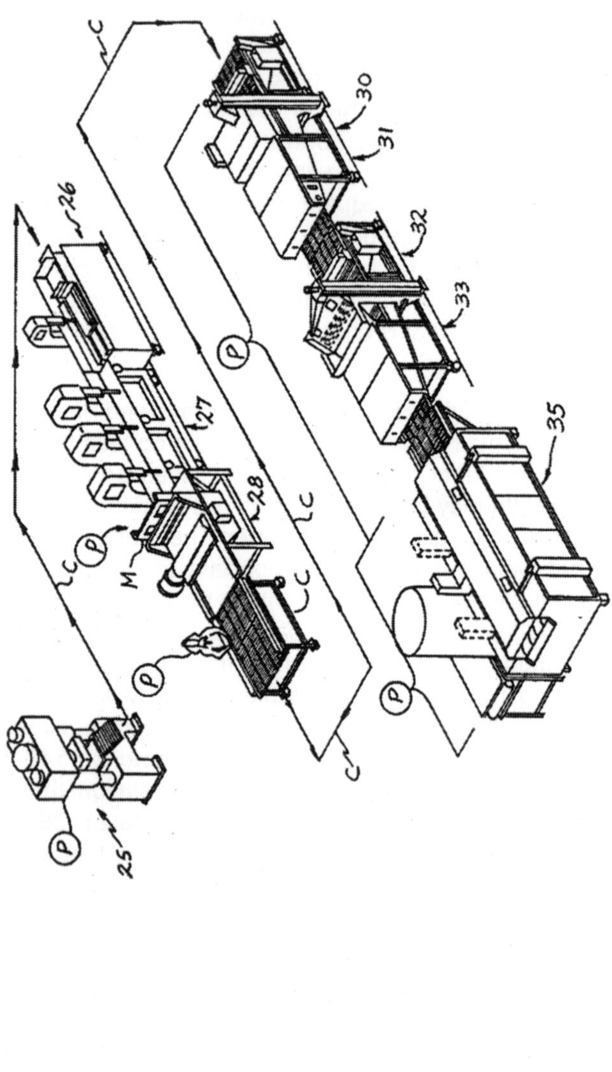

Fig. 4.3. Isometric View of a Processing Line for Processing Convenience Foods by the Process of the present Method and which Line Utilizes Presently Commercially Available Equipment;

Referring now to Figs. 4.2 and 4.3 the novel method of processing convenience foods of the present method will now be described.

As seen in the flow diagram of Fig. 4.2. a typical processing line for practicing the process of the present method as identified in its entirety at 200, may include several of the same types of equipment at several of the process stations as previously utilized in the process line 100 of Fig. 4.1. which is in present use today.

For example, processing line 200 of the present method may incorporate the use of initial processing stations 10, 11 and 12 for receiving the raw food product selected to be processed; temporary cooling of the food product at a suitable temperature to prevent spoilage and for cold water washing and trimming the food product.

The individual food product pieces are then presented to a conveyor C at station 21 which may include conventional equipment such as an overhead hopper or the like for automatically spreading said pieces evenly across the usable width of the conveyor C. The conveyor as thus loaded carries the individual pieces into a suitable quick freeze unit at station 22 which unit may be any one of a number presently commercially in use, such as a nitrogen or CO_2 freezer unit wherein the individual food pieces are quick frozen to a suitable temperature which at present is within a temperature range of approximately -10° to +10° Fahrenheit.

From freeze station 22 the frozen food pieces may be placed, if desired, into a temporary freezer storage room at station 23 or alternatively may be conveyed directly by a conveyor C to weigh-batch equipment at station 24, which equipment may comprise any suitable type of weighing apparatus such as a hanging scale or a platform or pan-type scale at which a preselected batch weight of the frozen food product is determined, as for example, a batch weight of sixteen (16) pounds. As will be understood other batch weights may also be selected

As aforementioned, to the present time in the food processing industry to which this method relates, it has been generally believed that it is not possible to form a frozen block of vegetable and/or fruit food products in their natural state by reason that they lack natural binding material such as protein that is in fish or poultry and which enables the processor to form a frozen block of such food product in the manufacture of fish or poultry convenience food products.

However, the present applicants have discovered surprising and unusual results in that it is possible to form a frozen block of vegetable or fruit in their natural state by taking such in the size (bite size or the like) that is commercially available in the frozen food department of a typical market which as known in the art may conventionally be either raw or blanched, i.e. partially cooked, and while said products are at a temperature within the range of approximately -10° to +10° Fahrenheit and then placing them into the mold cavity of a press at station 25, as depicted in Fig. 4.3., and exerting substantial pressure on said products in the range of approximately 100-1500 lbs/in ^{2} a satisfactory frozen block of food product is formed wherein the individual food pieces adhere to each other sufficiently to enable said block to be subsequently fabricated as will be hereinafter described. It is believed tha during this pressing operation binding of the individual food pieces occurs by reason that ice crystals in the frozen food pieces react with ice crystals on adjacent food pieces to affect welding of said pieces together sufficiently to adequately bind the same together into an integral block.

The press is operated to compress the individual food pieces into a frozen block B of food product in which the food pieces are pressed to thus form a substantially homogeneous food product dispersion throughout while the food product remains frozen. In the compression the individual food pieces retain their initial piece shape and texture with only possible very minor distortion, if any at all.

The block B, as will be understood, may be of any desired geometric configuration, one selected configuration being a polygonal solid as illustrated in Figs. 4.4-4.6 which may have a typical rectangular cross-sectional dimension of approximately four inches by ten inches with a length of approximately twenty inches. The press is capable of forming the block B at food product temperatures as low as -10° Fahrenheit.

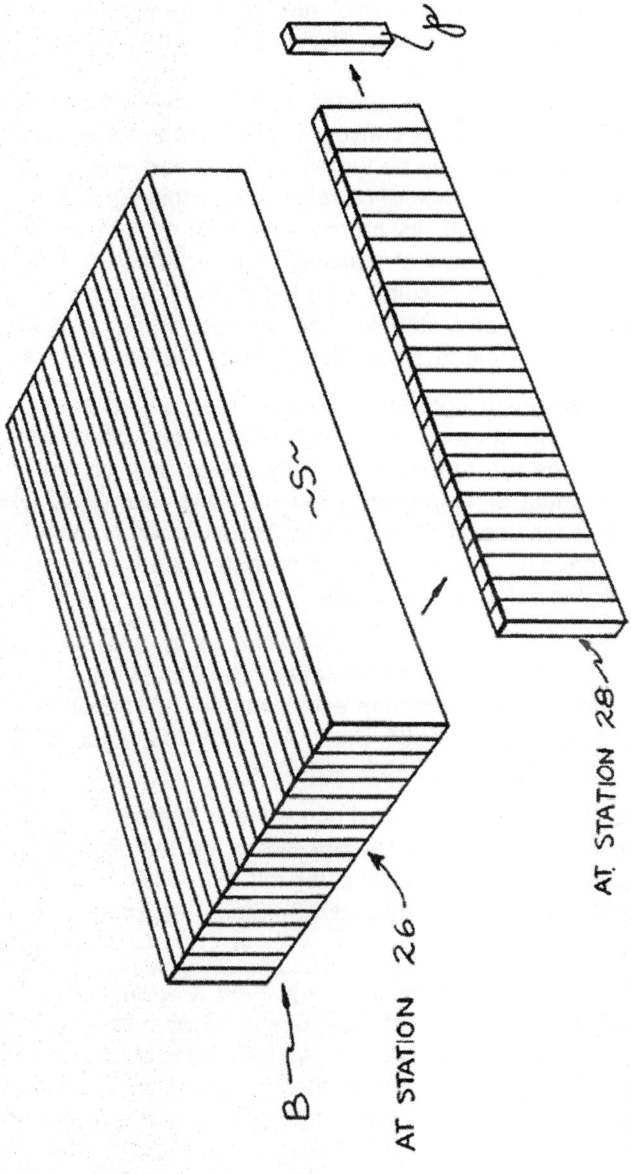

Fig. 4.4. Isometric View of a Frozen Pressed Block of Convenience Foods Formed in the Process of this Method and showing One Possible way to Divide it into Sticks or Fingers

The block B is then placed onto a conveyor C and presented to station 26 whereat it is sawed into slabs, as identified at S in Figs. 4.4 and 4.5. A suitable saw as illustrated in Fig. 4.3. at station 26 is an Automatic Feed Band Saw Model AFBS manufactured by Pearce Equipment, Inc. of Danvers, Mass. The slabs S are then carried by conveyor C to a second saw station 27 whereat each slab may be turned on its narrow side or edge and cut into four slabs each of correspondingly thinner thickness. Turning of the slab onto its narrow side may be automatically accomplished by the saw at station 27 or performed manually. One such saw capable of suitable performance is depicted in Fig. 4.3. at station 27 and identified as a Triple Band Saw also manufactured by Pearce Equipment, Inc. of Danvers, Mass.

The slabs exiting from station 27 are then deposited into a vertical magazine M as seen in Fig. 4.3. at station 28, at which station the slabs are further individually sawed or chopped into individual product or finger-size pieces p. One exemplary type of equipment for use at station 28 for this purpose is identified as a Vertical Cut Portion Cutter manufactured by Pearce Equipment, Inc. of Danvers, Mass.

The individual pieces are then conveyed by a conveyor C to a first batter stage at station 30 whereat the pieces are covered with a suitable liquid batter, one exemplary suitable machine for this purpose being the XL34 Batter Machine manufactured by Stein Associates, Inc. of Sandusky, Ohio.

The battered pieces are next conveyed to station 31 whereat a suitable first breading coat is applied to the battered pieces. One suitable exemplary machine for this purpose is the XL34 Breading Machine as manufactured by Stein Associates, Inc. of Sandusky, Ohio.

The breaded pieces are then conveyed to a second batter and breading stage as indicated at 32 and 33 whereat a second batter coat and breading coat are applied, wherein the second breading coat may be more coarse than the first coat. The second batter coat may be applied at station 32 with similar type of Stein equipment as at station 30 and the second breading coat may be similarly applied at station 33 with equipment similar to the breading machine at station 21.

The pieces as thus battered and breaded may then be presented to a cooking station 35 whereat they may be deep fried, or alternatively conveyed by conveyor C directly to a suitable fast freeze station 36 whereat they may be quick frozen in an uncooked state. Inasmuch as the food pieces are processed while they are in a frozen state as presented to the various work stations 26-33, they should still be in a frozen state when exiting from the second stage breader at station 33 and conveyed to freeze station 33 and they may be simply lowered slightly in temperature to the desired temperature for storage of ±10° Fahrenheit.

An optional coating such as tempura and/or a dehydrated fruit coating may, if desired, be applied at station 43, which coated product may be either fried or frozen directly at station 36.

A suitable fryer for use at cooking station 35 may be the FB/FD Custom Direct Fired Fryer as manufactured by Stein Associates, Inc. of Sandusky, Ohio.

After frying, the individual food pieces are conveyed by conveyor C to the fast freeze station 36 to be quick frozen. Any suitable freezer equipment may be employed at station 36 as for example the same type of equipment utilized at freezer station 22.

After quick freezing at station 36, the individual food pieces are conveyed to station 41 for packaging by piece count.

The packing operation in the block processing method of the present invention varies considerably from that of a conventional processing line 100 as depicted in Fig. 4.1. Since in the present process all product pieces are the same size and shape, packages may be designed to accept any number of pieces desired. Then, when product is properly oriented according to package design, the correct count of pieces is obtained. But very importantly, because product pieces are identical, it is possible to control package weight by count. Occasional check weighing may be undertaken at station 42 to indicate whether packages are within desired weight tolerances. This information can be fed back to automatic batter mixers or portioning devices as schematically indicated by the dotted line L weight control which may continually correct for weight tolerances. By slight variations in batter viscosity, or portion thickness of vegetable sticks, package weights can be held to very close tolerances, and the judgment function of package fillers is reduced, therefore these workers can produce more than the workers of stations 37 or 40 of the conventional processing line 100 of Fig. 4.1.

From the packaging station 41, the package food pieces may be conveyed to a second packaging station 50 whereat they are placed into a master carton of larger volume and then placed into a temporary freezer storage at station 51 while awaiting future shipment at station 52.

Several alternate processing steps are anticipated particularly in the initial stages of the block processing method of the present invention as is illustrated in line 200 especially when the industry becomes mature enough to support and recognize the variations that may be made thereto. For example, it is believed that it will be possible to receive already cleaned and trimmed vegetables in frozen bulk, as at station 10a, which may then eliminate work stations 11, 12, 21, and 22. It is also conceivable that certain processors will concentrate on making standard sized blocks which will then be made available to the processors of the present invention so that frozen blocks of the same size could be received as at station 10b which may be temporarily stored in freezer storage 29 to be subsequently presented directly to the saw equipment at station 26 to further eliminate stations 23, 24, 25 in the final processing plant.

It will also be noted as seen in FIGS. 4.2 and 4.3 that only station 41 for package filling can be considered as labor intensive, while at six other stations 12, 24, 25, 26, 27 and 42 require some labor.

As also seen in the processing line of Fig. 4.3., an attendant as depicted by letter P may be stationed at station 28 to load themagazine M if it is to be hand fed and between stations 27 and 28 to monitor the conveyor C. Monitoring attendants P may likewise be provided at the block press station 25 and in the area of the line between batter station 30 and fryer station 35.

As will be understood in the art, many different shapes and/ or sizes may be selected for the individual portion or finger pieces, several of which are illustrated in Figs. 4.4 and 4.5. As seen in Fig. 4.4., the frozen compressed food block B is divided into a

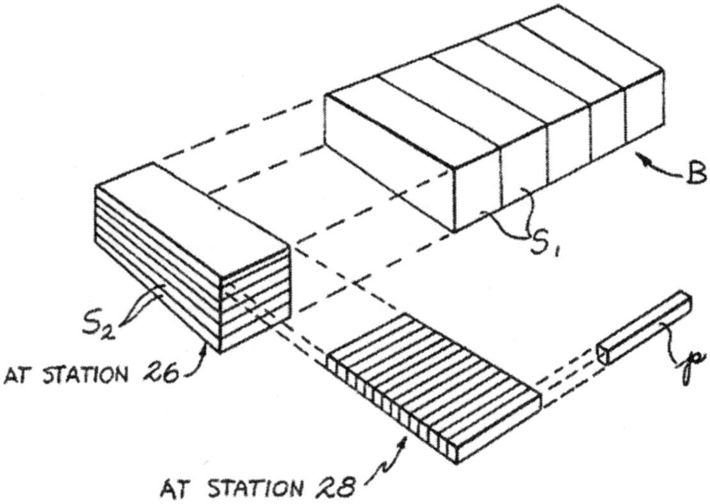

Fig. 4.5. Isometric View of a Frozen Pressed Block of Convenience Foods showing a Second Possible Way to Divide into Sticks or Fingers

plurality (thirteen) of slabs S with each slab extending longitudinally of the block B and with each slab S being cut or chopped into twenty-four individual portions of finger pieces p wherein the dimension of each piece is approximately four (4) inches by three-quarters inches square.

The block B of Fig. 4.5. of the same dimension as the block of Fig. 4.4. is shown initially divided into five slabs S_1, each of which is then again divided in the same transverse direction into seven (7) slabs S_2 and then cut or chopped into individual portions or finger pieces p, the dimensions of which each are approximately four (4) inches by one-half inch square.

It is also contemplated that a block B may be formed of multiple layers of different food products and wherein it may also be desirable to retain each different food product within the boundaries of its respective layer. Such a layered block B is illustrated in Fig. 4.6., and merely as an example, said block is seen to comprise three layers a, b and c wherein layer a may be broccoli, layer b cauliflower and layer c a selected cheese. While not shown it is also contemplated that several or more

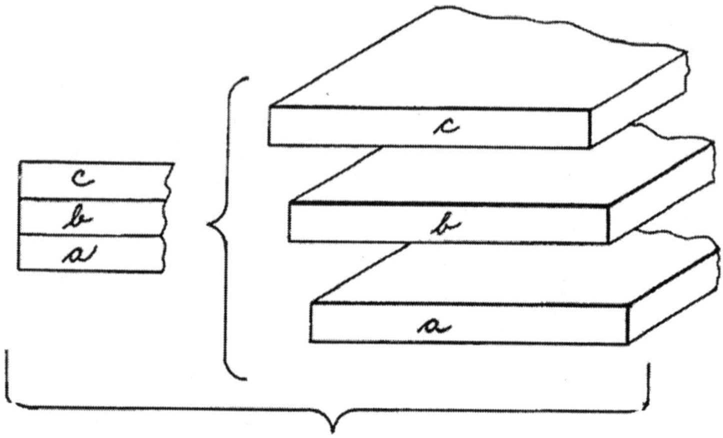

Fig. 4.6. Isometric View of a Frozen Pressed Block Formed of at least Three Different Convenience Foods which may be Layered within the Block

different food products may be substantially evenly dispersed throughout the block B so that the resultant individual portion may consist of a plurality of different food products either layered or dispersed therethrough. It is also contemplated that other food products in their natural or processed state such as bacon pieces may be mixed with a suitable vegetable with the latter constituting the major ingredient of the end product may be readily adaptable to the present process.

The new and novel "finger-food" product thus produced by the process of the present invention is thus seen to comprise the selected food product in its natural and frozen state and constitutes all or substantially all of the end food product in the resultant finger-food and has a natural taste and mouth feel characteristic of the selected food product.

5

Method for Producing Frozen Vegetable Food Material Having Soft Texture

It would in general be difficult for the aged to eat hard food materials. Moreover, the aged in general has such a strong demand that when taking a meal, he also enjoys, like the usual people, the shapes and colours of the food materials used in dishes, at the table, in addition to the taste thereof.

Under the existing circumstances, however, it is one of the leading mainstreams that the meals for the aged are prepared in the paste-like or liquid-like forms, in which all of the ingredients thereof have been softened even to such an extent that the ingredients have almost lost their original shapes while taking into consideration the convenience of the aged such that he can easily eat the same. Therefore, it is common that when the aged is at table, he cannot satisfactorily enjoy the shapes and colours of the food materials or the ingredients of a meal and accordingly, such a meal would be enjoyable for the aged. For this reason, it is rarely the case that the meals for the aged can stimulate the aged person's appetite and accordingly, this would exert a variety of evil influences on the aged such as the gradual decrease in their physical strengths. Moreover, if such ingredients are cooked even to such an extent that they are in the paste-like or liquid-like states, it would be quite difficult, for the aged, to enjoy the colours of a meal provided by the food materials thereof.

Furthermore, it would be quite desirable for the aged that he can commercially easily obtain, at home, soft food materials obtained by preliminarily having softened hard food materials in order that the aged, by himself, can easily prepare the meal for the aged in his own house.

There has recently been known a method for preparing a food material which is softened even to the interior or further to the center thereof, which comprises the steps of freezing a raw or preheat-treated food material, thawing the frozen food material, and then immersing the material in a dispersion of a pectin-decomposition enzyme under reduced pressure to thus make the pectin-decomposition enzyme penetrate even into the center of the material.

This rapid enzyme-introduction method can make the enzyme penetrate into the central portion of a food material and therefore, it would be expected that not only the superficial portion, but also the central portion of a food material can uniformly be processed (for instance, the softening of the material) within a very short period of time.

In the meantime, the authors of the process have tried to prepare a food material according to this rapid enzyme-introduction method, packing the same in a container as it is, then storing it in a refrigerator and finally putting it on the market as a softened food material. In such case, however, the authors have found that the food material thus treated suffers from the following problems: The food material is inevitably and gradually further softened in the course of its circulation; the material is too soft at the time of cooking the same or even hard food material such as bamboo shoot or carrot is softened to such an extent that the shape can immediately be damaged. Alternatively, it would also be tried to put the food material into a container as it is and to subsequently freeze the food material therein, but the softening of the material may proceed to some extent even in this case. Moreover, the food material in such a condition should be thawed prior to the cooking of the same. However, this is quite inconvenient for the aged since such an operation requires much time.

For this reason, it would be quite convenient for the aged that a food material, in which any softening of the material never proceeds and which is in a softened condition while maintaining the original shape and colour peculiar to the material, can be cooked without any additional treatment and this would be quite important to make the life of the aged comfortable and plentiful.

The authors of the process conducted intensive studies to develop a food material suitably used for the preparation of a meal for the aged, which is prepared by an enzyme-treatment like that described above, which can maintain a fixed and desired softness, even on the market, and which can also maintain the shape, colour and good resistance to the teeth even when it is immediately cooked without any excess treatment.

6

Preparation of Frozen Food (Cooked Burdocks)

Pretreatment of Burdocks

Raw burdocks which had been washed with water and whose skin had been removed (the hardness of raw burdocks was found to be 3.8×10^6 N (as determined by the use of Texturometer manufactured and sold by TAKEMOTO Company)) were chopped or cut along the longitudinal direction thereof into small pieces each having a length ranging from 5 to 30 mm.

Heat-Treatment

The chopped raw burdocks were heated at 90° C. for 30 minutes while they were immersed in water in an amount of 8 times the volume of the chopped raw burdocks.

Freezing Treatment

After the chopped raw burdocks were removed from the immersion water (water-drainage), they were cooled with water and then frozen at –20° C. for 40 minutes using a quick freezer. Thus, ice crystals were formed within the tissue of the burdock. Then, the quantity of the moisture present on the surface of the chopped burdock in its frozen state was reduced by blowing cold air (–20° C.) onto the surface of thereof for 48 hours to thus improve the penetration of an enzyme into the tissue of the burdock.

Preparation of Enzyme-Containing Dispersion

Macellozyme 2A (containing 39% of pectinase incorporated therein, available from Yakult Pharmaceutical Industry Co., Ltd.) was blended with and dispersed in water to thus form an enzyme-containing dispersion having an enzyme concentration of 0.3%.

Enzyme-Impregnation Treatment

The frozen and chopped burdocks were immersed in the 0.3% enzyme-containing dispersion in an amount of 3 times the volume of the burdocks, followed by the initiation of the reduction of pressure and the continuation of the pressure-reducing operation at a pressure ranging from 0 to 80 hPa (0 to 60 mmHg) over 20 minutes.

Treatment with Enzyme to Cause Enzyme Reaction

The enzyme-treated burdocks were then released from the reduced pressure, removed from the enzyme-containing dispersion (drainage of the dispersion) and subsequently allowed to stand for 16 hours in a refrigerator maintained at 10° C. At this stage, the hardness of the burdock was found to be 1.8×10^5 N (the value as determined using Texturometer manufactured and sold by TAKEMOTO Company)).

Enzyme-Deactivation Treatment

The burdocks, which had been subjected to the enzyme-treatment at a low temperature, were heated at 95° C. for 10 minutes while they were immersed in water in an amount of 3 times the volume of the burdocks to thus inactivate the enzyme.

Freezing Treatment

The resulting enzyme-treated burdocks were subjected to cooling operations in a vacuum and then frozen at –40° C. for 30 minutes. This would permit the removal of any excess moisture, the instantaneous freezing of the burdocks would improve the handling thereof such as packaging and the resulting product would be prevented from being damaged. Moreover, the frozen goods do not lose their original shape even during the circulation process and the thawing of the same surely provides a soft burdock food.

7

Seasoning Individually Quick Frozen Vegetables

With the growth and industry-wide adoption of individual quick freezing (IQF) of vegetables and like produce prior to storage in suitably frozen totes and packaging thereafter as convenient, it has become desirable to apply an organoleptically appealing sauce to the individually frozen produce. Such sauces may be applied in a bar or tube form as an individual portion centered in the body off the individually quick-frozen charge to the frozen food carton. However, for many applications, employment of such a sauce-form is unnecessary and undesirable because of non-uniformities in applying the correct volume for seasoning purposes. It would be desirable to apply the sauce as a plug but to do so invites variations in sauce applications, particularly at high production rates.

It is among the objects of the present method to provide a process whereby seasonings can be uniformly applied to individual and discretely frozen food produce and mixtures of such produce such as vegetable mixtures and combinations thereof with other like frozen foods such as meat, fruits and nut meats.

A more specific object of the method is to provide a process whereby the sauce can be charged to the vegetable in a controllable manner at high production rates to an extent whereby the sauce applied in the package per se onto discrete frozen produce does not migrate to the bottom of the package and occasion freezing of container contents to the carton wall or other container panel structure. A further benefit and hence object of the method is to control the application of such a seasoning sauce to frozen food as packaged whereby additional and complementary garnishes or toppings such as bread crumbs or croutons separately packaged in a pouch will not be "wetted" by the migration of the sauce applied to the food despite the presence of the package of topping in the frozen food container.

In accordance with the present method a frozen vegetable or a mixed vegetable combination or like frozen product is prepared by methods commonly understood in the art and designated IQF to provide relatively discrete frozen produce which typically will be recovered from a tote bin in a free flowing form at a temperature ranging between 10°F and -10°F. This produce will be individually portioned and introduced into individual frozen food cartons which optionally will have included therein at the bottom thereof a foil pouch of suitable topping such as bread crumbs or croutons. The vegetable or other free flowing food product in the opened container carton or like structure will then have applied in the form of an aqueous "plug" or extrudate having a freezing point of 15°-26°F. a viscous suspension composed of seasoning, water and hydrocolloid such as a pregelatinized starch, the extrudate being maintained at a temperature below 40°F and typically between 30°-35°F. and being applied centrally of the frozen charge as it moves to receive the seasoning portion. The suspension is formulated with a viscosity of 1000 to 17,000 cps., preferably about 3500 to 5500 cps. upon standing at 30°-40°F. for up to 2 hours stemming from the inclusion of a colloid such as pre-gelatinized starch in a quantity therein sufficient to assure that the reduced temperatures of application the sauce quantity will not migrate or "bleed" to adhere to the container walls or otherwise collect upon being applied. Rather, the suspension will, upon intercepting contact with the IQF goods at below 10°F, undergo heat transfer therewith and migrate gradually thereover in a controlled manner such that the sauce quantity freezes in a period of less than ten minutes essentially in place on the goods and centrally of the charge.

A vegetable combination product consisting of 1 part sweet red peppers, 21/2 parts pearl onions, 8 parts spinach, and 13½ parts zucchini is loaded volumetrically into a carton already containing a poly-foil pouch of crouton topping made as described in aforesaid co-pending application of Bartenbach. Each of these vegetables was previously individually quick frozen and packed in bulk at 0°F; they were then removed from refrigerated tote premises in the stated ratios and fed to a standard rotary vegetable loader at a temperature of 5°F.

A series of cartons were mechanically conveyed to a carton closure system. Prior to closure, 2½ parts sauce by weight of the aforesaid combination are added to each of two moving cartons simultaneously, the sauce filler moving with the cartons to insure uniform sauce distribution at the geometric center thereof; the filler moves back to fill the next succeeding two filled cartons on the line and the operation is repeated. The sauce consists of 1 part pre-gelatinized tapioca starch, 1 part propoxylated tapioca starch, 15 parts water, and 3 parts spices and flavorings (hydrolyzed vegetable protein, salt, sugar, onion powder, garlic powder and oregano). The sauce had previously been prepared by first pre-blending all dry materials. This pre-blending dispersed the starches within the other dry ingredients thereby reducing the probability of starch agglomeration within the sauce. This mix was then slowly added to chilled water at 35°F. under recirculation and rapid agitation. Agitation and recirculation were stopped when the correct sauce viscosity has been reached (1000-7000 cps), ideally 4000 cps. The sauce was then placed under slow agitation with minimum recycling during application at the filler stations.

The sauce issues from each applicator nozzle as a unitary plug approximately three-eighths inch in diameter and 1½ inch in length, the sauce being flowable and yet cohesive as it is deposited under gravity plus a moderate head pressure of about 10 psig. As the sauce comes into contact with the vegetable combination, the latter is moving and engages the lower free end of the plug occasioning a pulling and slight elongation as the plug is deposited in place. The carton is moved at a speed such as to fill 160 cartons per minute, each filler providing the parallel filling with 80 plugs per minute. The plug has a freezing point of about 21°F. The plug of sauce froze in place within 10 minutes.

The packaged product when thawed and cooked developed a viscous sauce appearance by the addition of 0.06 parts of water to 1 parts of the sauce-vegetable combination and 0.12 parts butter, the vegetable moisture and added water serving with boiling and 3 minute simmer to thicken the sauce by the gelatinization of the propoxylated tapioca starch.

In all of these applications it will be essential that the freezing of the sauce as formulated and its viscosity consonant with this freezing point are regulated by formulation so that the sauce can be cooled to below 40°F prior to extrusion and yet will remain sufficiently fluid to permit ease of extrusion onto the charge of frozen food. Collaterally the produce will be at a temperature below 10°F and sufficiently reduced in relation to the sauce as applied that the latter will reasonably rapidly freeze in the region of application; accordingly, there should be a temperature differential at least 15°F between the frozen goods and the sauce.

8

Freezing of Bakery and Dessert Products

BAKERY PRODUCTS

Bake off technology and bakery products

Bakery products (termed BCG) such as bread, viennoiserie, and many other specialities remain an important input in a well-balanced diet, being at the base of the pyramid of nutrition. Consumers prefer freshly baked products, which are traditionally prepared by baking from scratch. In addition, consumers are searching for a larger variety of products including ethnic products, health promoting products, nonallergenic products (i.e. gluten-free bread) with a high level of 'freshness' ('freshly baked') and organoleptic qualities. In parallel, the reduced availability of skilled bakers and the cost of shop space mean that traditional bakers have difficulties to match production with demand. The food industry has been proposing several alternatives to solve this problem. The corresponding technologies called 'Bake Off Technologies' (BOT) encompass several baking processes. The spirit of BOT is to keep the technological and time-consuming operations at the industrial level and the final preparation of products before retailing is carried out in small shops equipped with a minimum of equipment (thawing–proofing chamber, oven) and with minimally skilled personnel.

The market share of BOT is growing at a very high rate (more or less around 10% per year), whereas the overall bread consumption is almost constant; there is thus a transfer from traditional baking (scratch baking) towards BOT. The main technologies of bread making are listed in Table 8.1. The three key technologies of BOT are the *Unfermented Frozen dough* (UFD), the *Partially Baked Frozen Bread* (PBF) and the *Partially Baked Unfrozen Bread* (PBUF). UFD requires skilled personnel but can also produce products with a quality comparable to scratch baking. At least 3 hours are needed to prepare bread with UFD technology. UFD products are the most preferred frozen bakery products in France. PBF or PBUF do not require highly skilled personnel. Usually PBF and PBUF, breads are thawed before being baked in a convection oven. Partially baked (PBF and PBUF) products can be prepared in less than 1 hour but their production is energy demanding. The fermented frozen dough (F-FD) technology has not been extensively developed due to quality problems. This technology, also called 'ready to bake', is promising; however, if temperature abused in the cold chain, the surface of the dough pieces might reach the melt point and stick together, resulting in an unacceptable crust after baking.

In 2003, the European bread market was divided into 47% for traditional scratch baking, 6% for bread production in supermarket (traditional scratch baking), 36% for industrial fresh breads and 11% for industrial baked and part-baked products. France, Italy and Germany represent 75% of the European bread market. Concerning frozen breads, the market share in volume at the European level in 2003 was 63% for FPB, 32% for UFD and 5% for FBF. The production was divided into 6% for traditional scratch bakers, 19% for out-ofhome consumption, 20% for affiliated bakers and downtown vending shops and 55% for supermarkets. Among these mean values, differences exist from one country to another. For example, in France, only 24% of fresh bread comes from industrial bakeries, whereas in UK 51% of the production of fresh bread comes from industrial bakeries (in total 88% of the overall bread production is industrial in the UK).

Frozen dough

Breads made from frozen dough are exposed to a global loss of volume in the final product. The final volume of a bread is

Table 8.1 Terminology and acron>rns of ttie conventional and Bake Off Technology bread-mate^

Name	Acronym	Brief description of the procexs
Fully baked unfrozen or conventional direct bread making	FB-U	Main steps are mixing - rest - dividing - shaping - fermentation - baking - refrigeration
Fully baked frozen	FB-F	The bread is obtained from FB-U and is frozen
Partially baked	PB-UF	The bread is obtained from FB-U except that baking is stopped before crust colouration. Bread is cooled and is stored in packaging at room temperature.
Partially baked frozen	PB-F	The bread is obtained from FB-U except that baking is stopped before crust colouration. Bread is cooled and is frozen in packaging at freezing conditions (i.e. –20°C)
Unfermented frozen dough	U-FD	Doughis prepared as for FB-U; the rest period is shortened and care is token to prevent excessive fermentation before freezing, which is done as soon as possible after shaping.
Fermented frozen dough	F-FD	Dough is prepared as for FB-U; the fermentation started and is stopped before full development. The fermented dough is then frozen. Rapid freezing is usually recommended. Baking is usually earned out in one process (frozen - ready to bake) or after thawing

a function of the fermentation step and from the oven rise. The expansion during fermentation, which is one of the most important phases of the bread making process, is linked to three main properties: the activity of the yeast, the rheology of the dough and the presence of miniature bubbles embedded in the dough during mixing. The expansion during baking is linked to the following key points: the condition of the dough at the end of fermentation, the baking conditions and the rheology of the dough during the baking process (dough–crumb transition and dough–crust transition at surface). Two types of studies are available in the literature focussing either on the formulation and/or on the process.

Process conditions

Process parameters that have been examined are, for example, the mixing conditions, degree of fermentation prior to freezing freezing temperature, freezing rate storage conditions, thawing rate.

Formulation

The basic formulations can be quite different from one study to the other, using or not, for example, shortening. The quality of the basic ingredients first seems to be an important issue. The quality of the gluten can be as important as its amount, as shown by the researchers. Flour with higher gluten is usually recommended for frozen dough (i.e. higher then 12%). This can be obtained by using specific blends of flour or by adding vital gluten.

Another point of interest is the yeast.Yeast amount is usually higher for frozen dough; often multiplied by a factor of 2. Nevertheless, specific studies have focused on the development of freeze tolerant yeast. Specific properties of the yeast appear to be important such as trehalose content or lipid content for example. Improvers for baking are often used and are made of a mix of selected ingredients such as specific amylases, gluten and ascorbic acid. Such mixes are developed and adjusted constantly by specialised companies and they vary from one country to another depending on the quality of the flour (for example, humid weather during growing might develop a higher amylasic activity, dryer weather may result in more damaged starch and in possibly better 'strength' of the dough due to a modified amount and quality of gluten). Mixes are also developed for specific applications such as frozen dough and part-baked applications. Amylases facilitate the release of free sugars for the fermentation. Gluten and ascorbic acid make the rheology of the dough more tolerant to freezing. A specific study showed the combined effect of mixing time, ascorbic acid and á-amylases on selected quality parameters (fermentation rate, bread volume). They observed that the bread volume was positively correlated not only to ascorbic acid amount but also to the mixing time. Other technical parameters, such as the length of the dough stick at the end of the moulding machine, show that the dough is more elastic with a higher amount of ascorbic acid. Shortening and emulsifiers have attracted a lot of interest. The most encountered emulsifiers are diacetyl tartrate ester of monoglycerides (DATEM) and sucrose esters. Such substances are most of the time combined with the use of shortening. They have a combined effect and help in making the gas bubbles that are embedded in the dough during mixing, and that develop during fermentation, smaller and more numerous, giving the dough more tolerance to freezing. This results also in a foamier crumb texture (numerous cells of uniform diameter). Such a 'foamy' crumb has not been researched for specific products such as French baguette (crispy rolls) for which the consumers expect a crumb with irregular alveolar structure.

Recently, the use of gums and hydrocolloids have attracted research efforts. One of the expected roles of hydrocolloids is to immobilise water in order to reduce the 'freezable' water (or free frozen water) in the dough, resulting in an improved tolerance to storage. Some researchers found that hydrocolloids can also have an effect of the retrogradation of starch. The use of hydrocolloids in frozen dough tends to improve their stability during storage. Researchers observed that guar gum and DATEM improved bread volume and texture and resulted in a reduced staling rate. Nevertheless, they were not able to counterbalance the negative effect of frozen storage on dough microstructure. Hydrocolloids are therefore thought mainly to interact with water distribution in the dough and with dough rheology, offering in principle a better tolerance to frozen storage.

FROZEN PART-BAKED BREAD

Introduction

The market share for frozen part-baked bread is growing and this product can be considered as the success story of BOT. This is probably because of its convenience and because the technology is kept under control at an industrial level. Therefore, its production can be managed with well-defined protocols and quality targets, and its final transformation requires minimally trained personnel. One may also mention that this concept of 'frozen and partially baked' applies to several other products such as frozen pizza, quiches and pies. Literature references related to frozen part-baked bread are scarce. There are some French references related to this product but the information available remains very general. A French patent concerns the process of partial baking. This patent is mainly related to the baking conditions; it describes an optimised baking temperature profile adapted to the production of part-baked bread. Researchers present specific data on special breads (ethnic breads). Part-baked breads can indeed offer shops the possibility to sell several types of breads, without having the constraints (as in the case of scratch baking) of adjusting the production to the demand of consumers. Specific problems (detachment) might arise when grains or seeds are applied onto the surface of ethnic breads. A technological study was carried out by researchers who demonstrated that partial baking process induced higher water loss than conventional direct baking (4% versus 2.5%). These authors compared different baking conditions (10 min/210°C, 15 min/190°C, 20 min/170°C) and observed that thewater loss increased with the duration of the baking process. More recently, Researchers studied the impact of storage on the microbial quality and on the moisture distribution of part-baked breads.

Quality loss during frozen storage has been assessed by researchers in a 9-month trial. The change in quality during the first month of storage was acceptable but it degraded further subsequently. The impact of frozen storage was also studied by researchers. Miniature dough samples were set in DSC pans and were stored at –18°C for 7, 15 and 30 days. They were baked *in situ* and were kept as 'bread' samples and stored at 4°C for

2, 4 and 7 days. Amylopectin retrogradation, which is an indicator of bread staling, increased during storage at 4°C after final baking and then stabilised after 7 days of storage. It was observed that this staling phenomenon increased with increasing storage duration. Researchers studied the impact of the amount of yeast and of vegetable shortening on the organoleptic quality and on the texture of frozen part-baked bread. Increasing the amount of yeast resulted in a more aerated crumb, whereas increasing the shortening resulted in a softer crumb. Researchers studied the optimisation of the baking parameters for partially baked bread.

Crust flaking of part-baked bread

One of the quality problems for frozen partially baked products is the quality of the crust in terms of colour, glossiness and crispiness, Sometimes, flaking off of the crust (crust flaking also called crust peeling) is mentioned by industry. There is very limited literature available on this problem. The crust is a very specific part of a crispy roll (typically a French Baguette) and may contain up to one-third of the dry matter. The hydrothermal treatment undergone by the bread during baking is applied to a crust dry area where non-gelatinised starch is still present. This affects the organoleptic perception of the consumer and also the nutritional value of the bread.

The impact of process conditions on crust flaking has been studied by LeBail *et al.* (2005). The impact of fermentation condition (50% and 90% air humidity at 27°C), chilling condition after partial baking (50–55% and 90–95% air humidity at 20°C) and freezing condition (blast air freezing, bread centre temperature 35°C, 45°C

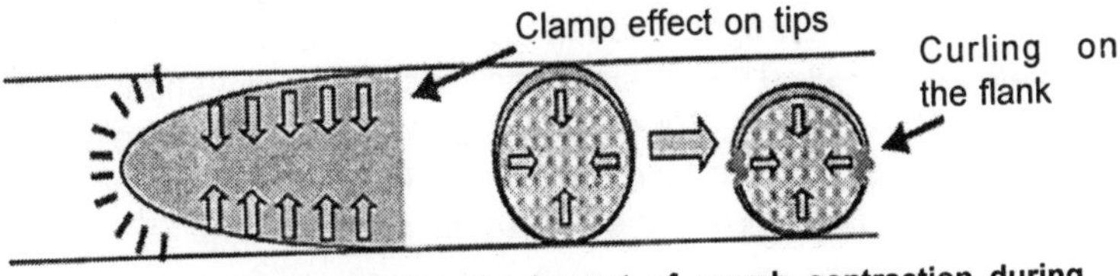

Fig. 8.1: Scheme showing the impact of crumb contraction during bread chilling and freezing. The clamp effect is developing on the tip of a crispy roll. In parallel, crumb contraction induces curling of the surface of the flank of the product, which has the thinner and therefore less mechanically resistant crust.

or 55°C at the freezer entrance) on crust flaking of part-baked bread was investigated. Crust flaking was evaluated by crushing a baguette on the top and on the sides and collecting the crust flakes. Crust flakingwas quantified from the mass ratio of crust to bread. An experimental design procedure was used to compare the relative effect of the selected parameters. It was found that the chilling condition after partial baking was the most influential parameter on crust flaking. This showed that chilling is only second in order of importance as the reason for crust flaking. Other parameters were not significantly influential; nevertheless, flaking was minimised by placing the product in the freezer at –35°C rather than at a higher temperature. This study showed that crust flaking was reduced if higher air humidities were used during fermentation and chilling. The authors observed that the size of the crust flakes increase with increasing crust flaking ratio. An important observation is that even though crust flaking was only fully revealed by the final baking process, the phenomenon may be predicted and was obviously visible at the end of the freezing process. Two hypotheses are proposed by the authors to explain crust flaking;

Assumption (a): Ice concentration below the crust

Assumption (b): A thermo-mechanical problem between the crust and crumb.

The first assumption is driven by the fact that during freezing, the centre of the bread remains hot for a certain duration while the freezing front is travelling from the surface of the bread. This situation induces a strong vapour pressure gradient, which results in moisture diffusion from thewarmer locations (centre) toward the cooler location (freezing front). The accumulation of ice on the freezing front might expose the crumb–crust interface to mechanical stress. This assumption has been investigated by Hamdami *et al.* (2004a, 2004b, 2004c); they found that the small amount of water collected by the freezing front was not significant enough to be considered the cause of crust flaking.

The second assumption is driven by the fact that bread contracts during chilling and freezing. This fact can be visible on baked bread especially on the flanks of a baguette (curling of the surface). Crust flaking mostly occurs on the flanks and on the tip of a baguette. The scheme proposed in Fig. 8.1 explains the clamp effect that develops on the tips and the curling of the flanks with thinner crust thickness and therefore these two result in deformation caused by crumb contraction.

The evidence of crumb contraction was first assessed using magnetic resonance imaging (MRI) by Lucas *et al.* (2005). They found MRI signal amplitude to increase below the crust during chilling and freezing; they attributed it to densification of the crumb–crust material. More recently, the impact of selected enzymes on crumb contraction was studied by Ribotta and LeBail (2007c). Relative strains corresponding to crumb contraction can reach a few percent during the chilling and freezing phases. The strain (contraction of the crumb) seems to be related to the retrogradation phenomenon which corresponds to the recrystallisation of macromolecules that are gelatinised during baking. The contraction of the crumb exposes the crust to stresses. Contraction stops once the crumb reaches the glass transition temperature. In this study, crumb contraction was studied using a Dynamic Mechanical Analyser operated as a dilatometer. A piece of crumb (8-mm thick) was exposed to a temperature scan (3°C per min) from 20°C to –70°C while crumb contraction was continuously logged.

Additional work showed that crumb contraction seems to be related to amylose recrystallisation, which occurs during the post-baking chilling process. Specific technological aids such as enzymes or adapted processing conditions may reduce the contraction of the crumb; work on this is in progress. It also seems that the milder the baking process, the greater the contraction of crumb. Optimisation of the partial baking condition may therefore also be an objective of further research.

Conclusion on frozen part-baked bread

One can easily see that the production of high-quality frozen part-baked bread remains a challenge for the food industry. The concept of quality varies from one country to another. Texture of the crust is obviously a central characteristic that is difficult to control; possibly each step of the process has its own role in the final crust quality. The quality of the flour, the mixing conditions, the fermentation conditions, condition of the batter at the end of fermentation, the partial baking conditions, the chilling conditions, the freezing conditions, the storage conditions, the final baking conditions are process parameters that may impact the final quality of the crust. The formulation is also very important and may need adaptation from traditional formulations for frozen part-baked production.

Freezing of partially fermented dough

Partially fermented dough (also called 'ready to bake' or 'ovenrise') has appeared in the market over the last decade and has become especially popular over the last 5 years. The objective of using partially fermented dough is to make a product that may ideally be transferred directly from the freezer to the oven.

Usually conventional blast air freezing equipment is used for freezing of prefermented dough. A high freezing rate is recommended in the literature, and so an efficient freezer should be used. Cryogenic freezing may be used, even though the operating cost of such equipment is hardly justified by the low cost of the bakery products.

The degree of fermentation before freezing plays an important role. The structure of the dough, which is made of closed cells will collapse due to gas contraction during freezing and. the volume that is lost has to be recovered during the thawing and baking phases. Hanneforth *et al.* (1994) recommend a fermentation ratio of 1/3 to 1/2 in comparison to full fermentation (volume ratio between non-frozen dough and fermented dough). Research work carried out by Rasanen (1998) investigated the frozen storage stability of pre-fermented frozen bread dough during frozen storage for 14 days at –20°C. Shorter fermentation time (25 min versus 40 min) prior to freezing improved the freeze–thaw stability of frozen dough with a 20% increase in loaf volume, a more uniform pore structure and a thicker network of gluten around gas bubbles, making them more resistant to freezing stress. No differences in storage stability of frozen dough were observed immediately after 25- and 40-minute prefermentation with most of the damage (expressed as the impact on the final bread volume) occurring during the first week of storage. A reduced moisture content (minus 2% versus optimum content in fresh dough) resulted in a higher volume. The use of hydrocolloids was also evaluated as a solution to minimise the dehydration of the dough by ice coarsening (increase in the mean size of ice crystals) during frozen storage.

LeBail (unpublished) carried out a set of specific experiments to assess process conditions for partly fermented dough. The experimental processing conditions are presented in Table 8.2. Preproving was between 1 hours (half of optimal proving time) and 2 hours (full optimal proving time). Dough formulationwas 100 g flour (type 55), 58 gwater, 2.2 g salt and 3 g compressed yeast. Fermentation ('proving') was carried out in a fermentation cabinet at 30°C with a relative humidity of 80%. Pre-fermentation was either 1, 1.5 or 2 hours and the corresponding final fermentation after frozen storage was 1 hour, 30 minutes or 0 minute so that the total fermentation time (including prior to freezing and post-frozen storage) was 2 hours. This total fermentation duration of 2 hours did not include thawing time after frozen storage. Displacement transducers were used to measure the expansion of the dough during fermentation (see Fig. 8.2). A typical plot of dough expansion Is presented in Fig. 8.3. Freezing was carried out in a blast air tunnel (air velocity 4 ms^{-1}) at –20°C or –40°C; dough sticks were withdrawn once the centre temperature became –20°C. The dough was thawed in a fermentation cabinet and was considered as completed once the centre of the dough stick (baguette 3.2 cm diameter after shaping–modelling) was 20°C. Storage was for 1 day at –20°C to focus on the effect of freezing *per se*. Baking was done in a ventilated oven at 230°C. Total baking duration was 15 minutes with steam injection at the beginning of baking and opening of the oven extraction after 5 minutes.

The experimental results showed that the lower the freezing rate the higher the dough collapse during freezing. In parallel, the higher the expansion ratio during the fermentation prior to freezing, the higher the dough collapse during freezing. These results are logical as rapid freezing permits the dough stick to stabilise and result in a much better preserved dough volume. Ahigher expansion ratio prior to freezing result in a more fragile dough with a higher gas ratio. A higher contraction is thus expected during freezing. An experimental design has been used to assess the interaction of the selected parameters. The highest bread

Table 8.2: Experimental conditions used to assess the impact of preproving time on bread volume in the case of partially fermented frozen bread dough.

Experiment #	Preproving time	Freezing temperature (°C)	Time fo reach -18°C at centre (min)
1	1 h	-20	86
2	1 h	-40	32
3	2 h	-20	103
4	2 h	-40	39
5	1 h 30 min	-30	45
6	1 h 30 min	-30	43
7	1 h 30 min	-30	48

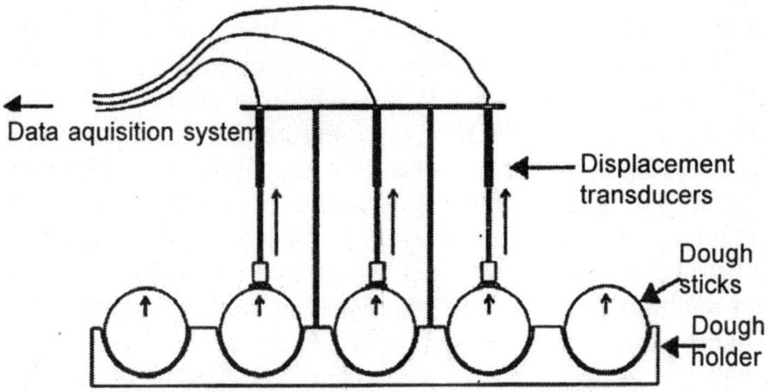

Fig. 28.2. Scheme showing o cross-section of ihe dough sticks installed in the dough holder. Displacement transducers were used to measure the vertical expansion of the dough stick continuously.

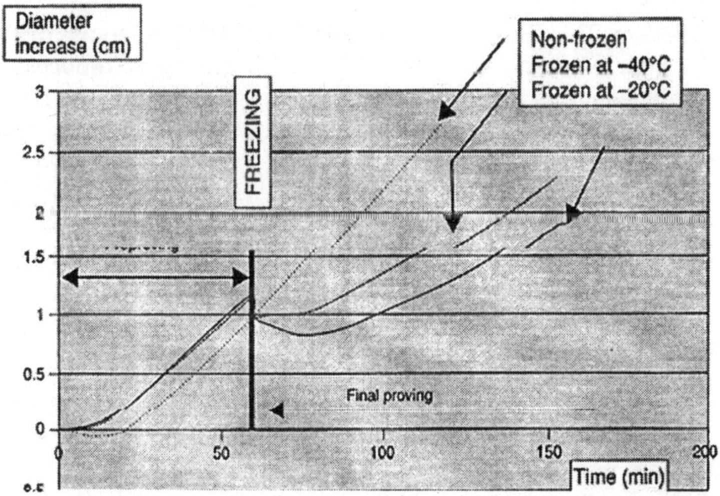

Fig. 8.3 Expansion (vertical rise) of a dough stick in the case of a prefer mentation of 60 minutes followed by frozen storage of 1 day at –20°C and second fermentation of 60 minutes. The graph does not show the thawing period before the second final proving- Fermentation was stopped when the diameter increase was around 20 mm (overall volume expansion ratio was 2.5 for an initial diameter of 3.2 cm). A higher final volume at the end of the 2-hour fermentation was observed for the fastest freezing rate. A significant volume reduction was observed in comparison to direct fermentation (non-frozen conditions).

volume was obtained with the highest freezing rate and with the lowest pre-fermentation time. One of the other problems with pre-fermented frozen dough is that during fermentation, the dough tends to dehydrate, resulting in a reduction in the initial freezing temperature. The initial freezing temperature of a dough is around –3°C/–4°C; therefore, the initial freezing temperature of the surface of the dough stick might be reduced by a few °C due to dehydration. During frozen storage, a rupture of the cold chain might induce a partial thawing of the surface of the dough sticks, which might stick them together. Such an incident would result in unacceptable crust in the finished product.

Conclusion

The industry has developed several bakery technologies to keep as much technology and know-how at the industrial level as possible, so as to ensure good control of the final quality of the product. This 'Bake Off Technology' is growing by about 10% every year whereas the share of scratch baking is reducing. Nevertheless, this technology still has quality problems and has a high energy demand, approximately double that required for scratch baking. New products such as pre-fermented frozen dough have therefore appeared in the market in the last decade. Nevertheless, new innovative technologies are still expected to enhance the convenience, organoleptic quality and to reduce the energy demand of these products.

FROZEN DESSERTS

This section describes frozen desserts, but the discussion will be limited to those desserts that are consumed frozen, e.g. ice cream and its low-fat versions: frozen yogurt, sherbets and sorbets. These desserts typically contain dairy ingredients and are frozen in a scrapedsurface freezer. In addition, there are several types of desserts that can be frozen, including bakery desserts (cakes, pies, etc. – unbaked, pre-baked or ready-to-eat), starch-based or gelatin-based custards and puddings, raw and prepared fruits, sweetened whipped toppings, and many more. These products are all characterised by thawing before consumption. In these products, the freezing steps must be optimised to maintain the quality parameters that were inherent in the original product before freezing, to deliver to the consumer a final product that has not been affected by the freezing process. As with most other frozen products, freezing time and storage temperature are the most important parameters to be optimised. Rapid freezing promotes small ice crystals, which minimise structure disruption and water dislocation. Low and constant storage temperatures maintain this population of ice crystals by minimising ice recrystallisation. Desserts often provide a challenge due to formulation as a result of high sugar content. This creates a low freezing point due to solute effects and freeze-concentration, which results in a high content of unfrozen water at typical storage temperatures, in comparison to products like vegetables or meats. Thus, it is especially imperative that desserts be maintained at the lowest storage and distribution temperatures possible. Functional ingredients, such as polysaccharide stabilisers or modified starches, may be used to help control water redistribution and ice recrystallisation. The rest of this section will focus on desserts that are consumed frozen, with the discussion specific to ice cream, unless otherwise noted.

Ingredients

The range of compositional variables found in most frozen dairy dessert mix formulations is shown in Table 8.3. The composition of frozen dairy dessert products in most countries is standardised and regulated.

Fat

The fat content is an indicator of the perceived quality and/or value of the ice cream. The fat component of the mix increases the richness of flavour of ice cream, produces a characteristic smooth texture by lubricating the palate, contributes to making the structure and aids in producing desirable melting properties. Milk fat – from cream, sweet (unsalted) butter, frozen cream, condensed milk blends or whey cream – is the principal and only fat source for dairy ice cream formulations. Vegetable fats can also be used as fat sources in non-dairy ice cream. Blends of oils are often used in ice cream manufacture to gain on physical characteristics, flavour, availability and cost. Palm kernel oil, coconut oil, palm oil, sunflower oil, peanut oil, fractions thereof, and their hydrogenated counterparts are all used to some extent. Regardless of the source, it is important that a considerable quantity of the fat be crystallised at the time of whipping/freezing. During freezing of ice cream, the fat emulsion that exists in the mix will partially coalesce or destabilise as a result of the presence of crystals of fat, emulsifier action, air incorporation, ice crystallisation and high shear in the freezer, thus establishing a three-dimensional network of fat throughout the product that entraps air and provides shape retention and meltdown resistance.

Milk solids-not-fat

The milk solids-not-fat (SNF) or serum solids contain the lactose, caseins, whey proteins, minerals (ash), vitamins, acids, enzymes and gases of the milk or milk products from which they were derived. The proteins are essential for their functional contributions of emulsification, aeration and water holding capacity/viscosity enhancement. An excess of lactose, however, may lead to problems due to excessive freezing point depression or lactose crystallisation, leading to a textural defect. Thus, SNF sources should be chosen to optimise protein functionality but limit lactose content. Traditionally, the best sources of milk SNF for high-quality products have been fresh concentrated skimmed milk or spray dried low-heat skimmed milk powder. Others include those containing whole milk protein (e.g. condensed or sweetened condensed whole milk, milk protein concentrates, dry or condensed buttermilk), those containing casein (e.g. sodium caseinate), or those containing whey proteins (e.g. dried or condensed whey, whey protein concentrate, whey protein isolate).

Sweeteners

Sweeteners improve the texture and palatability of ice cream and enhance flavours. Their ability to lower the freezing point of a solution imparts a measure of control over the temperature–hardness relationship. The most common sweetening agent is sucrose, alone or in combination with other sugars. In determining the appropriate blend of sweeteners to use, the sweetness, freezing point depression and contribution to total solids – all have to be considered. Sucrose and lactose are most commonly present in ice cream in the supersaturated or glassy state, with few crystals being present. In many ice cream formulations, sweeteners derived from corn syrup are substituted for all or a portion of the sucrose. The use of corn starch hydrolysis products (corn syrups or glucose solids) in ice cream is generally perceived to provide greater smoothness by contributing to a firmer and more chewy body, to provide better meltdown characteristics, to reduce heat shock potential, which improves the shelf-life of the finished product, and to provide an economical source of solids.

Functional additives (stabilisers, emulsifiers)

Ice cream stabilisers are a group of hydrocolloid ingredients (usually polysaccharides) used in ice cream formulations to produce smoothness in body and texture and retard or reduce the growth of ice and lactose crystals during storage, especially during periods of temperature fluctuation, known as heat shock. Thus, by physical means, they effectively increase the shelflife of ice cream. They also increase the viscosity of the mix, aid in suspension of flavouring particles in the semi-frozen ice cream, produce a stable foam with easy cut-off and stiffness at the barrel freezer for packaging, slow down moisture migration from the product to the package or the air in frozen product, and contributes to preventing shrinkage of the product volume during storage. Stabilisers commonly used include: locust bean (carob) gum, guar gum, carboxymethyl cellulose, sodium alginate, xanthan, and gelatin. Each stabiliser has its own characteristics and often two or more of these stabilisers are used in combination to lend synergistic properties to each other and improve their overall effectiveness. Carrageenan is a secondary hydrocolloid used to prevent serum separation in the mix, which is usually promoted by one of the other stabilisers. Hence, it is found in most stabiliser blends Small-molecule surfactants (emulsifiers) are usually integrated with the stabilisers in proprietary blends but their function and action are very different from those of the stabilisers.

They are used to: (a) improve the aeration properties of the mix; (b) produce an ice cream at extrusion with good shape retention properties (referred to as 'dryness') to facilitate moulding, fancy extrusion and novelty product manufacture; (c) produce a smoother body and texture in the finished product; and (d) produce a product with good shape-retention properties during melting.

Their mechanism of action can be summarised as follows: they lower the fat–water interfacial tension in the mix, resulting in protein displacement from the fat globule surface, which in turn reduces the stability of the fat globule to partial coalescence that occurs during the whipping and freezing process, leading to the formation of an aggregated fat structure in the frozen product which contributes greatly to texture and melt-down properties. Emulsifiers used in ice cream manufacture are of two main types: mono- and di-glycerides and sorbitan esters. Of the latter, polysorbate 80 is a very strong promoter of fat destabilisation in ice cream and is used in many commercial stabiliser/emulsifier blends.

Flavours

Liquid flavours and colours, those that are to be homogeneous throughout the frozen product, are added to the flavour tank prior to scraped-surface freezing while particulate flavours are added post-freezing. While there are numerous flavours that exist for ice cream, there are a few limitations, such as the effect of the flavour addition on protein stability in the mix (ethanol, for example), the effect on freezing point depression (in the case of high sugar flavours), the water activity balance between the frozen ice cream and the ingredient (as it affects water migration), hardness of the flavour ingredient at product consumption temperatures, etc.

Processes

The manufacturing process for most of these products is similar. It involves the preparation of a liquid mix; whipping and freezing this mix dynamically under high shear to a soft, semifrozen slurry; incorporation of flavouring ingredients to this partially frozen mix; packaging the product, and further freezing (hardening) of the product under static, quiescent conditions. Swept (scraped)-surface freezers are used for the first freezing step, while forced convection freezers, such as air blast tunnels or rooms, or plate-type conduction freezers are used for the second freezing step.

Mixing, pasteurisation, homogenisation and aging

Ice cream processing operations can be divided into two distinct stages: mix manufacture and freezing operations (Fig. 8.4). The manufacture of ice cream mix involves the following unit operations: combination and blending of ingredients, batch or continuous pasteurisation, homogenisation and ageing. Ingredients are chosen to supply the desired components, e.g. cream or butter to supply fat, on the basis of availability, ease of handling, desired quality and cost. An algebraic solution of the formulation is required, since many of the ingredients supply more than one component.

Pasteurisation is designed to kill pathogenic bacteria. In addition, it serves a useful role in reducing the total bacterial load and in solubilising some of the components (proteins and stabilisers). Both batch (>~69°C for<–30 min) and continuous (high temperature–short time, HTST, >~80°C for ~15–25 s) systems are in common use. Homogenisation is responsible for the formation of fat emulsion by forcing the hot mix through a small orifice under pressures of 15.5–18.9 MPa (2000–3000 psi gauge), depending on the composition of the mix. Small fat globules are needed to establish the appropriate degree of fat partial coalescence. A large increase in the surface area of the fat globules is responsible in part for the formation of the fat globule membrane, comprised of adsorbed materials that lower the interfacial free energy of the fat globules.With single-stage homogenisers, fat globules tend to cluster as bare fat surfaces come together or adsorbed molecules shared. Therefore, a second homogenising valve is frequently placed immediately after the first with applied back pressures of 3.4 MPa (500 psi gauge), allowing more time for surface adsorption to occur.

An ageing time of 4 h or longer following mix processing prior to freezing is recommended to produce a smoother texture and better quality product. The temperature of the mix should be maintained as low as possible without freezing (≤4°C). Ageing allows for hydration of milk proteins and stabilisers (some increase in viscosity occurs during the ageing period), crystallisation of the fat globules and membrane rearrangement. The appropriate ratio of solid:liquid fat must be attained at this stage, a function of temperature and the triglyceride composition of the fat used, as a partially crystalline emulsion is needed for partial coalescence during the whipping and freezing steps. Emulsifiers generally

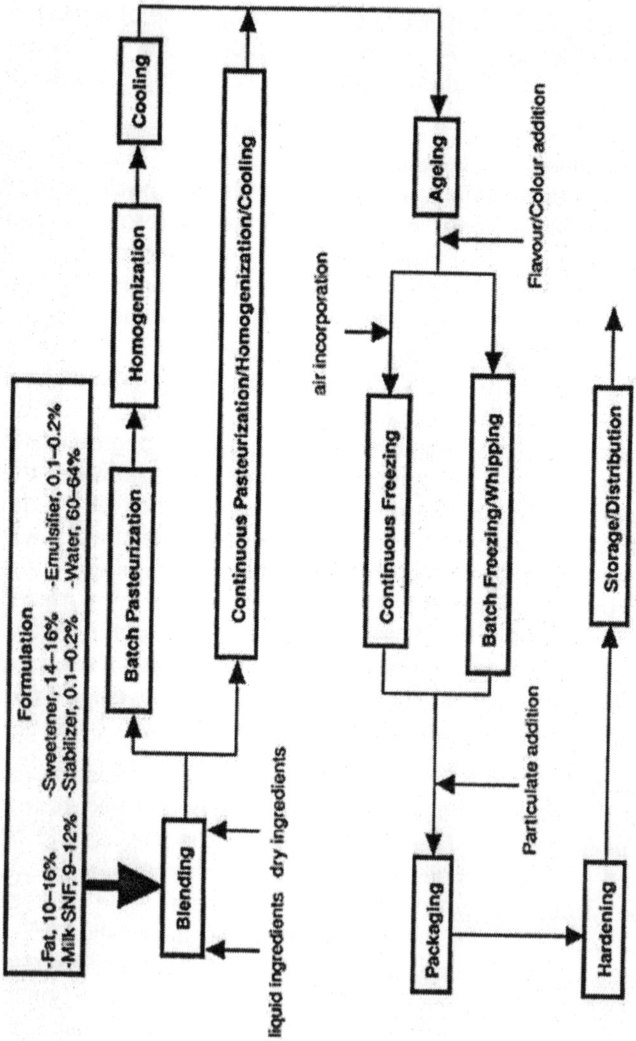

Fig. 8.4. Flow diagram of the ice cream manufactyring process

displace milk proteins from the fat surface during the ageing period.

Dynamic freezing

Ice cream freezing also consists of two distinct stages: passing mix through a swept (scraped)- surface heat exchanger under high shear conditions to promote extensive ice crystallisation and air incorporation; and freezing the packaged ice cream under conditions that promote rapid freezing and small ice crystal sizes. The concomitant freezing and whipping process is one of the most important unit operations for the development of quality, palatability, and yield of the finished product. Flavouring and colouring can be added as desired to the mix prior to passing through the barrel freezer, and particulate flavouring ingredients, such as nuts, fruits, candy pieces, or ripple sauces, can be added to the semi-frozen product at the exit from the barrel freezer prior to packaging and hardening. Continuous freezers dominate the ice cream industry. In this type of process, mix is drawn from the flavouring tank into a swept-surface heat exchanger (Fig. 8.5), which is jacketed with a liquid, boiling refrigerant (e.g. ammonia). Following the incorporation of air into the mix, the water in the mix is partially frozen as the mix and air combination passes through the barrel of the scraped-surface heat exchanger. Rotating knife blades scrape the ice layer off the surface and dashers keep the product agitated, which incorporates the air phase as tiny bubbles and maintains discrete ice crystals as they grow in the bulk liquid. Residence time for mix through the annulus of the freezer varies from 0.4 to 2 minutes, freezing rates can vary from 5 to 27°C min^{-1}, and draw temperatures of "6°C can easily be achieved. Incorporation of air into ice cream, defined by its 'overrun' or increase in volume, as a percent of mix volume, is a necessity to produce a desirable body and texture. As a guide, maximum overrun should be 2.5–3 times the total solids content to avoid possible defects in the finished ice cream. In older systems, the pump configuration resulted in a vacuum either at the pump itself or on the mix line entering the pump. Air was then incorporated through a spring-loaded, controllable needle valve. Newer types of freezers utilise compressed air, which is injected into the mix. This type of air handling system allows for

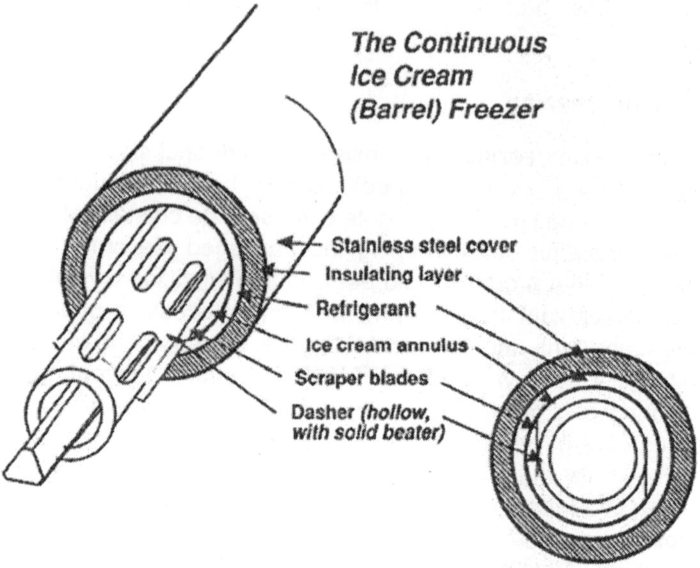

Fig. 8.5 Continuous Ice cream (Barrel Freezer)

filtration of the air prior to entering into the mix and for better control of overrun.

Batch freezing processes differ slightly from the continuous systems just described. The barrel of a batch-swept surface heat exchanger is jacketed with refrigerant and contains a set of dashers and scraper blades inside the barrel. It is filled to about one-half volume with the liquid mix. Barrel volumes usually range from 2 to 12 L. The freezing unit and agitators are then activated and the product remains in the barrel for sufficient time to achieve the desired degree of overrun and stiffness. Whipping increases with time and cannot exceed the amount that will fill the barrel with product (i.e. 100% overrun when starting half full). Batch freezers are used in smaller operations where it is desirable to run individual flavoured mixes on a small scale or to retain an element of the 'homemade'-style manufacturing process. They are also operated in a semi-continuous mode for the production of soft-serve type desserts. A hopper containing the mix feeds the barrel as product is removed.

Static freezing

Following dynamic freezing, ingredient addition, and packaging, the ice cream is immediately transferred to a hardening chamber (–30°C or colder, either forced convection or plate-type conduction freezers) where most of the remainingwater freezes. Rapid hardening is necessary for product quality, as it helps to maintain the small ice crystal size distribution thatwas created in the scraped-surface freezer. When hardening is slow, there is too great an opportunity for small ice nuclei formed to recrystallise, resulting in larger ice crystals and a coarser product. Many factors need to be considered during the hardening process. The main factors affecting heat transfer are the temperature difference between the product and the freezing medium, the area of product being exposed to the freezing medium, and the heat transfer coefficient for the particular operation. The temperature of the ice cream when placed in the hardening room should be as cold as possible. Draw temperatures from the barrel freezer are limited by the necessity of flowability for packaging the product. The addition of ingredients and the packaging operation should not increase the temperature of the ice cream as it is drawn from the barrel freezer any more than necessary. The temperature of the hardening chamber is also critical for rapid freezing and smooth product. The surface area of the Ice cream also needs to be considered, and is especially important when packaging in large packages or in shrinkwrapping product bundles. Palletising or stacking of product should not interfere with rapid air circulation and fast freezing. Convective heat transfer coefficients are greatly increased through the use of forced convection systems. The evaporator should be free of frost from the outside and oil from the inside of the coils as these act to reduce the heat transfer coefficients. Following rapid hardening, ice cream storage should occur at low, constant temperatures, usually at –25°C.

Structure and stability

The whipping and freezing processes occurring concomitantly in the scraped-surface freezer together account for the formation of the freeze-concentrated, unfrozen, continuous phase and all of the discrete phases of ice cream structure: the ice crystals, the air bubbles and the partially coalesced fat globule structure

(Fig. 8.6).This structure, in turn, dictates the final texture as consumed. The ice phase is of critical importance to the quality and shelf-life of frozen products. The objective of ice cream manufacturers is to produce ice crystals of size that is below, or at least not significantly above, the threshold of sensory detection at the time of consumption: 40–50 μm. Consequently the freezing steps of the manufacturing process and the temperature profile throughout the distribution system are the critical factors in meeting this objective.

The dissolved sugars, lactose, and salts, result in an initial freezing temperature in the mix of about –2.5°C, depending on their concentration. From Raoult's law, the freezing point is a function of both the concentration and the molecular weight of the solutes. As water freezes out of solution in the form of pure ice crystals, solutes are excluded from the growing ice and concentrate in an ever-decreasing amount of water. Water and its dissolved components are referred to as the serum or matrix of the mix. Because the freezing point of the serum is a function of the concentration of dissolved solids, the formation of more ice concentrates the serum and results in an ever-decreasing freezing temperature for the remaining serum.

Thus at temperatures several degrees below the initial freezing temperature, there is always an unfrozen phase present. Ice cream hardness is a function of temperature due to its effect on this conversion of unfrozen water to ice and further concentration of the serum phase surrounding the ice crystals, which gives ice cream its property that it can be scooped and chewed at freezer temperatures. Composition-based freezing curves for ice cream can readily be calculated.

The dynamic whipping and freezing process is also responsible for the formation of a fat network or structure in the product. Ice cream is both an emulsion and a foam. The milk fat exists in tiny globules that have been formed by the homogeniser. There are many proteins that act as emulsifiers and give the fat emulsion its needed stability. The emulsifiers actually reduce the stability of this fat emulsion, because they replace proteins on the fat surface. When the mix is subjected to the whipping action of the scraped-surface freezer, the fat emulsion begins to partially coalesce and the fat globules begin to flocculate (Fig. 8.6). The

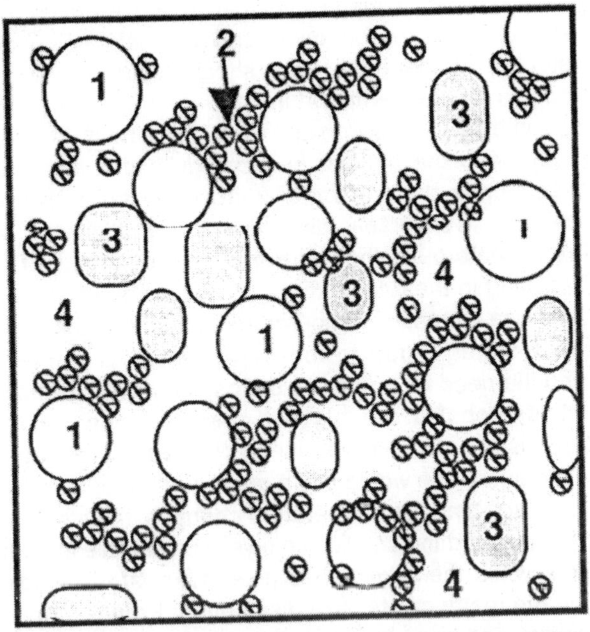

Fig. 8.6 Schematic diagram of the physical structure of ice cream: (1) air cells, (2) fat globules and partially coalesced fat surrounding air cells, (3) ice crystals, *(4)* unfrozen, freeze-concentrated solution of dissolved and suspended solids.

air bubbles that are being beaten into the mix are stabilised by this partially coalesced fat. This process is similar to that which occurs during the whipping of heavy cream as the liquid is converted to a semi-solid with desirable stand-up qualities and mouthfeel. In ice cream, the emulsion destabilisation phenomenon also results in desirable textural qualities both at the time of draw from the barrel freezer and during consumption, resulting in a smoother, creamier product with a slower meltdown.

During storage, the ice crystals that were created during manufacture undergo morphological changes in number, size, and shape. This is known collectively as recrystallisation and leads to a coarse, icy texture and the defect of iciness. Recrystallisation is probably the most important change producing quality losses and limitations in shelf-life. It also probably accounts for countless lost sales through customer dissatisfaction with quality. The majority of recrystallisation is stimulated by fluctuating temperatures (known as heat shock) and can be minimised by maintaining a low, constant storage temperature. Heat shock occurs readily in ice cream products. If the temperature during the frozen storage increases, some of the ice crystals melt, particularly the smaller ones as they have the highest free energy and lowest melting point. Consequently, the amount of unfrozen water in the serum phase increases. Conversely, as temperatures decrease, water does not renucleate but rather refreezes on the surface of larger crystals, resulting in the total number of crystals diminish and the mean crystal size increase. Temperature fluctuations are common during frozen storage, due to the cyclic nature of refrigeration systems and the need for automatic defrost. However, mishandling of product is probably the biggest culprit. If one tracks the temperature history of ice cream during distribution, retailing, and finally consumption, one would find a great number of temperature fluctuations. Each time the temperature changes, the ice to serum content changes, and the smaller ice crystals decrease in numbers or disappear while the larger ones grow even larger, leading to a change in the mean crystal size distribution. Proper formulation with stabilisers designed to combat heat shock is an essential defence against the inevitable growth of ice crystals.

9

Banana based Frozen-nondairy Dessert

Today's population is becoming more and more health and health food conscious. Witness the continuing ban on cigarette smoking and the increase of availability of organically grown foods. More and more Indians are desirous of cutting down on their intake of presevatives and food additives. In addition there is a segment of the population that is attempting to reduce its intake of fats and cholesterol. There is also a segment of the population that needs to exclude dairy products from its diet due to allergy. For these people and others there is a need for healthful desserts, that allows them to exclude the above named non-desired products from their diets.

It is an object therefore of this project to provide a nondairy based dessert that utilizes as its base ingredient quick frozen preferably ripe bananas.

It is another object of this method to provide a frozen dessert that can be made without the addition of food additives and preservatives.

It is yet another object to provide a frozen dessert that can be made substantially fat free.

The figure is a block diagram illustrating the preferred mode of manufacture of the frozen dessert of this method.

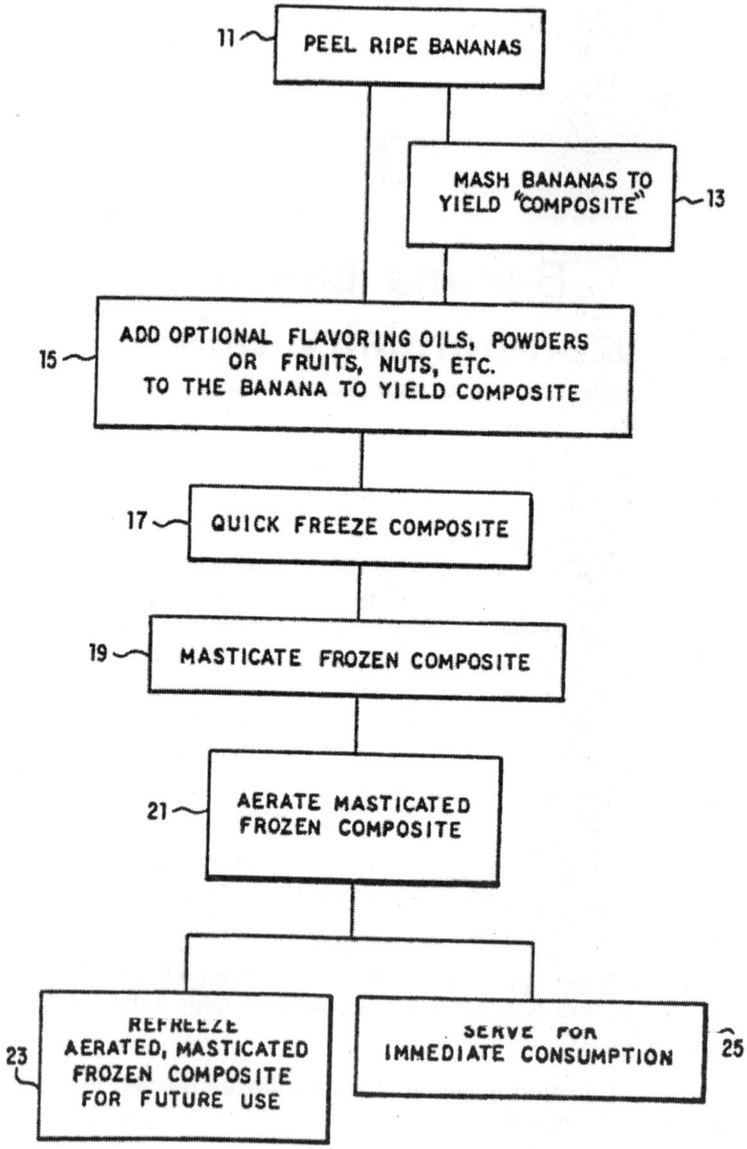

The method differs from all of these products which start with a liquid which is a mixture of some or all of the following; dairy products, water, fruit concentrates, sugar, emulsifiers, stabilizers, colours, and fats derived from vegetable, and/or animal sources. In these prior art products, the liquid is cooled and frozen while being whipped. The whipping action is what gives the products its overrun which is the entrainment of air therein. The percent of overrun is an expression of the amount of air that is frozen in said dessert.

The method preferably involves the steps of using whole ripe bananas singularly or mixed with other fruits, nuts, oils or powders or liquors at room temperature and the "quick freezing" of that mass to form a composite; (b) then storing the frozen composite in a conventional freezer at around 0°F. to -15°F., and when the frozen composite is either ready to be consumed or repackaged, first masticating and then whipping the composite into a mass to give desired overrun qualities. If the mass is to be repackaged for later consumption it is again quick frozen and stored in a conventional freezer.

In order to obtain the optimum dessert, care should be exerted in the selection of the bananas to be employed for the base i.e. the composite; of this dessert. Properly chosen bananas have just the right amount of starch, carbohydrates, cellulose, pulp and pectin to work best in this process. Thus the bananas should be stored such as to avoid extreme heat and cold. When bananas approach their freezing point, the skin turns brown and more importantly the starch therein will not effectively turn to sugar. Permitting the banana's starch content to break down into sugars (glucose, fructose and sucrose) is of utmost importance to maximize flavour. Thus it has been noted that when the banana skin is yellow green, 40% of the carbohydrates are in the form of starch while after ripening, only 8% are still starch, the rest having broken down into natural sugars. It is important also not to try to obtain the last bit of starch to conversion, since bananas left too long will have their sugar content start to ferment. The ideal ripening temperature is about 78°F, and temperatures below 55°F should be avoided.

In view of the high natural sugar content, and the presence of the banana pulp, there is little or no need for added sugar for either sweetening or for thickening purposes. The relative smoothness of the prepared pulp closely approximates the mouth feel that is obtained from the addition of fats, such as butter fat and emulsifiers and stabilizers to frozen desserts. Brown coloured small spots on a yellow skin is a good colorimetric indicator of adequate ripening for use in the process of this invention. Almost any variety of banana may be employed herein other than plantains and related varieties whose starch does not turn to sugar and which upon ripening assume a consistency of potatoes, i.e. relatively hard.

The bananas which may comprise all or part of the composite, are first peeled. They then may be mashed into a pulp, by hand or mechanically or quickly sliced into wafers of about thicknesses 1/16 to 3/8 inch thick, or if desired they may left in an unaltered though peeled state. The initial preparation, if any, should take place quickly such that oxygen induced browning discolouration is avoided. The choice of preparation mode will be related to the quick freeze mode to be employed. For example if ice cube type trays carrying banana in the compartments are to be utilized, placement of a wafer in each compartment of the tray, or a filling of the tray with banana pulp mark would be satisfactory. On the other hand, if the bananas are to be placed on an endless belt and moved continuously through a freezing chamber, then no initial preparation is required.

Whole bananas or banana chunks can be used as the composite, if the frozen dessert is to be solely banana. But if the dessert is to include other flavorants such as berries, nuts, etc, it is preferred that the banana be mashed to a pulp to aid in the ultimate incorporation of such flavorants prior to the freezing step.

Mashing of the banana, especially when it is to be united with other materials of a liquid or powder nature, is recommended. This eases the incorporation of the other ingredients, and permits placement of uniform amounts into little molds such as ice cube trays adapted for the plate freezing technique.

The standard commercially available banana puree is not acceptable for use in making the frozen dessert of this method. In making a puree, the reduction of the fruit to such small particle sizes causes the introduction of a significant amount of oxygen. This oxygen is the fuel for the enzyme polyphenoloxidase present in the banana, which aids very quickly to turn the banana puree brown. Thus commercially prepared banana puree is heat treated and subjected to an antioxidant such as ascorbic acid, to impede or prevent this browning reaction. On the contrary, avoid using an antioxidants in the desserts of this invention.

ALL BANANA

Let bananas of good quality ripen undisturbed until; most of the starch has turned to sugar. Then peel ripe bananas either mash the pulp or leave the banana whole while maximizing surface area and minimizing mass. The banana is put through the quick freeze process with target freezing time of less than 10 to 15 minutes. The frozen pulp is then stored in regular freezer at a temperature of around 0°F to -15°F, after being wrapped in plastic to protect the pulp from the ambient air which carry both moisture and contaminants. When needed, the frozen composite is masticated, homogenized and whipped to a target overrun of preferably about 60%, or to desired taste and consistency. The product can now be consumed or quick frozen again to be consumed later.

STRAWBERRY-BANANA

The procedure for using ripe bananas is the same as above. Strawberries are cleaned and cut into smaller pieces and blended with peeled ripe bananas. This composite is then poured into suitable molds then quick frozen followed by storage in a regular freezer prior to ultimate processing.

The proportion of strawberry to banana is defined only by individual taste. Using 8 ounces of banana as a constant and adding progressively more grams of strawberry up to 64 grams gives a progressively more strawberry flavor and colour. At 64 grams a nice red colour and clearly strawberry flavor is achieved. Although the strength of both the flavor and colour is enhanced after 64 grams it is not as dramatic as before. In taste tests it was found that at 112 grams the flavor starts to become too tangy and not as pleasant as before at smaller proportions. 64 to 96 grams seemed to be the most popular.

BANANA AND PINEAPPLE

The procedure and proportions are almost identical to strawberry except that the colour remained constant.

BANANA AND PECANS

The procedure for using ripe bananas is the same as mentioned earlier. It is important to note that the nuts to be used must be fresh. If they have started to turn rancid, beside the obvious taste consideration, the rancidity will accelerate the oxidation of the frozen composite. Pecans should be slightly chopped to ensure a more uniform mixture. When researcher used 8 ounces of banana as a constant and added more and more grams of pecan, the pecan flavor became more and more prominent up to the 14 gram point, at which it begins to overtake the banana flavor. As the amount of pecans increases the flavor becomes more and more intense. At 24 grams the banana influence appears lost. In taste tests around 18 to 24 grams of pecans per 8 ounces of banana was the most popular.

BANANA AND CHOCOLATE

Pure chocolate liquor was used. Using 8 ounces of banana as a constant, researcher added more and more chocolate in ½ gram increments. In taste tests, the preference was for between 5 and 7 grams. At 8 grams the cocoa flavor started to become to strong.

BANANA AND PEPPERMINT

Non-alcoholic natural peppermint flavor was used. 8 ounces of banana was again used as a constant and drops of flavor were added. Anything over 4 drops were too strong. The preferred formula utilized between 2 and 3 drops per 8 ounces of banana.

STRAWBERRY-BANANA

Approximately 8 ounces of ripe peeled banana were blended with 64 grams of fresh sliced strawberries in a large glass bowl by mashing the banana and stirring it with the strawberries. The mixture was spooned into several empty openings in a plastic ice cube tray and then covered with plastic and flash frozen by immersing the tray into a tank of liquid nitrogen. After 6 minutes the tray was removed and the cubed composite was found to be frozen solid and stored at -5°F.

The following day the frozen composite was then subjected to mastication procedure and whipped to entrain air. The increase in volume was found to be 60%, i.e. an overrun of 160%. The product, which was dark pink in colour was spooned onto a plate and served immediately.

BANANA

Sixteen ounces of mashed ripe banana were mashed and was spooned into a plastic ice cube tray and frozen. After quick freezing the tray it was removed from the nitrogen tank, and stored in a conventional home freezer for future use.

About two weeks later, 8 ounces of the frozen composite were masticated in a customized Champion Juicer and whipped with an electric mixer to an overrun of about 160% and then served. The balance of the frozen composite was returned to the home freezer in the zip lock bag.

BANANA

Eight ounces of ripe banana sections were placed in liquid nitrogen and allowed to solidify. After 6 minutes, the frozen composite was removed, and stored at -5° F. for one day and then masticated by a cheese grater and then whipped using a hand held electric mixer. Overrun was believed to be about 127%. The frozen dessert had a smooth frozen yogurt like mouth feel.

The following further examples illustrate the preparation of additional composites suitable for the preparation of frozen desserts according to the procedure described previously.

BANANA AND COCOA POWDER

As is known, chocolate liquor differs from cocoa powder in that the fat is removed in the formation of the cocoa powder.

Pure cocoa powder was used. Using 8 ounces of banana as a constant researcher added more and more cocoa in one-half gram increments. In taste tests, the best flavor was obtained between two and three grams of cocoa powder per 8 ounces of banana. At four grams of cocoa flavor was too strong. Colour was good for all mixtures.

BANANA AND WALNUTS

Researcher added incremental grams of walnuts to a constant 8 ounces of banana. The walnut flavor started to be noticed at 10 grams walnuts and became too intense at 20 grams. The best flavor was judged to be between 14 and 16 grams of nuts. The walnut as with other nut flavors masked the banana taste within the preferred range of the flavorant.

BANANA AND PECAN AND CHOCOLATE LIQUOR

Using the same method as previously described, with respect to banana and chocolate liquor I added incremental grams of pecan as well as chocolate liquor. It was found that at about 16 grams of pecans and about 5 grams of chocolate liquor provided the optimum flavor combination. Significantly greater amounts of either ingredient turned out to be overpowering to the palate while lesser amounts did not deliver the desired flavor. Colour was constant throughout the range of experiments.

BANANA AND ANISEED (LICORICE)

Whole aniseeds were added to 8 ounces of banana at one-quarter teaspoon intervals. At one-quarter teaspoon the anise was barely detectable and the best results were achieved between the range of one-half and three-quarter teaspoons per 8 ounce of banana. 1 and 1.25 teaspoons of aniseed were found to be too strong. [One teaspoon=1 gram].

10

Coated Frozen Cheese Granules

In India, many retail operations engaged in preparation and baking of pizzas desire to use cheese in a comminuted form. Consequently, producers of mozzarella and other cheese used on pizzas shred or dice block cheese for delivery to the pizza restaurants. To provide improved storage and keeping qualities, comminuted cheese for use on pizzas can be frozen and delivered in frozen or semi-frozen condition. However, the cheese must at least be thawed to the extent that the shreds or granules can be separated. Moreover, further thawing is needed to improve functionality.

The use of comminuted cheese in frozen or partially frozen condition on pizzas frequently results in baked products showing excessive browning and blistering. Not only is this appearance unattractive to the consumer, but the flavor and eating quality can also be adversely affected.

The recommended practice involves slow thawing of the frozen cheese. Where thawing is carried out during non-freezing refrigerated storage, as is a common practice, a minimum of two to three days of thawing-holding is usually required. Moreover, the best practice involves holding of the granular cheese for four to five days, until thawing is completed.

Because of the problems associated with the use of frozen comminuted cheese for preparing pizza, certain franchised cheese restaurants require that the comminuted cheese be packaged non-frozen in specially designed packages. This adds considerably to packaging and distribution expenses, although it does avoid the necessity of slow thawing.

As far as is known, no one heretofore has produced frozen comminuted cheese which can be applied to pizzas in frozen or partially frozen condition and baked to produce a pizza product of as good quality as with fully thawed cheese. The high standards of appearance, quality and taste for large scale pizza preparation have not been satisfied by the use of comminuted cheese which has not been completely thawed.

It has also been desired to modify the properties of granular cheese for use on pizzas and as toppings or ingredients in other baked food products. Such modifications include the incorporation of emulsifiers and flavor additives. Heretofore, however, no method or product has been provided in which such additives are provided as components of frozen comminuted cheese.

PROCESS

Shredded mozzarella cheese is prepared in a granule size of about 1/8×3/16×3/4 inches. The granules are subjected to IQF fluidized bed freezing in a "FLoFREEZE" Model 300 WS-ADF supplied by Frigoscandia Contracting, Inc., Bellevue, Washington. The freezing and fluidizing air which is blown upwardly through the bed of granules can have a velocity of around 400 ft/min. and a temperature of about -40° F. Frozen crusts form rapidly around the outside of the granules, viz. in one to two minutes or less. The time required for completion of the freezing is of the order of 7 minutes. The frozen granules leaving the fluidized bed have a temperature of around -20° F. Weight loss due to moisture evaporation during the freezing process is less than 0.5%. Baffles along the sides and over the fluidized bed to minimize loss of cheese fines are provided. The frozen granules are packed in bags and boxed for storage, for example, at a temperature from -10° to 0° F.

Coatings for the frozen cheese can include one or more of the following flavor additives: lactose, glucose, diacetyl, free fatty acids (i.e., butyric, propionic, capric, caproic acids), cheese flavors (cheddar, Swiss. Provolone, etc.), meat flavors (bacon, pepperoni, sausage, etc.), spices (basil, oregano, garlic, dill, cinnamon, fennel, etc.), vegetable flavors (tomato, onion, pimiento, pepper, etc.), and fruit flavors (strawberry, pineapple, cherry, lemon, etc.). Emulsifier additives, which may be used either alone or with the flavor additives, include: surfactants, disodium phosphate, silicone emulsifiers, and other GRAS-approved emulsifiers.

The following formulations are illustrative.

EMULSIFIER COATING SOLUTION

A silicone emulsifier is mixed with water to form a 0.05% emulsifier solution. This solution is sprayed on the frozen cheese granules at a rate of 1.75 parts of solution per 100 parts by weight of cheese. This should achieve a final content of around 0.09% emulsifier on the cheese.

SMOKE FLAVOR COATING SOLUTION

A smoke flavor is mixed with water to form a 4.5% solution thereof. The solution is sprayed on the frozen cheese granules at a rate of 2.2 parts by weight of solution per 100 parts of cheese. This should achieve a final content of about 0.1% smoke on the cheese, which will provide a smoked flavor when the cheese is cooked.

SWISS FLAVOR SOLUTION

A Swiss cheese flavor is mixed with water to form a 50% by weight solution. The solution is sprayed on the frozen cheese granules at a rate of 0.5 parts of solution per 100 parts by weight of cheese. This should achieve a final content of about 2.5% Swiss flavor on the cheese, to provide cheese with this flavor on cooking.

PROVOLONE FLAVORING OF MOSSARELLA

A cheese having the flavor characteristics of provolone on cooking is prepared from mozzarella cheese as follows. Mozzarella cheese is first shredded or diced to a granular form, as previously described. For example, two different kinds of mozzarella cheese may be combined in equal parts by weight, such as 70% skim mozzarella and 30% low moisture mozzarella to provide the granular cheese mixture which is subjected to rapid freezing as described above. After the granules are frozen, a series of two coatings is applied. The first comprises a 1% coating (based on the weight of the cheese granules) of an 0.85% solution of liquid smoke (Arrow P-50). After the first coating has been distributed in the form of a frozen layer around the cheese granules, a second coating is applied comprising a 1 to 1.5% application of an aqueous solution containing 2% defoamer and 1% sodium citrate dehydrate. A suitable defoamer is Union Carbide SAG 710 Food Grade, which is a silicone (dimethylpolysiloxane) emulsion.

CHEDDAR FLAVORING OF MOZZARELLA

A cheese having flavor characteristics similar to cheddar cheese on cooking is prepared from mozzarella cheese. In one embodiment, 100% part skim mozzarella cheese is converted to comminuted form. These granules after freezing are coated with two layers. The first layer comprises a 1 to 1.5% application of an aqueous solution containing 2% defoamer (Mazu) and 1% sodium citrate dehydrate. The same defoamer may be used as in the Provolone substitute. The second layer comprises a 2% application of a 50% solution of a cheddar cheese flavor including Annatto colouring. Suitable flavor ingredients.

The above solutions should be applied gradually while the frozen cheese granules are being mixed to distribute the solution over the outer surfaces of the granules. This produces thin frozen coatings around the outside of the granules while the granules remain in individual free-flowing condition. The silicone antifoamers tend to minimize blister formation and to increase oiling off in the baking of pizzas from the coated cheese granules.

In addition to commercial pizza preparation for sale in restaurants, the coated frozen cheese granules of the present method are applicable to the home baking of pizzas solid in frozen condition. A manufacturer preparing pizzas for sale through retail outlets to home consumers can apply the coated frozen cheese granules to unbaked, unfrozen pizza, then without thawing the cheese the rest of the pizza is frozen by any suitable procedure.

The unbaked frozen pizzas are distributed and sold in frozen condition. When a frozen pizza is purchased and baked at home without thawing, the advantages of this method for baking the cheese in frozen or partially frozen condition will be obtained. By applying the frozen coated cheese granules to unbaked, unfrozen pizzas, a further advantage is provided. The frozen granules do not absorb the tomato or other liquid sauces. This protects the baking properties of the cheese granules against deterioration by absorption of an acidic sauce.

11

Aerated Frozen Dessert Compositions

Aerated frozen dairy dessert products such as cream, ice milk, milk shakes, sherbet, yogurt, an the like, are popular due to their convenience, wide spread availability, nutritive value and appealing forms, flavors, and colours. Such dairy desserts may range in fat content from 0.01-18 wt %. A weight conscious society has further popularized non-fat and low fat preparations. In addition to consumer expectations of flavor, appearance, and particular physical properties of aerated frozen dessert products, the nature and composition of these products are regulated by various standards of identity promulgated by the. Food and Drug Administration and the individual states. The combination of rigid consumer acceptance criteria, regulatory standards and the complex nature of the interactions which produce an acceptable frozen dessert product, make it difficult to formulate an aerated frozen dessert having improved characteristics, particularly when formulating a reduced or non-fat product containing only natural components and ingredients without added traditional stabilizing gums.

It is particularly desirable for frozen dessert products to be stable against "heat shock," which is cyclic conditions of partial thawing and refreezing which occur during typical storage, shipping and handling of frozen dairy desserts. These cycles of fluctuating temperatures promote ice crystal growth in the dessert product, and a resultant gritty texture to the product. The gritty texture and mouthfeel, and diminished appearance detract from the overall general quality of the product.

Stabilizing gums and emulsifiers have been used in an attempt to improve the heat shock stability of frozen food products. Examples of stabilizing gums which have traditionally been used in ice cream include gum acacia, guar gum, locust bean gum, carrageenan, and the like. Often, microcrystalline cellulose and carboxymethylcellulose are used in combination with stabilizing gums to maximize their functional effectiveness. Emulsifiers help provide stability by facilitating the formation of an interface between the aqueous phase and the fat phase. Milk and egg yolk are both sources of natural emulsifiers. Commercially available emulsifiers are generally derived by chemical reaction with naturally occurring glycerides.

Though gums improve stability, the use of gums presents several drawbacks. The quantity of stabilizing gums required to provide effective heat shock stability often produces a frozen dessert product which has an unacceptable greasy and/or gummy mouthfeel. In addition, although stabilizing gums may be derived from naturally-produced substances, consumers tend to perceive a product which contains gums to contain artificial rather than all natural ingredients.

Ultrafiltration of the milk component of dairy desserts has been used in an attempt to reduce lactose crystallization in the frozen dessert products.

Others also discloses low and non-fat dairy desserts prepared with ultrafiltered skim milk. To provide fat-like benefits for improved heat shock stability, high levels of whey protein concentrate, being at least 50% undenatured, are added to the compositions to provide a whey protein to casein ratio dramatically different than that observed in milk.

Therefore, an object of the present method is to provide a composition comprising all natural ingredients without added stabilizing gums, which is capable of being processed into an aerated frozen dairy dessert product. Another object is to provide aerated frozen desserts which are heat shock stable over a range of fat content, and which have a high degree of creaminess, and organoleptic qualities comparable to high fat frozen desserts such as ice cream. Yet another object is to provide a method of making the dairy dessert compositions and frozen dairy dessert products of the invention.

The dairy dessert compositions of the method may be used to provide frozen, aerated dessert products, such as ice cream and yogurt desserts, which possess organoleptic characteristics of high-fat ice cream. The all-natural ingredient compositions and dessert products contain milk protein, a sweetening agent, partially hydrolyzed starch, and water. The compositions and dessert products are free of added stabilizing gums which have traditionally been added to frozen desserts.

A source of milk protein is added to the compositions as a source of high molecular weight compounds to provide body and texture to the dessert compositions, and decrease sensitivity to temperature fluctuations and increase stability to heat shock of the aerated frozen dessert products. Primarily, milk proteins include casein and whey protein. It is preferred that the milk protein component has a casein to whey protein ratio according to that found naturally in skim milk, or about 4:1. The dessert compositions contain about 4-20° wt-% milk protein, more preferably about 5-12 wt-%, most preferably about 6-10 wt-%. Milk protein may be derived from any suitable milk source, as for example, skim milk, condensed skim milk, ultrafiltered skim milk concentrate or retentate, nonfat dry milk powder, lactose-reduced nonfat milk, milk protein isolate, and the like. Milk protein substitutes such as milk protein, casein, soy milk, soy protein, milk replacers, and the like, may also be used. Whole milk and buttermilk may also be added.

The compositions also include a partially hydrolyzed starch component which is an acidic or enzymatically hydrolyzed starch material, as for example, potato starch, corn starch, wheat starch or rice starch, which will provide thickening or body to the composition. The compositions include about 6-16 wt-% partially hydrolyzed starch having a dextrose equivalent (DE) of about 5-35, preferably about 10-30 DE, with an about 15-26 DE partially hydrolyzed corn starch being more preferred. Compositions prepared according to the invention but which contain cor syrup having a DE value of higher than about 36 DE tend to have an unacceptably thin consistency, an unacceptably high degree of sweetness, and a high level of heat shock instability. Corn syrups having a value of less than about 36 DE have been found to provide dessert compositions and products having improved heat shock stability and creaminess while having an acceptable level of sweetness.

The higher amount of partially hydrolyzed starch material relative to the milk protein component in the compositions also contribute to the enhanced stability of the frozen dessert products to heat shock. The ratio of partially hydrolyzed starch to milk protein in the compositions is about 0.8-2.75:1, more preferably about 1-2:1.

A premix composition suitable for preparing the dairy dessert products, may include about 6-16 wt-% partially hydrolyzed starch, preferably a corn syrup solid derived from a corn syrup having a dextrose equivalent of about 5-35, preferably about 10-30 DE, more preferably about 15-26 DE, and an effective amount of milk protein to provide a ratio of partially hydrolyzed starch to milk protein of about 0.8-2.75:1. It is preferred that milk protein is present in the premix in an amount of about 4-20 wt-%, more preferably about 5-12 wt-%, most preferably about 6-10 wt-%. An effective amount of sweetening agent and water may be combined with the premix to provide the dessert compositions of the invention.

The dessert compositions further include a natural or artificial sweetening agent such as sucrose, fructose, aspartame, and the like. The compositions may include about 0.01-18 wt-% sweetening agent, being preferably sucrose.

The compositions contain about 30-44 wt-% total solids, and about 0.01-18 wt-% butterfat. Optionally, cream and/or a blend of egg yolk with sugar, may be added to the compositions for flavor enhancement. Egg yolk is beneficial as a natural emulsifier, and incidentally to improve the stability of the frozen dessert products. Other ingredients which may be added to the compositions and dessert products of the invention include, as for example, flavorings, condiments such as nuts, fruits, and candies, and colourings.

PROTOCOL FOR PREPARING FROZEN DESSERT PRODUCTS

Frozen aerated ice cream and yogurt desserts were prepared by mixing together the ingredients according to the weight percentages (wt-%) indicated in the Tables as shown below, to make 10,000 lbs. batches. Ingredients in liquid form were used to facilitate blending, although dry ingredients may be used.

The listed ingredients, other than vanilla, yogurt premix, condiments, flavoring and colouring, were placed in a blend tank and stirred until the mixture was thoroughly blended. To facilitate mixing of the ingredients, the UF5X skim milk retentate was first blended with a portion of condensed skim milk in a ratio of about 85:15, respectively. The mixture was pasteurized by high temperature short time (HTST) pasteurization at about 180+ F. for approximately two minutes, followed by two-stage homogenization at about 1500 psi. during the first stage and about 500 psi. during the second stage. Pasteurization may be by batch method, HTST, or any suitable method. The mixture may be homogenized according to any suitable method.

The mixture was then cooled to about 40°F. The vanilla aliquot was then added. For preparation of yogurt desserts, the indicated aliquot of yogurt premix, was added. The dessert mixtures may be aged, or held, for 0-24 hours. The mixtures for the examples herein were held for about 4-16 hours at about 40°F.

The mixtures were then placed into a standard ice cream freezer, agitated to provide an overrun of about 20-40%, and extruded at about 20-25°F. The aerated desserts were placed in containers and held in a -30°F freezer for about 1-2 hours.

Optionally, after aging, the dessert composition may be placed in containers, frozen, and/or held at freezing temperatures for a desired period of time, and then aerated to provide a frozen dessert product.

Optionally, after aging, the dessert mixture may be spray-dried according to any suitable method, and the composition later reconstituted and aerated to make a frozen dessert product. Also, the composition could be prepared with dry blended ingredients and later reconstituted to produce convenient frozen desserts suitable, for example, in food service applications.

Pursuant to this protocol, frozen desserts of the invention may be prepared by substituting amounts of the appropriate ingredients in the foregoing steps.

PREPARATION OF YOGURT PREMIX

To make 10,000 pounds of the yogurt premix, the following ingredients were placed in a blend tank and blended together:

	Pounds	Total Solids (wt %)
cream, 40 wt % fat	(500)	45.3
condensed skim milk	(5540)	32.0
water	(3960)	—

The mixture was HTST pasteurized at about 185° F for about 17 seconds. Pasteurization may otherwise be by batch method, or any other suitable method. The mixture has then two-stage homogenized at 1500 psi. in the first stage, and 500 psi. in the second stage, and held at about 185° F for approximately 30 minutes. Homogenization of the mixture may be by two-stage homogenization, or any other suitable method.

The mixture was then allowed to cool to between about 90°-114°F, and inoculated with about 500 grams of a mixture of *Streptococcus thermophilous* and *Lactobacillus bulqaricus* cultures. Other suitable lactic acid producing bacterial cultures include, for example, *Streptococcus lactis*, and *Lactobacillus acidophilius*. The inoculated mixture was agitated for approximately 30 minutes to about evenly mix in the cultures. The mixture was then allowed to ferment without agitation at between about 90°-114°F. for approximately 10-12 hours until the titratable acidity (TA) reached about 1.1-2.0. Titratable acidity, as used herein, is the % acidity in the product and is expressed as the % of lactic acid. The resulting yogurt premix was allowed to cool with agitation to about 40°F.

TABLE 11.1

	Frozen Dessert Compositions [1]						
	1	2	3	4	5	6	7
UF5X skim milk blend[2]	37.95	0.00	0.00	23.00	23.70	42.80	0.00
Condensed skim milk	21.00	29.10	29.10	15.67	0.00	0.00	23.50
Cream (40% fat)	0.00	7.45	7.45	7.36	37.44	6.30	37.47
Sugar-egg yolk blend[3]	4.00	4.00	4.00	4.00	4.00	4.00	4.00
corn syrup, 26DE[4]	14.00	0.00	0.00	14.00	8.00	11.00	0.00
corn syrup, 36DE[5]	0.00	15.01	0.00	0.00	0.00	0.00	0.00
corn syrup, 63DE[6]	0.00	0.00	14.72	0.00	0.00	0.00	0.00
Sucrose	11.40	13.32	13.32	13.32	9.07	12.00	13.40
Water	11.05	30.52	30.81	22.05	17.19	3.30	21.03
Yogurt premix[7]	0.00	0.00	0.00	0.00	0.00	20.00	0.00
Vanilla	0.60	0.60	0.60	0.60	0.60	0.60	0.60
TOTALS	100.00	100.00	100.00	100.00	100.00	100.00	100.00

Breakdown of compositions							
Total solids	40.00	40.00	40.00	40.00	40.00	40.00	40.00
Lactose	5.83	5.16	5.16	4.24	2.46	4.16	5.04
Fat	1.11	4.00	4.00	4.00	16.00	4.00	16.00
Milk protein (mp)	8.42	3.50	3.50	5.59	4.50	8.34	3.45
26DE corn syrup solids (css)	10.85	0.00	0.00	10.85	6.20	9.53	0.00
26DE css:mp	1.29:1	0.00	0.00	1.94:1	1.38:1	1.02:1	0.00

1 The weight-percentage (wt %) of each ingredient is based on the total weight of the composition.

2 Ultrafiltered (UF) 5X skim milk blend was prepared by blending together about 85 wt % UF5X skim milk retentate with about 15 wt % condensed skim milk.

3 Sugar-egg yolk blend was prepared by blendingtogether about 10 wt sucrose with about 90 wt % egg yolk. Egg yolk substitutes, especially cholesterolfree substances, may be used to replace the egg yolk component

4 Staley 200 liquid 26DE corn syrup (about 22.5 wt % water).

5 Staley 300-liquid 36DE corn syrup (about 20 wt % water).

6 Staley SWEETOSE 4300 liquid 63DE corn syrup (about 18.4 wt % water).

7 The yogurt premix was prepared according to Example II.

TABLE 11.2

	Ingredient Percentages[1]			
	Solids	Total Protein	Lactose	Fat
UF5X skim milk retentate	22.50	16.58	4.00	0.30
UF5X skim milk blend[2]	23.93	15.82	5.95	0.29
Condensed skim milk	32.00	11.50	17.00	0.21
Cream (40 wt % fat)	45.70	2.00	2.80	40.00
Sugar-egg yolk blend[3]	48.70	14.40	0.00	24.00
Corn syrup, 26DE[4]	77.50	0.00	0.00	0.00
Corn syrup, 36DE[5]	80.00	0.00	0.00	0.00
Cornsyrup, 63DE[6]	81.60	0.00	0.00	0.00
Sucrose	100.00	0.00	0.00	0.00
Liquid sucrose	66.50	0.00	0.00	0.00
Water	0.00	0.00	0.00	0.00
Vanilla	0.00	0.00	0.00	0.00
Yogurt premix[7]	22.00	7.20	7.20	2.00

1 The weight-percentage (wt %) of each ingredient is based on the total weight of the composition.

2 UF5X skim blend was prepared by combining about 85% UF5X skim milk retentate with about 15% condensed skim milk.

3 Sugar-egg yolk blend wasprepared by blending together about 10 wt sucrose with about 90 wt % egg yolk.

4 Staley 200 liquid 26DE corn syrup, about 22.5 wt % water.

5 Staley 300 liquid 36DE corn syrup, about 20 wt % water.

6 Staley SWEETOSE 4300 liquid 63DEcorn syrup, about 18.4 wt % water

7 The yogurt premix was prepared according to Example II.

An aliquot of the cooled yogurt premix was then added to the dessert composition to provide an aerated frozen yogurt dessert The pH of the final dessert composition was about 6.2. Also, other commonly produced cultured dairy products may be substituted for the yogurt portion to yield other cultured frozen dessert products The ingredients and methodology employed in the production of these optional other cultured premixes could, of course, be dependent upon the particular cultured frozen dessert product being produced

Pursuant to this protocol, yogurt premixes may be prepared by substituting amounts of the appropriate ingredients in the foregoing steps.

AERATED FROZEN DESSERTS

Aerated frozen ice cream desserts, compositions 1-5 and 7, and yogurt dessert, composition 6, were prepared by mixing together the ingredients according to the wt-% indicated in Table 11.1.

COMPOSITION OF INGREDIENTS

Compositions of ingredients listed in Table 11.1 are summarized in Table 11.2.

12

Non-fat Frozen Dairy Product

Physically, ice cream is the most complex of dairy products, being a three-phase system consisting of air, liquid and solids. The desirable structure of ice cream, expressed in terms of body and texture, is due to the physical effects of homogenization, whipping and freezing and to the type, source and pretreatment of the mix ingredients. Ice cream can be classified as a foam, or a physico, chemical system containing a gas (air) dispersed in a liquid. Ice cream is a complicated foam, the continuous phase representing a partly frozen emulsion, the ice crystals and the solidified fat globules being embedded in the unfrozen water phase. Typically, in conventional ice cream formulations, the higher the fat level, the more pleasing and appetizing the texture and flavor are considered to be. In accordance with the Standards of Identity of the Food and Drug Administration, ice cream must contain at least 10% of milk fat. The texture, flavor and mouthfeel characteristics of ice cream, containing at least 10% milk fat, are considered substantially superior to the texture and flavor of frozen desserts containing lower levels of fat, producing an overall consumer preference which is substantially higher than very low fat or non-fat frozen dessert products which seek to mimic the characteristics of ice cream.

There has been substantial technical effort directed to the development of low fat and non-fat frozen desserts in order to provide consumers with products having reduced calories and reduced fat content while preserving the organoleptic appeal of fat-containing frozen desert products. Such efforts include the use of various types of indigestible fat-like materials, such as sucrose polyesters and polyglycerol polyesters which pass through the digestive system without absorption and without contributing calories or the effects of saturated fats, such as butterfat.

Early efforts to provide non-fat frozen dairy desserts were directed to simple formulations wherein the fat normally present in ice cream was replaced with additional non-fat milk solids. The data is directed to a non-fat frozen dairy dessert which allegedly has comparable body, texture and flavor which are comparable to high butterfat-containing frozen diary dessert of the same total solids content as ice cream. The solids content normally provided by butterfat is replaced by a combination of increased non-fat milk solids and low dextrose equivalent (DE) corn syrup solids. Non-fat milk solids contents are present in the range of 10% to 19%, sugar is present in the range of 9% to 13%, corn syrup solids are present in the range of 9% to 13%, stabilizer is present in the range of 0.2% to 0.5% and an emulsifier is present in the range of 0.04% to 0.15%. The non-fat frozen dairy dessert proposed in the data is highly desirable in that the contents of the dairy dessert are substantially natural products normally found in ice cream and highly modified or complicated materials are not required in the product. However, the non-fat frozen dairy dessert data has not met with commercial success due to short shelf life and stability.

Efforts to produce non-fat frozen dairy dessert have grown increasingly more complex and numerous efforts have been expended to provide a non-fat frozen dairy dessert containing milk solids which has comparable body-texture and flavor to ice cream containing 10% milk fat. Substantial work has been carried out over an extended period of time with bulking agents, such as powdered and microcrystalline cellulose, in fat-containing a reduced fat food product including frozen dessert formulations.

Accordingly, it is an object of the present method to provide non-fat frozen dessert products having organoleptic, stability and body features comparable to those of fat-containing frozen dessert products. It is also an object of the method to provide essentially non-fat frozen dessert formulations which have a high degree of shelf and flavor stability. It is a further object of the present method to provide non-fat frozen dairy dessert products from natural materials which have properties comparable to frozen dairy dessert products having more than 7% butterfat.

In its composition aspect, the present method provides a milk protein based, non-fat aerated dessert which has the organoleptic characteristics of high fat ice cream. Also, the present method provides liquid mixes from which these desserts can be prepared by conventional agitated freezing. The frozen dessert compositions comprise milk solids not fat, sweetener, low dextrose equivalent (DE) corn syrup solids, and starch. Optionally, the frozen dessert compositions may contain a stabilizer, high DE corn syrup solids, dextrins and artificial sweeteners. The high DE corn syrup solids may have been treated to convert a substantial portion of the dextrose to fructose. In its method aspect, the method resides in the process for preparing the non-fat frozen dairy desserts and liquid mixes therefor from the components of the composition to provide a frozen, aerated, dairy-based dessert product having surprising qualities in view of the simple and inexpensive nature of the components used in the preparation thereof. Each of the composition components and essential characterizing product features and preparation steps are described in detail below.

In an important embodiment, the composition of the present method which can be used to prepare non-fat frozen aerated dessert products generally has the following components as set forth in Table 12.1.

TABLE 12.1

Ingredient	Range
Milk Solids Not fat	12-16
Sucrose	10-14
Corn Syrup Solids (25-36DE)	10-14
Unmodified Starch	0.75-2.0
Stabilizer	0.1-0.5
Water	q.s

Skim milk has about 9% milk solids not fat. Accordingly, skim milk cannot be used as the sole source of milk solids not fat for the compositions of Table 12.1 without being treated or supplemented with additional milk solids not fat. In one method of providing a suitable level of milk solids not fat, the skim milk may be concentrated by condensation in accordance with well known processes to produce condensed skim milk having from about 20% to 35% total solids. It has been determined, however, that an acceptable product can be made through use of dried milk solids not fat, i.e., dried skim milk or a combination of skim milk and dried skim milk.

The corn syrup solids used in the compositions of the present method are low dextrose equivalent (DE) corn syrup. Low DE corn syrup has a high viscosity and can be used in a water phase at relatively high concentrations. Corn syrup is produced from a suspension containing 35%-40% or corn starch in water. The suspension is fed to an autoclave and sufficient hydrochloric acid is added to provide a concentration of about 0.02 NHCl. The autoclave is heated by introduction of steam until a temperature of about 150° C. is reached. The mixture is held at this temperature for a period of time sufficient to produce the required degree of hydrolysis. This is specified analytically by the percentage of reducing sugar in the dry solids of the hydrolysate and ranges from about 20% to about 60% depending upon the type of product desired. The contents of the autoclave are then neutralized to pH 4-5 by the addition of soda ash. The neutralized hydrolyzate further refined by filtration and treatment with activated carbon and is then evaporated to provide a heavy syrup. The final syrup contains about 75%-80% dry solids. Corn syrup may also be dried to form corn syrup solids with moisture contents of approximately 5%.

Corn syrup is specified on the basis of reducing sugar content on a dry basis. This is designated as dextrose equivalent or DE, when calculated as dextrose. Corn syrup is marketed with various concentrations of solids usually determined by density determination and designated in degrees Baume' (Be'). Typically, cornstarch syrups are marketed at densities of 41°-45° Be'.

In accordance with the present method, low DE corn syrups or corn syrup solids are used in the compositions of the method.

By low DE corn syrups is meant those corn syrups having a DE of from about 25 to about 36. Such low DE corn syrups have a very high viscosity and relatively low sweetness. The relatively low sweetness is the result of having low levels of reducing sugars, such as dextrose and maltose, and relatively high levels of non-reducing sugars such as trisaccharides and higher saccharides. The low DE corn syrup is preferably used in the compositions of the invention at a level of from about 10% to about 14% on a dry solids basis.

The starch may be any unmodified food starch, such as cornstarch, potato starch, rice starch or tapioca starch. The starch used in the compositions of the present method is preferably unmodified cornstarch either a native or a cold-water swelling cornstarch. The cornstarch is preferably cold-water swelling to provide further ease in the preparation of the white mix of the method which is used to prepare the aerated frozen dessert products, although native ungelatinized starch may be used. When native starch is used, it is first cooked to gelatinize the starch prior to use.

Stabilizers are not required in the non-fat frozen dessert products of the method. However, the use of stabilizers may improve the texture and stability of some compositions. The stabilizers useful in the present methodb are those well recognized and understood for use in the manufacture of ice cream. Such stabilizers include carboxymethyl cellulose, alginates, xanthan gum, carob bean gum, guar gum, locust bean gum, carrageenan, gum tragacanth, and gelatin. In addition to those stabilizers which are well known for the use in the manufacture of ice cream, a preferred stabilizer for use in the present method is pectin. The use of pectin as the stabilizer in the present method is particularly preferred since pectin is a natural product derived from fruit.

In the method of the present method, the water required for the manufacture of the white mix is added to a kettle provided with an agitating device. The preferred agitating device is a Lanco mixer which is provided with a rotating disc at the bottom of the mixer bowl. The disc is provided with a series of upwardly extending projections which causes the mixer to operate in the manner of a large blender. The Lanco mixer is preferably operated at its highest speed.

The water is heated to a temperature of from about 100° F. to about 160° F., preferably about 150° F. The order of addition of the individual ingredients is not important. The ingredients may all be added to the heated water at the same time, provided that the starch used is a cold-water swelling starch or has been gelatinized by cooking. A white mix is formed after a period of agitation of from about 10 to about 40 minutes. The following order of addition, however, is preferred.

The stabilizer and cold-water swelling starch are added to the heated water and agitation is commenced and continued for a period of from about 2 to about 15 minutes, preferably about 10 minutes. The sugar is then added and agitation is continued for an additional 5 to 10 minutes. Dry corn syrup solids or corn syrup, condensed skim milk and dry milk solids not fat (if used) are added and agitation is continued for an additional 2 to 10 minutes, preferably 5 minutes, to provide the white mix. The white mix is then pasteurized under suitable time and temperature conditions, preferably at a temperature of from about 180° F. to about 225° F. for 30 to 60 seconds, most preferably at a time of about fifty seconds. The heated white mix is then homogenized in a two-stage homogenizer at a total pressure of 2,200 psig and 500 psig second stage. The white mix is then cooled to a temperature of 160° F. to 180° F. and is decanted into containers and cooled to about 40. F. The white mix is held at 40° F. for a period of about 6 to about 100 hours. The cooled white mix is then aerated under agitating conditions in a conventional ice cream freezer. The aerated ice cream mix has an overrun of from about 80% to about 100% and exits from the ice cream freezer at a temperature in the range of from about 18° F. to about 23° F. The aerated ice cream is then placed in containers and hardened at a temperature in the range of from about -10° F to about -25° F for a period of from about 20 hours to about 40 hours, prior to distribution.

Method

A 150 lb. batch of vanilla ice cream was made using the following components at the indicated levels:

Ingredient	Level/lbs.
Condensed skim milk (30% solids)	65
Cold-water swelling unmodified starch Staley Miragel ™	1.59
Corn syrup 25 DE, 42 Baume	19.23
Sucrose	18
Pectin	.18
Water	46
	150

The water was heated to 150° F. and placed in a Lanco mixer. The Lanco mixer was set to the highest speed and the pectin, starch and sucrose were added. After 10 minutes of agitation the corn syrup and condensed skim milk were added. After 2 minutes of additional mixing a white mix was formed. The white mix was HTST pasteurized at 220° F. for 50 seconds. The white mix was homogenized at 2200 psig total pressure and 500 psig second stage and cooled to 40° F. for 10 hours. 230 ml of natural vanilla flavor was added. The white mix was then pumped to a scraped wall ice cream freezer. The white mix exited from the freezer at a temperature of 22° F. and 100% overrun. The aerated frozen white mix was placed in containers and hardened at -20° F. for 24 hours to provide vanilla ice cream.

13

Method of Preparing a Frozen Dairy Desserts

This method relates to a method of preparing a thickener-free consumption ice or frozen dairy dessert from a mixture of fermented milk constituents, including whey protein-rich products, and sugars, and optionally emulsifying agents, flavouring material and other conventional components by mixing those ingredients and freezing the mixture under aeration.

Such a method is known, except that in that method always microcrystalline cellulose is utilized in the mix as a stabilizer and thickener. A yogurt based frozen dairy dessert without thickener is mentioned in a publication. The formulation comprises, in addition to saccharose, exclusively milk derived products, i.e. in addition to ordinary yogurt 5 different whey products, obtained by lactose hydrolysis, from whey and from purified lactose, by ion exchange extraction, by ultrafiltration and still other techniques. This technique is rendered unattractive by the large number of ingredients, some of which are not available unless at high cost.

Accordingly, one can attempt to employ a slightly simplified formulation, using as an ingredient, in addition to ordinary yogurt, a whey protein preparation, which may or may not be combined with conventional thickeners,. But there are objections to such thickeners, which, in general, must be specified as such or by a code on the package, because the consumer tends to be suspicious regarding such ingredients that are not familiar to him.

From a whey protein-enriched yogurt of a normal type, fermented at elevated temperature with cultures containing Lactobacillus bulgaricus and Streptococcus thermophilus, a thickener-free yogurt based frozen diary dessert be prepared by freezing under aeration, which yields a palatable frozen dairy dessert of fairly good texture. But then the product exhibits the disadvantage of a relatively low "overrun" which in general is substantially less than 80%.

"Overrun" is the increase in volume of the frozen frozen dairy mass caused by the air incorporated as a result of the aeration of the mix during freezing, expressed as a percentage by volume of the volume without aeration. Such frozen dairy dessert with low overrun has a firm but at the same time actually too solid a texture, it has a not so desirable high calorie content and is relatively costly, all as compared with an equivalent volume of frozen dairy dessert with high overrun rates.

It has now been found that a yogurt based frozen dairy dessert with high overrun can be obtained by starting from a mixture of milk constituents, in which the ratio of whey proteins to casein proteins is at least 50:50, fermenting said mixture to a pH between pH 4.3 and pH 5.5 and, after mixing all ingredients, aerating the mix in that pH range and freezing it to form ice cream with an overrun of at least 80% by volume, particularly at least 100% by volume.

It has been found that conventional yogurt cultures generally continue fermentation until a pH below 4.3 has been reached: mostly fermentation stops at approximately 4.0-3.0. During cooling, too, fermentation continues, though much slower, until the final pH typical for the starter culture is reached. Even in the frozen state, enzymatic processes may still continue.

When pH falls below 4.3, the air-retaining ability of the freezing yogurt mix without vegetable stabilizers proves insufficient to retain more than a limited volume of air of approximately 60-70% in the freezing mix. But when a culture of lactic acid bacteria is used which by nature have a limited acid-forming ability such that fermentation stops in the desired range between pH 4.3 and pH 5.5, a tart yogurt frozen dairy dessert can be prepared which freezes well with an overrun of more than 80% by volume.

Particularly useful for this purpose are the well known ABT cultures, which chiefly contain germs Lactobacillus acidphilus, Lactobacillus bifidus and Streptococcus thermophilus such starters are conventional for the preparation of so-called acidophilus and bifidus milk products, fermented milk products with a different flavour and a different texture from the normal yogurt types prepared with Lactobacillus bulgaricus and Streptococcus thermophilus. Also, this acidophilus bifidus milk contains more dextrorotatory lactic acid than normal yogurt. Furthermore, the microorganisms in the ABT cultures tend to stop the production of lactic acid at a slightly higher pH than the Lactobacillus bulgaricus starters. The so-called AB starters also exhibit this property.

When the weakly acid-forming culture does not produce sufficient acid, the pH can, if desired, be lowered by adding for example lactic acid, particularly after the temperature has first been lowered to below 5° C. In that case the acid addition can be performed without objections, to a pH of approx. 4.3, without an undesirable texture developing in the ice cream owing to local protein agglomeration.

Similarly, a pH that has fallen somewhat too low can readily be corrected by means of alkaline reactive agents, but this does not correct any change of taste that has thereby occurred or any texture change of agglomerated casein proteins that has already occurred.

Yogurt based frozen dairy dessert according to the method invented can best be prepared with a solids content between 35 and 45% by weight, with a total protein content between 4 and 12% by weight.

A composition is preferred wherein such an amount of milk constituents is utilized that at least 2% by weight of casein protein is present in the mixture. In the form of whey products, whey powder, which may or may not be desalinated, desugared, lactase-treated or as whey protein concentrate or whey protein isolate, such much whey protein is then employed in the mix that in total at least 2% by weight of whey protein is present, preferably more.

But an increase of the whey protein content above the 50:50 ratio of whey protein to casein protein may, as was found, yield a particular effect on the texture and the properties of the frozen dairy dessert. In particular, it was found that when the ratio of whey protein to casein protein is equal to or higher than 66:34 the frozen dairy dessert may exhibit a surprising behaviour upon melting. Although the yogurt based ice cream traverses the transition from the solid state to the liquid state then, the form of the frozen dairy dessert remains well intact. A portion of frozen dairy dessert melting on a dish hardly sags, if at all; a yogurt based frozen dairy dessert lolly hardly drips. Consumption ice or yogurt based frozen dairy dessert of normal quality sag upon melting or drip, while the yogurt based frozen dairy dessert products prepared according to the invention in the aforementioned ratio of whey protein to casein protein are much stabler in retaining their form.

One starts from fat or oil which is not derived from milk. Thus frozen dairy dessert of a less expensive type can be made, the disadvantage being, however, that the taste of a yogurt based frozen dairy dessert based on real milk fat is generally rated higher than that of a yogurt frozen dairy dessert of consumption ice quality.

The taste of the frozen dairy dessert obtained can be varied by admixing conventional ice cream ingredients, such as flavouring, fruit, nuts, chocolate and the like. Provided such admixtures are of the proper bacteriological quality, they can be added after pasteurization of the frozen dairy dessert mix. This is advantageous when admixing fruit, nuts and the like, in that the texture of the mixture is not disturbed by a homogenization process. The choice of the bacteria culture which the product is fermented with, also affects the taste. Besides a culture containing Lactobacillus acidophilus as well as L. bifidus and Streptococcus thermophilus (ABT culture), a culture with just the lactobacilli, a so-called AB culture, can be chosen.

Method

From 8.8 kg skim milk powder, 3.5 kg whey protein concentrate (75% protein) and 66.8 l water a milk solution was prepared, to which 32.9 kg cream (42.5% fat) was added. The milk prepared at 50° C. was deaerated at that temperature for 3 h, followed by heating to 80° C. and two-step homogenization at 250 atm/

50 atm. After cooling to a suitable fermentation temperature, a starter culture of a conventional starter of the type ISt for fermented milk products was added to this milk. After 15 h incubation at a temperature of 35° C., pH had dropped to 4.0 due to the formation of lactic acid. To the fermented product 21 kg saccharose and 7 kg dextrose were added. Agitation rendered the mass homogeneous, the sugar going into solution and the base for yogurt based frozen dairy dessert exhibiting a smooth thin-fluid viscosity. The liquid was pasteurized at 80° C. in a through-flow pasteurizer with a residence time of 30 sec and subjected to two-step homogenization at 50 atm/0 atm.

Freezing of portions of this frozen dairy dessert mix by means of a scraped heat exchanger conventionally used for that purpose yielded yogurt based frozen dairy dessert of good quality with an agreeable tart flavour and good consistency, but with a volume overrun of about 65%.

14

Ice Cream Maker

Portable or personal ice cream making apparatus have suffered from the following disadvantages:

The ice cream must be made from a liquid mass formed of expensive dairy products;

The time required for making the ice cream is too long and the work required is too extensive;

Finally, the cost of the personal or portable ice cream making apparatus is very expensive in view of the complicated structures required for the transfer of heat from the liquid mass to the refrigerant for the purposes of freezing the liquid mass in making the ice cream.

Typically, the prior art systems require a liquid mass made of the diary products which are conventionally used to make ice cream. The devices are, for the most part, very slow in making ice cream and, where the object of the prior devices was to make the ice cream making process quicker, the elaborate heat exchange elements which have been provided add considerably to the costs of these prior devices.

It is therefore an object of the method to overcome the aforementioned disadvantages of the prior art.

Yet another object of the method is to provide a new and improved apparatus for making a frozen dessert of the ice cream type.

Still another object of the method is to provide a new and improved apparatus for making a frozen dessert of the ice cream type which is adapted to use commercially available pudding mixtures as the liquid mass for making the ice cream.

Yet another object of the method to to provide a new and improved apparatus which utilizes a unique structure for facilitating the heat exchange between the liquid mass and the refrigerant for increasing the speed with which ice cream can be made.

Still another object of the method is to provide a new and improved ice cream maker which is adapted for personal use and which is easily carried by the user and is simple to use.

Referring now in greater detail to the various figures of the drawings wherein like reference numerals refer to like parts, an ice cream maker embodying the invention is shown generally at 20 in Fig. 14.1.

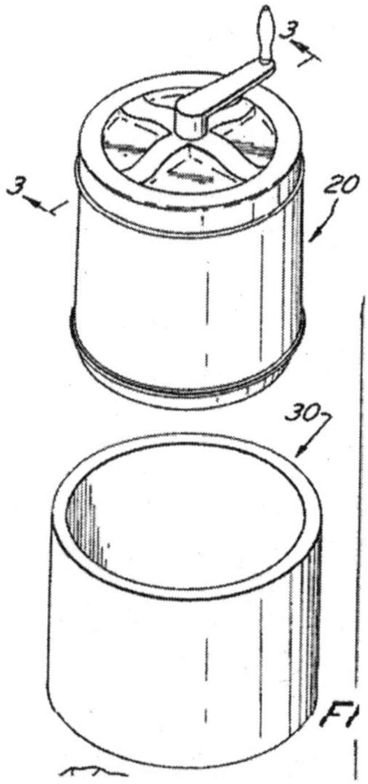

Fig. 14.1 An exploded perspective view of the ice cream maker embodying the method and the holder therefore

As best seen in Figs. 14.1 and 14.2, the ice cream maker 20 basically comprises a vessel or tub 22, a dasher 24, a cover member 26 and a hand crank 28. Referring to Fig. 14.1, a cup shaped flexible holder 30 which is preferably made of styrofoam is also provided for holding and insulating the ice cream maker when ice cream is being made therein.

The vessel 22 is preferably comprised of a thermoplastic such as a low density polyethylene and acts as a receptacle for a liquid mass from which the ice cream type of dessert can be made. The vessel 22 is basically comprised of a base member 32 and a generally cylindrically shaped top member 34. As best seen in Fig. 14.3, the vessel 22 basically comprises a generally vertical and cylindrical wall 36, a horizontally disposed bottom wall 38 and a generally cylindrical upstanding post 40 which extends coaxially with the cylindrical wall 36 and is secured at its lower most end of thevessel.

The top portion 34 of the vessel is thus formed of a cylindrical outer shell 42 which extends vertically and is integral with a top panel 44 which is annular and disposed horizontally and is in turn integrally secured to an inner cylindrical shell 45. Shell 45 and shell 42 in combination with the panel 44 act to form the hollow wall 36. The inner shell 45 is integrally secured at its lowermost end to an annular bottom panel 46 which is also disposed in a horizontal plane and is connected to the cylindrical shell 48 which forms post 40. The shell 48 has integrally secured at the top thereof a circular end panel 50 which includes a recess 52.

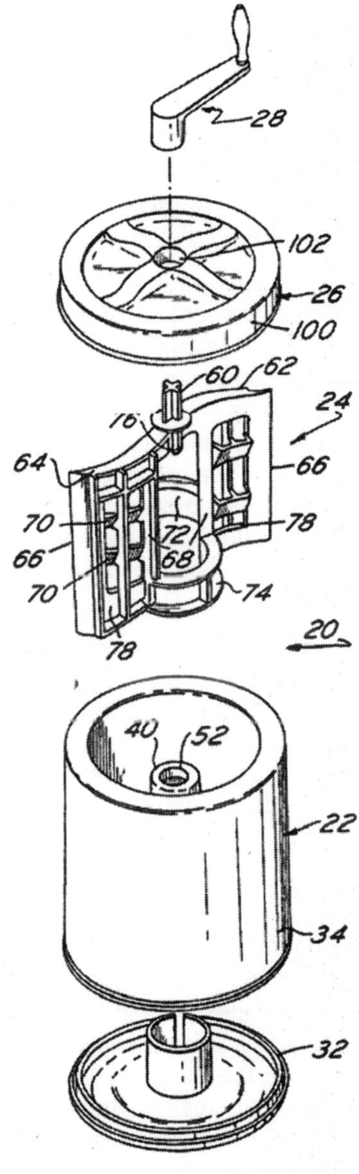

Fig. 14.2 An enlarged exploded perspective view of the ice cream maker

The base member 32 includes a generally horizontally disposed panel 54 which includes ridges 56. At the center of the base 32 is a cylindrical projection 59 which is disposed at the center of the base and extends coaxially with the cylindrical shell 48 which forms post 40. At the periphery of the base 32 a cylindrical collar 58 which is integral with panel 54 is provided to facilitate securement between the top and base portions 34 and 32, respectively, of the vessel.

As best seen in Fig. 14.6, the lowermost end of the outer cylindrical sheet 42 of the vessel has a somewhat pointed edge which is adjacent a flange 60 and the annular collar 58 includes a complementary recess for receipt of the end of the shell 42. The flange 60 rests on a shoulder 62 and the shell 42 and is preferably joined to the annular collar 58 of the base 32 by a spin weld. The cylindrical projection 59 includes vertically extending slots 61. The projection 59 fits within the shell 48 when the base 32 is secured to top portion 34. The slots 61 permit passage of a refrigerant between the hollow walls 36 and 38 and the post 40.

As can best be seen in Fig. 14.3, the welding of the top member 34 to base 32 forms a sealed compartment within the walls 36, 38 and post 40. Prior to the spin weld of the base to the top portion of the vessel, a refrigerant is placed inside the post 40 and the wall 36 so that the refrigerant is sealed therein by the securement of the base to the top portion of the vessel.

The dasher 24, preferably comprises a thermoplastic such as high impact polystyrene and is best seen in Fig. 14.2 and basically comprises a crank shaft 60 which is integral with an S-shaped bracket 62 which supports a pair of scraping members 64 and 66. Each of the scraping members basically includes an outer scraper 66 and an inner scraper 68 which are connected together by a pair of veins 70. The veins 70 are integrally connected between the scrapers 66 and 68 but are disposed at opposing angles with respect thereto in order to enable circulation and create turbulance of the liquid mass within the vessel as the scrapers are rotated about the post within the vessel 22. Integrally securd to the veins 70 is a vertically extending rib 69. Rib 69 is provided on each of members 64 and 66 for structural rigidity.

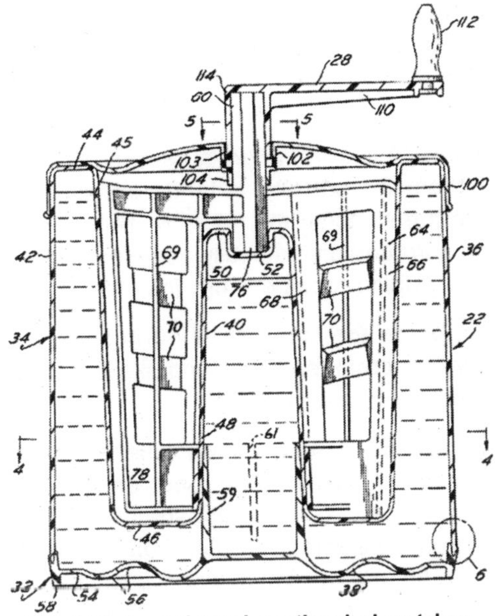

Fig. 14.3 An enlarged sectional view taken along the line 3—3 of Fig. 14.1

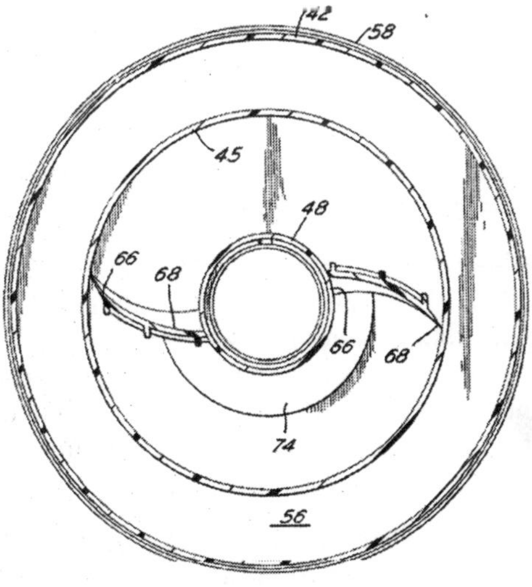

Fig. 14.4 Sectional view taken along the line 4—4 of Fig. 14.3

The dasher 24 also includes a pair of semi-circular brackets 72 and 74. The upper bracket 72 is integrally secured to and centrally of the inner scraper 68 of the scraping members 64 and 66.

The bracket 74 is also integrally secured to the inner scraper 68 at the bottom thereof and extends laterally in the opposite direction from the scraping member 68. The brackets 72 and 74 embrace and surround diametrically opposed surfaces of the post 40 when the scraping members are inserted into the vessel 22.

Disposed below the crank shaft 60 is a projection 76 which depends from the crank shaft 60 and like the crank shaft 60 is of a cross-shaped cross-section.

The scrapers 66 and 68, when inserted in vessel 22, are disposed respectively against the inner shell 54 of wall 36 and the shell 48 of post 40. As the crank shaft 60 has applied thereto a clockwise torque, the scrapers 66 and 68 ride along the surfaces of the shell 50, 45 and 48. Thus, when a liquid mass is provided within the wall 36, walls 38 and between post 40 and the refrigerant within the sealed compartment within the vessel 22 is frozen, the ice formed against the shells 45 and 48 is scraped off to increase the speed of freezing the entire mixture provided within the vessel.

Referring back to Fig. 14.1, the cover member 26 is preferably comprised of a thermoplastic such as low density polyethylene and includes a cylindrical skirt 100 which extends about the cover 26. As best seen in Fig. 14.3, the skirt 100 overlaps the topmost edge of the wall 36 of the vessel 22 when the ice cream making apparatus is assembled as seen in Figs. 14.1 and 14.3.

As also best seen in Fig. 14.2, the cover member includes an opening 102 at the center thereof through which the crank shaft 60 of the dasher extends. As best seen in Fig. 14.3, the opening 102 includes an enlarged portion 103 and a narrow portion 104. Only the crank shaft 60 fits within the reduced portion 104 while the hand crank 28, which is fitted over the crank shaft 60 also fits within the enlarged portion 103.

The hand crank 28 is preferably comprised of a thermoplastic such as high impact polystyrene and basically includes an arm 110 and a handle 112. At the opposite end of the arm 110 is a socket 114 which, as best seen in Fig. 14.5, receives the crank shaft 60.

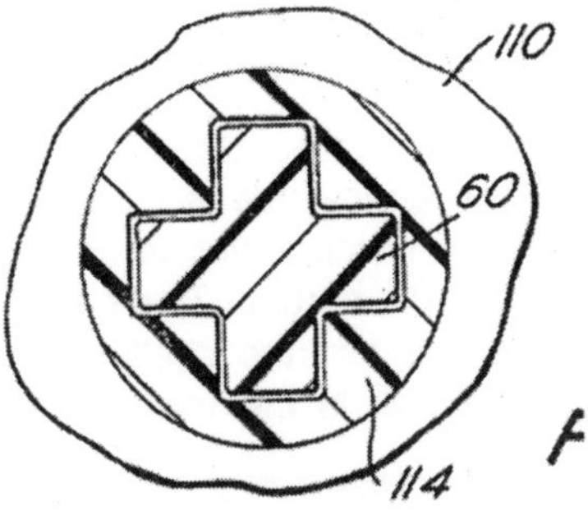

Fig. 14.5 An enlarged sectional view taken along the line 5—5 of Fig. 14.3

In operation, the vessel 22 is placed in the freezing compartment of a refrigerator for approximately 12 hours.

When a frozen dessert is ready to be made from a liquid mass, the vessel is removed from the freezer and is placed within the holder 30 which is cup shaped and is adapted to snuggly receive the vessel 20. Since the holder 30 is insulated, very little heat can be drawn into the vessel 20 from the outer shell 42 thereof. The liquid mass from which the frozen dessert is made is then placed within the vessel 22 between the wall 36 and the post 40. The dasher 24 is then placed in the vessel with the depending projection 76 inserted in recess 52 of post 50 and the brackets 72 and 74 embracing the post 40. The vessel is then placed in the freezer for approximately 30 minutes and is then removed. The cover member 26 is then placed over the top of the vessel 22 with the crank shaft 60 extending through opening 102 of the cover member 100. The crank shaft 28 is then assembled on the crank shaft 60 by inserting the socket 114 over the end of the crank shaft 60. The hand crank is then rotated clockwise looking down at the ice cream maker 20 and a dessert having a frozen consistency

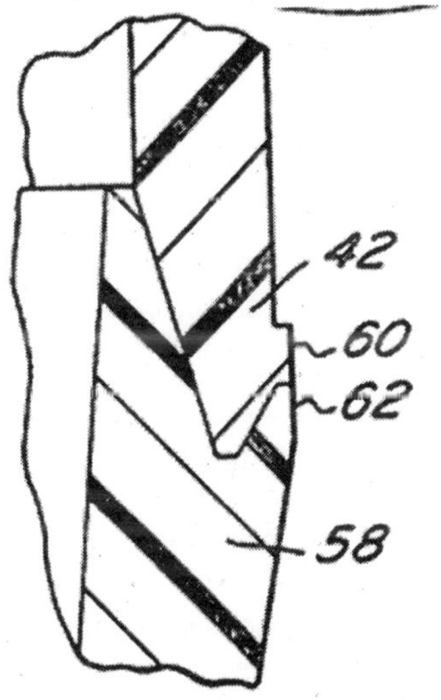

Fig. 14.6 An enlarged view of the section taken within the area 6 of Fig. 14.3

similar to ice cream is then quickly formed from the liquid mass within the vessel 22.

It should be noted that the thickness of wall 36 of vessel 22 is tapered towards the top and the diameter of post 40 is tapered toward its top while scraping members 62 and 64 are tapered toward the bottom. This causes a better fit between the scraping members and the shells 45 and 48 as well as ease of placing the dasher in the vessel.

The speed of production of the dessert is enhanced by the formation of ice against the shell of the vessel 22 which is a part of the post 40 and the wall 36 which provides a large surface area through which heat may be removed from the liquid mass. In addition, the scraping causes a very quick transmission of the heat from the liquid mass as the frozen material is placed within the body of the liquid mass quickly by the scraping action. This also enables more quick freezing of the liquid mass that is against the shell of the vessel.

The refrigerant may be any conventional coolant which freezes at a temperature of less than 25° F. such as brine. The freezing point is preferably below 25° F. to enable the freezing of the liquid mass to form the dessert.

It can therefore be seen that the ice cream maker is not only inexpensive but also, can operate on inexpensive liquid masses to provide an ice cream type of dessert. No electricity is required since the ice cream maker is merely inserted into the freezing compartment of a refrigerator. The refrigerant, because it is self contained, does not cause any mess and requires little cleaning up afterwards.

15

Method of Making Frozen Patties

The frozen food industry is continually seeking to develop and introduce new frozen food products. A recently developed frozen food product is a portion controlled patty prepared from shrimp, sometimes referred to herein as a shrimp steak. The frozen product is prepared from small (Titi) sized imported shrimp. Titi size shrimp is the commercial term for tiny shrimp which have a count of 90 to 130 shrimp per pound. The patties are prepared by combining Titi size shrimp with suitable flavorings and thereafter printing the shrimp into portion-controlled patties.

The use of imported shrimp, however, presents a considerable problem to the industry in that imported shrimp received from any available foreign source is often found to be infected with extremely high bacterial count. This is attributed to the fact that handling of shellfish at ambient temperatures is extremely difficult without contributing bacterial contamination. Even though the foreign shrimp are frozen after harvesting, they incur sufficient handling at ambient temperatures to incur an extremely high bacterial count. The table below illustrates the bacterial counts which are encountered from shrimp imported from various sources:

While it is true that cooking of the shrimp reduces the counts of bacteria found in the shrimp, the above table is an indication that the conditions under which the imported shrimp are harvested and transported are not bacteriologically sound. It would be desirable to provide a more careful control of microbiological contamination of shrimp prior to the incorporation of the shrimp into a product, such as a shrimp steak. Better control of microbiological contamination could be maintained if domestic shrimp were used to prepare the shrimp steaks. However, domestic shrimp are generally too large to be used in preparing shrimp steaks and a grinding step increases the possibility of microbiological contamination. It would therefore be desirable to provide a method for grinding shrimp or other shellfish that limits the possibility of microbiological contamination.

Also, known methods for preparing frozen portion controlled patties from shrimp are not entirely suitable. In accordance with known methods, a processor receives shrimp as frozen blocks. The blocks of shrimp are then permitted to thaw while immersed in cool water by the processor for a period of 5 to 7 hours until the shrimp have become completely unfrozen. The shrimp are then mixed with suitable flavoring materials. It is then necessary to spread the shrimp onto pans and to chill the shrimp to a temperature of about 35° F. to provide a suitable consistency for printing of the shrimp mixture into portion controlled patties. After chilling, the shrimp are transferred from the pans to the hopper of a printing machine and are printed or molded into portion controlled patties which are then breaded. The printing operation is sometimes difficult to control due to a tendency of the shrimp mix to stick to the printing apparatus.

Each of the steps indicated above are potential sites for bacterial contamination. It would be desirable to provide a method for preparing portion controlled patties of shellfish wherein the potential for bacterial contamination is reduced. It would also be desirable to provide a method for preparing shellfish patties from sections or segments of shellfish which are considered too large to be directly incorporated into a patty.

Accordingly, it is an object of the present method to provide a method for preparing frozen portion controlled patties from shellfish. It is another object of the invention to provide a method for preparing frozen shrimp patties. It is a further object of the method to provide a method for preparing shellfish patties wherein the bacterial contamination is reduced. It is a still further object of the invention to provide a method for preparing frozen patties

	Total count (72°C)	Coliform	Yeast	Mold	Staphylococcus	Coagulase	Salmonella
Titi size shrimp from India	68,000,000	10	20	10	3,000,000	Negative	Negative
Titi size shrimp from China	20,000,000	300	6,700	10,100	1,000,000	Negative	Negative
Titi size shrimp from Venezuela	12,000,000	10	10	10	3,900,000	Negative	Negative

from shellfish wherein the shellfish are too large to be directly incorporated into a patty.

Commercially available blocks of frozen shrimp are used in the method . The shrimp may be any size or from any source, but it is preferred to use shrimp which are harvested off the coast of Maine. Such shrimp are harvested during a season which extends from about the first of January to the last of March each year. By utilizing shrimp which are harvested during seasonally cold months, it is possible to provide reduced bacteriological counts on the shrimp. Also, by using domestically harvested shrimp, it is possible to insure that the shrimp are processed and frozen within a reduced period of time and to thus reduce the bacteriological count even further.

More particularly, in the method , frozen blocks of shrimp are ground to the desired particle size in suitable apparatus, such as high energy impact grinding apparatus, or an auger type meat grinder. When high energy type grinding apparatus, such as a hammer mill, is used to effect a reduction in particle size of the shrimp, it is preferred to maintain the temperature of the shrimp below at least about 28° F. At higher temperatures, the work energy imparted to the shrimp during grinding may increase the temperature of the shrimp to thawing conditions and the possibility of contamination is increased. The operation of high energy compact-type grinding apparatus is such that efficiency of grinding of the frozen shrimp is increased as the temperature of the shrimp is decreased below freezing. As the temperature of the frozen shrimp which are to be fed to the impact type grinding apparatus is lowered below freezing they become more friable and easier to grind. Consequently, in a particularly preferred embodiment of the method , frozen shrimp are removed from freezing apparatus and are ground to the desired particle size in high energy impact-type grinding apparatus before the temperature of the shrimp has risen substantially above that temperature maintained in the freezing apparatus. For this embodiment of the invention the temperature of the shrimp is not increased above about 10° F. during the grinding step.

When auger-type meat grinding apparatus is used to effect grinding of the shrimp it is necessary that the shrimp be at a temperature of from about 15° F. to about 28° F. during grinding.

At lower temperatures, the meat grinder will not usually operate. Therefore, when a meat grinder is to be used, frozen shrimp which are removed from commercial freezers at a temperature of - 10° F. are permitted to warm for a period of about 2 to 3 hours to permit the temperature of the shrimp to increase to within the indicated range.

The particle size and texture of the ground shrimp may be varied by the selection of grinding apparatus and the selection of conditions of operation of the apparatus. For example, an auger-type meat grinder operates by accepting material from a hopper and extruding the material by the action of the auger through a plate which is provided with a plurality of holes. The selection of the size of holes in the plate determines the fineness of grind. This type of apparatus provides fairly fine particles with a shredded, compacted appearance.

It is sometimes desired to provide at least a portion of the particles of shrimp produced by grinding of a size that is comparable to the Titi size of shrimp. This size particle is most easily produced with high energy impact type grinding apparatus, such as a hammer mill. In a preferred embodiment of the invention the conditions of grinding frozen shrimp in a hammer mill are adjusted to provide ground shrimp having about 20 percent by weight of particles which are comparable to Titi size shrimp with the remaining particles being smaller.

The shrimp particles are then transferred to suitable mixing apparatus where they are combined with other ingredients for preparing the portion controlled patties. Because of the low temperature of the shrimp particles, the ingredients which are introduced to the mixer to be mixed with the shrimp particles tend to lump and to prohibit uniform dispersion of the ingredients with the shrimp particles. Single and double arm dough mixers are found to be most suitable, and sigma-type mixers are also suitable.

During the mixing step the particles of shrimp are maintained at a temperature below freezing. It will be readily understood that when the other ingredients to be mixed with the shrimp particles are at ambient temperature that the level of the other ingredients that can be added to the shrimp particles is limited to that level which will not raise the temperature of the mix above freezing.

For example, when the temperature of the shrimp particles is about 28° F., the shrimp particles should comprise at least 80 percent by weight of the mix. Lower levels of shrimp particles may be used if the temperature of the shrimp particles is reduced or it the temperature of the other ingredients is reduced prior to mixing.

It is desirable to incorporate a binding agent into the mix which is to be made into the patties. A preferred binding agent is an alginate, either sodium or calcium alginate. The use of a binding agent, however, is not essential if a more loose, open texture is desired in the final product. When used the binding agent is added at a level of from about 0.2 to about 0.5 percent by weight of the mix.

The mix of ingredients at a temperature below about 28° F. is then transferred to suitable printing or molding apparatus. The printing apparatus preferably includes means for breading the printed patties with a light coating of bread or cracker crumbs. After printing, the patties of shrimp, at a temperature still below freezing, are packaged and the packages are immediately transferred to freezing apparatus where the temperature is reduced to a level suitable for cold storage, such as below about 0° F.

Method

The process of the method is used to prepare 100 pounds of a shrimp mix suitable for making portion controlled patties. The shrimp mix has the following ingredients:

Ingredients	Weight Percent
Frozen shrimp portion controlled	87.44
Cracker meal	9.62
Spices	2.97
Calcium alginate	0.44
Water	0.44

The shrimp are removed from a freezer which is maintained at a temperature of -10° F. The frozen shrimp are allowed to stand for a period of 2 hours until they have reached a temperature of 15° F. The shrimp are then removed from the polyethylene bags in which they are packaged and are loaded into the hopper of an auger-type grinding machine. The grinding machine is equipped with a plate provided with a plurality of 3/4-inch holes.

The ground shrimp at a temperature of 22° F. are collected in a sterilized stainless steel container and are transferred to a double paddle mixer. The cracker meal, spices, calcium alginate and water are preblended and are then gradually added to the ground shrimp, as the mixer is operated to provide a shrimp mix. After blending, the shrimp mix at a temperature of 25° F. is transferred to a printing machine. The shrimp mix is then printed into portion controlled patties which are subsequently battered and breaded.

The portion controlled shrimp patties are then packaged and transferred to a freezer for storage. After storage for a period of 6 weeks the shrimp patties are examined to determine the level of microbiological contamination. The total microbiological count is less than 4,000. The shrimp patties are then prepared for eating by deep frying at a temperature of 350° F. for 3 minutes. A delicious product is obtained with a mild shrimp flavor.

16

Method for Making Frozen Drinks

The present method relates to an improved means of making milkshakes and other frozen drinks. Currently the two commercially prevalent methods of making milkshakes and other frozen drinks are: 1) placing frozen ingredients such as ice cream scoops or ice or frozen fruit into a blending/mixing receptacle, then adding liquid such as milk or juice or water, and then blending them together, or 2) using a dispensing freezer of the type in which liquid ingredients are automatically fed into a freezing cylinder, agitated by a dasher in the cylinder during the freezing operation, and then dispensed when desired through a front discharge valve.

The first method, while delivering an excellent quality milkshake or frozen drink, takes too much time and labor to be viable in high volume fast-food restaurants, where a major portion of the potential market lies. The second method, using a dispensing freezer, dominates the fast-food market, yet possesses several serious short-comings. The required dispensing freezer equipment is expensive to purchase, and very time consuming and expensive to clean and maintain. In addition, the quality of product this equipment produces, by its nature, does not recreate the "old fashioned" style lumpy/slushy texture that can only be achieved by blending frozen ingredients together with liquid ingredients and then serving immediately. Consumers do not respond nearly as favorably to the homogeneous texture produced by the dispensing freezer equipment as they do to the old fashioned texture, and therefore, these dispensing freezer drinks do not sell well, holding less than 3% market share of total restaurant beverage sales today.

The overall goal of this method is to enable the creation of a consumer preferred old fashioned texture milkshake or other frozen drink that will fit into the operational constraints of today's high volume fast-food restaurants. In order to meet the operational constraints of today's fast-food restaurants this method was developed to achieve three objectives.

The first objective is to create a milkshake or other frozen drink in 30 seconds or less. In the fast-food market literally every second of preparation time is critical. By enabling preparation time to be reduced by even a few seconds, a number of features of this method are significant improvements over the existing art.

The second objective is to provide a frozen drink machine which requires very little labor for cleaning between servings or at the end of the day, and which improves safety from bacterial concerns. Both of the existing methods of preparation require excessive amounts of clean-up time, either between servings in the case of the blended method, or at the end of the day in the case of the dispensing freezer. In addition, because this cleaning is often poorly done, or neglected entirely, consumers are often put at risk of consuming unsafe food products. This is a serious health risk which this method addresses in new and novel ways.

A third object of the present method is to achieve levels of whipping/aeration of the frozen drink of at least 15% of total volume. This level of whipping is important for two reasons. First, it is critical to keeping ingredient costs of this new method in competitive alignment with milkshakes and frozen drinks produced by dispensing freezers, which are whipped to this level of aeration and higher. Second, whipping also substantially improves flavor delivery of a frozen drink by improving a consumer's ability to taste the drink as their sense of smell senses the frozen drink's aroma trapped inside the tiny bubbles created by the whipping process.

The present method is a frozen drink machine and a method for making frozen drinks from a frozen substance which has been frozen into a cup. According to the method and the machine of the present method, a cup containing a frozen substance is positioned in a cup support located in the frozen drink machine. A rotatable blade having features for grinding the frozen substance and for aerating the ground frozen substance is lowered into the cup, grinding the frozen substance while a liquid is simultaneously introduced into the cup. In an alternative embodiment, a second blade is provided which incorporates air into the liquid before the liquid is introduced into the cup.

Generally speaking, the milkshake and frozen drink machine according to the present method allows milkshakes and other frozen drinks to be quickly made by breaking up frozen blocks of ingredients into small frozen particles, and combining them with an added liquid. The ingredients to be frozen into frozen blocks are pre-mixed in liquid form, placed into serving cups which are the same serving cups in which the finished milkshake or frozen drinks are to be served, and then frozen into blocks conforming to the insides of the serving cups and stored.

When a milkshake or other frozen drink is to be made, a serving cup containing the frozen block is positioned in the machine. A rotating blade is lowered into the cup and bores through the frozen substance in the cup. Milk or another liquid is added to the cup for blending with the frozen substance, which is broken up into small frozen particles by the boring blade. The machine introduces air into the liquid or the liquid plus frozen particle mixture in order to give the milkshake or frozen drink its proper volume, texture, and flavor delivery.

For the rest of this detailed description, the details of the machine and method will be provided with milkshakes as the end-product being produced, though it is to be understood that end-products such as smoothies or a variety of other frozen drinks can be made by the machine and method described herein.

Cup and Ingredients

A serving cup 200 of the type which may be used in the method and apparatus according to the present method is shown in Fig. 16.1. The exterior surface of the cup 200 includes a plurality of ridges 202.

When ready for use in the machine according to the present method , the cup 200 contains milkshake ingredients which are frozen into a block 204 which conforms to the shape of the cup. The block 204 includes an upper surface 206. The frozen substance preferably comprises all the ingredients required to make a milkshake, with the exception of the milk and the air (which gives the milkshake its volume and texture, and improves flavor delivery). Specifically a cup which will yield a sixteen fluid ounce volume milkshake typically contains a frozen block of approximately six fluid ounces of the same ingredients found in ice cream, but with no air incorporated. It should be pointed out that this differs from placing ice cream in the cup, because ice cream, by definition, contains air which is incorporated during freezing. For instance, the ice cream typically used in old-fashioned scooped type milkshakes typically contains approximately 45% air by volume.

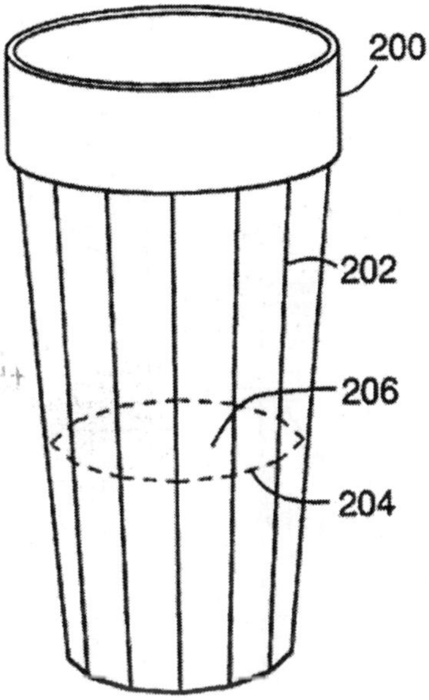

Fig. 16.1 Perspective view of a milkshake cup according to the present method .

The ingredients are frozen into the cup 200 and form a block of frozen substance that typically fills the cup by less than 50% of its total volume. As will be appreciated below, the full volume of the cup is used to contain milkshake once the milk and air are introduced into the cup during a milkshake making operation.

Milkshake and Frozen Drink Machine

Referring to Figs. 16.2 and 16.3, the frozen drink machine 10 according to the present method is comprised generally of

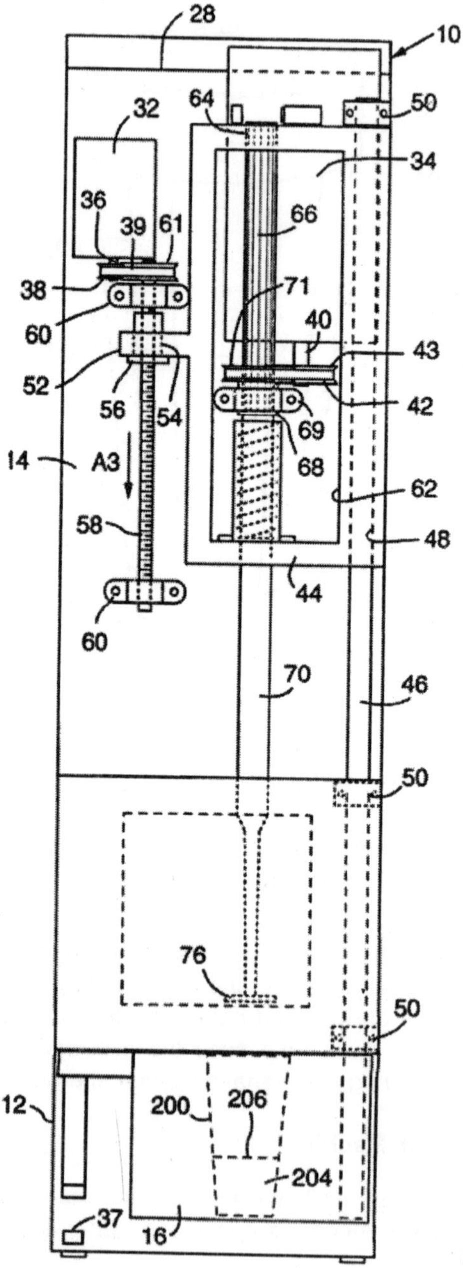

Fig. 16.2 Front elevation view of a frozen drink machine according to the present method , in which a front panel is removed to expose the carriage and blade drive assemblies.

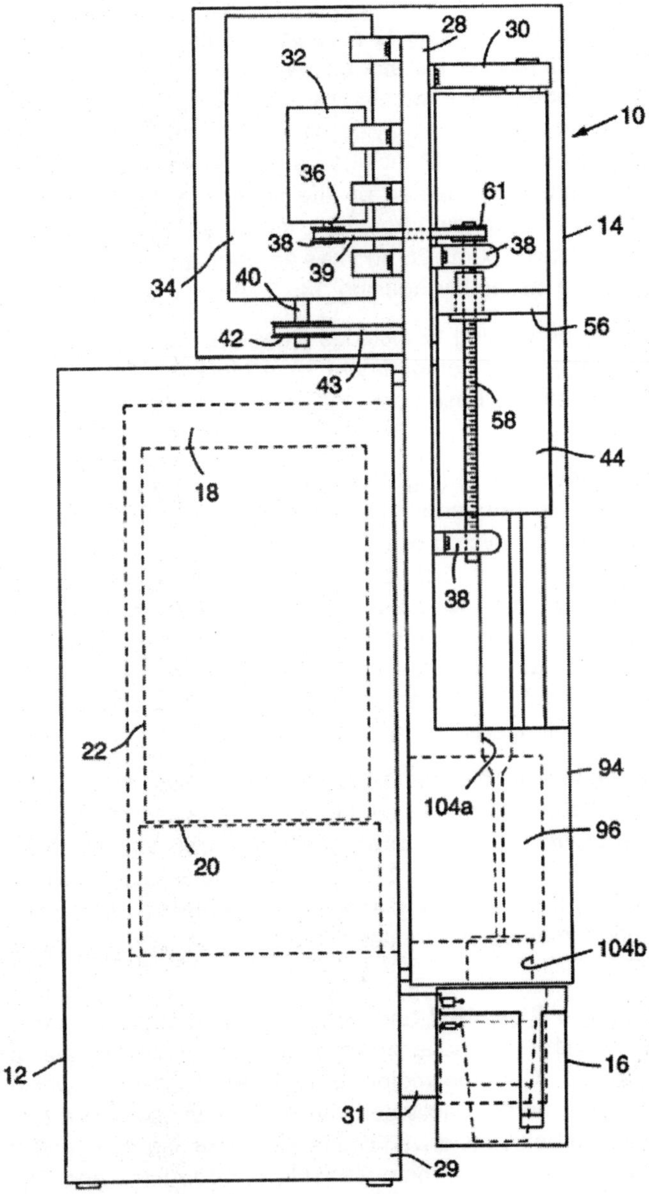

Fig. 16.3 Side elevation view of the frozen drink machine of Fig. 16.2.

a refrigerator housing 12, a blending assembly housing 14, and a cup housing 16.

The refrigerator housing 12 may be a commercially available self-service bulk milk refrigerator dispenser of the type commonly found in cafeterias. For example, the Norris Dispenser Company Model N-5 milk refrigerator may be used. Referring to Fig. 16.4A, the refrigerator housing 12 includes a refrigerated compartment 18 having a shelf 20. Seated on the shelf is a box of milk 22 having a tube 24 extending from its lower face. Tube 24 extends through a peristaltic pump 26 and has an open end 27 positioned within blending assembly housing 14.

Refrigerator housing 12 includes a base portion 29 which lies below the refrigerated compartment 18. A block 31 (FIGS. 3 and 4A) extends from the base portion 29 and supports a pair of limit switches 33a, 33b.

A microprocessor 35 (Fig. 16.4A) is contained within the base portion 29 of the refrigerator housing 12. As will be discussed in detail below, the microprocessor 35 receives information from the limit switches 33a, 33b and other sensors which monitor operation of the milkshake machine, and manages the operation of the milkshake machine. A starting switch 37 is located on the front of the refrigerator housing 12 and is interfaced with the microprocessor 35 to deliver starting signals to the milkshake machine when triggered by a user.

Referring to Fig. 16.3, blending assembly housing 14 is hinged to the refrigerator housing 12 so that blending assembly housing 14 can be pivoted into the open position shown in Fig. 16.4A in order to allow the milk box 22 to be replaced. A support frame 28 is mounted to the blending assembly housing 14. Upper and lower support members 30 extend laterally from support frame 28.

Referring to Figs. 16.2 and 16.3, two motors are mounted to frame 28 within the housing 14: a carriage motor 32 and a blade motor 34. Carriage motor 32 includes a shaft 36 which spins when the motor is activated. Shaft 36 is coupled to a first pulley 38 and a belt 39 is driven by first pulley 38. Carriage motor 32 is preferably a stepper motor capable of 1500 RPM and 140 ounce-inches of torque.

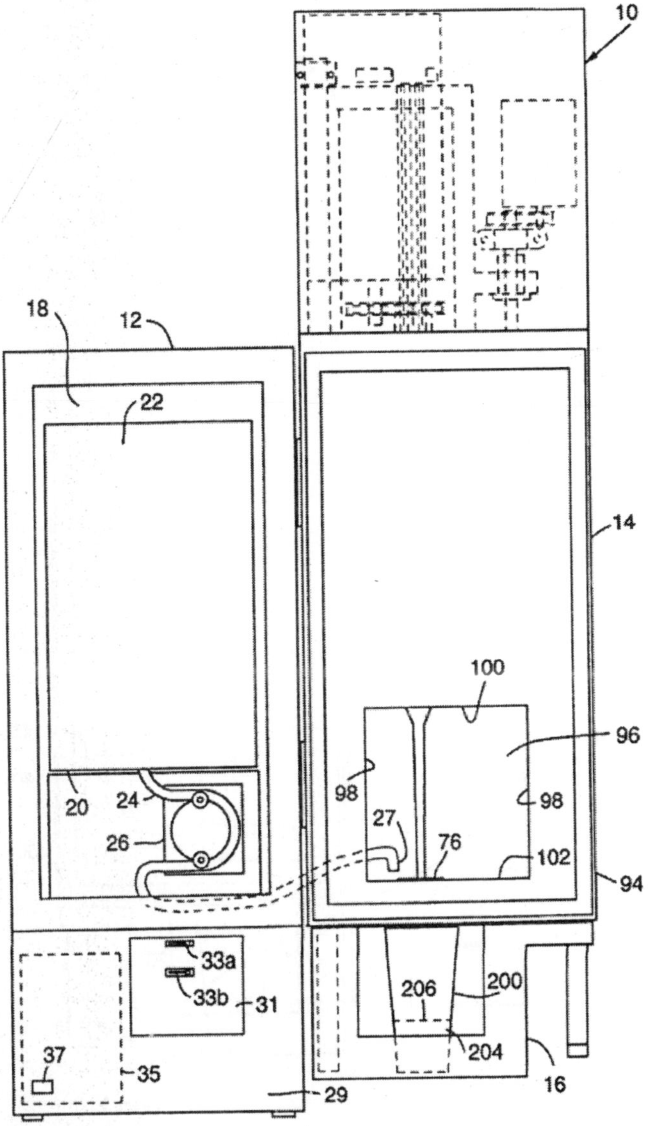

Fig. 16.4A A front elevation view of the frozen drink machine of Fig. 16.2 in which the blending assembly housing has been pivoted to an open condition to expose the interior of the refrigerator housing and to further expose the back side of the blending assembly housing.

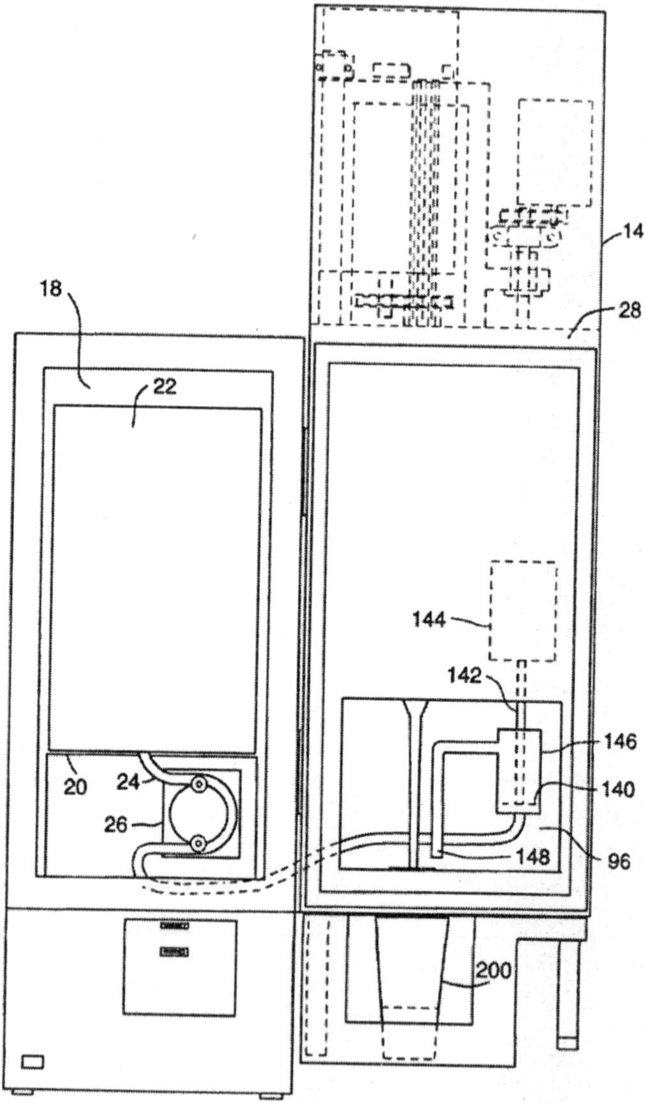

Fig. 16.4B A front elevation view, similar to the view of Fig. 36.4A, of a second embodiment of the frozen drink machine, in which an assembly for pre-whipping milk before it is added to the frozen substance is included.

Blade motor 34 is preferably a one horsepower motor capable of up to 3400 revolutions per minute. It includes a rotatable shaft 40 which is coupled to a second pulley 42 such that activation of the blade motor 34 results in rotation of the second pulley 42. A belt 43 is driven by second pulley 42.

A carriage 44 is located within the housing 14. An elongated rod 46 (Fig. 16.2) extends through a bore 48 in the carriage 44 and is fixed to the support members 45. Rod 46 is secured to the blending assembly housing 14 by a number of mounting blocks 50. The bore 48 is proportioned such that the carriage 44 can slide easily along the rod 46, and linear bearings (not shown) are pressed into the ends of bore 48 to aid the sliding motion.

Referring to Fig. 16.2, carriage 44 includes a laterally extending member 52 having a bore 54. A ball nut 56 is secured within the bore 54, and a vertical screw drive 58 extends through the ball nut 56. The screw drive 58 is mounted to the support frame 28 by a pair of mounting members 60.

A third pulley 61 is attached to one end of screw drive 58. Belt 39 is coupled to pulley 61 such that rotation of pulley 38 results in corresponding rotation of third pulley 61. Thus, activation of carriage motor 32 results in rotation of screw drive 58. When screw drive 58 is rotated in this manner, ball nut 56 is caused to travel vertically along the screw drive 58 and to thereby move the carriage 44 vertically upward or downward, depending on the direction in which the screw drive is rotating.

Carriage 44 is a substantially rectangular frame having a rectangular center opening 62. A bore 64 extends through the upper end of the carriage 44 and into the opening 62. A splined spindle shaft 66 is slidably disposed in the bore 64. Splined shaft 66 extends through a bearing 68 which is mounted to the support frame 28 by a support 69. A fourth pulley 71, which is internally splined, is attached to the bearing 68 and belt 43 is coupled to fourth pulley 71. Thus, rotation of second pulley 42, such as by activation of blade motor 34, causes resultant rotation of splined fourth pulley 71.

During rotation of splined pulley 71, the splines in splined shaft 66 and splined pulley 71 are rotationally engaged with one another such that rotation of splined pulley 71 causes rotation of splined shaft 66. This engagement, however, does not prevent the splined shaft 66 from sliding vertically within the splined pulley 71 and bearing 68 during vertical movement of the carriage 44.

Splined shaft 66 includes a smooth section 70. A collar 72 (Figs. 16.5A and 16.5B) surrounds and is fixed to the smooth section 70 of shaft 66. Shaft 66 further includes a tapered section 74 and a blade 76 attached to the tapered section 74.

Referring to Fig. 16.5A, smooth section 70 of shaft 66 extends through a sleeve 78 mounted to the carriage 44 within the opening 62 (opening 62 shown in Fig. 16.2). A shoulder 82 is formed at the top of sleeve 78.

A compression spring 80 surrounds the shaft section 70 and is housed within the sleeve 78. Spring 80 has a first end 84 which abuts the shoulder 82 and a second end 86 which abuts collar 72. When carriage 44 advances downwardly in the direction indicated by arrow A1, and blade 76 reaches the surface 206 of the frozen substance 204 in the cup, spring 80 becomes compressed between shoulder 82 and collar 72 as indicated in Fig. 16.5B. Gradually, shaft 66 slides downwardly, as indicated by arrow A2 in Fig. 16.5B, through the sleeve 78 until spring 80 returns to its relaxed condition shown in Fig. 16.5A.

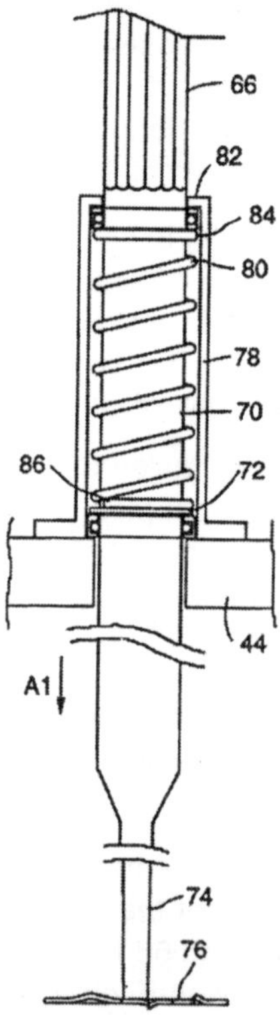

Fig. 16.5A A front elevation view of a portion of the carriage, the sleeve mounted to the carriage, and the blade shaft extending through the sleeve and the carriage. The sleeve and carriage are cut-away to more clearly illustrate the structure of the shaft and the contents of the sleeve.

Referring to Figs. 16.6A and 16.6B, an optical detector 88 is mounted to the top of carriage 44. Optical detector includes a light source 90 and a receiver 92 which detects light emitted by light source 90. Optical detector 88 is positioned to detect whether the upper end of splined shaft 66 is extending above the carriage 44. When the upper end of the shaft 66 extends above the carriage 44, receiver 92 is prevented from receiving light emitted by light source 90. When the carriage 44 is lowered and the upper end of the splined shaft 66 can be detected by the optical detector 88, it indicates that the blade 76 has not yet reached the bottom of the serving cup 200 which contains the milkshake ingredients.

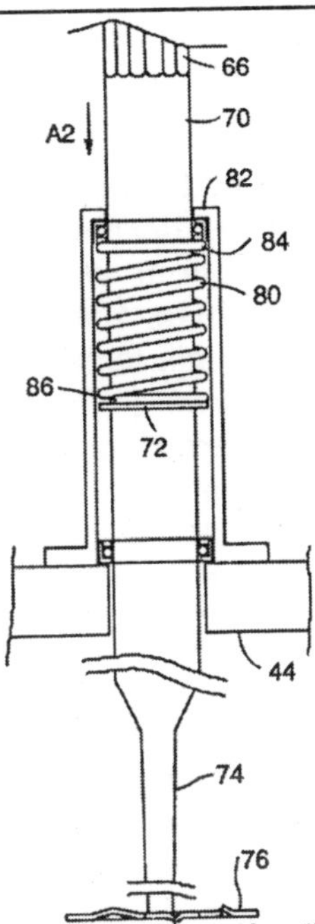

Fig. 16.5B is a front elevation view, similar to the view of Fig. 16.5A, in which the spring is in a compressed state.

Optical detector 88 is electronically coupled to microprocessor 35 (Fig. 16.4A). When the blade 76 reaches the bottom of the serving cup 200 during use of the milkshake machine, this information is received by the microprocessor 35 and used to control the milkshake making operation as will be discussed below.

Referring to Figs. 16.3, 16.4A and 16.7, support frame 28 has a lower portion 94 positioned above the cup housing 16. Lower portion 94 includes a cooled recessed section 96 which, when the blending assembly housing 14 is pivoted to the closed condition shown in Fig. 16.3, faces the portion of the refrigerated compartment 18 which lies below shelf 20. Because the refrigerated compartment 18 is cooled by its internal refrigeration unit, and because the recessed section 96 is exposed to the refrigerated compartment 18, the recessed section 96 is likewise cooled to a temperature of approximately 40° F. or below.

Recessed section 96 is bounded by three side walls 98, a top wall 100 (Fig. 16.4A), and a bottom wall 102. Openings 104a, 104b shown in Fig. 16.3, are formed in top and bottom walls 102. These openings permit the blade 76 to extend into the recessed section 96 and to pass from the recessed section into the cup 200.

A solenoid latch 103 having a plunger 105 (Figs. 16.8A and 16.8B) is attached to lower portion 94 of housing 14. The solenoid latch 103 works in a conventional manner. Plunger 105 is spring biased in the elevated condition shown in Fig. 16.9. When solenoid latch 103 is energized, plunger 105 slides vertically downward to the latched position shown in Figs. 16.8A and 16.8b.

Referring to Fig. 16.9, cup housing 16 includes a side section 106 which is hinged to the rod 46. Cup housing is pivotable about the rod 46 between the closed position shown in Fig. 16.2 and the open position shown in Fig. 16.9. A handle 107 is provided to permit the cup housing to be easily pivoted between the

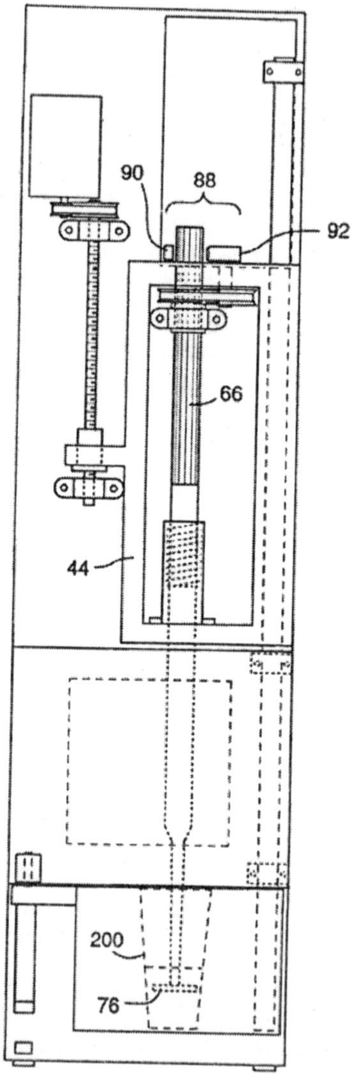

Fig. 16.6A Front elevation view of the frozen drink machine of Fig. 16.2 showing the carriage at the end of its downward travel and showing the blade moving downwardly within the serving cup.

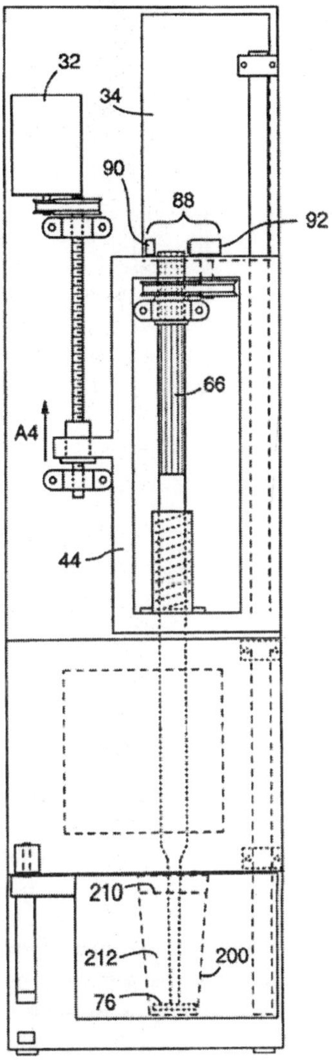

Fig. 16.6B Front elevation view of the frozen drink machine of Fig. 36.2 showing the carriage and the blade at the ends of their respective downward travels.

closed and open positions. When the solenoid plunger 105 is in the latched position shown in FIG. 8A, it prevents the cup housing from being moved to the open position.

Referring to Fig. 16.9, cup housing 16 includes a tray 108 which is provided with a cut-out 110 for receiving a serving cup 200. The portion 114 of the cup housing 16 above the tray is open.

Cup housing 16 further includes an outer wall 112 which, when the cup housing is in the closed position, causes the cup 200 to be enclosed between the outer wall 112 and base portion 29 of refrigerator housing 12. Moreover, and as best shown in Figs. 16.8A and 16.8B, when the cup housing 16 is in the closed condition, the block 31 which is attached to refrigerator housing 12 extends into the open portion 114 of the cup housing 16. The wall 112 and the block 31 are important because they prevent access to the cup during the processing cycle, when it would be very dangerous to disturb the cup due to the sharp blade spinning at high RPM inside the cup.

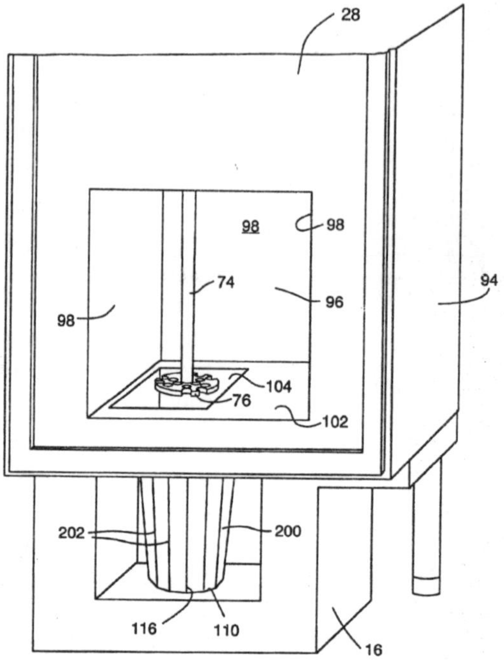

Fig. 16.7 Perspective view of the cup housing according to the present method .

Referring again to Figs. 16.8A and 16.8B, when a cup is positioned in the cup housing and the cup housing placed in the closed condition, the cup depresses at least one of the limit switches 33a, 33b. A short cup 200b, shown in FIG. 16.8A, will depress only lower limit switch 33b, whereas a tall cup 200a, shown in Fig. 16.8B will depress both lower and upper limit switches 33a, 33b. The switches 33a, 33b provide a means by which the presence of a cup in the cup housing may be detected. As will be described in detail below, when at least one of the switches 33a, 33b is closed, the microprocessor activates solenoid latch 103, causing the cup housing 16 to be locked in the closed condition and generates starting signals which cause the frozen drink making cycle to begin.

The limit switches 33a, 33b also deliver information to the microprocessor 35 (Fig. 16.4A) concerning the size of the cup

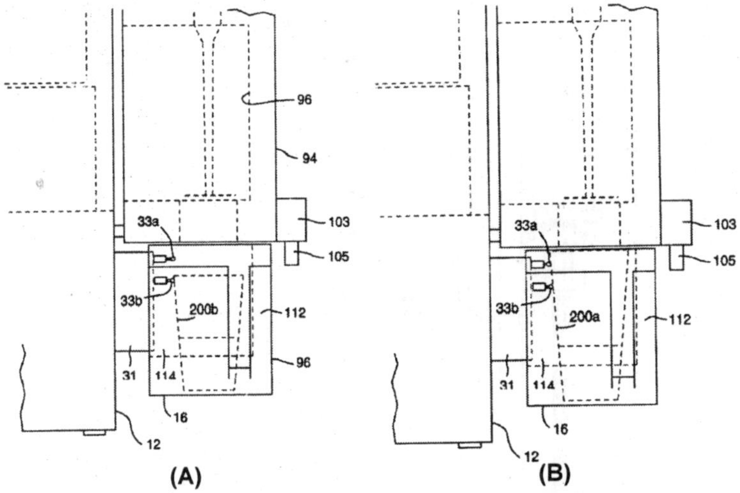

Figs. 16.8A and 16.8B Side views of the cup housing of the frozen drink machine of Fig. 36.1, showing small and large cups, respectively, positioned in the cup housing.

which is positioned in the cup housing. As detailed below, this will ensure that the appropriate quantity of milk is delivered into the cup for the size milkshake which is to be made. Also, because the surface 206 (Fig. 16.1) of the frozen block 204 is lower in a smaller cup than in a relatively larger cup, the microprocessor can ensure that the blade 76 is lowered to the proper height before it is caused to begin spinning.

Referring to the perspective view of Fig. 16.7, cut-out 110 includes ridges 116 around its perimeter. These ridges are designed to engage with like ridges 202 on the outside surface of the serving cup 200. This prevents cup 200 from rotating within the cut-out 110 as the rotating blade advances through the frozen substance.

Blade

Figs. 16.10A and 16.10B are top and side views, respectively, of blade 76. Blade 76 is preferably a 2.5 inch diameter stainless steel blade having a circular shape and a thickness of approximately 0.080 inches. Three-eighth inch diameter holes

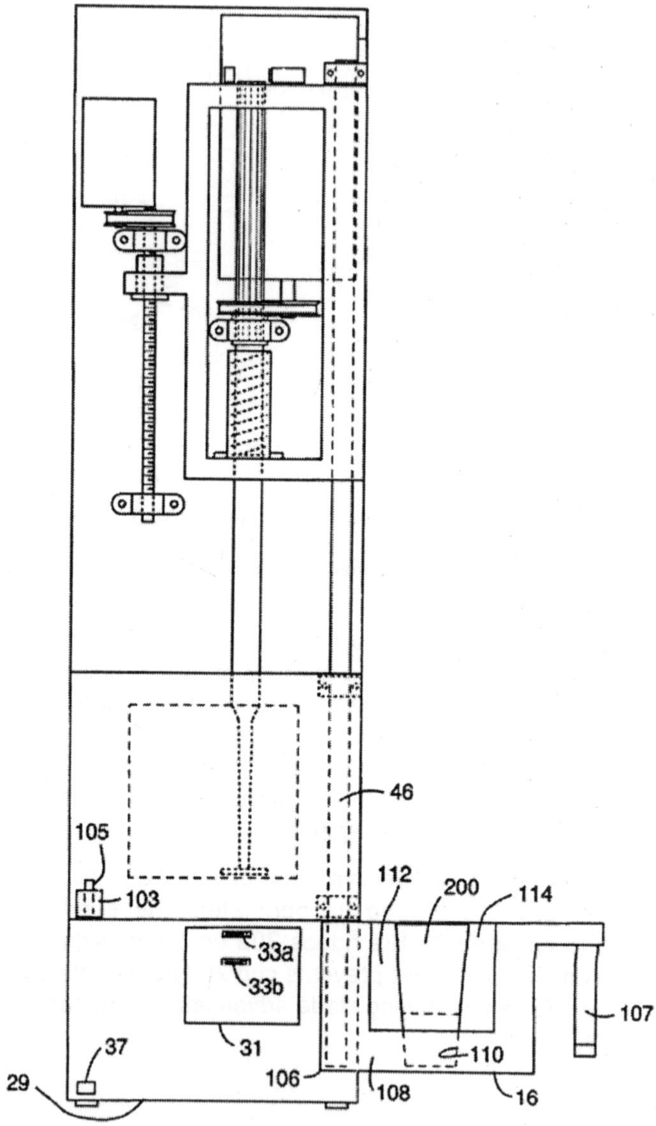

Fig. 16.9 Front elevation view, similar to the view of Fig. 16.2, in which the cup support assembly is pivoted into the opened condition.

118a, 118b and 118c are spaced 120° apart rotationally and at specific radiuses from the center of the blade such that as the blade makes one complete rotation, the entire surface area of the frozen substance will have been passed over by three holes. Holes 118a are centered 0.041 inches from the blade's center, and holes 118b and 118c are spaced 0.062 inches and 0.083 inches from the blade's center respectively. Depressed regions 120, best shown in the cross section view of Fig. 16.10C, are formed immediately adjacent to each of the holes, located on their trailing edge as the blade rotates. These regions are depressed by 0.080 inches. The holes and the depressed regions are arranged such that as the blade 76 is rotated and advanced into the frozen substance in the cup 200 (Fig. 16.1), the holes 118a-c and depressed regions 120 grate through the frozen substance much like the grating action of a cheese grater. It should be appreciated that the blade of Fig. 16.10A is configured such that clockwise rotation of this blade produces the desired grating effect. This arrangement also provides for easy manufacture in a stamping operation, and maintains the mechanical strength of the blade so that its outside edges are not deflected upward by the force of the frozen substance being bored through. Other arrangements with differing size or shaped holes will also work well.

Three waves are formed in the blade. As shown in Figs. 16.10A and 16.10C, each of the waves 122 includes a center crease 124 which is elevated above the plane of the blade and side creases 126 which lie in the plane of the blade. The creases 124 and 126 are approximately 1/2 inches in length and extend radially from the perimeter of the blade. A distance along the perimeter of the blade of approximately 1/2 inch separates each pair of side creases 126. During high speed rotation of the blade, the waves 122 increase the whipping effect of the blade by causing an alternately high and low pressure zone at the blade's edge, creating turbulent eddies which cause a whipping effect.

Three pairs of cutouts 128 are formed along the perimeter of the blade 76, spaced 120° from each other. Each pair includes a first cutout which has a depressed trailing edge 130 and a second cutout which has an elevated trailing edge 132. During a milkshake making operation, the trailing edge 130 is depressed

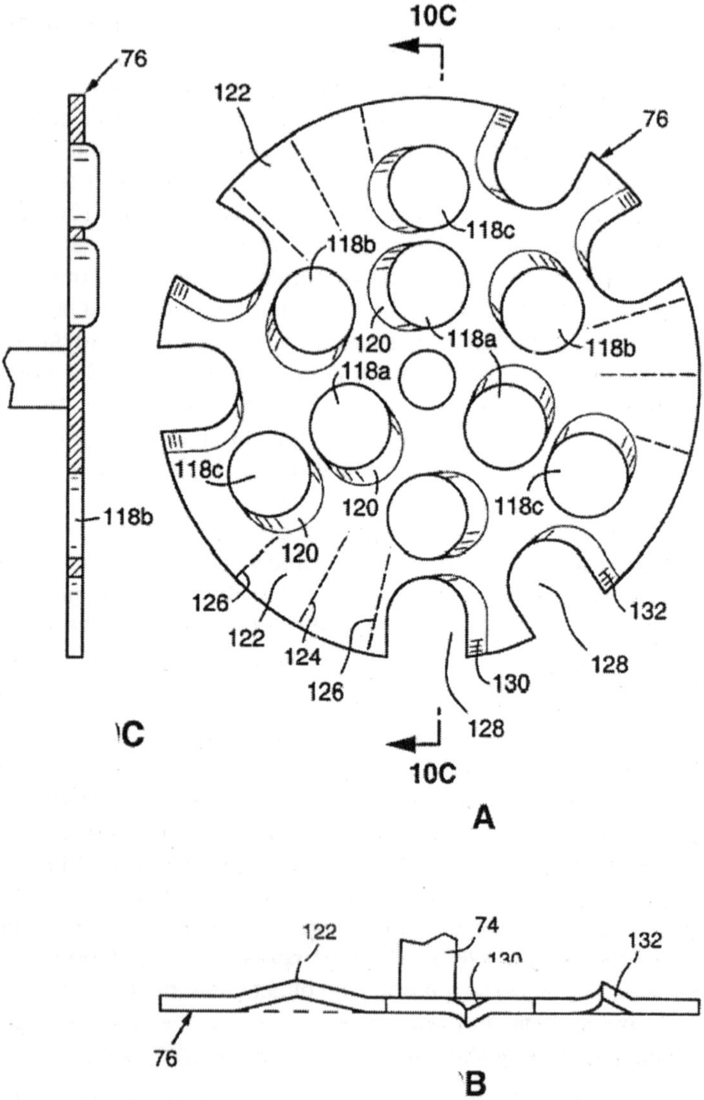

Figs. 16.10A and 16.10B Top plan view and a side elevation view, respectively, of a blade according to the present method.
Fig. 16.10C is a cross-sectional side view of the blade of Figs. 16.10A and 16.10B, taken along the plane designated 10C—10C in FIG. 16.10A.

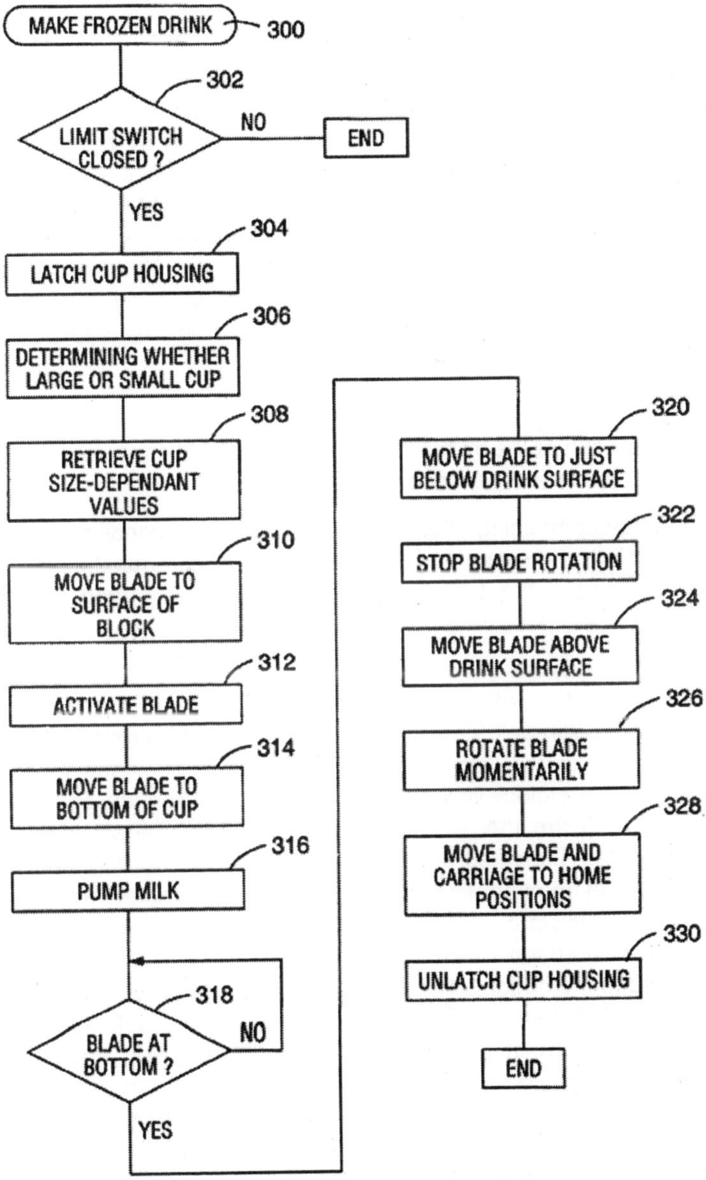

Fig. 16.11: Simplified flow diagram showing the functions of the microprocessor of the present method

to act as a grating surface to bore through the frozen substance at the outermost radius of the blade. The trailing edge 132 is elevated to act as a inverted ramped surface to force milkshake downward in the cup and thereby minimize the amount of milkshake that is driven up the interior walls of the cup by centrifugal force. Moreover, by directing milkshake ingredients above the blade, which are carried to the outer edge of the blade by centrifugal force, to then be forced downward and under the blade as the rotating blade moves upward, the elevated trailing edge 132 helps prevent the blade from carrying ingredients up and out of the cup as the blade is lifted from the cup.

Operation

Operation of the frozen drink machine according to the present method will next be described.

First, cup housing 16 is pivoted to the opened condition shown in Fig. 16.9 and a cup 200 containing the frozen substance 204 is positioned in the cutout 110. Cup housing 16 is then pivoted to the closed position shown in Fig. 16.2.

Next, carriage motor 32 is activated. Activation of carriage motor 32 causes rotation of carriage motor shaft 36 and pulley 38, and through belt 39 further causes rotation of pulley 61 which is attached to the vertical screw drive shaft 58, causing it to rotate. Counterclockwise rotation of screw drive shaft 58, when viewed from the top, causes carriage 44 to advance vertically downward as indicated by arrow A3 in Fig. 16.2. Carriage 44 has spindle shaft 66 mounted to it such that when carriage 44 advances vertically downward, spindle shaft 66 advances downward as well, with one exception which will be explained shortly. As blade 76, attached to the bottom of spindle shaft 66, approaches the surface 206 of the frozen substance 204, blade motor 34 is activated causing rotation of pulley 42, and through belt 43, rotation of pulley 71 which is attached to spindle shaft 66, causing it and blade 76 to spin. Downward travel of carriage 44 continues and blade 76 makes contact with the surface 206 of the frozen substance and begins boring down through it.

At the time boring begins, the milk pump is activated and begins pumping milk into the cup through tube 24 for mixing and whipping with the small frozen particulate being created by the boring action of the blade. Approximately six ounces of milk is pumped into the cup over a period of approximately three to five seconds, depending on the desired consistency of the finished milkshake.

The downward travel of the carriage 44 is generally driven at a rate faster than the blade 76 can bore through the frozen substance in the cup. This disparity in downward travel rates causes the downward travel of the spindle shaft 66, to which the blade 76 is attached, to be slower than the downward travel of carriage 44. This forces the spindle shaft 66 to move upward within its mountings on the carriage 44 and for spring 80 to be compressed as shown in Fig. 16.6A. The carriage 44 is driven to its lowest most point of travel, as shown in Fig. 16.6B, and then the carriage motor 32 is deactivated.

The blade 76 continues to grate and blend the frozen substance 204 within the cup 200 as it moves downward in the cup, driven by the gradual relaxation of the compressed spring 80 (Figs. 16.5B and 16.6A) acting on spindle shaft 70. When the optical detector 88 senses that the spindle shaft has progressed all the way to the bottom of the cup as shown in Fig. 16.6B, the boring stage of the process is complete.

The reason for this spring release arrangement is to allow for a high rate of travel speed of the carriage 44 from its uppermost position at the beginning of the cycle to the bottom of its travel. This is advantageous because it allows the blade 76 to bore as quickly as the frozen substance will allow. Softer frozen substances can be bored through more quickly. Without this spring release arrangement, time would be wasted as the carriage 44 would have to be driven downward as slowly as the hardest frozen substance could be bored through in order to be sure the blade motor 34 is not stalled out by an excessive torque requirement to continue the blade's rotation. An additional advantage is that the exact rotational speed for the carriage motor 32, driving the downward travel of the carriage during boring, becomes less critical. This simplifies the controls required for this motor.

Given these two advantages of the spring release it can be appreciated that the same advantages could be accomplished through a variety of other means, including placing the spring mechanism on the screw drive shaft or its mountings rather than on the spindle shaft, or placing a slip clutch in the connection of the carriage motor to the screw drive shaft which would slip as the spindle and carriage's downward travel was caused to slow down by the resistance of the boring blade against the frozen substance.

With the boring stage complete, as signaled by the optical detector 88 when the blade 76 reaches the bottom of the cup, the carriage motor 32 is caused to reverse polarity and is activated to begin to move the carriage, and with it, the spindle drive shaft and blade, upward as indicated by arrow A4 in Fig. 16.6B. At this point in the process the rotating blade 76 acts as a mixing and whipping agitator, with the important feature of being formed such that its slim cross-sectional profile does not cause excessive rotation of the entire contents of the cup. The carriage motor 32 raises the carriage, and with it, the rotating blade up through the milkshake, completing the mixing and whipping of the frozen particulate and milk into a milkshake as it travels vertically through it.

Some formulations of milkshake benefit from a second vertical pass of the mixing/whipping blade through the milkshake, in which case the mixing blade's vertical travel is stopped one inch below the surface 210 of the milkshake 212 (labelled in Fig. 16.6B), and the polarity of the carriage motor 32 is again reversed and the blade 76 is moved back down to the bottom of the cup. Upon reaching the bottom, the polarity of the carriage motor 32 is again reversed and the blade is moved back upward in the cup 200 to a point one inch below the surface 210 of the milkshake 212.

With the mixing and whipping process complete, and the blade reaching the point one inch below the surface 210 (Fig. 16.6B) of the milkshake 212, the blade motor 34 is deactivated and a braking force applied to the blade motor to slow its rotational speed. This slowing of the blade's rotational speed prevents splattering of milkshake out of the cup as the blade breaks through the surface 210 of the milkshake 212. With the rotation slowed, the carriage moves up to a point where the blade is approximately one half inch above the surface 210 of the milkshake 212, but still below the top lip of the cup, and stops momentarily. With the carriage stopped momentarily, the blade motor is reactivated momentarily, causing the blade to spin and fling any remaining milkshake material off the blade and back into the cup below its upper lip. After a momentary spinning of approximately one half second, the blade motor 34 is deactivated, and the carriage motor 32 reactivated to bring the carriage and blade upward to its original position above the cup. At this point the process is complete and the cup can be removed for serving by opening cup housing 16 and removing cup 200 from the recess 110.

As shown in Fig. 16.2, when the carriage 44 and blade 76 are in their original positions, the blade 76 and the narrow portion 75 of shaft 70 are disposed within recessed section 96 of the housing 14. As described above, this section of the housing is cooled by the refrigerated compartment 18 and is thereby maintained at bacteriologically safe temperatures. Accordingly, blade 76 and shaft section 74 need not be washed between milkshake making operations, even if the milkshake making operations are separated by several minutes or hours. The cooled compartment minimizes the risk that residual milk left on these components will sour and/or promote bacteria formation.

MICROPROCESSOR CONTROL

The functions of the microprocessor 35 in controlling the frozen drink making operation will next be discussed with reference to Fig. 16.11. A frozen drink making operation is commenced at step 300 when a user presses the start button 37 (Fig. 16.2). Next, the microprocessor 35 detects whether at least one of the limit switches 33a, 33b (Figs. 16.8A and 16.8B) is closed, which indicates the presence of a cup 200 in the cup housing 16. If a limit switch is closed, the microprocessor 35 causes activation of the solenoid latch 103, step 304, such that plunger 105 moves to the latched condition shown in Fig. 16.8A to latch the cup housing 16. If a limit switch is not closed, the microprocessor terminates the milkshake making procedure or it may alternatively continue monitoring the limit switches for a predetermined period of time.

Next, at step 306 the microprocessor 35 determines whether a tall cup 200a (Fig. 16.8B) or a short cup 200b (Fig. 16.8A) is positioned in the cup housing 16 by determining whether only one limit switch 33b is closed, indicating a small cup, or whether both limit switches 33a, 33b are closed, indicating a large cup.

At step 308, the microprocessor retrieves certain cup size-dependent values from look up tables stored in its memory. For example, because a larger quantity of milk is needed for a large milkshake than for a small milkshake, one of the stored values is the length of time for which the peristaltic pump 26 will be made to pump milk into the cup 200. The other stored values include (1) those indicating the distance to be travelled, or the amount of time for travel, by the carriage 44 to position the blade 76 at the surface 206 of the frozen block 204, which will be higher for a large cup than it will for a small cup; (2) those indicating the distance to be travelled (or the amount of time for travel) by the carriage from the surface 206 of the frozen block 204 to the bottom of the cup; (3) those indicating the distance to be travelled (or the amount of time for travel) by the carriage to lift the blade from the milkshake to a height just below the upper surface 210 (Fig. 16.6B) of the milkshake 212; and (4) those indicating the distance to be travelled (or the amount of time for travel) by the carriage to lift the blade from the milkshake to a height just above the upper surface 210 of the milkshake 212.

During steps 310 through 316, the stored values retrieved at step 308 are used to generate control signals which control the carriage motor 32, blade motor 34, and peristaltic pump 26. Specifically, the microprocessor at step 310 instructs the carriage motor 32 to advance the carriage by the appropriate number of steps to position the blade 76 just above the surface 206 of the frozen block. At step 312 the microprocessor further directs the carriage motor 32 to advance the carriage 44 by the appropriate number of steps which will cause the blade 76 to move to the bottom of the cup (step 314). At step 316, the microprocessor delivers control signals to cause the peristaltic pump 26 to pump milk into the cup through opening 37 for the amount of time which will deliver the proper quantity of milk into the cup. It should be appreciated that if the embodiment of Fig. 16.4B is used, the microprocessor would also initiation rotation of whipping motor 140 at this step in the process and whipped milk would be delivered into the cup through outlet 148.

At step 318, the microprocessor looks to the optical sensor 88 and awaits a signal from the optical sensor indicating that the blade 76 has reached the bottom of the cup (Fig. 16.6B). When the blade 76 has reached the bottom of the cup, the microprocessor instructs (steps 320) the carriage motor 32 to move the carriage 44 vertically upward by an amount which will position the blade 76 approximately one inch below the milkshake surface 210.

Next, the microprocessor directs the blade motor 34 (step 322) to deactivate and thereby slows the rotation of the blade 76. As described above, this prevents splattering of milkshake out of the cup as the blade breaks through the surface 210 of the milkshake 212.

Next, at step 324, the carriage motor 32 is caused to advance the carriage 44 such that the blade 76 is approximately one half inch above the surface 210 of the milkshake 212, but still below the top lip of the cup 200. With the carriage stopped momentarily, the microprocessor reactivates the blade motor 34 for approximately 0.5 seconds (step 326), causing the blade to spin and fling any remaining milkshake ingredients off the blade and back into the cup below its upper lip. At step 328, which occurs after the reactivation of the blade motor 34, the carriage motor 32 is instructed to move the carriage 44 and blade 76 into their original positions above the cup 200. Finally, at step 330, the microprocessor 35 causes deactivation of the solenoid latch 103, causing plunger 105 to move to the unlatched position shown in Fig. 16.9, allowing the cup housing 16 to be opened by a user.

Alternative Embodiment

As described above, it is important to the milkshake consistency to have air whipped into the milk or milkshake before the milkshake is served. This may be accomplished in the manner described with respect to the first embodiment, in which aeration of the milk and/or milkshake occurs due to the action of the blade 76 within the cup.

Alternatively, the milk may be whipped by a separate whipping blade which acts on the milk before the milk is introduced into the cup 200. Referring to Fig. 16.4B, a whipping blade 140 may be provided for this purpose. Whipping blade 140 is mounted to the end of a shaft 142 which is rotatably coupled to a whipping motor 144. Motor 144 is mounted to the support frame 28.

The whipping blade 140, shaft 142 and motor 144 may be of the type commonly found on traditional milkshake blenders, such as the Model 936 made by Hamilton Beach. Whipping blade, shaft, and whipping motor are mounted within the blending assembly housing 14 such that the whipping blade 140 and the shaft 142 extend into the refrigerated section 96 and such that whipping blade 140 extends into a vessel 146.

The tubing 24 which extends from the box 22 of milk is connected to the vessel 146 such that milk is pumped by the peristaltic pump 26 into the bottom of vessel 146. Air is introduced into the milk by the whipping action of the whipping blade 140. Further pumping of the peristaltic pump 26 causes the milk to exit the vessel 146 via an outlet 148 directed into the cup 200. These components are preferably disposed within the refrigerated section 96 in order to prevent possible souring of the milk and bacterial formation.

The remaining features of the embodiment of Fig. 16.4B are identical to those of the embodiment of Fig. 16.2 and will not be described in detail.

17

Frozen Dessert Dispensing Apparatus

This method relates to an apparatus for dispensing food products such as ice creams, yogurts, sherberts and other frozen or semi-frozen dessert confections. This method also relates to an apparatus for dispensing food products from collapsible containers.

Soft serve frozen and semi-frozen confections are widely used in the food industry and have a broad customer appeal. Although Ice creams are the most widely known product dispensed in a soft serve form, an expanding market based on alternative frozen and semi-frozen confections, such as yogurts, also exists. The most common means of dispensing soft serve confections is by extrusion into an edible cone or other suitable container, and the confection is generally intended for immediate consumption.

It is well known that soft serve confectionary products can be easily extruded from dispensing apparatuses to a variety of patterns or shapes. The most common means of dispensing a frozen confection has been the extruding of a continuous ribbon or rod that can be coiled on itself to form a cone having a beehive-type shape. Moreover, the soft serve confectionary products ideally have sufficient strength to retain the extruded shape for a sufficient time to allow for consumer consumption.

It is accordingly an object of the present method to provide a frozen dessert dispenser capable of extruding a frozen or semi-frozen confection from a collapsible container.

Another object of the method is to provide a device for dispensing confections or desserts that eliminates the problem of the collapsible container collapsing into its dispensing outlet during use.

It is a further object of the present method to provide a device for dispensing confections or desserts that is sanitary, mechanically simple, easy to clean and easy to use.

More particularly, the present method provides a frozen confection dispensing apparatus comprising a housing having an interior therein including means to maintain the interior at a preselected temperature; at least one receptacle disposed within the housing for receiving a collapsible container therein, the receptacle having a first opening at one end and a second opening at the opposite end, said first opening being sized to receive said collapsible container therein, said receptacle including means to prevent said collapsible container from collapsing into said first opening during use; said collapsible container including a soft serve frozen confection therein, said collapsible container having an outlet of sufficient size to allow extrusion of said soft serve confection therefrom; and, means to collapse said collapsible container.

For a better understanding of the nature and objects of the present invention, reference should be made to the following detailed description and the accompanying drawings, in which:

Fig. 17.1 shows a frozen confection dispensing apparatus 10 of the present method with an outer casing 11. A dispensing section 12 having a conduit casing 13 extends through a container door 14 of the apparatus 10. Extending outward from the conduit casing 13 are two valves 20 operably responsive to valve handles 84. Even though two dispensing valves 20 are shown, it is realized that the dispensing apparatus 10 of the present invention may include one or a number of dispensing valves 20 depending on the design of the unit. The dispensing valves 20 are linearly aligned at each interval across the conduit casing 13. Each dispensing valve 20 (Fig. 17.3A) is disposed for controlling the flow of product from each collapsible container 22. The valve 20 excepting its handle 84 is disposed within the dispensing section 12 so that the valve 20 is in the refrigerated portion of the apparatus, thereby maintaining any frozen dessert therein in a frozen or near-frozen condition at all times prior to dispensing. Access to the interior of the apparatus 10 is aided by the use of a door handle 16.

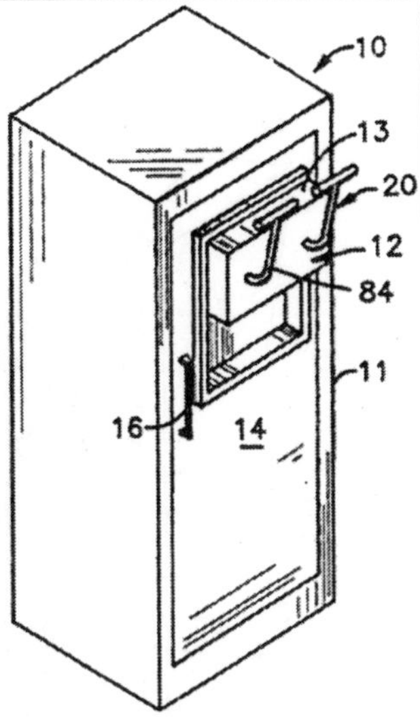

Fig. 17.1 shows an exterior view of the frozen confection dispensing apparatus according to the present method

The outer casing 11 of the apparatus 10 is ideally insulated to reduce heat transfer from the exterior environment to the interior of the apparatus 10. The interior temperature of the apparatus 10 should ideally be maintained within a preselected temperature range generally sufficient to keep frozen confection in a condition that it can be easily extruded from the collapsible bag or container. The preselected temperature will generally be in the range of from 10° F. to about 12° F., but may be lower or higher depending on the physical properties of the frozen dessert being dispensed. When the outer casing 11 is properly insulated, only a small freezing unit is needed to adequately compensate for heat gained from the exterior environment acquired from the outer casing 11 and the opening of the container door 14. Moreover, appropriate refrigeration means, which are well known in the art, are in use within the interior of the dispensing apparatus 10 to maintain the temperature in the preselected range.

Fig. 17.2 is a partial interior view of the dispensing apparatus 10. The container door 14 is open to reveal storage area 38, which contains multiple replacement collapsible containers 22 collected together into a transport package 42. The transport package 42 is generally constructed of a thermally insulated material.

Generally, frozen dessert or confection is bagged in a collapsible container 22, collected with other similar units in a

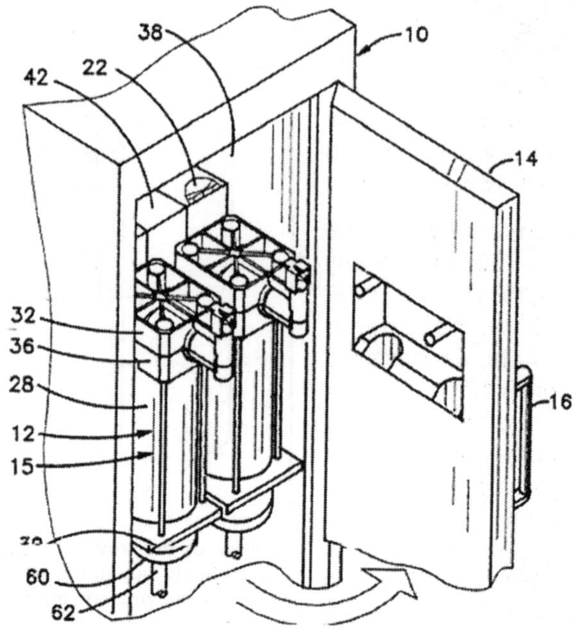

Fig. 17.2 Partial interior view of the dispensing section and shows the receptacle for a collapsible container of the present method

transport package 42 and shipped in a hard frozen state at generally sub-zero degrees Fahrenheit. The transport package 42, containing the frozen confection, is placed in the storage area 38 where it is allowed to slowly thaw to the preselected dispensing temperature range. After the frozen confection has been tempered and the temperature has been brought to the preselected temperature, (or tempered) the temperature of the confection is maintained at this level to prevent localized melting and refreezing that could result in an unappetizing crystallization of the soft serve frozen confection.

The dispensing section 12 includes a plurality of dispensing assemblies 15, only two being shown. Each dispensing assembly 15 includes a receptacle 28 for receiving the collapsible container 22 (Figs. 17.3, 17.3A, 17.4, 17.4A) therein. The receptacles 28 are elongated sleeves generally made of stainless steel, fiberglass or the like, with openings in each end thereof. As shown in Fig.

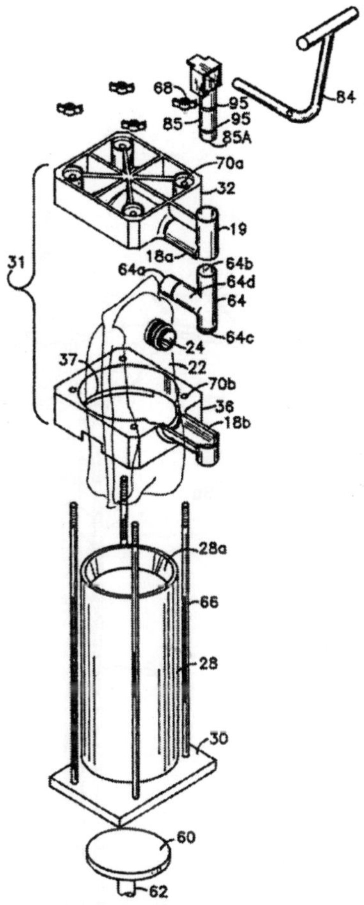

Fig. 17.3 Exploded view of the collapsible container and receptacle for the collapsible container of the present method

17.3, the top opening 28a is the opening to receive the collapsible container 22 therein. The bottom opening, or second opening 28c (Fig. 17.3A) receives the piston 60 therein as discussed hereinafter.

A receptacle support plate 30 is mounted to the interior of the dispensing section 12 for holding the receptacle 28 thereon. The receptacle support plate 30 has an opening therethrough of substantially the same diameter as the inside diameter of the receptacle 28 and the circumferential diameter of the piston 60 so as to receive the piston 60 therethrough.

As best shown in Figs. 17.3 and 17.4, the collapsible container 22 is held in place in the receptacle 28 during use by a pressure lid assembly 31. The pressure lid assembly 31 includes a pressure lid 32 and a pressure lid mount plate 36. The mount plate 36 is provided with a centrally disposed opening 37 therein that receives the discharge end of the collapsible container 22, the end including the collapsible container outlet 24. The pressure lid 32 in combination with the pressure lid mount plate 36 are provided with semi-circular outwardly extending conduit portions 18a and 18b, which together form a T-shaped dispensing conduit that receives the collapsible container outlet 24 therein. The T-shaped dispensing conduit 18a, 18b also receives the T-

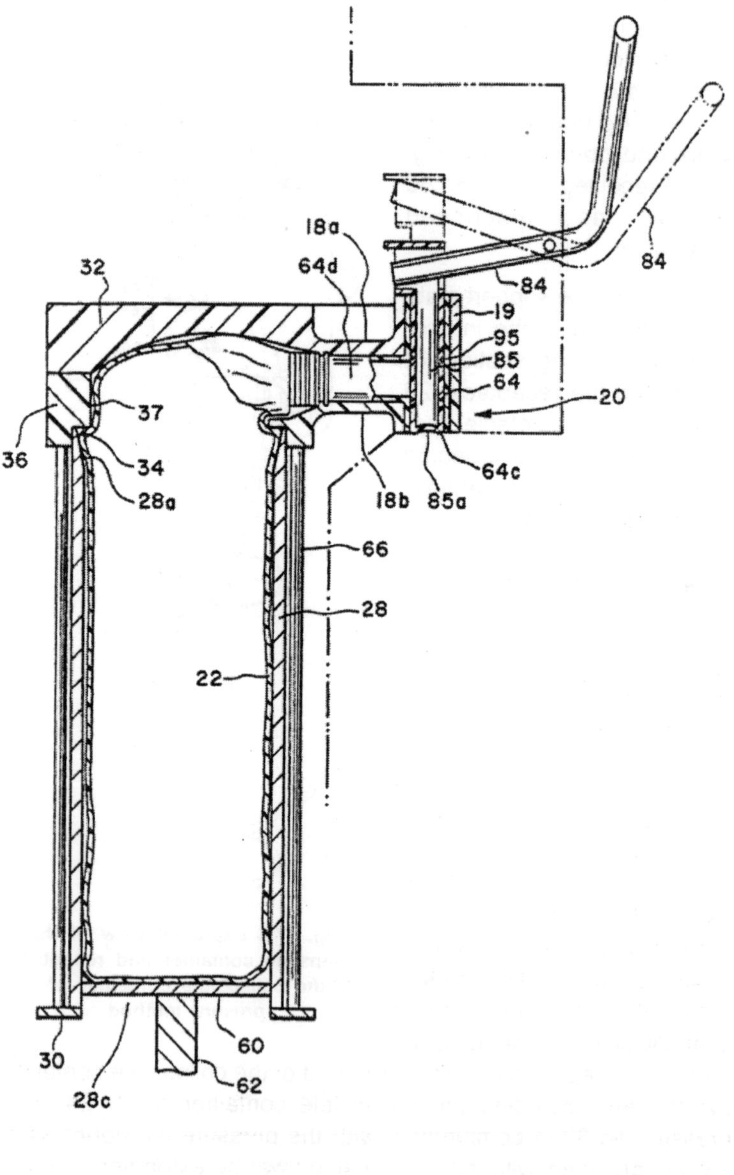

Fig. 17.3A Partial cross-sectional view of a receptacle and collapsible container of the present method shown in Fig. 17.3

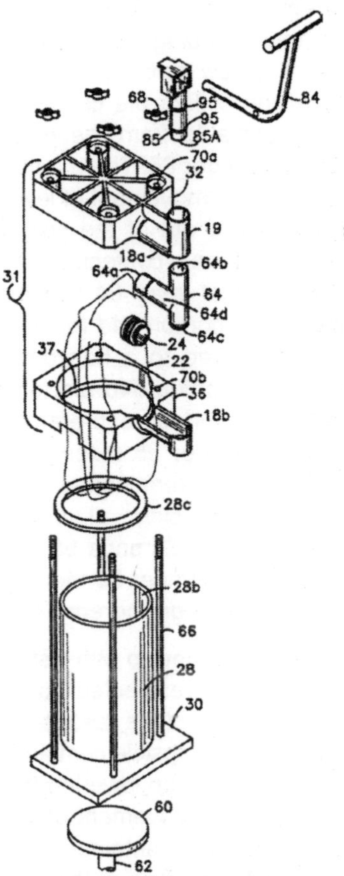

Fig. 17.4 Exploded view of another preferred embodiment of the receptacle and collapsible container of the present method

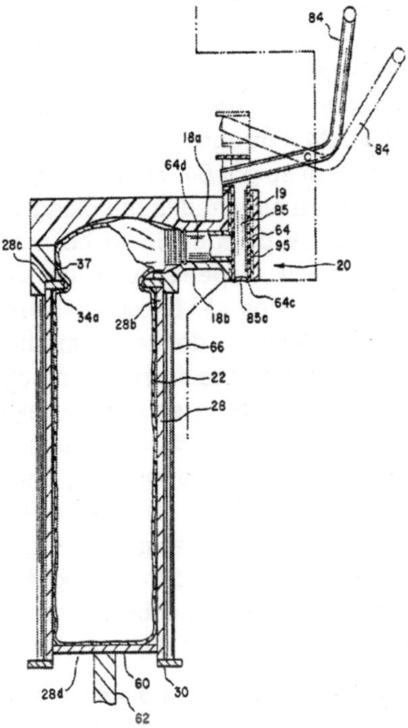

Fig. 17.4A Partial cross-sectional view of the receptacle and collapsible container shown in Fig. 17.4

shaped spigot 64 therein. The T-shaped spigot 64 is provided with a cylindrical hollow inlet leg portion 64d that is disposed within the dispensing section 12. An opening 64a is in flow communication with the collapsible container outlet 24, preferably with the collapsible container outlet 24 being received within the inlet opening 64a in sealing relationship therewith.

The spigot 64 is also provided with a cylindrical hollow head portion in flow communication with and transverse to leg 64d.

An opening 64b is disposed at one end of said head portion to receive a vertical action plunger 85 therein plunge 85 may be solid, but a preferred plunger 85 has a hollow core. The frozen confection or dessert that flows out of the collapsible container outlet 24 through leg portion 64d is blockable from the head portion of spigot 64 by the vertical action plunger 85. The manual lever 84 is attached to the plunger 85 whereby movement of lever 84 causes plunger 85 to be movable in and out of the spigot 64 to allow dispensing of the soft serve frozen confection. As shown in Figs. 17.3A and 17.4A, the manual lever 84 can be raised (shown in dotted lines) above the leg portion 64d to allow dispensing of the frozen confection or lowered to a horizontal position (shown in solid line) below the leg portion 64d blocking flow of the confection through the spigot 64. In a preferred embodiment, the terminating end 85a of plunger 85 extends to and is horizontally aligned or flush with the terminating end (opening) 64c of spigot 64 so that in dispensing, all of the confection is forced from spigot 64. Moreover, "O" rings 95 are provided to circumscribe the outer surface of plunger 85 thereby sealing the plunger 85 from confectionary leakage therearound.

Generally, the handle 84 is in actuating relationship with piston 60 so that upon handle 84 being raised to a preselected point, the piston 60 is actuated and engages the bottom of the collapsible container 22, forcing the confection out of the collapsible container 22 through the collapsible container outlet 24. Upon lowering the handle 84, the piston 60 is disengaged and the movement of the piston upwardly for engaging with the collapsible container 22 is therefore stopped and the plunger 85 blocks the flow of the soft serve confection through the spigot 64. In a preferred embodiment piston 60 is operable in response to a variable pressure source so that as the lever 84 is raised higher, additional pressure is applied to the collapsible container 22 through piston 60.

The pressure lid mount plate 36 and the pressure lid 32 are mounted onto the receptacle 28 for the collapsible container 22 by a plurality of elongated threaded members 66 and accompanying wing nuts 68. The pressure lid 32 and the pressure mount plate 36 are provided with a plurality of apertures therethrough identified as 70a and 70b, respectively. Each elongated threaded rod member 66 is passed through aligned apertures 78a and 78b and a wing nut 68 is screwed onto the threaded rod member 66 and tightened down, thereby holding the pressure lid 32 and the mount plate 36 onto the receptacle 28.

As shown in Figs. 17.3 and 17.3A, at the top opening 28a of the receptacle 28, the opening is tapered so that at the outer extremity of the opening 28a, the diameter is greater than the diameter of the opening 37 thereby defining a groove 34 at the juncture of the mount plate 36 and the receptacle 28. This groove 34 prevents the upward movement of the collapsible container 22 when the piston 60 is actuated to force confection out of the outlet 24 and collapse the container 22. The collapsible container 22 tends to gather at the groove 34 and thereby does not collapse into the outlet 24, which would interfere with or block the flow of soft serve confection from the collapsible container 22.

Figures 17.4 and 17.4A show an alternative means for the prevention of the collapsing of the collapsible container 22 into the outlet 24 when in use. In this embodiment the receptacle opening 28b is not tapered but is straight or of substantially the same diameter as the opening 37 in the mount plate 36. Moreover, a metallic or relatively hard plastic O-ring 28c having an inside diameter less than the diameter of the opening 28b is placed on the receptacle between the receptacle 28 and the mount plate 36. A recess 34a is thereby formed between the opening 28b and the O-ring 28c to prevent the movement of the collapsible container 22 therepast when the confection is being dispensed therefrom.

In the removal of a collapsible container 22, wing nuts 68 are removed from the elongated threaded rod members 66 and the pressure lid 32 is separated from the pressure lid mount plate 36, thereby disengaging the pressure lid 32 from the spigot 64. The spigot 64 is then disengaged from the collapsible container outlet 24 and the pressure lid mount plate 36 is lifted away from the receptacle 28, thereby leaving the collapsible container 22 to be removed from the receptacle 28. The T-shaped spigot 64 and plunger 85 are then cleaned and replaced in the pressure lid plate 36 as the spigot 64 and plunger 85 are the only parts that come in contact with the flowing frozen confection. And, in many cases, since the T-shaped spigot 64 and plunger 85 are relatively inexpensive plastic pieces, the spigot 64 and plunger 85 may be discarded and new ones inserted.

In the insertion of a full collapsible container 22 into use, the full collapsible container 22 is placed or dropped into the receptacle 28 and the pressure lid mount plate 36 is placed onto the receptacle 28 with the elongated threaded rod members 66 passing up through the appropriate apertures 70b. Once the pressure lid mount plate 36 is secured upon the receptacle 28, the spigot 64 is placed upon the semi-circular conduit 18b and the collapsible outlet 24 is inserted within the opening 64a. Apertures 70a are then aligned with the elongated threaded rod members 66 and the pressure lid 32 is then placed over and onto the pressure lid mount plate 36 with the semi-circular conduit portion 18a receiving the spigot 64 therein with the end opening 64b being inserted into the tubular portion 19 of the semi-circular conduit portion 18a. Wing nuts 68 are then threaded upon the threaded rod members 66 and tightened down to secure the bag in place.

18

Miscellaneous Laminated Frozen Food Product

It is known that rapid freezing of many liquids, especially liquid comestibles, retains many of the constituents either lost altogether, or at the best changed in some deleterious fashion, when the liquid is frozen slowly. It has also been found that as a rule, the more rapid the freezing, the more nearly does the thawed frozen product resemble the original liquid prior to freezing.

This method discloses a method of extremely rapid freezing, and the product it produces is superior to present fast frozen products, because it is not only frozen very rapidly, but is immediately subcooled to a degree that prevents partial melting and resultant evaporation as well as the more rapid sublimation to be found with products nearer the melting point.

For example, liquid eggs are usually frozen in cans requiring from 18 to 72 hours to complete the freezing; by the method disclosed herein several seconds are all that is required to freeze the eggs and subcool the product.

By the method and with the equipment disclosed hereinafter, a thin layer of liquid egg has been frozen in approximately 2 seconds, and then subcooled to the desired degree in another 2 to 3 seconds. As this product is too thin to handle as a separate ribbon or when processed into flakes, another layer of liquid egg is spread on the top of the already frozen and subcooled layer which immediately freezes to the layer beneath it, and this layer in turn is promptly subcooled. Proceeding in this fashion enough layers are added to make a ribbon of the thickness desired for subsequent handling.

As these layers are extremely thin, the total resistance to heat flow through the freezer and the layers varies little with the additional layer thus spread, as the number of layers required in most cases is small. For example, frozen ribbons of liquid egg between four and six one hundredths of an inch thick, comprising four layers, well bonded together to form a single homogeneous frozen egg ribbon, has been frozen in 10 to 15 seconds.

Subsequent handling takes one of two general forms; the frozen product may be converted into flakes, and thus packed and marketed, or the subcooled ribbons may be stacked in the form of a bar, wrapped and packaged. As long as the bar is maintained at its subcooled temperature, the ribbons will maintain their separate identity, and will thaw most rapidly, as the entire surface of each ribbon will be presented to the material being cooled. Contrast this with the present methods of thawing, requiring so long a time that bacteria growth is favored, or if the chunks of frozen material be taken from the can and broken up, labor and possible injury to the egg results.

Both the bar and the flakes disclosed herein have the advantage of large surface and quick thawing, the bar has the added advantage of having a volumetric density almost equal to that of the solid mass.

An object of this method is to obtain improved frozen products. Another object of this method is to produce frozen products that may be very rapidly thawed, when further processed. Still another object is to provide frozen comestibles that can be readily packaged for present day frozen food markets.

Referring particularly to Fig. 18.1 of the drawings, the freezer has an evaporator 1 assembled with an evaporator frame 3 in the manner more fully described hereinafter. The subassembly of evaporator 1 and evaporator frame 3 is supported by a base frame 5 bolted to it by means of brackets 7. Wooden skids 13 form an insulating foundation for the metal base frame 5. This frame has two central support members 6 and 8 which carry two centrally supported tubular arms 10, which in turn, support slant

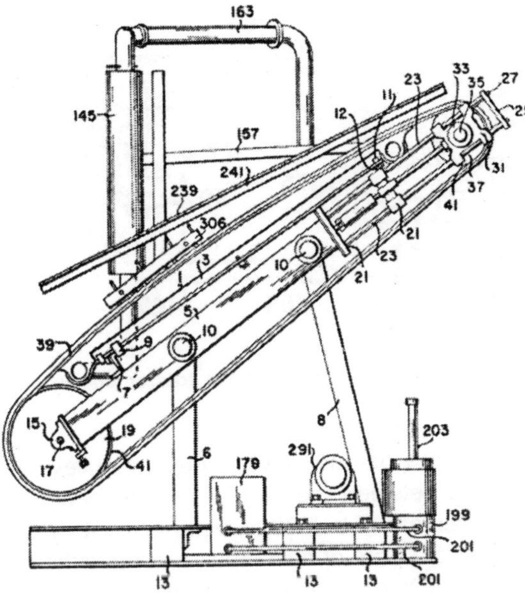

Fig. 18.1 Side elevational view of a freezer embodying my method

portions of the frame 5 cantilevered on both sides. The slant portion carries a freezing subassembly. The evaporator subassembly is mounted in a slant position as shown. Pads of rubber 9 provide cushioned mountings on the brackets 7 that permit final adjustment of the alignment of the evaporators 1 by means of bolts 11, which by means of their nut 12 control the compression of the pads 9.

As best shown in Fig. 18.1, a weldment 21 is bolted to the upper end of frame 5 and supports four parallel guide rods 23, two on each side. The guide structure is completed by end plates 25 secured to the ends of guide rods 23 by screws 27. Bearing block 31 is bored to slide on guide rods 23, thus permitting the bearings to move longitudinally of the slant frame. Each of the pair of bearing blocks 31 has a bearing 33 for an idler shaft 35. Mounted upon a free turning shaft is an idler pulley 37. A drive pulley 19 of considerably greater diameter than the idler pulley 37 is keyed to a shaft 17, which is rotatably mounted in the pair of bearings 15 secured to the lower ends of the slant members

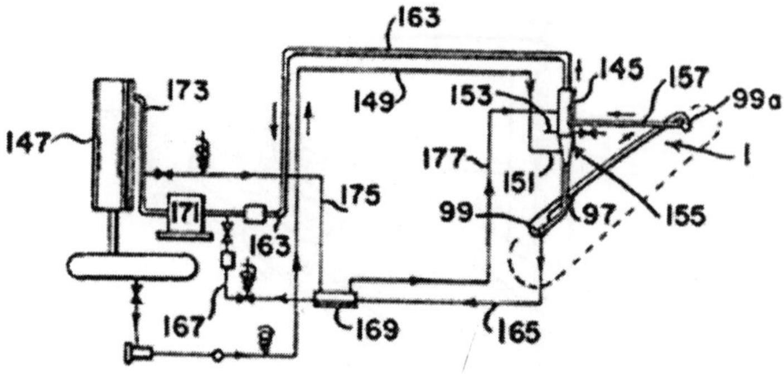

Fig. 18.2 The refrigeration system of the freezer shown in Fig. 18.1

of frame 5. Freezing belt 39 is supported by pulleys 19 and 37 and is tensioned between them as will be described more fully hereinafter. Movement of belt 39 is imparted to it by drive pulley 19. Pulleys 19 and 37 are of rigid metal and have their cylindrical faces covered by a layer 41 of an elastomer, such as rubber (see Fig. 18.9). Pulley 19 is driven as described hereinafter in connection with Fig. 18.8. The frame 5 is built so that the line between the centers of the shafts of the pulleys 19 and 37 may make with any horizontal line any angle between 45° above to 45° below horizontal. As pulley 19 turns, it drives the belt 39 so that it is drawn along the curved top surface of the evaporator. The portions of the belt in contact with the evaporator is maintained at a low temperature. As shown in Fig. 18.6, the belt is held under tension by rods which bear upward against bearing blocks 31. The force on the inner rod 43 is produced by a coaxial spring 45 which is screw adjusted for changing the pressure. The force on the outer rod 43 is produced by a coaxial hydraulic cylinder 47 which is automatically controlled as described hereinafter. The belt is driven by pulley 19 in a clockwise direction in Fig. 18.1; that is, with the upper run moving to the right.

As shown in Figs. 18.4 and 18.5 4 and 5, each edge of belt 39 has bonded to it a continuous molded dam structure 49 of an elastomer, e.g., rubber. As shown in the cross sectional view of Fig. 18.4, this dam structure has portions on both sides of the belt; the one portion to retain the liquid or fluid 40 (product)

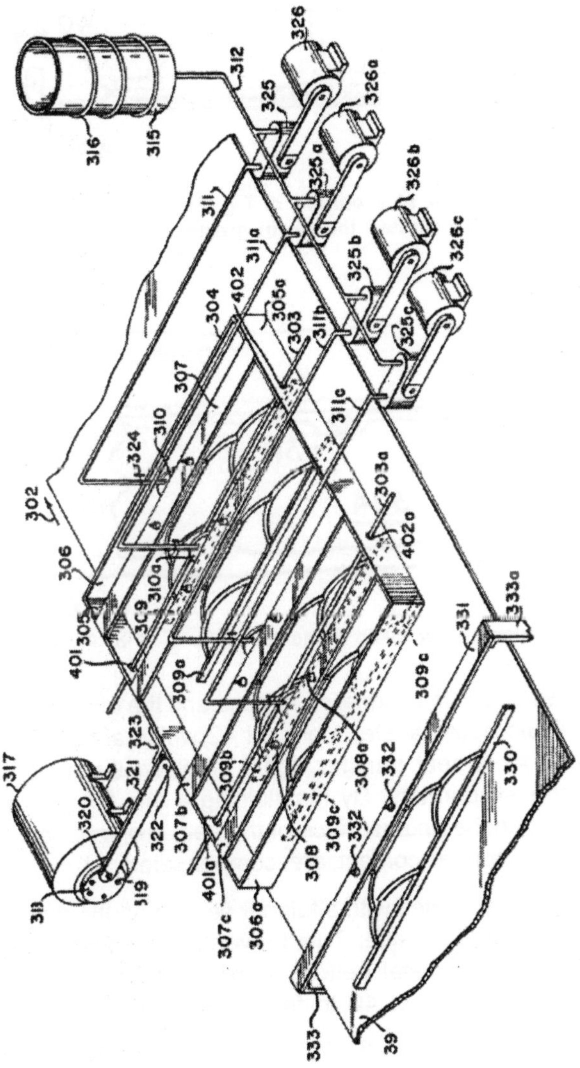

Fig. 18.3 The system employed for feeding liquid to be frozen to the freezer

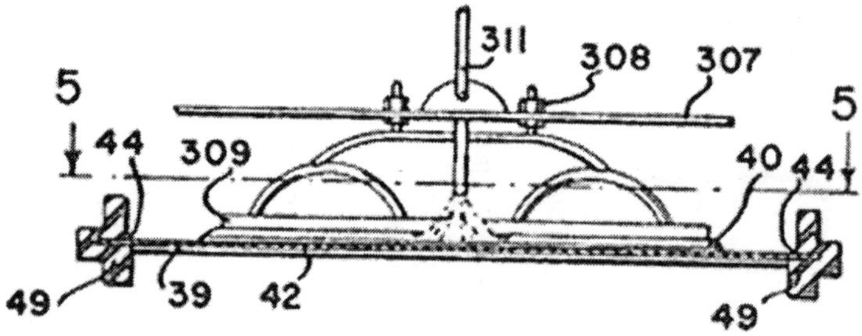

Fig. 18.4 An enlarged view of a portion of Fig. 18.3 showing the dam structure illustrated therein in greater detail

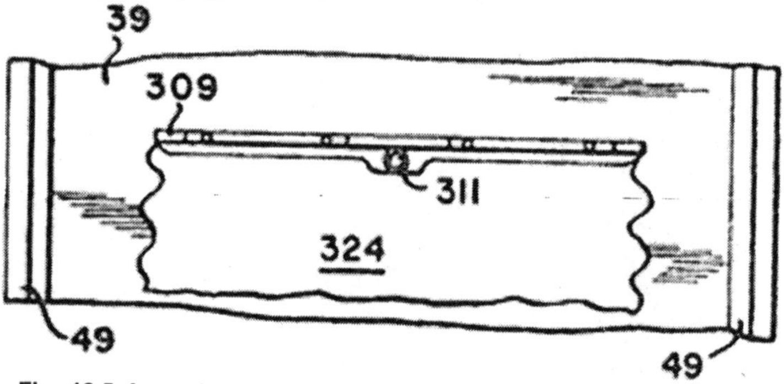

Fig. 18.5 A sectional view taken along the lines 5—5 of Fig. 18.4

being congealed upon the congealing surface and the other portion to retain the liquid heat transfer lubricant 42 which acts both as a lubricant and as a heat transfer agent between the metal of the belt and the evaporators. By maintaining a thin film of heat transfer lubricant on the undersurface of the belt, any irregularities in the surface in normal contact are compensated for.

The dams 49 are formed with a thinner section on the product side than on the lubricant side. This prevents the edges where the dams 49 meet the metal belt 39 at points 44 from getting cold enough for the product 40 to freeze along its edges.

From drive pulley 19, shaft 17 fastened to it by key 18, is extended inwardly beyond bearing 15 (see Fig. 18.1 and 18.9) where sprocket 51 is keyed to it. Sprocket 51 is driven from upper jack-shaft 53 by chain 55 and sprocket 56 which is keyed to jack-shaft 53. Jack-shaft 53 is turned by sprocket 57, driven by chain 63 from motor 291, gear-motor sprocket 59 and gear motor shaft 61. Jack-shaft 53 turns in two bearings 65, bolted one on either side to the center post of frame 5. A lower jack-shaft 67 turns in two bearings 69 which are similarly bolted to the center post of frame 5. Jack-shaft 67 is turned by sprocket 71 from chain 63. A hydraulic pump sprocket 73 is driven from this jack-shaft by a chain 79 and a sprocket 75, and 73 and chain 79. The sprocket 81 of the lubricant pump is also driven by chain 63. Vertical adjustment of sprocket 81 produces the proper tension in the chain 63. Proper tension in chain 55 is maintained by vertical adjustment of bracket 87 which supports an idler sprocket 83 and its pivot 85.

REFRIGERATION OF EVAPORATOR

Fig. 18.2 is a diagrammatic representation of the refrigeration system for the evaporator 1 which omits accessories such as controls, oil separator and others well known in the art. Liquid refrigerant from condenser 147 is fed through conduit 149 into the surge drum through valve 151 which is controlled by level responsive element 153 so that the level in the surge drum is maintained at level 155, which is the optimum operating level. The refrigerant liquid flows by gravity from the surge drum into the evaporator 1. The refrigerant vapour formed in the evaporator flows through conduit 157 into surge drum 145, displaced by liquid refrigerant under the static head at level 155. The liquid refrigerant flows through an orifice in a nozzle into each of the evaporator tubes 97 to provide proper distribution of refrigerant between the tubes and to increase velocity and turbulence therein resulting in a higher rate of heat transfer. The refrigerant vapour returns to the compressor 171 via the surge drum 145 where any liquid carried with it is separated out before it enters the suction line 163. Oil return is obtained by bleed off tubes 165 from the lower evaporator header through the oil still 169 and back into the suction line to compressor 171. Oil still 169 is heated by a small amount of discharge gas from compressor discharge line 173 through tubes 175 and 177 to the top of surge drum 145.

Lubricant System

Fig. 18.7 is a diagrammatic representation of the system which maintains a thin film of heat transfer lubricant between the evaporator and the belt. This lubricant may be an antifreeze compound such as an aqueous solution of propylene glycol. A supply of lubricant is maintained in reservoir 179. When the belt is driven, pump 181 supplies lubricant to the leading end of the evaporator 1, through filter 182 via capillary 183 and a feed block (not shown).

Pump 181 is driven by sprocket 81 as previously described with reference to Fig. 18.8. Used lubricant is returned to reservoir 179 via a drain line.

When the refrigerant flow is stopped a timer keeps the belt 39 running for a preset period. During this period solenoid valve 197 opens diverting all lubricant from the discharge of the pump 181 to reservoir 179 while the above described lubricant system returns the lubricant in use to reservoir 179 also to prevent loss of lubricant by overflow on shutdown.

Since the lubricant used is water soluble, it may be gradually diluted by moisture condensed from the air as the ice maker operates. Further, since the freezing point is raised by dilution, this accumulation of water must be constanting removed to avoid possible freeze-up. Since the boiling point of the lubricant and water mixture is a function of its water content a rectifier 199 is used, maintained at a practically constant temperature by means of an electric immersion heater and thermal switch. The temperature of the rectifier is set to correspond to the boiling point of the desired concentration of lubricant solution. A small convection flow in tubes 201 maintains the solution concentration in reservoir 179 substantially the same as that in rectifier 199 without heating the solution in the reservoir. Thus when the solution is diluted in the reservoir 179, it is also diluted in rectifier 199 depressing its boiling point below the rectifier temperature. The boiling in the reservoir drives water out of the solution, thus concentrating it until its boiling point reaches the predetermined rectifier temperature, at which time the boiling stops. A reflux condenser 203 having glass ball packing is used over the rectifier to minimize loss of lubricant carried off by the escaping steam.

HYDRAULIC TRACKING SYSTEM

Fig. 18.6 is a diagrammatic representation of the hydraulic tracking system which automatically keeps belt 39 centered on evaporator 1 and drive pulley 19 and idler pulley 37 as it runs. A reservoir 205 holds a supply of hydraulic fluid. Pump 207 (driven by sprocket 73 in Fig. 18.8) draws fluid from reservoir 205 to build up pressure in pressure line 209, limited by a pressure regulator 211 which bleeds into a drain line 213 to return spent fluid to reservoir 205. The belt is tracked by using this pressure in the following manner: a control valve 215 is operated by a roller arm 217 which follows the molded edge 49 of belt 39. When belt 39 starts to the left of center it causes arm 217 to turn control valve 215 so as to permit more fluid into cylinder 47 increasing the tension slightly in the left side of the belt 39

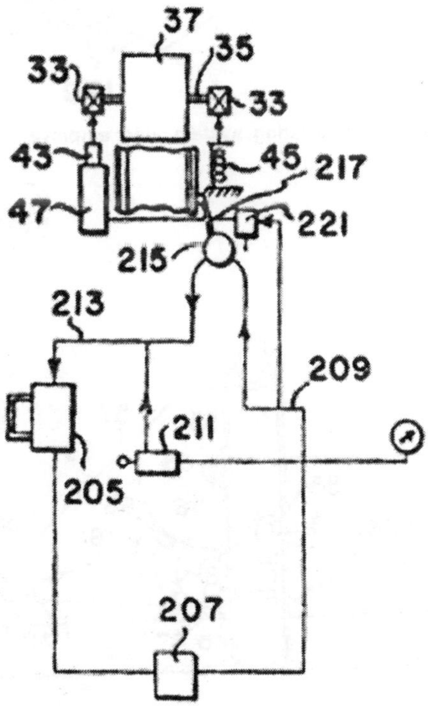

Fig. 18.6 The system for tracking employed in the freezer of Fig. 18.1

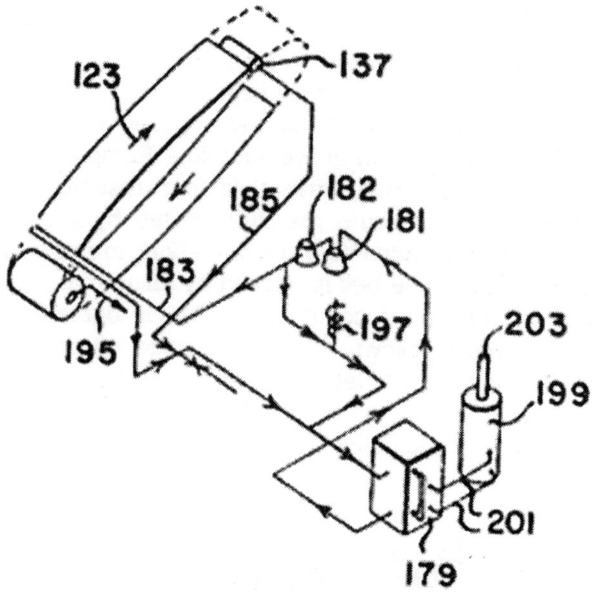

Fig. 18.7 The belt lubricating system also employed in the freezer

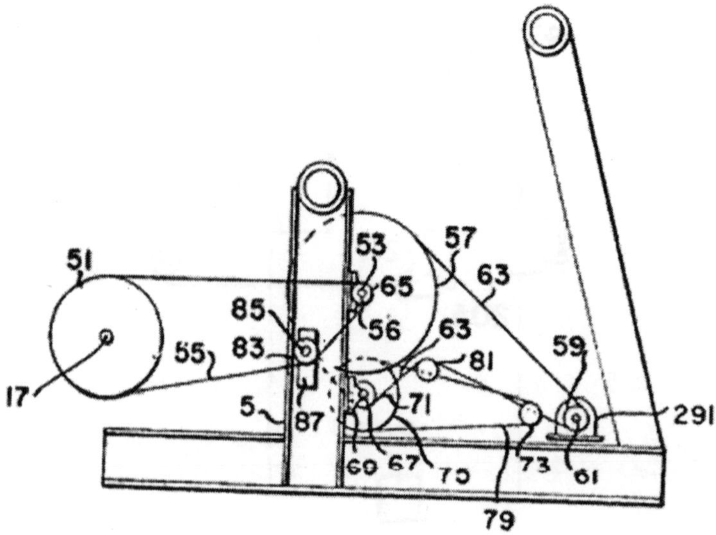

Fig. 18.8 The drive system employed in the freezer apparatus

which moves the belt back to the center position. When belt 39 starts to the right of center it causes arm 217 to turn control valve 215 so as to vent fluid from cylinder 47 decreasing the tension slightly in the left side of the belt 39 which moves the belt back to the center position. Spring 45 maintains a practically constant preset tension on the right side of the belt. The changes in tension on the left side of the belt required for tracking are referenced to this tension and are so slight that they have no noticeable effect on the belt. A check valve 201 is provided between the control valve 215 and the cylinder 47. This valve remains open as long as there is pressure in line 209. When the pump stops and its pressure falls, check valve 221 closes to hold cylinder 47 in the proper position for restarting without excessive tracking movement.

FEEDING THE LIQUID TO BE FROZEN

The feed of the liquid to be frozen is all important. The liquids vary greatly in viscosity, density, surface tension, and size and amount of suspended solids. Viscosity, density, and surface tension in turn vary with the temperature range through which the liquid passes as it is being cooled on the belt just prior to freezing. In Fig. 18.3 there is disclosed an arrangement which is applicable to a large number of liquids.

Referring now to Fig. 18.3, the freezing belt 39, travelling in the direction of the arrow 302, passes under the following structure. Attached to the main frame 5 are two rods, 303 and 303a, on which slides in bearings 401 and 402, and 401a and 402a, a frame 304 comprising longitudinal members 305 and 305a, and transverse members 306 and 306a. A number of brackets 307, (307b, 307c), are attached to the longitudinal members 305 and 305a, and these carry by means of adjustable screws and nuts, such as 308 and 308a, a number of belt wipers 309, 309a, 309b, and 309c. The belt wipers are similar to automobile windshield wipers; but when intended for food freezing, the blades are made of some material other than natural rubber, such as silicone rubber.

The brackets 307 et seq. carry clamps 310, 310a, 310c, which in turn carry the open ends of the flexible tubes 311, 311a, 311b, 311c. The other end of each of these tubes 311 et seq. is connected to one of a series of pumps 215 et seq. driven by motors 326, et seq. Suction of the pumps 325 et seq. is connected through a header 312 to a reservoir 315, which holds the product to be frozen. As a temperature control is a vital part of the process, reservoir 315 is maintained at the required temperature by either heating or cooling coils 316.

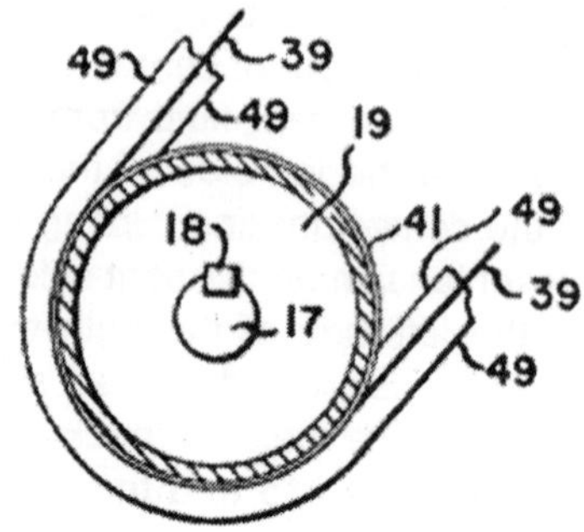

Fig. 18.9 is a fragmentary view of the drive pulley used in the freezer shown in Fig. 18.1

Frame 304 is made to reciprocate laterally by means of a motor 317, carrying a disk 317, in which are a number of holes 319, in one of which a pin 320 can be inserted, giving a reciprocating motion to the link 321, pivoted at 322 to a bracket 323 attached to the frame 304.

Valves, cocks or some similar devices, 324, 324a, 324b, 324c are used to control the flow of the liquid being frozen. With certain products, such as liquid eggs, albumen will tend to clog up the cock, requiring a greater force to drive it through the cock. For this type of product the construction shown is preferable, as it permits changes in pressure in any one line without affecting any other line, in other words, it permits independent pump action.

The method of operation is: the liquid to be frozen, 328 is fed through the tube 311 (see Fig. 18.5) and is spread by the wiper blade 309 forming a small puddle in front of the wiper, where it is instantly frozen (324). It is scalloped on the edges because of the reciprocating motion of the wiper described hereinabove. The size of these "scallops" can be controlled, as the amount of reciprocation is controlled by the hole 319 in which the pin 320 is placed, as each hole 319 is at a different radius from the center of the disk.

In case, during adjustment, or because of some other incident not normal to the operation, some liquid overflows the ends of the wipers 309, it is caught by longer stationary wiper 330, held by bar 331 by adjustable screws and nuts 332. Bar 331 is attached to the main frame 5 of the machine by brackets 333, 333a.

For certain products, because of lesser viscosities, the product to be frozen may be flowed on to the belt 39 through a nozzle attached to each of the tubes 311, et seq. These nozzles may be made of glass, stainless steel or other special material.

The reciprocating of the wipers prevents the blades from being frozen to the moving belt by the quick freezing of the liquid; it also assists materially in flowing the liquid towards the ends of the blades, and producing a thin film of uniform thickness to be frozen.

Referring now to Fig. 18.10, it will be seen that the frozen product 324 is in the form of a homogeneous ribbon, sufficiently thick to peel from the belt 39 as it passes over the deflecting pulley 37, as it has been built up during freezing as described hereinabove by spreading upon a quick frozen and subcooled extremely thin ribbon another thin liquid ribbon, which in turn is very rapidly frozen; and this process has been continued until

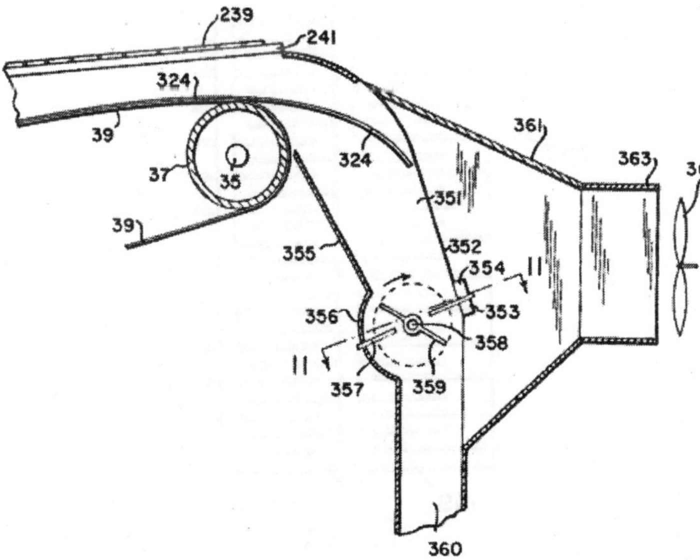

Fig. 18.10 Apparatus to make flakes from the frozen ribbons formed in accordance with the teachings of my method

the ribbon is sufficiently thick to permit peeling of the frozen composite ribbon. It may be discharged into a cold room, and then broken or cut into lengths manually or by a machine. These ribbons may be stacked and wrapped and sold as a bar. If the bar has been kept at the required subcooled temperature through the handling, packing and storage, the individual ribbons will not freeze or stick together, and when the package is opened, the individual ribbons will separate and present to the material being processed the complete surface of each individual ribbon. The entire bar will then thaw extremely rapidly.

To further process the ribbons into flakes, (see also Fig. 18.11), a chute 351 is provided against one side 352 of which ribbon 324 rubs and breaks into relatively large pieces which fall until they are caught by pins 354 and 357, held in brackets 353 in the sides of the chute 351. Pins 359, rapidly rotating on shaft 358 break these pieces of frozen material into flakes, by hurling

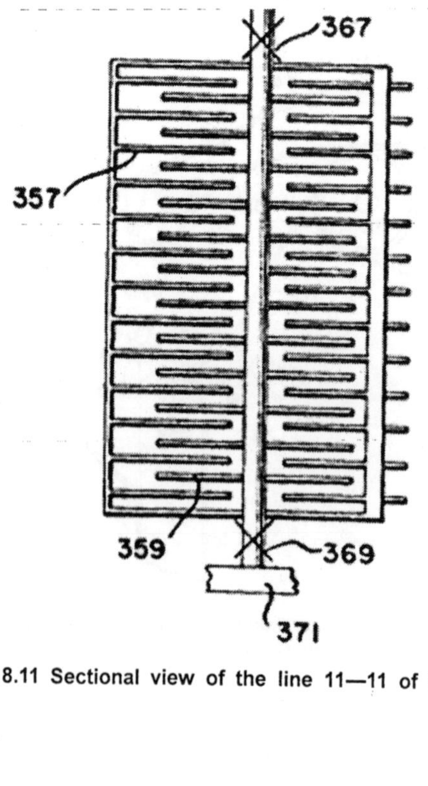

Fig. 18.11 Sectional view of the line 11—11 of Fig. 18.10

them against the stationary pins 354 and 357, whereupon the flakes thus formed fall through the outlet 360 into a refrigerated storage. Shaft 358 is driven by pulley 371 and turns in bearings 367 and 369.

To prevent the subcooled ribbon touching a warm side of the chute an evaporator 363 is provided and a duct 361, together with a fan 365 blowing the air through the evaporator and thence against the chute 351. This air is circulated all about the chute, and the methods of doing this are so well known in the art that they are not further described herein.

In the embodiment of Fig. 18.12 an arrangement is provided for cutting the ribbon 324 into predetermined lengths and assembling them in subcooled condition for storage and shipment. With this arrangement a cutter unit 401 has a cutter blade 403 positioned adjacent the side wall 405 of an assembly tray 407. Knife 403 is carried by a mounting arm 409 which is swingably supported by a pivot 411. A tension spring 413 urges arm 409 upwardly and a rotary cam 415 is turned at spaced intervals of time to swing knife 403 downwardly against the tension of spring 413. During each downward movement knife 403 severs the end of ribbon 324 and produces a rectangular sheet 417 of the frozen product. Ribbon 324 is shown below in Fig. 18.13 as it projects from the freezing surface and is moving at a constant speed. The interval between successive impacting actions of cam 415 is such as to permit the desired length of the ribbon to project beyond the knife to substantially the opposite wall 419. Hence, the ribbon 324 is cut into predetermined lengths and the sheets are assembled in a stack. When a predetermined number of the sheets have been

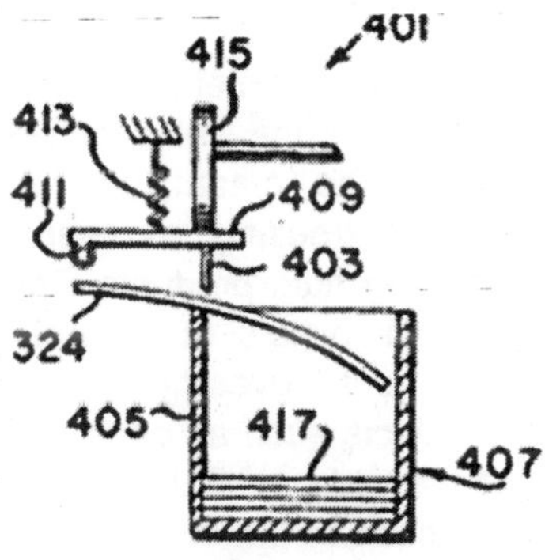

Fig. 18.12 Schematic view of an arrangement for cutting the frozen ribbons of this method into strips

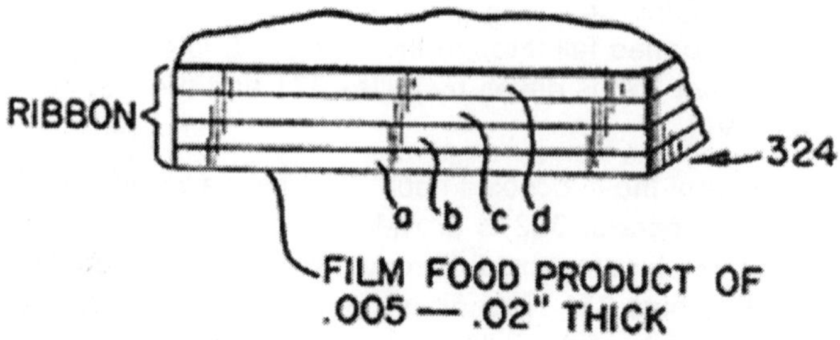

Fig. 18.13. Ribbon 324 as it projects from the freezing surface

assembled the stack is removed and packaged. The entire assembly of Fig. 18.12 is positioned within the subfreezing atmosphere of the air stream in hood 361 and the packaging operation is also at a subfreezing temperature.

The present method is applicable to a wide range of products, i.e., eggs or the yolks or whites of eggs, fruit and vegetable juices, coffee, cream, and various liquid and viscous products. The term “freezing” as used herein covers the broad range of congealing fluid products. The water in such products is frozen into small crystals. In general, each film freezes immediately and is “dry” as it moves beneath the next set of wipers. Illustratively, for products such as eggs, the thickness of each film of the fluid is of the order of 0.01 to 0.02 inch and the ribbon is peeled at a thickness of the order of 0.05 to 0.25 inch. For most products, the ribbon has a thickness which is not greater than 0.1 inch. As a specific example, when freezing coffee having 10 percent solids by weight the film thickness is 0.005 to 0.01 inch and the ribbon is peeled at 0.04 to 0.05 inch.

19

Frozen Comestibles

Food technology in recent years has focused on providing high quality food products which are low in calorie content and low in cost. In this regard, the frozen dessert industry has attempted to provide reduced-fat products which have organoleptic properties similar to the same products having a normally higher fat content. This objective is particularly difficult to achieve in frozen food products because the product is subjected to low temperatures which can have an adverse effect on the blend of ingredients.

Ice cream, for example, is a frozen dessert recognized for its smooth, creamy texture achieved by delicately balancing formulated ingredients and processing steps to provide the desired coldness, melt-down, mouthfeel and other taste characteristics.

Primary components of ice cream products are the dairy-based ingredients. In earlier times, milk and cream provided the basic ingredients, i.e., milk protein, milk sugar, milkfat (butterfat), emulsifiers and stabilizers, necessary for making ice cream products. In current commercial operations, ice cream formulations can also include nonfat milk solids, milk fat, sugar and water to replace some or all of the traditional ingredient milk/cream, as well as other non-dairy ingredients such as egg yolks, emulsifiers and stabilizers.

By definition, ice cream must contain not less than 10% milk fat and 20% total milk solids. Unfortunately, milk fats add a significant amount of calories to the ice cream. Ice milks have been introduced to reduce the amount of calories in the product. Ice milks are formulated to be low in milk fat and to include primarily nonfat milk solids. Some ice milks, however, contain high percentages of nonfat milk solids which can impart a gritty or chalky mouthfeel. This drawback is chiefly due to the high levels of solids which do not melt in the oral cavity. In addition, the higher concentrations of crystallized lactose present in nonfat milk solids can also contribute to inferior organoleptic qualities.

Thus, ingredients and methods are constantly being sought to provide a reduced fat frozen comestible with a creamy texture and a lubriciousness characteristic of a higher fat content food product.

It is, therefore, a purpose of the present method to provide a frozen food product which has organoleptic properties characteristic of a fat-containing product.

It is another purpose of the present method to provide ice cream or ice milk products having substantially reduced fat content and a creamy texture which can be stored for relatively long periods of time without deterioration.

The present method includes frozen food products prepared with an oleaginous-containing matrix formed by melt-spinning an oleaginous substance with a carrier material. The oleaginous substances used in this method can include edible oils such as vegetable oils including soybean, corn, canola and the like. Alternatively, fats such as meat fats, hydrogenated vegetable oils, and even butter fat can be used. The oleaginous substances make up from about 2 to about 40% by weight of the matrix, with amounts of from about 10 to about 30% being preferred and amounts of from about 15 to about 25% being most preferred.

Carrier materials which can be used for the matrix are saccharides such as sucrose or saccharide-based materials such as maltodextrins and/or water soluble cellulosic materials such as methyl and ethyl cellulose. In further aspects of the method, the matrix includes one or more adjunct materials such as natural or artificial flavors, spices, sweeteners and/or hydrogels such as xanthan gum or alginates to enhance the matrix and/or products to which the matrix is included.

The oleaginous-containing matrix can be incorporated in a variety of frozen food products. For example, the matrix can be included with partially frozen or fully hardened homogenized pasturizing mixtures containing fat, milk solids other than fat, sweeteners, flavoring substances, emulsifiers and the like. Frozen desserts prepared in accordance with the present invention can be firm, solid products, or can be pumpable, semi-solid products such as soft-serve type products. Frozen desserts of the present invention also include, but are not limited to, products similar to conventional ice cream, frozen custards, i.e., the so called French ice creams, mellorines, ice milks and sherbets.

The present method further includes the method of making frozen food products. The method includes subjecting a feedstock material and oleaginous substance to conditions of high temperature and shear sufficient to form a matrix which includes oleaginous materials. This oleaginous-bearing matrix can then be incorporated into the frozen food product. In order to prepare a frozen dessert, the matrix described above can be combined with a dessert material to provide various products such as ice-cream-like products.

The present method also includes matrices composed of an oleaginous substance, a carrier material, and one or more ingredients that are commonly used in conventional frozen food products. It is preferred that these ingredients be substantially non-aqueous. Water is not an ingredient useful in forming these matrices. The matrix in this form may be consumed as the dry non-descript matrix or may be mixed with a liquid such as water, milk, a milk product, or the like, to form a creamy product which has a taste and texture approximating ice cream or other frozen food product. Products made in this way may be refrigerated or frozen if desired. Alternatively, the dry matrix may be compressed, by itself or in conjunction with additional dry ingredients, to tablet form that can be dissolved in the mouth or chewed, thereby also imparting the taste and texture qualities of a conventional frozen food product.

As a result of the present method, frozen comestibles can be provided which have desirable organoleptic properties and a selected fat content. For example, ice-cream-like products can be made which are low in fat yet have a smooth, creamy and non-gritty mouthfeel similar to that of a fine custard. In addition, the creamy texture and smooth consistency can be maintained for long periods of storage.

In one particularly interesting aspect, a portion of the frozen food product's fat content is replaced with a matrix containing a much lower amount of fat without a detectable loss of flavor or mouthfeel. In certain products, up to 50% of the usual fat content can be replaced without compromising gustatory qualities.

In the present method, an oleaginous-bearing matrix can be formed by subjecting carrier feedstock and oleaginous substance to conditions of temperature and shear to form the matrix. This can be accomplished by melt-spinning oleaginous substances with carrier materials. The matrix is included in various low fat frozen products.

The following methods serve to provide further appreciation,. Unless indicated otherwise, the Econo Floss machine referred to above was used to form the spun-matrix. Operating temperatures were approximately 200° C., and spinning speed was approximately 3,600 r.p.m.

Method 1:

25% Fat Matrix

In this method, butter oil and corn oil were combined with sucrose and processed to form a matrix as set forth below for incorporating in a frozen food product. Normally, butter oil and corn oil are substantially nondispersible. Consequently, a mixture such as that set forth in this example would not be a likely candidate for dispersing in a food product, especially a frozen food product where the inability to effect thorough mixing is exacerbated by freezing the product.

Ingredients	Weight	Percent Weight (lbs)
Butter Oil	12.5	2.0
Corn Oil	12.5	2.0
Sucrose	75.0	12.0

All of the ingredients were first thoroughly mixed. The resulting mixture was subjected to elevated temperatures and shear of the Econo Floss machine to provide the oleaginous-containing matrix.

Method 1A

The matrix obtained in method 1 was incorporated into a 10 gallon mixture of low calorie ice cream. The total amount of oleaginous substance in the resulting product was about 5% of the overall composition. Ice-cream normally contains about 12 to 16% fat. Thus, the frozen product of the present method contained about 60% reduction in oleaginous substance.

The product itself was a velvety, fine custard of creamy textured ice-cream. Moreover, the product maintained its texture for long periods of storage, e.g., about 1 year, without experiencing recrystallization or organoleptically perceptible deterioration.

Method 2

This method shows the preparation of a dry delivery product, having medium fat content, useful for the preparation of food products in accordance with the present method.

Ingredients	Weight, Grams
1. Finely Ground Fructose	60.0
2. Corn Syrup Solids (Hubinger DE42)	132.0
3. Non-Fat Milk Solids (Carnation)	90.0
4. Cream Solids (Dietrich Milk Prod.)	6.0
5. Best Mix Stabilizer (Germantown Mfg.)	1.35
6. Medium Chain Triglyceride Oil	6.0
7. Vanilla	3.0
8. Cream	0.30
9. Carboxymethylcellulose (Aqualon)	0.30
10. Sugar Gum (Supercol U NF, Aqualon)	0.30

All ingredients except the medium chain triglyceride oil and the cream were blended in a Cuisinart® mixer. Then the triglyceride oil and the cream were added to the blend and mixed in thoroughly. The blend was then processed in a three inch diameter cable heater flash flow apparatus, at 3600 rpm with a cable temperature setting of approximately 105° C. Large white flakes of processed product were generated.

Fifty grams of the flake product was gently stirred into 150 grams of skim milk. The liquid mixture was poured into freezer trays and put in a freezer until solid. This procedure resulted in a frozen product having the taste and texture of a good frozen soft ice cream.

Fifty grams of the flake product was gently stirred into 75 grams of water and the resultant mixture was frozen to produce a frozen product having a taste and texture of a very acceptable frozen soft ice cream.

The flake product provides a dry delivery system which can be easily mixed with a comestible liquid such as water, milk or aqueous emulsion of a food oil to produce an acceptable product.

The processed flake matrix appears to provide a much more stable suspension of the ingredients in a liquid than the ingredients provide when blended but not processed. The unprocessed blend was compared to an equal amount of processed flakes, when each was added to skim milk in the above ratio. Upon four hours holding in a soft serve machine the unprocessed blend showed evidence of separation and breakdown whereas the sample made from processed flakes maintained its integrity and had a fuller creamier mouth feel.

These processed flakes have also been pressed into tablet form. When the tablets are put in the mouth they dissolve to produce a very pleasant creamy taste.

Method 3

This method shows the preparation of a dry delivery product, having low fat content, useful for the preparation of food products in accordance with the present method.

Ingredients	Weight, Grams
1. Finely Ground Fructose	60.0
2. Corn Syrup Solids (Hubinger DE42)	138.0
3. Non-Fat Milk Solids (Carnation)	90.0
4. Best Mix Stabilizer (Germantown Mfg.)	1.35
5. Medium Chain Triglyceride Oil 6.0	
6. Vanilla	3.0
7. Cream	0.30
8. Carboxymethylcellulose (Aqualon)	0.30
9. Sugar Gum (Supercol UNF, Aqualon)	0.30

20

Apparatus and Method for Dispensing Frozen Aquarium Food

Aquariums housing fish or other aquatic creatures are widely used as decorative displays in homes and businesses. Aquariums may be used to keep fresh water fish or other creatures or, alternatively, salt water or marine fish or other aquatic organisms. One of the problems facing owners or operators of aquariums is the proper and consistent feeding of fish with food of a high nutritional content. Aquarium owners have the option of manually feeding their fish several types of fish food, such as dry flake food, freeze-dried food, or frozen food.

In conjunction with aquariums, an automated food dispensing device may be used by the owner or operator of the aquarium. Automated food dispensing devices for aquariums offer several advantages to aquarists, in that they free the aquarists from the required duties of feeding fish or other aquatic organisms at predetermined or regular times during the day. An automated food dispenser also provides free time to the aquarist, thus allowing the aquarist to devote time to other activities such as, for example, vacation, other business duties, or other recreational activities. Additionally, automated food dispensers allow aquarists the freedom simply not to have to touch their aquarium for days or even weeks at a time.

A variety of systems for automatically dispensing food for an aquarium has been developed. Automated feeding devices for aquariums are widely used currently and are made by a variety of manufacturers. Examples of such feeding devices include the Daily Double model available from the company Penn-Plax; the Rondomatic model by Tetra; the Feed-Air model by Eheim; and the Fishmate model by Animate. Such automated feeding devices have varied configurations allowing automated feeding from, for example, seven days up to thirty days, or more.

For example, one general approach to automated dispensing of aquarium food includes a feeding unit which is placed on a platform or ledge above the surface water of an aquarium. The food dispenser unit includes a receptacle bin for holding food. Typically, dry flake food is loaded into the bin. This bin is rotatably mounted on a horizontal shaft connected to a motorized control chassis. The bin includes a small aperture or hole at the top. At predetermined times, the controller in the chassis causes the motor to rotate the shaft one full revolution. This causes the food-containing bin to rotate about its longitudinal axis. As the bin rotates, the hole in the bin begins to rotate downward. As the hole approaches the surface of the water, food within the bin falls out of the hole and into the aquarium. The shaft continues rotating until it completes one whole revolution of 360 degrees, resulting in the bin being placed in the same position in which it started, with the hole or aperture at the top.

As discussed above, aquarists have several choices of the types of food that can be given to fish. Salt-water or marine fish (and other creatures) have nutritional requirements which are better satisfied with the use of frozen foods. To a lesser extent, the same is true of fresh-water fish or other freshwater organisms. Frozen food can provide better for the health and longevity of fish and other marine life, especially as compared with non-frozen foods, such as dried flake food or freeze-dried foods.

The desire to use frozen fish food raises several issues which existing conventional food dispensers, such as those discussed above, cannot solve. Conventional automated feeding devices for aquariums suffer from a major drawback and shortcoming, in that all existing automatic feeder designs are capable of dispensing only non-frozen foods to the fish or other aquatic creatures. Existing food dispensers cannot accommodate frozen food and cannot keep the frozen food unthawed. Frozen fish food, by its nature, must remain cold or else it will create unwanted water build-up, will cause undesirable mess and odor problems, and will lose nutritional value as it begins to rot.

If an aquarist has a salt-water aquarium, then such an aquarist is only able to use existing automated food dispensers which fail to provide the nutritional benefits of frozen food. Similarly, if an aquarist wishes to provide frozen food to fish in a freshwater aquarium, such an aquarist would be unable to do so with conventional food dispensers. For example, an aquarist with a salt-water aquarium who wishes to leave the aquarium untended for a length of time (for example, during a vacation) is currently only able to provide dry flake or freeze-dried food with an existing automatic food dispenser, which may lead to nutritional deficiencies and health problems for the fish, including the possibility of death. Further to this example, such an aquarist's other option is to risk having another person, who may or may not be familiar with aquariums, tend for the feeding of the fish manually, which poses a risk of either overfeeding or underfeeding, and thus creates a risk of health problems, including possibly death, for the fish.

In sum, aquarists wishing to provide frozen food to their fish are simply unable to gain all the benefits of an automated food dispenser, discussed above.

Accordingly, an automated system and method for dispensing frozen food to an aquarium is desired.

In accordance with one aspect of the method , an automated frozen food dispenser is positioned on a ledge or platform above the surface water of an aquarium. The dispenser includes an insulated housing which envelops, thermally insulates, and, in one embodiment, is molded to fit and retain the interior elements of the dispenser. In one embodiment, the housing may be fashioned of expanded rigid polystyrene plastic. Inside the housing or shell are a series of horizontal compartments which are filled with a predetermined quantity of frozen food. The frozen food may be in the form of a pellet or any similar quantity of food, and alternatively may be any assortment of a plurality of types of frozen foods.

In one embodiment, the compartments are formed by radially dividing an annular channel with regularly spaced divider walls, whereby the walls of the channel and the divider walls make up the walls of each channel. Thus, the compartments form a wheel. The compartments in this embodiment sit atop a circular plate of equal or slightly greater diameter as the diameter of the compartment wheel. This circular plate forms the bottom floor for each of the compartments. As discussed below, the bottom circular plate has a hole, equal in size to the dimensions of one compartment, formed directly above a trap door which leads to an external conduit to the bottom of the dispenser unit. This trap door has a spring-loaded hinge so that it remains in a closed, horizontal position until acted upon. This trap door is also thermally insulated.

Alternatively, the compartments may be fashioned by laterally subdividing a horizontal, circular grooved channel with regularly-spaced divider walls between each compartment and its neighbors. The bottom of each compartment, in this embodiment, includes a trap door which is spring-loaded so as to remain in the closed or horizontal position unless acted upon. The trap door of each compartment is heat-insulated.

In any embodiment, the compartments may be fashioned as pockets or trays, sufficient to contain and hold a quantity of food. In alternative embodiments, the arrangement of compartments may be altered and need not be in an annular shape, for example the compartments may be arranged in a row on a movable conveyor belt.

In the embodiments utilizing a wheel of compartments, the annular configuration of compartments are mounted on a spoke and hub system, thus enabling the series of compartments to rotate around a central hub. The hub is vertically mounted on the interior, surface of the insulating housing. A plurality of spokes, appropriate to the size of the compartment wheel, radially connect the hub to the grooved channel forming the compartments.

In this system, a rotation controller, attached to the grooved channel forming the compartments, causes the grooved channel to rotate at a predetermined rate. This rotation controller may comprise a motor controlled by programmable control circuitry which causes the grooved channel to rotate at either a predetermined rate or at predetermined times.

In the embodiment in which the wheel of compartments is placed on a circular plate, the rotation controller rotates the compartments over the plate so that each compartment (along with the food stored therein) comes to rest, one at a time, in a position directly above a hole formed in the bottom circular plate. As each compartment rotates into position over the hole, the food in the compartment falls through the hole and onto the thermally-insulated trap door mounted directly below the hole and in the floor of the interior of the dispensing unit.

In this embodiment, a motor-driven piston is positioned directly above the compartment which is directly aligned above the trap door leading to the opening in the bottom of the insulating shell. At a predetermined schedule, the piston dispenses the frozen food out of the compartment by moving downward, through the space defined by the compartment, through the hole in the circular bottom plate, and ultimately forcing open and downward the trap door. The frozen food falls through the trap door and is then dispensed through the vertical conduit to the opening in the bottom of the insulating shell, and thus into the aquarium.

In the embodiment in which each compartment has its own trap door, the compartments are rotated by the rotation controller such that the compartments, one at a time, come to rest holding their frozen food over a vertical conduit leading to an aperture or opening fashioned in the bottom of the insulating shell.

In this embodiment, a motor-driven piston is positioned directly above the compartment which is directly aligned above the opening in the bottom of the insulating shell. At a predetermined schedule, the piston dispenses the frozen food out of the compartment by forcing open and downward the trap door at the bottom of the compartment. The frozen food is then dispensed out of the compartment, through the vertical conduit to the opening in the bottom of the insulating shell, and thus into the aquarium.

In any embodiment, after the frozen food is dispensed, the piston retracts vertically upward, thus allowing the spring-loaded trap door to shut again. All the trap doors are thermally insulated in order to maintain the low temperature desired for the interior of the dispenser unit. The piston retracts to a sufficient height to allow the wheel of compartments to rotate freely, so that the next compartment may be presented under the piston and over the hole in the bottom of the shell.

In one embodiment, the motor and control elements for the piston are mounted on the exterior and on top of the housing. This arrangements prevents the heat generated by the piston's controller from affecting the temperature of the frozen food. In this arrangement, the piston is arranged so that it moves in a vertical channel or tube extending from the top of the dispenser down to and including the vertical conduit leading to the bottom exterior of the dispenser.

The temperature of the interior of the dispenser unit is maintained at a low level through the use of internal cooling devices. In one embodiment, one or more thermo-electric coolers are used. In another embodiment, one or more thermo-electric coolers are used in conjunction with a heat sink. A thermo-electric cooler or refrigerator is a semiconductor device which uses the Peltier effect to move heat to when a current is applied, and will act as a heat pump and move heat away from a source towards an opposite direction. In one embodiment, one or more thermo-electric coolers are mounted in the insulating shell above the center hub of the compartment wheel. The thermo-electric coolers are mounted so as to draw heat away from the center of dispenser unit, towards a hole in the top of the dispenser unit. The two thermo-electric coolers may be stacked, one on top of the other, in a vertical tube above the center of the compartment wheel. The thermo-electric coolers will move heat from the center of the dispenser to the top of the system. Above the uppermost thermo-electric cooler is a heat sink which is attached to the top exterior of the insulating shell. The thermo-electric coolers are attached to the heat sink, and the heat sink will dissipate heat removed from the inside of the dispenser unit, by the thermo-electric coolers, and out into the atmosphere outside the entire dispenser unit.

In one embodiment, the heat sink is fashioned of aluminum. In another alternative embodiment, the heat sink may include an electric fan which further acts to dissipate heat from the heat sink to the outside air.

Use of the same reference symbols in different figures indicates similar or identical items.

Fig. 20.1 shows an automated frozen food dispenser 2 positioned above the surface water of an aquarium 1. Aquarium 1 may be either a fresh-water aquarium or a salt-water aquarium. Aquarium 1 may be any conventional residential, commercial, or industrial aquarium, and may be used to keep alternatively fresh water fish or salt water or marine fish or other aquatic organisms. Aquarium 1 may be of any predetermined size. Frozen food element 36 is shown in Fig. 20.1 being dispensed into aquarium 1. Food 36 may be any conventional form of frozen food suitable for salt water or marine fish, fresh water fish, or other aquatic organisms. Alternatively, food material 36 may be any mixture of a plurality of types of frozen food suitable for fish or other aquatic creatures, or may be any nutrition supplement or even medicine, fungicide, water conditioner, or other additive appropriate for aquarium 1 or the organisms being kept therein.

Dispenser system 2 includes a bottom aperture or hole 34 (shown in Fig. 20.2). System 2 is positioned above aquarium 1

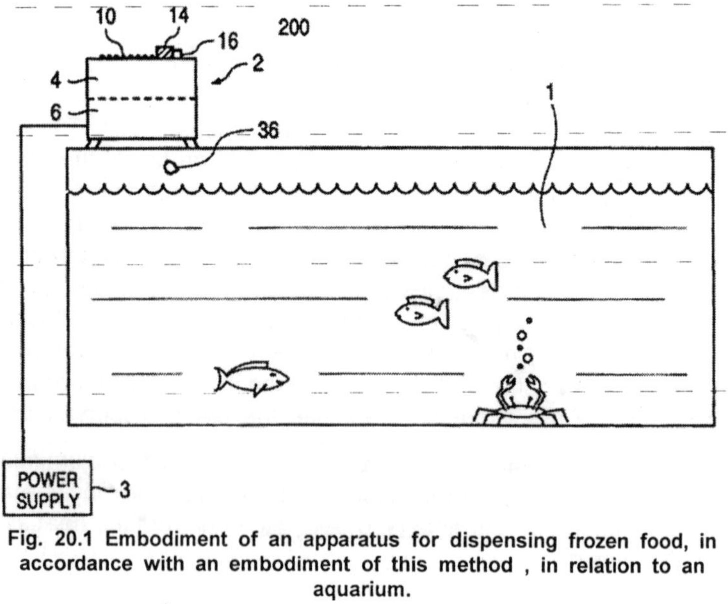

Fig. 20.1 Embodiment of an apparatus for dispensing frozen food, in accordance with an embodiment of this method , in relation to an aquarium.

on a ledge or platform, such that bottom aperture 34 is positioned above the surface of the water in aquarium 1. As shown in FIGS. 20.1 and 20.3, frozen food material 36 is dispensed from system 2 through aperture 34 and into aquarium 1.

Dispenser 2 is connected to power source 3, which may be any conventional power source, such as a an electrical outlet, a battery or any commercial or industrial source of power. Power source 3 is connected to the motorized control and electrical elements comprising dispenser system 2 as appropriately required. Alternatively, power supply 3 may be, for example, a battery integral or internally stored and mounted on, within, or as part of dispenser system 2.

Fig. 20.2 shows primarily the features of system 2 which are externally visible. The dispenser 2 includes an insulated housing or shell, which envelops and thermally insulates the interior elements of the dispenser 2. In one embodiment, the insulated shell is in two parts 4 and 6 roughly corresponding to an upper and lower half, respectively. These two parts 4 and 6 can be

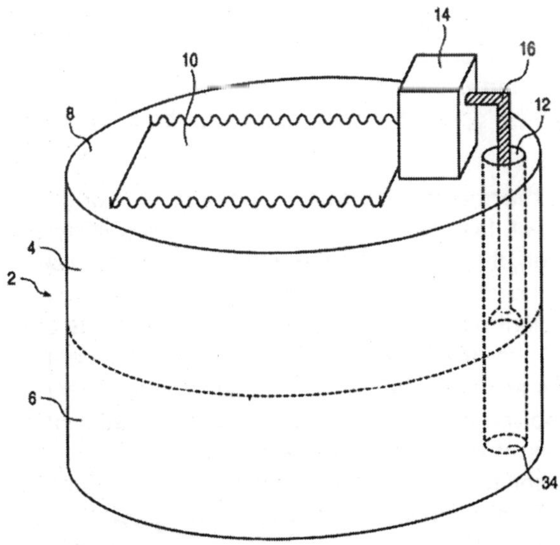

Fig. 20.2 Perspective view of features of a system for dispensing frozen food in accordance with an embodiment of this method.

manually separated to allow access to the interior of the dispenser, for example to fill the dispenser compartments 26 with food 36 or to set the configuration of rotation controller 22 (see Fig. 20.3). Alternatively, the insulating housing may be laterally divided into right and left portions, or any other configuration appropriate for allowing access to the interior of system 2 without substantially affecting the thermal insulating properties of the housing.

Food dispenser 2 includes a top aperture 12 and a bottom aperture 34 formed in the insulating shell. Aperture 34 is an opening in the bottom surface of lower portion 6 of dispenser 2. Top aperture 12 is an opening in top surface 8 of upper portion 4 of dispenser system 2. Top aperture 12 forms a tube or channel within which piston 16 is introduced vertically into the interior of system 2. Piston-controller 14, shown in this embodiment mounted on top surface 8, operates on and controls the movement of piston 16 upward and downward. Heat sink 10 is attached to the top surface 8 of the upper portion 4 of insulating housing for system 2.

The thermally insulating and enveloping housing may be manually opened between upper part 4 and lower part 6, and alternatively one or more hinges may connect upper and lower portions 4 and 6 so that they form a clamshell or similar shape which can be opened to gain access to the interior elements of system 2.

The thermally insulating housing or shell is, in one embodiment, fashioned out of expanded rigid polystyrene plastic. Alternatively, the insulating housing may be any thermally insulating material, including an external casing or shell to provide support and sufficient rigidity to retain the internal elements of dispenser system 2. In one embodiment, thermally insulating housing sections 4 and 6 are formed of expanded rigid polystyrene plastic to envelop the internal elements of system 2 with approximately two inches of insulating material on all sides and are formed in such a fashion so as to support and retain the interior assemblies of food dispensing system 2 discussed below.

Fig. 20.3 shows one embodiment, in cross-section view, of external and internal elements of frozen food dispensing system 2 in relation to one another.

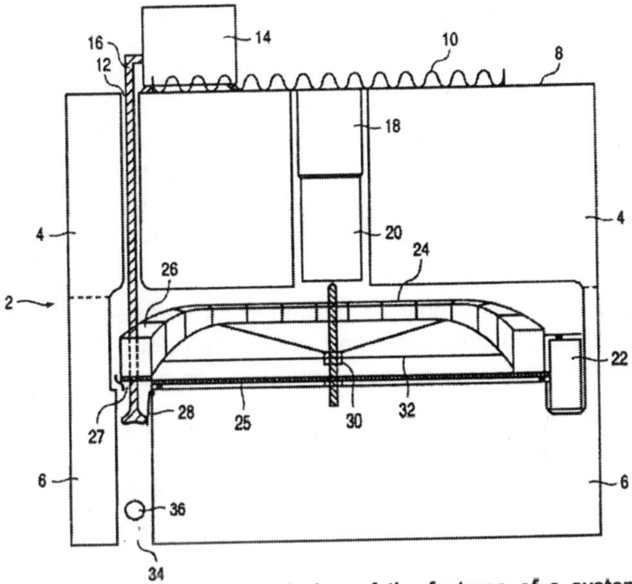

Fig. 20.3 Vertical cross-sectional view of the features of a system in accordance with an embodiment of the method.

A series 24 of horizontally aligned compartments 26 are arranged within a central chamber inside food dispensing system 2. This collection of compartments 24 comprises containers sufficient to hold a predetermined quantity of frozen food 36 within each compartment 26. Each compartment 26 is of equal size and dimension as each other compartment 26 forming the collection of compartments 24. Alternatively, compartment 26 may be fashioned as a pocket, a tray, or any shape appropriate to contain and hold a predetermined quantity of frozen food 36.

Frozen food 36 may be in the form of a pellet or any appropriate quantity of food. As discussed above, alternatively element 36 may be any assortment of any plurality of types of appropriate frozen foods, nutrion supplements, or any desired additive appropriate for aquarium 1.

In one embodiment, the collection of compartments 24 are fashioned by radially subdividing a horizontally arranged annular channel with regularly spaced divider walls set laterally between each compartment 26 and its neighbors. The divider walls and the walls of the grooved channel form the walls of each compartment 26. The collection of compartments 24 sits atop, but is not fixedly attached to, a bottom circular or annular plate 25 of equal or greater diameter as the collection of compartments 24. As discussed below, the collection of compartments 24 rotates, while bottom plate 25 does not. Plate 25 forms the bottom surface for each individual compartment 26. Plate 25 is mounted on and fixed in position in relation to the interior surface of lower portion 6 of insulating housing.

Plate 25 has a hole 27 formed in its surface, and this hole 27 is directly aligned with and above trap door 28. Hole 27 is of equal or substantially equal area or size as compartment 26.

Trap door 28 is spring loaded along its hinge so that it will remain closed and in a horizontal position unless acted upon. Further, trap door 28 is heat insulated or otherwise fashioned so as to participate in thermally insulating the interior chamber of dispenser system 2.

In another embodiment, the collection of compartments 24 are fashioned by radially subdividing a horizontal circular grooved channel with regularly spaced divider walls set laterally between each compartment 26 and its neighbors. The divider walls and the walls of the grooved channel form the walls of each compartment 26 and each individual compartment 26 has a unique trap door 28 formed as its bottom surface. Each trap door 28 is spring loaded along its hinge so that it will remain closed and in a horizontal position unless acted upon. Further in this embodiment, each trap door 28 in each compartment 26 within the collection of compartments 24 is heat insulated or otherwise fashioned so as to thermally insulate the frozen food 36 stored within each compartment 26.

As shown in Fig. 20.3, the collection of individual compartments 26 are formed in an annular or circular shape forming a wheel 24. This annular configuration of compartments 24 is mounted on a spoke and hub system 30 and 32. Hub 30 is vertically mounted on the interior surface of lower portion 6 of the insulating housing. A plurality of spokes 32 radially connect hub 30 to the wheel of compartments 24 sufficient to support the wheel of compartments 24 and allow them to rotate around hub 30. One of ordinary skill will understand that the number of spokes needed to adequately support and rotatably connect the collection of compartments 26 will depend on the number compartments 26 and size of wheel 24.

Rotation controller 22 is connected to the wheeled collection of compartments 24. Rotation controller 22 may comprise an electric motor, which uses gears or a friction wheel to engage the surface of compartments 24 so as to cause the wheel of compartments 24 to rotate at a predetermined rate or at predetermined times. Rotation controller 22 may be mounted within the insulating housing portions 6 or 4. Alternatively, rotation controller 22 may be mounted on the exterior surface of insulating housing portions 4 and 6, in which case an aperture or opening must be provided to allow the gear or friction wheel assembly of rotation controller 22 to engage and cause to rotate the collection of compartments 24.

Although rotation controller 22 is shown mounted to the side of compartments 26 in FIg. 20.3, alternatively, rotation controller 22 may be mounted above, below, or in any appropriate position in relation to either the collection of compartments 24 or spoke and hub system 30 and 32, as long as rotation controller 22 is engaged in such a way to effectuate rotation of the compartments 26.

Rotation controller 22 causes the compartments 26 to rotate at a predetermined rate or at predetermined times appropriate to the desired feeding cycle for aquarium 1. As noted, rotation controller 22 may comprise an electric motor controlled by control circuitry, which causes the collection of compartments 24 to rotate at either a predetermined rate or at predetermined times or schedule. Rotation controller 22 may be user programmable and reprogrammable so as to allow variation in the rate of rotation and thus feeding.

Rotation controller 22 causes the compartments 26 to rotate such that each compartment 26, one at a time, comes to rest in a position directly above hole 27 in bottom plate 25. Food is transferred from compartment 26 to aperture 34 and thence to the aquarium 1 as follows:

As rotation controller rotates wheel 24, each compartment 26 will in turn pass over hole 27. Food element 36 in compartment 26 will fall through hole 27 and onto the surface of trap door 28.

Piston 16, in its rest state, is withdrawn into top aperture 12 such that piston 16 does not touch and is not within the space defined by compartment 26. At a predetermined time or schedule after food element 36 has fallen onto trap door 28, piston controller 14 actuates piston 16 by pushing piston 16 downward through top channel 12 such that piston 16 will enter the space defined by compartment 26. Piston 16 will continue downward until it impacts frozen food element 36. Piston 16 will continue further downward until the force of its downward motion causes trap door 28 to open. Piston 16 will complete its downward motion such that it allows food element 36 to fall or be introduced into bottom aperture 34. Piston 16 pushes aside trap door 28 and frozen food element 36 egresses through bottom aperture 34 and thence into the aquarium 1 below as shown in Figs. 20.1, 20.3, and 20.4B.

Fig. 20.4A and 20.4B demonstrate the action of piston 16 before and during operation of the above-described feeding sequence. In Fig. 20.4A, rotation controller 22 has rotated wheel 24 over plate 25, such that a compartment 26 has come to rest above and directly aligned over hole 27 and trap door 28. Food element 36 has fallen through hole 27 onto trap door 28.

Piston 16 is withdrawn above compartment 26 and rests within channel 12. In one embodiment, the bottom flattened portion of piston 16 rests against the bottom opening of aperture 12 so as to seal aperture 12 and thermally insulate the compartments 26 from the exterior atmosphere. In one embodiment, all of piston 16 or the flattened head portion thereof may be fashioned from a thermally insulating material. As shown in Fig. 20.4A, trap door 28 is in the closed or horizontal position. Trap door 28, in this position, prevents food element 36 from falling into bottom aperture 34. The spring-loaded hinge of trap door 28 is sufficiently resistive so as to support the weight of food element 36.

As shown in Fig. 20.4B, piston 16 has been actuated by piston controller 14 in a downward motion. Piston 16 has moved downward through top aperture 12, through the space defined

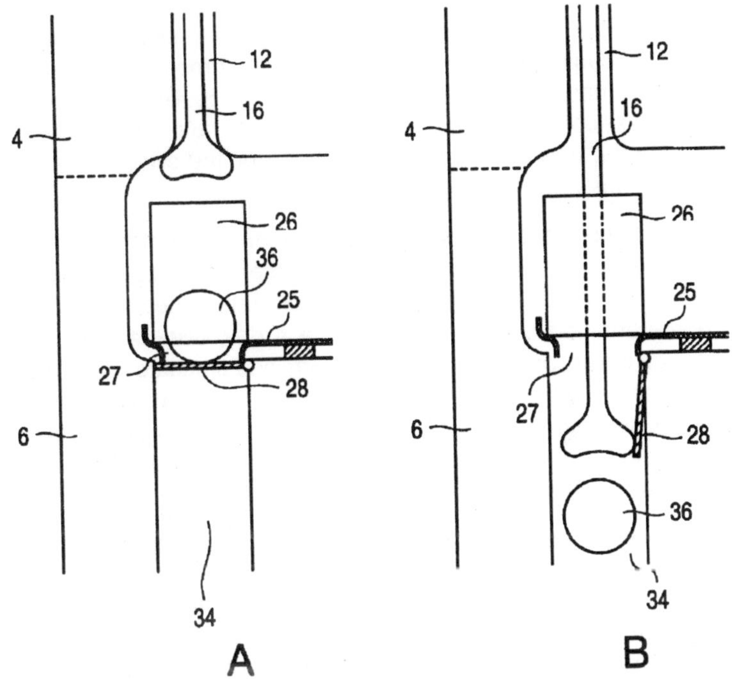

Fig. 20.4A and 4B show piston and compartment sub-assemblies during and before operation in accordance with an embodiment of the method.

by compartment 26, and further downward so as to force trap door 28 to open. The spring-loaded hinge of trap door 28 should not be so resistive as to prevent piston 16 from opening door 28. The downward action of piston 16 thus allows food element 36 to fall or be introduced into aperture 34 and thence into the aquarium 1.

To prepare for the next feeding cycle, piston controller 14 will actuate piston 16 and raise piston 16 upward and out of the position shown in Fig. 20.4B. Piston controller 14 will move piston 16 in an upward direction so as to withdraw the piston entirely from the space defined by compartment 26 and back to its starting or rest position as shown in Fig. 20.4A. Once piston 16 is removed, trap door 28 will return to its closed position due to its spring-loaded hinge. After piston 16 has withdrawn from the space defined by compartment 26, rotation controller 22 (shown in Fig. 20.3) will cause the wheel of compartments 24 to rotate a sufficient amount to cause the next neighboring compartment 26 to present itself underneath piston 16 as shown in Fig. 20.4A. The food 36 in this next compartment 26 will fall through hole 27 in plate 25 and onto the now closed trap door 28. Thus, the cycle will repeat itself for the next feeding.

Piston controller 14 may comprise an electric motor controlled by control circuitry, including a clock or timer, which causes piston 16 to move upward and downward at predetermined times or on a predetermined schedule (e.g., once a day, twice a day, once every six hours, or some other predetermined time interval). Piston controller 14 may be user programmable and reprogrammable to allow variation in the rate of feeding. Care should be taken to coordinate the schedule of the movement of piston 16 with the rotation of the wheel of compartments 24.

In one embodiment, piston controller 14 and rotation controller 22 are separate elements as shown in Fig. 20.3. In another embodiment, a master controller may be used to simultaneously control the actuations of piston controller 14 and rotation controller 22. In the embodiment where piston controller 14 and rotation controller 22 are separate elements, piston controller 14 and rotation controller 22 are programmed or mechanically configured so as to operate in synchronicity such that piston 16 withdraws from the space defined by compartment 26 before rotation controller 22 causes the wheel of compartments 24 to rotate. Appropriate configuration for piston controller 14 and rotation controller 22 should ensure that piston 16 does not interfere with the rotation of the compartments 26.

As shown in Fig. 20.4A, when piston controller 14 causes piston 16 to withdraw upward out of compartment 26, the trap door 28 will return to its closed and horizontal position due to the reflexive properties of the spring loaded hinge of trap door 28. Alternatively, trap door 28 can comprise any suitable mechanical or electro-mechanical recoil mechanism sufficient to cause trap door 28 to return to a closed and horizontal position after piston 16 has been withdrawn away from trap door 28 and upward towards top channel 12.

Fig. 20.3 shows piston controller 14 mounted on the top surface 8 of upper portion 4 of the thermally insulating housing of food dispensing system 2. In this embodiment, the placement of piston controller 14 on the exterior of food dispenser system 2 prevents heat generated by piston controller 14 to affect the interior temperature of food dispenser unit 2. Alternatively, piston controller 14 may be mounted on the exterior side of the thermally insulating housing portion 4 or may be mounted within the interior of thermally insulating housing 4.

As discussed above, power supply 3 is connected appropriately to piston controller 14 and rotation controller 22.

In the alternative embodiment in which each compartment 26 has its own unique trap door 28 and in which there is no bottom plate 25, food element 36 is dispensed into bottom aperture 34 in a similar fashion. Rotation controller rotates the wheel of compartments 24 so that one compartment 26 comes to rest directly under piston 16 and directly above bottom aperture 34. Piston controller 14 actuates piston 16, so that piston 16 moves downwards. Piston 16 moves downward into the space defined by compartment 26 and further downward so as to force trap door 28 to open. The downward action of piston 16 thus allows food element 36 to fall or be introduced into aperture 34 and thence into the aquarium 1.

Piston 16 will be retracted by controller 14, allowing trap door 28 to close. After piston 16 is retracted, rotation controller 22 causes wheel 24 to rotate a sufficient amount to cause the next compartment 26 to come to rest directly below piston 16 and directly above conduit 34. Thus, the cycle may repeat itself for the next feeding.

Fig. 20.3 shows cooling elements 18 and 20 mounted above the collection of food compartments 24. Cooling elements 18 and 20 may comprise one or more cooling elements depending on the size of the food dispenser unit 2 and the consequent amount of cooling required. Although shown stacked one atop the other in Fig. 20.3, cooling elements 18 and 20 may be aligned side by side or in any other configuration appropriate to maintain the interior of dispenser 2 at a low enough temperature so that food element 36 will not thaw.

In one embodiment, cooling elements 18 and 20 are thermo-electric coolers or thermo-electric modules or refrigerators. In one novel aspect of the present invention, thermo-electric coolers are used in conjunction with other elements of the food dispensing unit 2 to allow frozen food 36 to be stored and maintained within the compartments 26 of dispenser 2 without thawing.

A thermo-electric cooler is a semiconductor device which makes use of the Peltier effect to move heat in a particular direction when current is supplied to the thermo-electric cooler. A thermo-electric cooler acts as a heat pump and moves heat away from a source and towards an opposite direction. A thermo-electric module takes advantage of the different electrically properties of different semiconducting materials to achieve this heat pumping effect. One advantage of using a thermo-electric cooler or thermo-electric module is that it is relatively small and is a solid state device. Thermo-electric coolers provide a cooling or refrigerating capability without the need for refrigerants, such as freon, or compressors. When power is applied to a thermo-electric module, heat moves in the direction of the current such that the heat is pumped from one side of the module to the opposite side. As shown in Fig. 20.3, thermo-electric coolers 18 and 20 are arranged so that when power is applied to elements 18 and 20 heat will move or be pumped from the bottom of modules 18 and 20 toward the top of dispenser unit 2 in the direction of heat sink 10.

In one embodiment, one or more thermo-electric modules 18 and 20 are mounted within a channel or tube formed in the upper portion of insulating housing 4 of food dispenser 2. Thermo-electric modules 18 and 20 may be arranged side-by-side or in any appropriate configuration. The thermo-electric coolers 18 and 20 draw heat away from the center interior portion of the food dispenser unit 2, including especially compartments 26 and food 36, toward the top of the unit. A hole in top surface 8 of upper insulating portion 4 allows the heat from thermo-electric modules 18 and 20 to be pumped to the exterior atmosphere.

In the embodiment shown in Fig. 20.3, two thermo-electric coolers 18 and 20 are stacked one on top of the other in a vertical tube or channel formed within the upper portion of insulating housing 4. The thermo-electric coolers 18 and 20 are connected through a hole in top surface 8 to heat sink 10. Heat sink 10 is also attached to the top exterior surface 8 of insulating housing 4. When power is applied, thermo-electric coolers 18 and 20 are adapted to transfer heat from the interior chamber of dispenser 2 to heat sink 10, such that heat sink 10 will in turn dissipate heat into the exterior atmosphere. Thus, frozen food elements 36 stored in each compartment 26 in the center of food dispenser unit 2 will remain unthawed due to the cooling effect provided by thermo-electric coolers 18 and 20. Insulating housing portions 4 and 6 also serve to maintain the necessary low temperature by thermally insulating the interior of the dispenser 2 from the external atmosphere. As discussed above, trap door 28 and piston 16 may also be formed of, or be lined with, thermally insulating material to assist in thermally insulating the interior of dispenser system 2. The cooling effect provided by thermo-electric coolers 18 and 20, in conjunction with the thermal insulation of the various parts of system 2, result in food elements 36 not thawing while waiting to be dispensed.

In one embodiment, heat sink 10 is fashioned of aluminum. Alternatively, heat sink 10 may include an electric fan which will further act to dissipate heat drawn away from the center of food dispenser unit 2 by thermo-electric coolers 18 and 20.

Thermo-electric coolers 18 and 20 are appropriately configured to receive power from power supply 3. Heat sink 10, if it uses an electric fan, is also appropriately configured to receive power from power supply 3.

Cooling elements 18 and 20 may alternatively comprise conventional cooling elements, such as a pipe system with a refrigerant, such as freon, connected to an external compressor mounted outside the exterior surface of food dispenser unit 2.

Many elements and subassemblies described above could be chosen or arranged differently while still embodying the present method. While those of ordinary skill will appreciate interchangeable substitutions for the elements discussed above, examples of alternative embodiments include:

Different numbers of cooling elements 18 and 20; different numbers of compartments 26 making up collection 24; different geometrical arrangement of the collection of compartments 24, such as in a row or line on a movable conveyor belt (in which embodiment, rotation controller 22 would be substituted for a conveyor belt mover); other control circuitry to control the operation of either piston controller 14, rotation controller 22, or both; different geometrical shapes for each compartment 26; coating any or all the surfaces of compartments 26, plate 25, trap door 28, piston 16, or the walls of aperture 34 with a suitable coating or resin to prevent sticking to frozen food element 36; different thickness or dimensions for the thermally insulating housing; different material for heat sink 10; different gears or other hardware for controlling the movement of piston 16 or the action of rotation controller 22; different hardware for causing the collection of compartments 24 to rotate, for example, using a grooved channel molded within the interior surface of insulating housing 6 lined with ball bearings, or providing wheels attached to the bottom of the collection of compartments 24; different hardware; different hardware or systems for programming or configuring piston-controller 14 or rotation controller 22; different electric motors for piston controller 14 or rotation controller 22; and other predetermined schedules for the rotation of the wheel of compartments 24 and activation of piston 16.

21

Frozen Cat Food

Cats are well-loved, popular house pets. Many cat owners are devoted to their cats and concerned about their health and well-being. To this end, they desire to feed their feline pets healthy and nutritious food that provides a complete and balanced diet that is particularly adapted to the nutritional needs of a cat. Some cat owners are particularly concerned that they also feed their pets food that is natural, that is, free of added minerals and supplements, chemical enhancers and preservatives, nutritionally useless fillers, etc. Many commercially available brands and types of cat food claim to be "all natural," or to provide a "complete and balanced" diet for a cat, but nevertheless still contain ingredients that are foreign to the natural diet of a cat or are useless fillers, such as corn meal or other carbohydrates which a cat is incapable or only minimally capable of digesting and extracting nutrients from.

The cat is an "obligate carnivore," that is, it must eat meat to sustain life or remain healthy. This fact makes it difficult, for several reasons, to maintain the health of a cat that is fed with food that contains only natural food ingredients, and does not include non-food supplements. First, the cat is unable to synthesize or produce numerous life-sustaining food chemicals, such as certain amino acids, minerals, and vitamins. It relies on an animal-based diet to obtain these chemicals from other animals, who produce or synthesize them in a form the cat can digest.

The basic nutritional needs of a cat are: protein from an animal food product; taurine, an essential amino acid; certain vitamins, minerals, enzymes and fatty acids; and water. The most difficult ingredient to provide in natural cat food in the recommended amount for a cat is the taurine. Taurine is especially important for cats in the prevention of blindness and heart disease. This amino acid is abundantly present in insects, present at much lower levels in land animals, and generally absent or present in trace amounts only in bacteria and plants. For example, the taurine content in plant foods is measured generally in the nmol range, that is, billionths of a mole, and measured generally in the micro-mole range, that is, millionths of a mole, in animal foods. Studies have shown that taurine also deteriorates when exposed to heat. Table 21.1 lists a number of food products and shows their taurine levels raw, baked, and boiled food. The greatest amount of taurine is available in raw food products, a lesser amount available in baked food products, and the least amount available in boiled food products.

Taurine is, however, abundantly present in seafood, particularly in shellfish, and most particularly in mollusks (clams, snails, octopus, squid, inkfish, scallops, etc.). For example, oysters provide 698 and claims 2400 mg of taurine per kg net weight of the respective food product. Shrimp, on the other hand, has levels of taurine that are comparable with land-animal food products. Table 21.2 lists a wide range of animal food products and their corresponding taurine levels. The levels are given for raw food product, and again, the levels of taurine drop significantly when the food product is baked or boiled.

The second reason that it is difficult to maintain the health of a cat fed with food that contains only natural food ingredients, is that the cat has difficulty digesting carbohydrates. The feline liver has normal hexokinase activity, but no glucokinase activity. In other words, it is incapable of converting the sugars in grains into glucose or other forms that it can then convert to energy. Being a carnivore, it has a tremendous ability to produce glucose from protein, but has only limited ability to convert glucose from grain into glycogen. As a result, the glucose it ingests is stored

Table 21.1

Item	Taurine content of selected foods (mg/kg, wet weight)*					
	Raw Mean	Raw Range	Baked Mean	Baked Range	Boiled Mean	Boiled Range
Beef Muscle	362	150-472	133	96-125	60	58-63
Beef Liver	192	144-270	141	68-184	73	36-95
Beef Kidney	225	180-247	138	130-144	76	68-88
Lamb Muscle	473	446-510	257	220-284	126	91-184
Lamb Kidney	239	128-440	154	81-290	51	47-55
Pork Muscle	496	394-690	219	126-390	118	91-184
Pork Liver	169	110-228	85	70-100	43	30-54
Chicken Muscle	337	300-380	229	140-310	82	71-180
Cod Fish	314	233-396	294	260-328	161	125-198
Oysters	698	390-1238	264	217-308	89	59-122
Clams	2400	1450-3700	1017	587-1700	446	264-794

as fat. In addition, unlike with humans, protein is the stimulus for insulin release in the cat, which has developed insulin resistance as it adapted to a high protein diet. This resistance maintains blood glucose levels during periods of fasting, which is convenient for a cat in the wild, but it is not healthy for a cat that eats a diet rich in carbohydrates.

The American Association of Feed Control Officials (AAFCO) is an organization that defines terms for labeling pet food products, e.g., "meat by-products." It also defines quantity determination for

Table 21.2

Food	Taurine content (in mg/kg)
Conch (Strombus gigas)	8500
Inkfish	6720
Blood Clam	6170
Shellfish	3320
Crab	2780
Prawn	1430
Sole	2560
Crucial carp	2050
Silver carp	900
Hairtail fish	560
Yellowfish	880
Octopus	3900
Cat, entire body	2000
Eel	910
Pork meat	1180
Pork heart	2000
Pork kidney	1200
Pork liver	420
Chicken breast	260
Chicken leg	3780
Quail muscle	95-280*
Quail serum	0.50-0.9* (in mg/L)
Tuna canned	3320
Low-fat plain yogurt	7.8 (in mg/L)
Shrimp	1150
Cheetah serum	0.8-6.3
Cat serum	6-14

label titles, e.g., "Chicken Cat Food," "Chicken Dinner for Cats," "Chicken-flavored Cat Food," sets criteria for the usage of "complete and balanced" on pet food labels, and recommends percentage or minimum/maximum amounts of various ingredients in pet foods, depending on age and activity level of the cat. Many conventional pet foods, even pet foods recommended by veterinarians and those that are advertised as food that meets AAFCO standards and provides a complete and balanced diet, are high-carbohydrate foods that are unsuitable for the cat. Such AAFCO-quality foods, particularly dry cat foods, typically contain meat by-product or meat by-product meal, grains, such as ground whole grain corn or ground brown rice, brewers rice, animal fat, corn gluten meal, meat flavor, and then a long list of non-food additives that provide the needed amino acids, vitamins, minerals, enymes, as well as flavor and aroma enhancers. A typical AAFCO-quality wet cat food that is labeled as a chicken-hearts-and-liver-in-gravy food comprises poultry broth, chicken hearts, chicken livers, turkey, wheat gluten, meat by-product, chicken liver, corn starch, soy flour, soy protein concentrate, natural and artificial flavors, salt, and then a long list of non-food additives. Many commercial cat foods contain no meat at all, but are made up completely of grain products and non-food additives that provide vitamins, minerals, amino acids, and flavor.

Many cat owners believe that good natural food is the foundation for maintaining health, for themselves, as well as for their pets, and desire a cat food that provides all the necessary ingredients to maintain a healthy cat. Such cat owners desire a cat food that contains all natural food products, that is devoid of non-food additives. Furthermore, such cat owners desire a cat food that is produced according to hygienic food standards, from high-quality food products. It is know that in the pet food industry, the ingredients used are often discarded waste products unfit for human consumption. These waste products are often diseased or decaying animal parts. Many pet owners would like to know that the ingredients used in the pet food they buy are of a quality standard deemed adequate for human consumption and have been handled and prepared under standards of hygiene that are equivalent to the standards required in the handling and processing of food for human consumption.

What is needed, therefore, is a cat food that contains ingredients that satisfy all the nutritional needs of the cat, that does not contain artificial or unnatural additives, whether in the form of vitamin and/or mineral supplements, flavor enhancers, fillers, etc. What is further needed is such a cat food that is high in animal protein and low in carbohydrates. What is yet further needed is such a cat food that is prepared according to high standards of hygiene, from food that is of a quality for human consumption.

Fig. 21.1 lists all the ingredients and the guaranteed crude analysis for four recipes or embodiments of the raw frozen cat food according to the invention. The recipes include chicken with clam; tuna with conch; turkey with clam; and duck with clam. A study of the lists of ingredients reveals that clams, vegetables, oysters, rice bran, lecithin, wheat germ, apple, flax seed, dried autolyzed yeast, dried kelp, flax oil, wheat germ oil, and cold liver oil are common ingredients in all four recipes. Chicken heart or turkey heart is included in each recipe. The variable ingredients are the main ingredients chicken, tuna and conch, turkey, and duck and chicken. The ingredients are listed in descending order of content by weight. Thus, it can be seen that animal flesh, be it poultry, fish, or mollusk, is the main ingredient in each recipe. None of the recipes includes any non-food additive. All of the recipes provide adequate amounts of protein, fat, fiber, and taurine, with low amounts of ash. None of the foods included in the recipes is there simply to provide bulk or texture. Each food provides at least one required nutrient. Dried autolyzed yeast, for example, is used instead of other yeasts because it is much higher in thiamine than other yeasts. Apple, broccoli, and peas provide folic acid and soluble fiber. Mushrooms are a non-animal source of vitamin D and are used to boost the level of vitamin D provided by other ingredients.

Four recipes or embodiments mentioned above were tested by Pet Food & Ingredient Technology, Inc. of Topeka, Kans., an independent research institute. Figures 21.2 and 21.3 show the

Recipe Ingredients	*Guaranteed Crude Analysis*
Chicken with Clam **Ingredients**: chicken, clams, water, chicken liver, vegetables (may contain peas: broccoli; beets; carrot; spinach; mushroom), oysters, apple, rice bran, wheat germ, flax seed, lecithin, chicken heart, dried autolyzed yeast, dried kelp, flax oil, wheat germ oil, cod liver oil	Protein 14.5% Min Fat 11.0% min Fiber 1.7% max Moisture 71.0% max Ash 2.4% max Taurine 0.11% min
Tuna with conch recipe **Ingredients**: tuna, conch, clams, water, chicken liver, vegetables (may contain peas; broccoli; beets; carrot; spinach; mushroom; asparagus), oysters, apple, rice bran, wheat germ, flax seed, lecithin, chicken heart, dried autolyzed yeast, dried kelp, flax oil, wheat germ oil, cod liver oil	Protein 19.0% Min Fat 7.0% min Fiber 1.4% max Moisture 73.5% max Ash 2.2% max Taurine 0.10% min
Turkey with Clam Recipe **Ingredients**: turkey, clams, water, turkey liver, vegetables (may contain peas; broccoli; sweet potato; carrot; spinach; mushroom) oysters, apple, rice bran, wheat germ, flax seed, oysters, lecithin, dried autolyzed yeast, dried kelp, flax oil, wheat germ oil, cod liver oil	Protein 15.0% Min Fat 9.0% min Fiber 1.4% max Moisture 71.0% max Ash 2.7% max Taurine 0.11% min
Duck with Clam recipe **Ingredients**: duck, clams, chicken, water chicken liver, vegetables (may contain peas; broccoli sweet potato, carrot, spinach, mushroom), duck liver, oysters, apple, rice bran, wheat germ, flax seed, lecithin, chicken heart, dried autolyzed yeast, dried kelp, flax oil, wheat germ oil, cod liver oil	Protein 12.9% Min Fat 11.0% min Fiber 1.4% max Moisture 71.0% max Ash 2.7% max Taurine 0.11% min

Fig. 21.1 is a table showing the various recipes of cat food according to the method and the corresponding guaranteed crude analysis.

	Raw Turkey Cat Food		
Product Composition:	Dry Matter	30.88	
	Moisture	69.12	
	Crude Protein, %	16.51	As is
	AH Fat, %	9.44	As is
	Ash, %	2.61	As is
	Crude Fiber, %	0.9	As is
	NFE, %	1.42	As is
	ME, kcal/kg	1429.95	As is
	ME, kcal/kg	4630.6670	DM adjusted

Fig. 21.2 Product composition of raw turkey cat food according to the method

product composition of two of the four recipes, as an illustration of various compositions of the raw frozen cat food according to the invention. In the raw turkey recipe, the water content is 69.12% and the dry matter 30.88%. The 30.88% of dry matter comprises 16.51% crude protein, 9.44% fat (acid hydrolyzed fat), 2.61% ash, 0.9% crude fiber, and 1.42% nitrogen-free extract (NFE, i.e., starch). The metabolizable energy (ME) in the product as fed, that is, as "wet" food, is 1429.95 kcal/kg, or 4630.67 kcal/kg of dry matter. In the raw chicken recipe, the water content is 71.42%,

	Raw Chicken Cat food		
Product Composition:	Dry Matter	28.58	
	Moisture	71.42	
	Crude Protein, %	15.21	As is
	AH Fat, %	8.45	As is
	Ash, %	2.02	As is
	Crude Fiber, %	2.3	As is
	NFE, %	0.6	As is
	ME, kcal/kg	1271.6	As is
	ME, kcal/kg	4449.2652	DM adjusted

Fig. 21.3 Product composition of raw chicken cat food according to the method

Nutrient	Units In DM	Growth & Repro. Minimum	Maintenance Minimum	Chicken Dry	Duck Dry	Tuna Dry	Turkey Dry
Protein	%	30	26	49.29	42.8	79	53.3
Arginine	%	1.25	1.04	3.146	3.04	5	3.81
Histidine	%	0.31	0.31	1.395	1.01	3.49	1.39
Isoleucine	%	0.52	0.52	2.043	1.75	3.19	2.17
Leucine	%	1.25	1.25	3.633	3.16	5.45	3.81
Lysine	%	1.2	0.83	3.406	3.13	6.08	3.97
Methionine-cystine	%	1.1	1.1	1.557	1.39	2.58	1.68
Methionine	%	0.62	0.62	1.07	0.94	1.97	1.2
Phenylalanine-tyrosine	%	0.88	0.88	3.276	1.33	2.45	1.62
Phenylalanine	%	0.42	0.42	1.88	1.75	3.04	2.17
Threonine	%	0.73	0.73	1.88	1.88	3.45	2.29
Tryptophan	%	0.25	0.16	0.422	0.44	0.82	0.55
Valine	%	0.62	0.62	2.335	1.91	3.71	2.36
Taurine (canned)	%	0.2	0.2	0.35	0.38	0.37	0.39
Fat	%	9	9	29.85	42.3	28	30.5
Linoleic acid	%	0.5	0.5	7.817	9.53	1.78	11.58
Arachidonic acid	%	0.02	0.02	0.13	0.35	0.23	0.26

Minerals							
Calcium	%	1	0.6	1.36	2.96	1.49	1.97
Phosphorus	%	0.8	0.5	1.297	2.16	1.37%	1.46%
Potassium	%	0.6	0.6	0.94	2.26	1	0.81%
Sodium	%	0.2	0.2	0.276	0.26	0.22	0.26
Chloride	%	0.3	0.3	0.42	0.42	0.67	0.46
Magnesium	%	0.08	0.04	0.12	0.12	0.14	0.12
Iron	mg/kg	80	80	89.68	92.58	88.52	83.87
Copper	mg/kg	5	5	6.76	7.31	5.5	5.4
Manganese	mg/kg	7.5	7.5	9.04	21.91	9.63	8.39
Zinc	mg/kg	75	75	116.4	131.3	113.71	134.5
Iodine	mg/kg	0.35	0.35	4	3.88	6.26	3.21
Selenium	mg/kg	0.1	0.1	1.622	0.51	2.45	0.97
Vitamins							
Vitamin A	IU/kg	9,000.00*	5,000.00	58449	53367	73248	51632
Vitamin D	IU/kg	750	500	1325	1253	3285	1251
Vitamin Ef	IU/kg	30	30	125	132	143	107.40
Vitakin Kg	mg/kg	0.1	0.1	0.65	0.65	.74	0.65
Vitamin B1 (thiamin)	mg/kg	5	5	6.23	6.33	8.63	6.39
Vitamin B2 (riboflavin)	mg/kg	4	4	8.11	9.22	7.56	7.97

Nutrient	Units In DM	Growth & Repro. Minimum	Maintenance Minimum	Chicken Dry	Duck Dry	Tuna Dry	Turkey Dry
Vitamin B5 (pantothenic acid)	mg/kg	5	5	56.44	34.61	61.5	24.3
Vitamin B3 (niacin)	mg/kg	60	60	185.534	112	340	156.8
Vitamin B6 (pyridoxine)	mg/kg	4	4	16.22	8.35	24.2	9.91
Folic Acid	mg/kg	0.8	0.8	1.81	1.39	1.36	1.08
Biotini	mg/kg	0.07	0.07	0.483	0.39	0.15	0.54
Vitamin B12 (cyanocobalamin)	mg/kg	0.02	0.02	0.065	0.42	0.29	0.16
Choline	g/kg	2.4	2.4	3.07	2.81	3.28	2.94

FIG. 21.4 is a nutrient list for the raw frozen chicken, duck, tuna and turkey cat food recipes according to the method, listing the major ingredients necessary to provide a healthy diet for cats in the growth and reproduction and maintenance life stages.

and the dry matter 28.58%. The dry matter comprises 15.21% crude protein, 8.45% fat, 2.02% ash, 2.3% crude fiber, and 0.6% NFE (starch). The ME in the product as fed is 1271.6 kcal/kg or 4449.27 kcal/kg of dry matter. The results show that the raw frozen cat food products are high in protein and fat and extremely low in carbohydrates, a composition that closely resembles that of a natural cat diet. For example, natural prey for cats in the wild include mice and other small rodents. A mouse is [?? how much} % crude protein and 30% fat.

Figure 21.4 is a nutrient list showing the proteins, fats, minerals, vitamins that a cat requires, and the amount (percentage or units/kg) of the nutrient found in the whole food with the water removed, that is, in the dry matter for the four recipes of the raw frozen cat food products: chicken, duck, tuna, and turkey. The columns "growth & reproduction" and "maintenance" list the AAFCO recommended daily amounts of the nutrient in dry matter for the particular life stage of the animal. The test results for the recipes are given in the columns chicken dry, duck dry, tuna dry, and turkey dry.

A careful review of the table shows that the amounts of certain nutrients in the columns chicken dry, duck dry, tuna dry, and turkey dry far exceed the recommended AAFCO amounts. AAFCO recommends a minimum of 30% protein for the growth and reproduction stage and 26% protein for the maintenance stage of a cat. These are minumum requirements. The cat is a carnivore, and, in the wild, would naturally be ingesting a much greater portion of protein food than the AAFCO recommended amounts. The recipes of the raw frozen cat food according to the invention provide protein as follows: >49% in the chicken recipe, >42% in the duck recipe, 79% in the tuna recipe, and >53% in the turkey recipe. Listed below the entry "protein" are the amino acids necessary to maintain a healthy diet for a cat. Again, a comparison of the AAFCO recommended amounts and the amounts provided in the four recipes according to the invention show that the raw frozen cat food provides amounts significantly greater than the minimum recommended amounts. The amount of taurine provided in the recipes is noted specifically here, because it is so difficult to provide sufficient amounts of taurine without adding it as a non-food supplement. The AAFCO recommended minimum daily amount for taurine in canned food is 0.2% in dry matter. The comparison is made here with canned food, because it comes closest to the raw frozen cat food according to the invention, which naturally contains 0.35% or more of taurine. By "naturally" is meant that the taurine is contained naturally in the food ingredients in the recipe. The raw frozen cat food provides at least the minimum daily amounts of all of the amino acids, fats, minerals, vitamins required to provide a healthy diet for a cat, and does so without using non-foode additives.

22

Hard Frozen Food Containing Alcohol

Alcoholic frozen drinks are soft ice or slushy beverages. Such drinks are typically prepared by blending alcohol, ice, and a drink mix in a blender. The result is a thick cold drink with small pieces of ice. It became known to sell such drinks in a ready made form that did not need to have the ice or alcohol blended in. Such drinks only needed to placed in the freezer for a certain period of time before being consumed.

The frozen desert is said to be portable and supportable on a stick, however such gelatin is soft and easily falls from the stick. It has now become known to include alcohol into a frozen gelatin type food. For example, Electric Jello™ is a product that comprises vodka (or another alcohol) mixed with a prepared gelatin before being frozen. These alcoholic gelatin products are made by adding alcohol after the gelatin has been heated, but before refrigerating. Still, alcoholic gelatin deserts do not freeze to a sufficient hardness to be held securely on a stick.

Research Findings teaches a frozen beer or wine stick that freezes to a "solid bar". Because beer and wine generally comprise less alcohol content than other harder liquors, they may freeze to a relatively harder state, however, bars produced essentially from beer or wine are still relatively soft and do not have the same flaky consistency as pops without alcohol.

Thus, there is a need for a hard frozen food containing a relatively high alcohol content.

The present method is directed to a frozen beverage having a combination of a drug and a gelling agent. The combination is maintained at a temperature of 120°F. for at least one minute. In a preferred embodiment, the frozen beverage is hard frozen in the form of a pop and contains ethyl alcohol as the drug and pectin as the gelling agent.

In another aspect, the present method includes methods of producing a frozen food by first cooking a gelling agent and a drug together, then mixing a flavor into the cooked combination. The combination can be dispensed into a freezer pop container and shipped and shelved in an unfrozen state.

Referring first to Fig. 22.1 , a prior art food is prepared by first heating 130 a water 110 and gelatin 120 mixture. This is

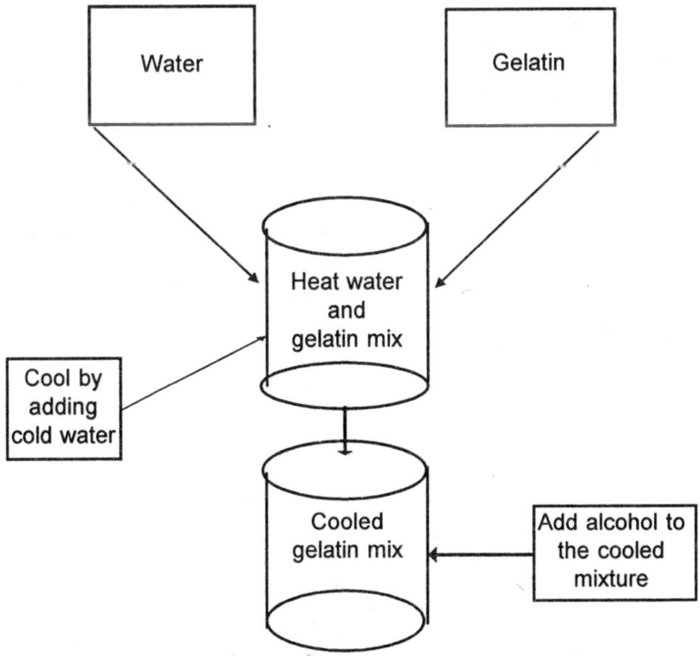

Fig. 22.1: Schematic showing steps in the production of a prior art food.

typically accomplished by boiling the water then adding the gelatin mixture, which may be flavored. It is important to recognize that addition of alcohol to the mixture only occurs after the mixture has been cooled by adding cold water 140. The mixture may be cooled by other means, however so long as the alcohol 150 is added when the mixture is in a relatively cool state 160.

The inventive subject matter exemplified by Fig. 22.2 depicts ingredients and steps in the production of a frozen pop. In a first

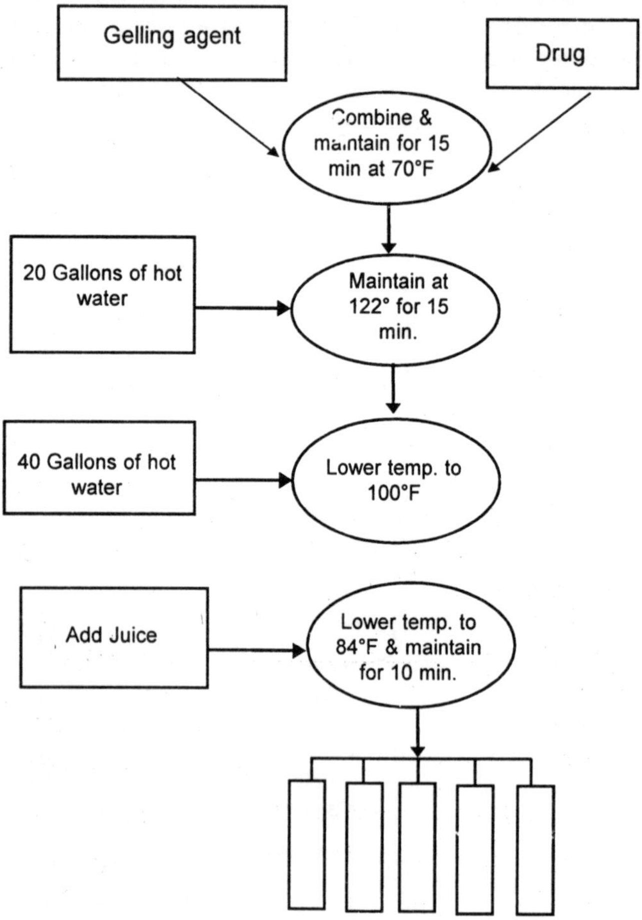

Fig. 22.2 Schematic for production of a frozen pop.

step, a gelling agent 220 is combined with a drug 210. A gelling agent is a compound that causes firmness or gelling. Gelling agents include pectin (a polysaccharide found in nearly all plant tissue), cellulose, carrageenan and gelatin. A drug is any molecule or composition of molecules that alters structure, metabolism, cell cycle and/or function of a diseased or otherwise negatively impacted cell or organ. For example, contemplated drugs include anti-neoplastic drugs (e.g 5-FU, taxol, etc.), anti-metabolites (e.g., trimethoprim, sulfonamides, etc.), antibiotics (e.g., beta-lactam antibiotics, tetracycline antibiotics, etc.), and anti-viral agents (e.g., ribavirin, T-20, etc.), immunomodulatory agents (e.g., steroids, cytokines, etc.), pro-, and anti-apoptotic agents, receptor blockers (e.g., beta blockers), enzyme inhibitors (e.g., statins), as well as ethanol (i.e. ethyl alcohol).

As depicted, the gelling agent and drug are combined and then maintained for 15 minutes at around 70°F. in step 230. Following this step, the drug/agent combination 250 is brought to a temperature of about 122°F. by adding 20 gallons of hot water 240. The drug/agent combination is maintained at about 122°F. for about 15 minutes in step 245. With regard to the temperature and the time in which the temperature is maintained, there is room for variance. For example, it is contemplated that the temperature can range from 105 to 150°F. and the time can range from 10 to 30 minutes. The time and temperature may be related in that a relatively high temperature may require relatively less time, and a relatively low temperature may require relatively more time—all within the ranges stated above.

"Maintaining" as defined herein means sustaining the heat (at about 122°F.) with the intent to sustain the heat. "Maintaining" is a purposeful act and does not include non-intentional maintenance within the range of required temperature. For example, if the substance were in a truck within which the temperature reached around 120°F. In an embodiment having an ethyl alcohol, the gelling agent bonds to the alcohol (OH) molecule during this stage 245. In such embodiments, it is preferred that a neutral (i.e. substantially clear and tasteless) alcohol be used such as that produced from grapes or from oranges.

Introduction of additional hot water 250 is used to lower the temperature of the combination to around 100°F. in step 260. Following this step, juice 270 is optionally added to provide flavor and to aid in consistency. A preferable juice contains real fruit (e.g. Dole™ Pineapple Juice) and may even contain pieces of real fruit. In any event, the addition of the juice brings the temperature of the mixture down to about 84°F. which is preferably maintained for about 10 minutes as shown in step 280.

For purposes of producing an alcoholic frozen beverage, it is advantageous to add flavoring (e.g. S&S Flavoring), to a neutral alcohol mixture in order to better replicate drinks produced with flavored alcohol and drink mixes. A neutral mixture can be frozen into units wherein each unit is sufficient for one drink. There are many benefits associated with using pre-frozen units including obtaining a more consistent flavor and texture, increasing the speed within which drinks can be made, and aiding in the auditing of the number of alcoholic beverages sold. For example, consumption of one frozen unit equals one drink sold.

The mixture is poured into molds 290 then frozen. The pops can be frozen to a hard state (e.g. a fruit pop or ice cube) or to some softer state such as a slush. Additionally, the mixture can be frozen in various containers or molds of various shapes and sizes. For example, it may be advantageous to freeze a mixture in a paper cup and eat it with a spoon rather than from a pop. Another embodiment may include freezing the mixture in the form of an ice cube and using the ice cube in a drink. Such frozen beverages can also be decorative having various colors and even brands or trademarks frozen into them. It is further contemplated that objects (edible and non-edible) can be frozen into a frozen beverage. Consider a frozen ice cube with an advertisement such as an ice cube having a Jack Daniels™ logo. It is preferred that an alcoholic mixture be placed into liquid brine and cooled to a temperature lower than –20° F.

The result of a mixture according to the steps outlined above is a frozen beverage generally having crystal flakes throughout and a relatively slow melting time compared to other frozen beverages.

The alcohol or other drug content of the product can vary widely from 1% or less, to 5, 10, or even 20% or more.

An item of manufacture may have been produced by performing the above steps with the exception of freezing the mixture. Thus, such items can be shipped and sold in an unfrozen state. By allowing such items to be shipped and sold unfrozen, many of the special handling and storage requirements are obviated. A consumer may either freeze the mixture at home or a vendor of the frozen beverage may freeze it before the consumer buys it. Moreover, where a pharmaceutical drug is concerned, the frozen beverage may be dispensed only by a pharmacist or doctor and it would be more convenient if such items did not require that they be frozen when dispensed. In any event, a frozen beverage is intended to be frozen before being consumed.

In another example, 25 gallons of 48 proof (24%) rum is mixed with 3 quarts of gelling agent (1 quart each of three different agents). The mixture of the rum and gelling agents sits for 5 to 15 minutes at approximately 70°F. Next, 20 gallons of hot water (at approximately 135°F.) is added to the mixture bringing the temperature to about 122°F. for 5 to 15 minutes. In the next step, the temperature of the mixture is brought down to about 100°F. by adding approximately 40 gallons of water. 75 gallons of pineapple juice is added to the mixture which then sits for approximately 10 minutes at around 96°F. At this point, rather than pass the mixture through a cooler system, the mixture was poured into molds at a temperature of about 88°F. The molds were placed into a freezer and frozen to a temperature of –20°F. Additionally, it may become necessary to add a defoamer to reduce the amount of foam caused by freezer impeller blades.

A further example begins with mixing 25 gallons of 80 proof Jose Cuervo™ tequila with three gelling agents. The mixture is maintained at around 70°F. for 15 minutes or more. Next, 20 gallons of hot water (135°F.) is added to the mixture and the mixture is maintained at around 122°F. for at least 15 minutes. 40 gallons of cooler water is added bringing the mixture temperature down to 100°F. before adding 75 gallons of strawberry margarita mix. The mixture is left to sit for around 10 minutes at 84°F. Following this step, the 80 degree F. mixture is poured into molds and frozen to –20°F.

During the process, the gelling agent is bonded to the drug and then the other ingredients (water, sugar, acid, flavoring, juice etc.) bond to the gelling agent. Even in a hard frozen alcoholic beverage, the alcohol does not actually freeze, but is encapsulated in the lattice formed by the other ingredients. Similar to candy with a liquid center, the hard shell protects the drug from escaping.

23

High Protein Frozen Food Product

It is known that high-protein diets can be beneficial for weight loss. In addition, high-protein, low carbohydrate diets have been recommended by some doctors for diabetes patients. One of the most difficult problems in maintaining a high-protein, low carbohydrate, low fat diet is the fact that most dessert or snack products which satisfy a craving for a sweet food contain large amounts of carbohydrates and fats and are low in protein content.

In addition to the high-carbohydrate, low-protein nature of many sweet foods, the organoleptic properties such as taste, and mouth-feel, of low-fat, low-sugar products are not satisfactory. The present invention relates to a high-protein, low-fat frozen food product having good organoleptic properties such as taste, mouth-feel and appearance and if required low available carbohydrate content. In particular, high protein frozen products tend to have a grainy mouth-feel which detracts from their acceptability as a frozen food in spite of their potential health benefits.

According to the present method , a high-protein, low-fat frozen food product is provided which can be made in a low available carbohydrate form. The frozen food product comprises:

(a) about 10% to about 25% by weight water soluble protein;

(b) about 0.2% to about 15% by weight natural and/or artificial flavors;

(c) about 6% to about 14% by weight of a bulking and/or sweetening agent;

(d) about 0.1% to about 2.0% by weight microcrystalline cellulose;

(e) about 0.1% to about 2.0% by weight pectin;

(f) water; and optionally:

(g) up to about 2.0% by weight stabilizer; and

(h) up to about 0.25% by weight acidulant.

A frozen food with a higher available carbohydrate concentration can be made by substituting a carbohydrate sweetening agent such as dextrose, fructose, high dextrose corn syrup, honey, concentrated fruit juices and the like for a part or all of the synthetic sweetener and bulking agent. The amount of carbohydrate sweeteners can be varied in conjunction with the synthetic sweeteners to provide a product with a protein available carbohydrate ratio within broad limits. The minimum amount of available carbohydrate in the product is determined by the amount of available carbohydrate in the natural flavors which can be used to manufacture the product. The products with the highest protein/available carbohydrate ratio are products which contain synthetic sweeteners and synthetic flavoring agents.

The frozen product has an excellent smooth, creamy mouth-feel, small ice crystal size and excellent flavor.

The high protein frozen product is produced using water soluble protein with a protein efficiency of at least 2.5. The water soluble protein provides a frozen product with a smooth mouthfeel rather than a grainy mouth-feel of insoluble protein. Although a frozen product with excellent mouth-feel requires use of soluble protein, a portion or all of the water soluble protein can be substituted with insoluble protein if mouth-feel is not critical and a grainy product can be tolerated. However, sole use of water soluble protein is preferred. Water soluble proteins such as POWER PRO® WPC, a water soluble high quality protein product of Land O'Lakes Corporation are useful in the practice of the invention. At least about 95-98% of the protein must be water soluble protein and it is preferred that all the protein be water soluble.

The water soluble protein must be soluble in the composition to the extent required, and not precipitate and be denatured under the acid conditions of the composition.

The amount of protein in the composition can range from about 10% by weight to about 25% by weight, preferably from about 11% by weight to about 21% by weight of the composition, more preferably from about 12% by weight to about 20% by weight, and most preferably from about 14% by weight to about 18% by weight.

The flavors used in the composition can be natural, artificial or mixtures thereof. Generally to achieve an intense, uniform flavor from batch to batch of the frozen product, a mixture of natural and artificial flavors is utilized. It is preferred that a mixture of natural and artificial flavors be utilized.

The natural flavors generally comprise macerated or pureed fruits and/or nuts; however, macerated or pureed vegetables can also be utilized. Fruits such as peaches, bananas, berries such as strawberries, blueberries, raspberries, plums, kiwi fruit (seeds removed), pears, pineapple, apples, coconut, oranges, lemons; nuts such as walnuts, hazelnuts, peanuts, cashews and the like are useful. Pureed vegetables such as carrots, celery, and tomatoes can be used to provide flavors generally not available in frozen products but which can provide an alternative to the sweet frozen products available.

The flavours imparted to the frozen product by natural flavoring materials are generally intensified or enhanced by addition of artificial flavoring agents and/or flavor enhancers. The artificial flavoring agents and flavor enhancers are added to the composition to provide a more intense and uniform flavor from batch to batch of the frozen product. The artificial flavors and flavor enhancers are well known to one skilled in the food formulation art and are dependent on the particular flavor desired. Examples of the myriad of natural and artificial flavors and flavor enhancers are shown in the examples and can be selected from: (A) flavor oils such as spearmint, cinnamon, oil of wintergreen (methyl salicylate), peppermint (menthol), clove, bay, anise, eucalyptus, thyme, cedar leaf, oil of nutmeg, allspice, oil of sage, mace, oil of bitter almonds, and cassia oil; (B) artificial, natural and synthetic fruit flavors such as vanilla, and citrus oils including lemon, orange, lime, grapefruit, and fruit essences including apple, pear, peach, grape, strawberry, raspberry, cherry, plum, pineapple, apricot and so forth; (C) aldehydes and esters such as acetaldehyde, benzaldehyde, anisic aldehyde, cinnamic aldehyde, citral, neral, decanal, ethyl vanillin, heliotrope, piperonal, vanillin, alpha-amyl cinnamaldehyde, butyraldehyde, valeraldehyde, citronellal, decanal, dihydrocarvyl acetate, eugenyl formate, aldehyde C-8, aldehyde C-9, aldehyde C-12, 2-ethyl butyraldehyde, hexenal, tolyl aldehyde, veratraldehyde, 2,6-dimethyl-5-heptenal, 2,6-dimethyloctanal, 2-dodecenal, p-methylanisol, and so forth.

The frozen food product contains a combination of bulking agents and sweeteners. The bulking agents can be non-nutritive or nutritive and are required to provide improved mouth-feel. In low available carbohydrate products, the non-nutritive bulking agents take the place of sugar. If it is required that the product contain sugar, all or a portion of the non-nutritive bulking agent can be replaced by sugar sweeteners.

Non-nutritive bulking agents include compositions such as mallitol, sorbitol, hydrogenated corn syrup, inositol and the like. A bulking agent is required to improve mouth-feel of the frozen product or the flavor when the bulking agent comprises a sweetener such as dextrose, fructose or the like. Artificial sweeteners such as (A) water-soluble naturally-occurring intense sweeteners such as dihydrochalcones, monellin, steviosides, glycyrrhizin, dihydroflavenol, and L-aminodicarboxylic acid aminoalkanoic acid ester amides, and mixtures thereof; (B) water-soluble artificial sweeteners including the soluble saccharin salts such as sodium or calcium saccharin salts, cyclamate salts, the sodium, ammonium or calcium salts of 3,4-dihydro-6-methyl-1,2,3-oxathiazine-4-one-2,2-dioxide, the potassium salt of 3,4-dihydro-6-methyl-1,2,3-oxathiazine-4-one-2,2-dioxide (Acesulfam-K), the free acid form of saccharin, and the like, and mixtures thereof; (C) dipeptide based sweeteners including L-aspartic acid derived sweeteners, such as 1-aspartyl-L-phenylalanine methyl ester (Aspartame) and materials described in U.S. Pat. No. 3,492,131, L-alphaaspartyl-N-(2,2,4,4-tetramethyl-3-thietanyl)-D-alanin amide hydrate (Alitame), methyl esters of L-aspartyl-L-phenyl-glycerine and L-aspartyl-L-2,5-dihydrophenyl-glycine, L-aspartyl-2,5dihydro-L-phenylalanine, L-aspartyl-L-(1-cyclohexene)-alanine, and the like, and mixtures thereof; (D) water-soluble. intense sweeteners derived from naturally-occurring water-soluble sweeteners, such as chlorinated derivatives of ordinary sugar (sucrose), e.g., chlorodeoxysugar derivatives such as derivatives of chlorodeoxy-sucrose or chlorodeoxygalactosucrose, known, for example, under the product designation of Sucralose®; examples of chlorodeoxy-sucrose and chlorodeoxygalactosucrose derivatives include but are not limited to: 1-chloro-12 -deoxysucrose; 4-chloro-4-deoxy-alpha-D-galactopyranosyl-alpha-D-fructofura noside, or 4-chloro-4-deoxygalactosucrose; 4-chloro-4-deoxy-alpha-D-galactopy-ranosyl-1-chloro-1deoxy-be ta-D-fructo-furanoside, or 4,12-dichloro-4,12 dideoxygalactosucrose; 12,62-dichloro-12,62-dide-oxysucrose; 4-chloro-4-deoxy-alpha-D-galactopyranosyl-1,6-dichloro-1,6-d ideoxy-beta-D-fructofuranoside, or 4,12 ,62 -trichloro-4,12 ,62 -trideoxygalactosucrose; 4,6-dichloro-4,6-dideoxy-alpha-D-galactopyranosyl-6-chloro-6-deoxy-beta-D-fructo-furanoside, or 4,6,62 -trichloro-4,6,62 -trideoxygalactosucrose; 6,12 ,62 -trichloro-6,12,62-trideoxysucrose; 4,6-dichloro-4,6-dideoxy-alpha-D-galacto-pyranosyl-1,6-dichl oro-1,6-dideoxy-beta-D-fructofuranoside, or 4,6,12,62-tetrachloro-4,6,12 ,62-tetradeoxygalacto-su crose; and 4,6,12,62-tetradeoxy-sucrose, and mixtures thereof; and (E) protein based intense sweeteners such as thaumaoccous denielli (Thaumatin I and II).

Microcrystalline cellulose is used in the present method to provide a smooth to creamy mouth-feel to the frozen product. It provides the function as a fat replacement or substitute to provide improved mouth-feel. Microcrystalline cellulose comprises fine particulate material which absorbs water and forms a paste which is used as a fat substitute. A preferred microcrystalline cellulose is Blanver's Best™ Formula 4 cellulose gel sold by Opta Food Ingredients.

Pectin, preferably low methoxyl pectin 35, is required in the composition of the present method to bind calcium and protein to protect the protein from coagulation due to low pH. Since the fruit flavoring materials used in the present invention are acidic, the pectin prevents formation of insoluble protein particles which can destroy the smooth creamy mouth-feel of the product.

The composition of the method is water based and can contain up to about 80% by weight water, preferably from about 45 to about 65% by weight water, and most preferably from about 50 to about 60% by weight water. Preferably water makes up the remainder of the formulation after addition of the non-aqueous materials.

The frozen product optionally contains up to about 2% by weight of a stabilizer to provide stability and maintain the smooth creamy texture of the product if it is to pass through many cycles in temperature. Temperature cycling encourages the growth of ice crystals which can cause the texture to become grainy. Inclusion of the stabilizer in the product is preferred but is not critical to the composition unless temperature cycling is expected to occur. However, inclusion of stabilizers in the composition contributes to the smooth creamy mouth-feel of the composition. Useful stabilizers include gums, but are not limited to material such as cellulose gum, guar gum, locust bean gum, carrageenin and the like. Gum stabilizers are well known to food chemists and can be readily selected to provide and maintain the smooth creamy texture of the frozen product of the invention.

The frozen product can contain acidulants such as citric acid, malic acid, tartaric acid and the like. The acids can be partially neutralized and act as flavor ingredients. If low sodium frozen products are required, potassium salts of the acids can be used.

The frozen products can be prepared by mixing the ingredients other than the protein, fruits, flavors, colors and acidulants, pasteurizing the mixture, cooling the pasteurized mixture, then adding the protein, fruits, flavors, colors and acidulants. A mixture containing the protein can also be pasteurized if the temperature is controlled closely to prevent coagulation and denaturing of the protein. However, the fruits, flavors, colors and acidulants are preferably added after the pasteurization. After all the ingredients have been mixed, the mixture is cooled and frozen in a desired shape. A preferred shape is a bar or a cup containing from about 85 to about 120 grams of frozen product.

Method 1: Peach Flavor Frozen Product

A mixture having the following composition was prepared.

Ingredient	Parts by Weight
Water	6831
Maltitol	1009
Pectin	31.6
Microcrystalline Cellulose	35.1
Merecol CLG1	4.9
Aspartame	2.3
SUNETT [2]	2.3
POWER PRO[5] WPG LoL	2017.9
Water	228
Red #4 (1.5% by weight solution)	26.6
Yellow #5 (5% by weight solution)	26.6

The above ingredients were dissolved in the water. The mixture was batch pasteurized under strictly controlled conditions (not to exceed 157° F.) for 30 to 45 minutes holding time at temperature. The pasteurized mixture was cooled and mixed with the remaining flavoring materials and thoroughly blended. The acidulant solution was slowly added with strong agitation to avoid contact of the protein with the strong acid solution to prevent protein coagulation.

Peach Puree	922.9
Vanilla Cookie Dough 660244[3]	32.3
Vanilla 680246[3]	9.23
Peach Flavor 533585	46.2
Citric Acid[4]	6.92
Potassium Citrate[4]	3.46

1 Merecol CLG - a mixture of natural gums (guar, locust, bean, carageena)
2 SUNETT™ - a synthetic sweetener Acelsulphane K
3 Cookie Dough - Vanilla Flavoring Agent: Peach Flavor
4 Citric Acid and Potassium Citrate were added as solution in 50 parts of water.
5 POWER PRO™ WPG - Water soluble whey protein

The mixture was poured into molds holding 93 grams of the mixture and frozen. The high protein frozen bar contained the following nutritional values.

Total Fat	0	gram
Cholesterol	0	gram
Sodium	30	milligrams
Total Carbohydrate	10	grams (10.7% by weight)
Fiber	0	gram
Sugar	1	gram
Protein	15	grams (16% by weight)

The bar had a smooth creamy mouth-feel and had a 15:1 protein to sugar ratio and substantially no fat.

Method 2: Strawberry Flavour Frozen Product

A mixture of the following ingredients was prepared according to the Method 1.

Ingredient	Parts by Weight
Water	8830.8
Maltitol	1009
Pectin	31.6
MC Cellulose	35.1
Merecol CLG	4.67
POWER PRO™ WPC	2018
Water	86
Strawberry Puree	898.3
Aspartame	1.8
SUNETT	1.8
Vanilla Cookie Dough [3] 680244	22.46
Vanilla[3] 680246	44.9
Strawberry[3] 61006	89.9
Raspberry[3] 600877	22.5
Red #40 (1.5% by weight solution)	112.3

Ingredient	Parts by Weight
Yellow #5 (5% by weight solution)	7.5
Citric Acid	10.28
Potassium Citrate	5.1
Water	50

3. Flavoring Agents

The mixture was poured into 92 gram molds and frozen to provide a frozen high protein product with a smooth mouth-feel and excellent flavor. Large ice crystals did not form after several months storage.

The nutritional analysis of the frozen product was:

Total Fat	0 gram
Cholesterol	0 gram
Sodium	35 milligrams
Total Carbohydrates	11 grams
Sugar	2 grams (2.2% by weight)
Protein	15 grams (16.3% by weight)
Fiber	0 gram

The protein to sugar ratio was 7.5 and the frozen product contained no fat.

Method 3: Pina Colada Flavour Frozen Product

A mixture of the following ingredients was prepared as in Method 1, poured into molds holding 88 grams and frozen.

Ingredient	Parts by Weight
Water	6830.81
MALTITOL	1009
Pectin	31.6
MC Cellulose	35.1

Ingredient	Parts by Weight
Merecol CLG	4.7
POWER PRO™ WPD LoL	2017.9
Water	464.4
Crushed Pineapple [3]	546.5
Coconut Cream [3]	131.2
Aspartame	2.19
SUNETT	2.19
Vanilla Cookie Dough [3] 680244	21.9
Vanilla [3] 680246	6.56
Pineapple Flavor [3] 609281	43.7
Coconut Flavor [3] 610571	43.7
Coconut Enhancer [3] 610627	43.7
Emulsifier	trace

3 Flavor Ingredients

Nutritional Values

Total Fat	1	gram
Saturated Fat	0.5	gram
Cholesterol	0	milligram
Sodium	25	milligrams
Total Carbohydrate	8	grams
Dietary Fiber	0	gram
Sugar	0	gram
Protein	15	grams (17% protein)

The frozen product had a smooth creamy mouth-feel and did not develop large ice crystals after storage for four months.

Method 4: Banana Flavor Frozen Product

A mixture of the following ingredients was prepared according to the Method 1.

Ingredient	Parts by Weight
Water	6830.81
MALTITOL	1009
Pectin	31.6
Microcrystalline Cellulose	35.1
Merecol CLG	4.87
POWER PRO™ WPC	2018
Banana Puree	947.7
Heavy Cream	155.4
Aspartame	0.95
SUNETT	0.95
Vanilla Cookie Dough [3] 680244	37.9
Vanilla [3] 680246	66.4
Banana Flavor [3] 601359	47.4
Banana Flavor [3] 52446	47.4
Emulsifier	0.1

3 Flavoring Agents

The mixture was poured Into molds holding 93 grams and frozen. The high protein bar contained the following nutritional values:

Total Fat	0.5	gram
Cholesterol	0	gram
Sodium	25	milligrams
Total Carbohydrate	11	grams
Sugar	1	gram
Protein	15	grams (16% protein)
Dietary Fiber	0	gram

The protein to sugar ratio was 15 and the protein to fat ratio was 30.

The frozen product had a smooth mouth-feel and excellent flavor. Large ice crystals did not form after five months storage in a freezer compartment of a home refrigerator.

The frozen product of the invention is a high protein, low fat frozen product with a smooth creamy mouth-feel and does not lose its smooth consistency when stored frozen for extended periods.

The properties of the product are unexpected since the product contains substantially no fat but has organoleptic properties (smooth, creamy, mouth-feel) associated with fat containing foods.

The frozen food can be prepared with a higher available carbohydrate (sugar) content by substituting sugar for ali or a portion of the non-nutritive bulking agents. In addition, small amounts of cream can be added to the frozen food composition to further increase the smooth creamy nature of the product.

Fruits and flavors such as banana, raspberry, blueberry, kiwi, orange, lemon, lime and the like can be used to flavor the frozen food product of the invention. The nutritional attributes of the product can abe further improved by including in the composition small amounts of natural or synthetic vitamins and minerals.

The product can also contain small or trace amouns of food grade emulsifier. Amounts of emulsifier up to about 0.006% by weight can be useful.

When the frozen product is provided in a cup, the mixture can be frozen in a continuous freezing apparatus, introduced into the cup and hardened in a freezing zone.

24

Microwave Heating of Certain Frozen Foods

Frozen food, reconstituted in a microwave oven, tends to spot heat. This is attributed to the different loss factors of frozen vs. unfrozen portions of the same food. Moreover, flat portions of food, as a sandwich, tend to edge heat—for unlike the middle portion of a sandwich which can only receive microwave energy from its top and bottom, the edge of said sandwich receives its energy from its top, bottom and side. To overcome spot, selective and edge heating, it is taught to operate at reduced power levels and/or provide a resting interval, but reduced power levels and resting intervals undesirably increase the cooking time and can result in undesirable dehydration of a food.

In microwave cooking, microwave energy concentrates at the ends of cylindrical foods (as egg rolls and hot dogs) and foods with protuberances (as the ends of fried chicken wings) which results in uneven, undesirable heating. Prior art teaches to cover ends, edges and protuberances with aluminum foil shielding to combat this problem.

The words "egg rolls" in this writing is meant to describe a cylindrical type, crusted, deep fat fried food whose filling may be of many varieties. For example, some fried "egg roll" type products may contain pizza type fillings and others may contain white and/or dark meat, boneless chicken. When fried, packaged in my novel package and frozen, said deep fat fried, boneless chicken rolls, pizza rolls, Chinese egg rolls and the like will result in a desirable snack food product line for vending operations. Notwithstanding this special deep fat fried, batter crusted, boneless chicken "egg roll" snack product, the words "fried chicken" and "fried foods" used herein encompass their common connotation.

In commercial and vending feeding, the faster an item can be heated, the longer it can be held hot, the convenience and simplification added by the package (for example, no requirement for knife and fork) and the ease of clean up are all important considerations which this invention is designed to afford.

Described is a food package whose structure is employed to contact and timely buffer, from direct exposure to microwave radiation, the outer periphery of certain food while said certain food is defrosted and heated in a microwave oven. It is expected that, at the termination of microwave heating, said food package will be spot, selective and edge heated rather than, without said food package, said food undesirably spot, selectively and edge heating. The part of said food package in direct contact with said food is fabricated of high-temperature-resistant material to permit said food's surface to reach browning and crusting temperatures. Means are provided in said high-temperature material so that liquid by-products, forced out of said food, can pass freely across said high-temperature material and thereupon lodge in liquid absorptive material.

It is an object of this method to describe a microwave oven heating package which can be employed during shipping, storing, serving and/or eating of certain foods.

It is an object of this method to describe a microwave heating package for reconstituting prefried, frozen convenience foods.

It is an object of this method to describe methods and apparatus for reconstituting in a microwave oven deep fat fried frozen chicken, Chinese and other type "egg rolls" and sandwiches.

It is an object of this method to describe methods and apparatus for reconstituting in a microwave oven baked and leavened products.

The foods referred to, herein, are foods which are by their nature will be contained by a microwave-permeable, perforated plastic film. Fig. 24.1 is an exploded, cross-section diagram showing the construction of food package 7 for reconstituting therein a frozen convenience food 1 in a microwave oven. Food 1 is enclosed in and contacted by a peforated plastic film 2 which in turn is enclosed in a microwave-permeable, water and food by-product absorptive material 3 where all is enclosed by a microwave-permeable, liquid-barrier plastic film 4 and, finally, all of which is enclosed by a microwave-permeable, heat-insulating material 5.

It is preferred to use a high-temperature plastic film 2 (as the Nylon and polyester plastic films in common use for gas and electric oven browning bags which operate at oven temperatures circa 350°F.) which has been made water and oil permeable by perforating a multitude of holes 6 therethrough. Holes 6 must be of such size as to permit film 2 to contain food 1 therein and of such number as to afford the free, random passage of water and oil through film 2 when said water and oil is in motion due to the exposure of food 1 to microwave radiation 8. The size of holes 6 taken with the thickness of plastic film 2 must not permit food 1 to sag through holes 6 in plastic film 2 and physically touch absorptive material 3. Holes 6 must not be of such small dimension as to support the capillary transfer of liquid through film 2.

Microwave-permeable, heat-insulating member 5 can be constructed of paper, cardboard or other material of low thermal conductivity—material useful for a hot pot holder. Microwave-permeable, liquid-absorptive material 3 is best constructed of blotting type paper or natural (as cotton) or synthetic (as plastic) fibres.

In operation (as seen in Figs 24.1 and 24.2) frozen food package 7 with food 1 therein is exposed to microwave radiation 8 whereupon steam (steam initially generated by spot, selective and edge heating of crust 16 and filling 17 portions of food 1) contained by plastic film 4 blankets and so defrosts the complete crust 16 of food 1. And while this is happening a second steam source starting deep in filling 17 of food 1 (e.g. core heating) drives before it, out of food 1, food by-products as said second steam source forces its way through the body of food 1 to and through crust 16. Said head of steam of said second steam source forces water, oil and other food by-products, that pass through

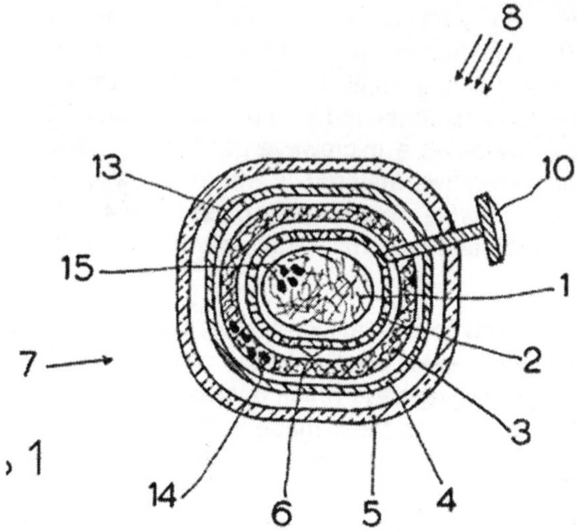

Fig. 24.1: An exploded cross-section diagram of the food package of this method

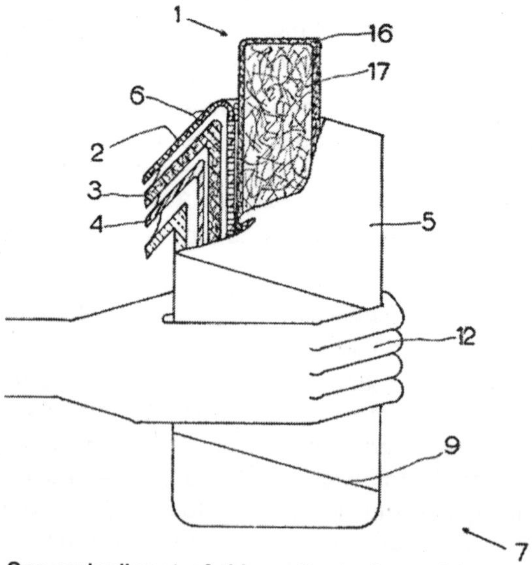

Fig. 24.2: One embodiment of this method , in partial cross-section, showing a hand holding a food package which contains an "egg roll" type food.

crust 1, through perforations 6 in perforated plastic film 2 whereupon said by-products are absorbed in microwave-permeable, absorptive-material 3. When the heating process is terminated and the microwave generator is turned off, said water, oil and food by-products, absorbed in absorptive-material 3, cannot transfer back to hot food 1 lacking a motive source. Trying to wet the crust 16 of food 1 are the wet portions of filling 17 and vapors emitting from the moisture caught in absorptive-material 3. Initially they cannot wet the crust 16 because crust 16, initially low in moisture and denser than filling 17, reaches baking temperatures. Crust 16 is an initial generator of water vapor (e.g. steam) when food package 7 is exposed to microwave radiation 8. Then, because of crust 16's low mass and density, crust 16 quickly dries and continued exposure to microwave radiation heats crust 16 to the highest temperature in heated food package 7. Water vapor can only condense on cool elements. Crust 16 once heated cools slowly for being dry it can not cool by evaporating water. Moreover, because saturated hot water vapor fills food package 7, held therein by liquid-barrier, plastic film 4, heat cannot easily transfer out of food 1 by conduction, convection, radiation or the evaporation and condensation of water. This action tends to make food 1 taste better for a longer time even though package 7 is not promptly opened.

Outer plastic film 4 is designed to contain a positive vapor pressure within food package 7 up to a preselected vapor pressure whereupon film 4 is best designed to rend and thereby vent steam above a preselected temperature and pressure. For example, in well known manner, outer plastic film 4 can be constructed of high-temperature, plastic film (e.g. nylon and polyester films) and designed to vent a a preselected temperature by blow out plugs 13 or can be constructed of a low temperature plastic (as polyethylene) formulated to melt at a predetermined temperature. Microwave-permeable, heat-insulating outer material 5 is optional and can be employed for such service as: (a) an aid in uniform internal heating, (b) heat-insulating package 7 from contact with cool oven surface and (c) as an aid in the easy handling of heated food package 7.

The time it takes to heat individual portions of food and the time it takes for said food to cool subsequent said heating is important in commercial feeding. While my food package is directed to commercial food applications, as vending, it is useful for domestic defrosting and heating. Food package 7 lowers the time it takes to defrost and heat and raises the time it takes a given product to cool subsequent heating.

In operation, food package 7 defines over heating food in the prior art apparatus and methods set forth because in food package 7 the microwave-lossy-liquid component (as water) is not trapped in a microwave-shielded collection chamber or trapped from recycling by proximetry to microwave-reflective material. In food package 7, by-product water and steam condensed to water are dispersed in liquid-absorptive material. By so dispersing water, there is created a bigger target area which captures more microwave radiation 8 and thereby hastens the evaporation or reevaporation of said water. Steam, per se, and fat are both relatively microwave non-lossy. Hence, fat is trapped and remains in liquid-absorptive material 3, and the steam, which fills the chamber defined by film 4, acts with material 3 and film 4 to create a blanket surrounding and heat-insulating food 1.

An advantage of food package 7 is that a portion of the oil on the surface of a fried food (for example, egg rolls, fried chicken, fried Monte Cristo sandwiches) cooked in food package 7 is forced through perforated plastic film 2 where it is trapped out of contact with food 1. The water and oil trapped in absorptive material 3 is blocked from contact with food 1 by the thickness of plastic film 2. The result is less oily, greasy cooked food which is desired by many. Because of perforated plastic film 2, when heated, food 1 is not left resting in a pool of grease and oil which would be undesirable to many. Said another way, fried food, heated in food package 7, is blotted of oil and does not require the subsequent draining and blotting characteristic of deep fat frying in gas and electric cooking. Notwithstanding the obvious advantage food package 1 has in reconstituting fried foods and other foods singled out herein, it is expected that many will find food package 1 highly useful in reconstituting numerous other type foods as a corn beef sandwich.

When desired, advantageously, a small amount of water or salt water 14 can be arbitrarily added to liquid-absorptive material 3 anytime before exposing food package 7 to microwave radiation

8. Water or salt water is dispersed by capillary action through liquid-absorptive material 3 and makes said material 3, generally, initially more microwave-absorptive than food 1. Hence, in heating up food package 7, initially, much of the power of microwave radiation 8 is expended in said small charge of salt water 14. Salt water 14 swiftly boils and its hot vapors blanch and completely defrost the surface of food 1. This action counters microwave spot heating and thermal run away effects that may occur without said salt water 14 charge. Employing salt water 14 as described permits faster heating through higher power operation where faster heating is the result sought. When salt water 14 is employed as described, it should be noted that perforated plastic film 2 takes on the additional function of not allowing salt water 14 to impinge upon food 1 thereby changing food 1's flavor.

The speed at which bread and rolls dry out after being heated in a microwave oven has long been considered as a shortcoming of microwave ovens. A method that discovered to obviate said shortcoming is to add extra-water 15 in the form of a water spray on a slice of bread or water injected into a roll. Small amounts of extra-water 15 can be added to risen baked goods before freezing at which time it is dispersed within the bread product by capillary action. Whereupon, after subsequent microwave defrosting and heating, said bread, roll or other baked and leavened product will not dry out as quickly as if the baked and leavened food was defrosted and heated in a microwave oven without said extra water 15 and/or food package 7. Surprisingly, adding extra-water 15 to stale bread has made said stale bread taste fresh when reconstituted. One must learn to choose the right amount of extra-water 15 to make the resultant defrosted and heated roll remain moist and taste as well as a freshly baked roll. It is preferrable to allow a charge of extra-water 15 time to disperse within a baked and leavened product before freezing. Ice is relatively non-lossy and, if said extra-water 15 is not allowed to disperse before freezing, after exposure to microwaves said quickly wetted and frozen baked and leavened product could be steaming hot with a small ice cube or puddle of water selectively placed within, an unsatisfactory condition.

There are innumerable type and size portions of the same type of food, different freezer temperatures, different microwave oven power levels and ambient conditions all which have a part in determining how long it will take to defrost and heat a given food in a given situation. For a particular situation, one must learn empirically how much water to add if any, the amount of absorptive material to use, etc. Researcher has discovered that once the time per ounce of food is discovered for a given freezer, package and microwave oven, this time per ounce holds well for other types of food and for different amounts of the same food. I have discovered that a thermometer (microwave oven type) inserted into food package 7, during its exposure to microwave radiation, to monitor the vapor temperature of the heating chamber, defined by outer plastic film 4, will indicate the average of many variables (e.g. a thermometer will report a colder freezer and a more powerful oven equal to a warmer freezer and a less powerful oven). Depending on the filling of a sandwich, one can defrost and heat a food package up to 120°F., or 190°F., or 220°F., etc. during a microwave exposure and then continue to monitor the temperature of unopened food package 7 until its temperature drops to a preselected temperature, for example, room temperature, 140°F., or 170°F., etc. for repeatable results. Using thermometer 10 for denser portions of food, as fried chicken, one can defrost the chicken and heat it to 212°F., boiling temperature, and continue heating until the temperature stops holding at 212°F. and raises to 220°F. whereupon microwave radiation 8 is turned off and the food package 7 opened when its temperature falls to 180°F. Using such programs as illustrated, thermometer 10 is useful to familiarize the uninitiated with the operation of food package 7 and is useful initially with each new type food defrosted and heated. Once the defrosting and heating time for a given type egg roll in a given situation is determined (using thermometer 10 or by simple experiment) the continued use of thermometer 10 becomes superfluous as the results become predictable.

Figure 24.2 illustrates one embodiment of the method showing a hand 12 holding food package 7 where food 1, illustrated in cross-section, is an egg roll with crust 16 and filling 17. After heating, food package 7 can be hand held as illustrated (made practical by the heat insulating properties of heat-insulating material 5). Fig. 24.2 illustrates food package 7's top opened using an easily ripped seam 9 designed into package 7 to provide "zipper" type means of opening package 7. Plastic film 2's perforations 6 and absorptive material 3's loose fibres are designed to easily tear apart as easily ripped seam 9 is ripped open. In Fig. 24.2, food package 7 is designed to be progressively torn away as the egg roll, food 1, is progressively consumed. The remains of food package 7, as food 1 is consumed above it, acts to protect the unconsumed portions of food 1 and keep it hot while protecting hand 12 from hot food 1 and the grease and oil by-products released during the heating of food 1.

It is expected that without the exercise of method one may manufacture food package 7 as one structure with perforated film 2, insulating material 3, outer film 4 and insulating material 5 as layers. Manufacturing all of food package 7 of plastic (e.g. plastic fibres for absorptive material 3 and plastic foam for heat-insulating material 5) the walls of food package 7 could be wrapped around food 1 and heat sealed shut.

25

Freeze Drying

Drying, like freezing, is primarily a method of food preservation, and is also one of the oldest methods of food preservation. An advantage of drying over freezing is that the dried product is shelf stable and thus generally requires only a sealed container to keep it for months or even years at ambient temperature. Refrigeration, on the other hand, requires a power supply, which if interrupted can jeopardise the safety and quality of the product. A further advantage of drying is that the removal ofwater reduces the weight and volume of the product, which aids storage and transport. The main disadvantage of drying, however, is that the product quality (resemblance to the original undried product) is generally not as high upon rehydration as frozen foods are upon thawing. Particular problems are changes in texture (for solid foods) and the loss of aromas.

Most drying processes involve the evaporation of liquid water to water vapour, but freeze drying instead occurs as a result of sublimation of ice directly to water vapour. The basic steps in a freeze drying process are briefly described as follows, and these will be examined in more detail in the rest of the chapter.

(i) The food is first frozen (usually on trays) which results in the formation of ice crystals within the food and the non-ice phase becoming freeze concentrated.

(ii) The frozen material is then exposed to a headspace with a partial pressure ofwater vapour well below the equilibrium vapour pressure of ice at the temperature of the material (see Fig. 25.1). This causes the sublimation of the ice crystals (primary sublimation) and also desorption of non-crystalline water present within the food matrix (secondary drying). The very low partial pressure of water vapour in the headspace is generally achieved by placing a condenser unit in close proximity to the food. The temperature of the condenser surface should be significantly lower than that of the drying material (typically –60°C)

(iii) In conventional freeze drying a vacuum is maintained in the freeze drying chamber, typically via the use of a vacuum pump. A common misconception is that the primary purpose for the vacuum pump is to remove water vapour. However, water removal is achieved far more effectively by the condenser. The vacuum pump is instead mainly used to remove air (and other non-condensable gases desorbed from the food) from the chamber. The reason is that the gases slow down the rate of transfer of water vapour from the food to the condenser.

(iv) As sublimation is an endothermic process, heat must be applied to the frozen food to sustain the sublimation

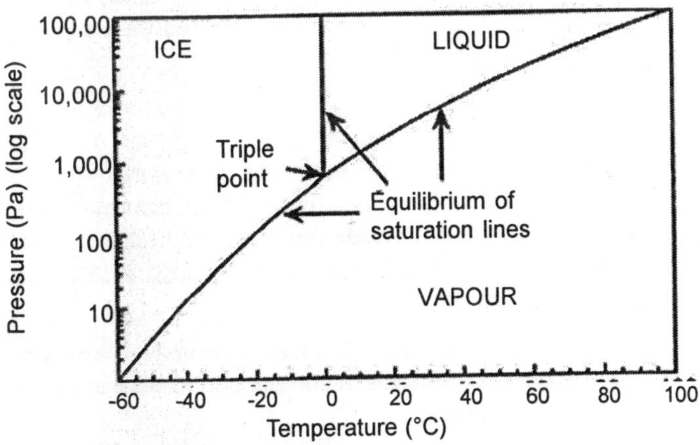

Fig. 25.1. Phase diagram of water showing the variation of equilibrium vapour pressure of water with temperature. At temperature below the triple point pure water exists as solid ice.

process. However, the temperature of the food must always be maintained below its 'collapse' temperature (which is related to the glass transition temperature). Not only must the ice crystals not melt, but also the frozen food matrix must maintain rigidity if a properly freeze dried food is to be obtained. The collapse temperature is not constant, but rises as the moisture content in the food matrix is reduced.

If the process is performed correctly then the resulting freeze dried product will have the following attributes:

(i) For a sufficiently dried product the collapse temperature will have risen far above ambient temperature. The product will therefore have a rigid structure at ambient temperature and be shelf stable.

(ii) If the sample has been consistently maintained below the collapse temperature throughout drying then the ice crystals will leave behind voids (which the crystals once occupied) as they sublime. This results in a highly porous structure with excellent rehydration properties as the water is sucked into the pores by capillary action on wetting. This enables relatively large objects such as meat steaks to be rehydrated more successfully than those dried using other methods. The presence of pores also speeds the sublimation process by providing easy routes for water vapour to escape the solid.

(iii) Freeze dried products are maintained at much lower temperatures than other drying processes. Reactions associated with the much higher temperatures that occur in other drying processes (such as the Maillard browning reaction) therefore do not occur to such a large extent in freeze drying.

(iv) Freeze drying is also good at retaining volatile flavour and aroma compounds in comparison to high-temperature drying processes.

(v) The formation of ice crystals during the freezing step can be problematic in materials which already possess a microstructure. This is a particular problem for cellular

(a)

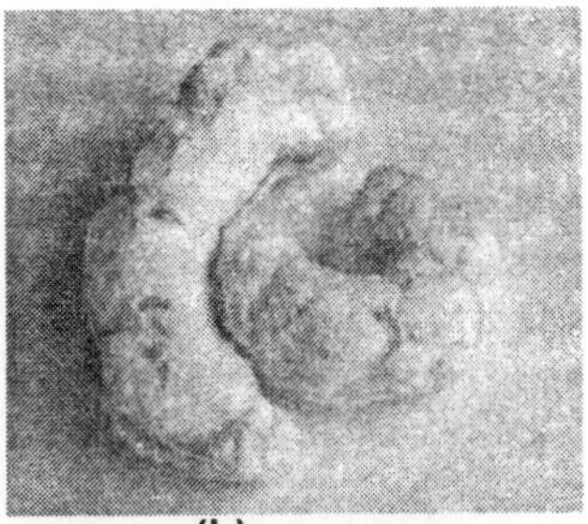

(b)

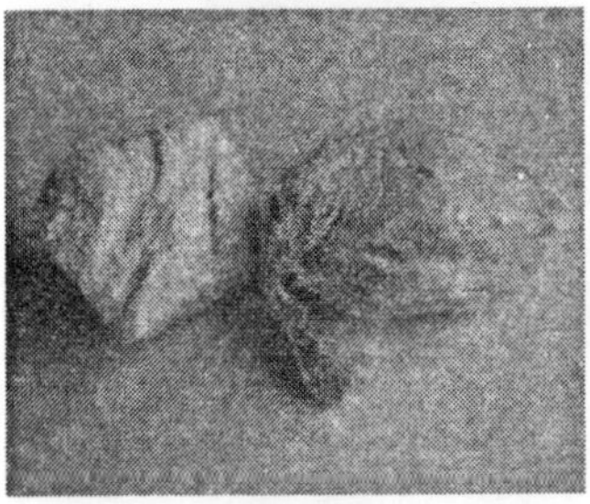

(c)

(d)

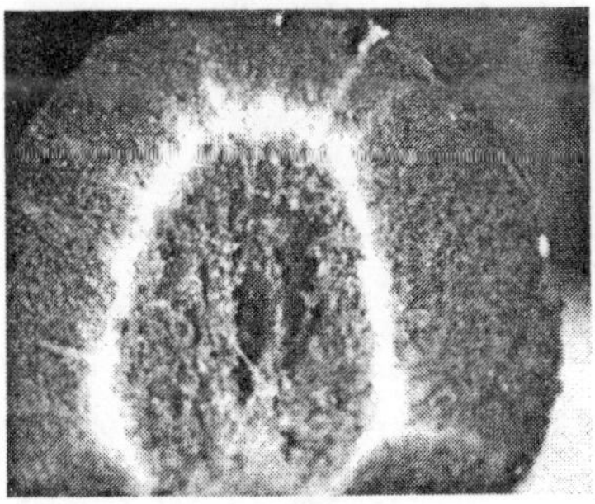

(e)

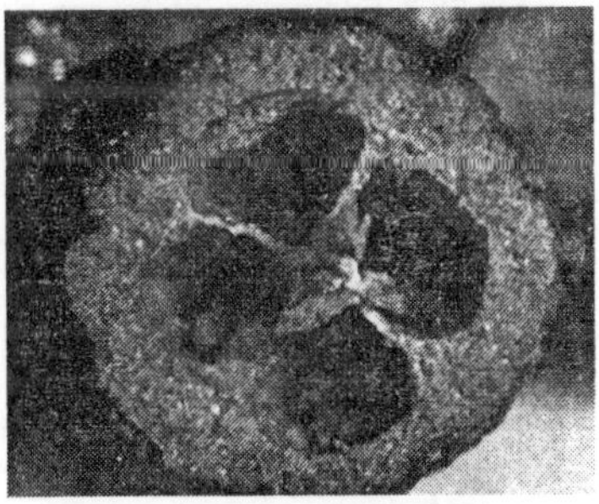

(f)

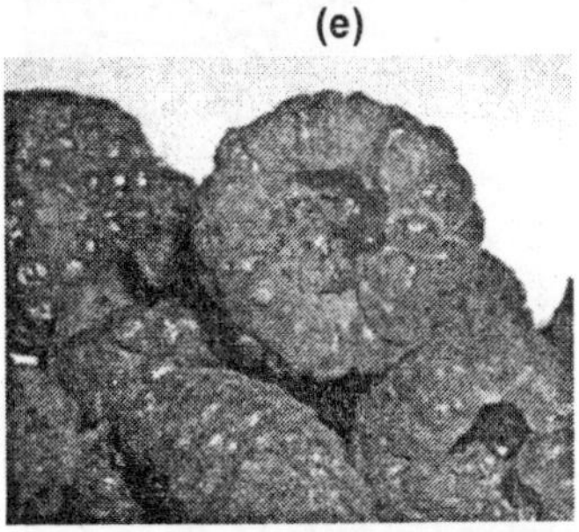

(g)

(h)

(i)

Fig.25.2 Examples of freeze dried foods. (a) coffee, (b) prawns, (c) chicken, (d) peach, (e) strawberry, (f) cranberry, (g) raspberries, (h) chives, (i) tarragon.

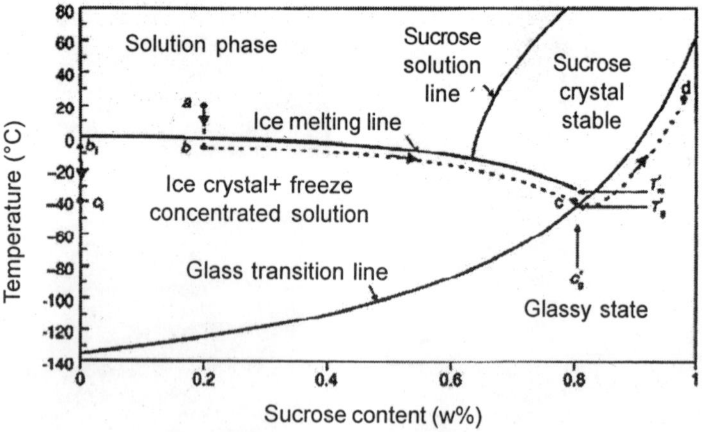

Fig. 25.3. State diagram of sucrose solution. A typical path of a 20% sucrose solution undergoing freezing [(a) to (c)] followed by freeze drying [(c) to (d)] is shown by dotted line

material such as plants and meat, but can be minimised by fast freezing, which produces small crystals.

Notwithstanding, the overall quality of freeze dried produce is usually superior to that of other dried foods for reasons (ii), (iii) and (iv). Almost any moisture-containing food can be freeze dried, including meat, fruits, vegetables and beverages. However, freeze dried products are usually more expensive than those obtained from other techniques for the following reasons:

(i) The drying chamber must be designed for vacuum operation. The main issues are structural strength (to resist buckling) and the avoidance of air leaks into the system (which brings undesired humidity as well as gas into the chamber).

(ii) The condenser presents a heavy refrigeration burden as it typically operates in the range between –40°C and –60°C, and must extract the same amount of heat in condensation from the condenser coils as that which is provided by heating to sublime the ice from the food. The food must also first be frozen which also incurs an energy cost.

(iii) Freeze drying is a slow process, taking many hours. This requires very large-scale equipment in order to produce acceptable throughput for bulk food manufacture. Consequently, both the capital and operating costs of freeze dryers are high. So although almost any moisture-containing food can be freeze dried, it is generally only niche foods that are freeze dried on a commercial basis. The most widespread examples include (see Fig. 25.2):

   (i) Freeze dried tea and coffee. Coffee is by far the most widely sold freeze dried product.

   (ii) Freeze dried meat and vegetables are popular in mountaineering, camping, military and astronaut rations and other 'instant' meals which are readily prepared by the simple addition of boiling water.

   (iii) Freeze dried fruits such as strawberries, cranberries and raspberries are an increasingly popular additive to breakfast cereals where milk is added.

(iv) Freeze dried herbs.

(v) Freeze dried pet food for dogs (meat), for cats (fish) and for fish (krill, worms).

In all these examples it can be noted that the freeze dried produce is more convenient to store or carry than the equivalent fresh or frozen produce, and this in many instances compensates for any reduction in quality.

THE FOOD MATERIAL SCIENCE OF FREEZE DRYING

In order to appreciate the requirements of a freeze drying process, it is important to understand howthe freezing and drying environments affect the food material. Perhaps the most important concept, which is key to sample collapse, is that of the glass transition.

The glass transition

The glass transition is a highly useful concept in understanding the behaviour of a wide variety of food materials. It was first used by (synthetic) polymer scientists to describe the relatively sudden change in mechanical properties of amorphous (non-crystalline) polymers from a hard, brittle, 'glassy' state to a soft 'rubbery' material as they are heated over a matter of only a few degrees Celsius. The change is fundamentally different to melting in that there is no enthalpy or volume change (as occurs when crystals melt) and that it only occurs in amorphous materials. The change nevertheless corresponds to a substantial increase in the mobility of molecules, which are almost immobile in the glassy state. The mid-point around which the change in properties occurs is commonly referred to as the glass transition temperature (Tg), although it is important to remember that the change in properties spans a small temperature range of approximately 10–20 K. The concept of a glass transition was not generally used in food science or food processing circles until the 1980s and 1990s, upon when it was extensively disseminated. The glass transition has now been observed in a wide range of amorphous food materials including sugars as well as food polymers such as proteins and starch. Many food materials are also able to crystallise but this does not tend to occur in freeze drying .

The use of state diagrams

The state diagram for an example system of sucrose and water system is shown in Fig. 25.3. It shows how the following vary with composition:

(i) The glass transition temperature.

(ii) The equilibrium melting temperature of ice below which ice is stable. Note that this falls below 0°C as the sucrose concentration increases due to freezing *point depression.*

(iii) There is also an equilibrium saturation line for sucrose crystals, to the right of which sucrose crystals are stable.

Similar diagrams can also be drawn for most food materials, including multi-component food systems, if all the non-aqueous components are treated as a single 'lumped' component for the purpose of using the Gordon–Taylor equation. This has been applied to fruits, which contain mixtures of cellular pulp, ascorbic and citric acids and various sugars, and tuna. Although the glass transition line may differ significantly for different materials (due to the different Tg of the dry material), the equilibrium melting line will not vary substantially.

The entire freeze drying process can be followed on this diagram. As an example take as a starting material a 20% sucrose solution at room temperature (at position marked 'a' on the chart).

Freezing

Removing heat from the solution initially causes it to cool to 'b', at a few degrees below the equilibrium melting line. A few degrees of sub-cooling is required to initiate nucleation and crystallisation of ice crystals ('bi'). The formation of an ice phase depletes water from the solution phase, which consequently becomes more concentrated with respect to sucrose. The solution phase thus now moves in the direction of 'c' on the chart. Due to the freezing point depression effect the temperature required to maintain ice formation declines steadily, and the solution becomes increasingly viscous as it becomes more concentrated. As the solution approaches the glass transition line at 'c' the solution becomes so viscous that ice crystallisation ceases and the composition of the viscous solution is now temporarily fixed at Cg. The ice phase will be at the same temperature at ci. This is the end of the freezing stage.

Point 'c' is known as the maximally freeze concentrated solution, as it is not possible to freeze concentrate further. There are a number of points to be made here:

(i) To ensure the maximum degree of freeze concentration, the solution must be held between Tm and Tg. At temperatures higher than Tm freeze concentration will cease at a lower concentration due to insufficient sub-cooling. At temperatures lower than Tg there is a risk that freeze concentration will cease when the glass transition is met at a lower concentration. However, if the temperature is again raised to the optimal temperature zone then the solution can be 'annealed' to rectify this.

(ii) Assuming the temperature is held between Tm and Tg, the maximum concentration of the freeze concentrated phase (Cg) is independent of the starting composition. However, the starting composition will determine the proportion of ice that can be formed, which can be calculated by a simple mass balance assuming a value of Cg.

(iii) The state diagram suggests that sucrose crystals can form at the eutectic point. However, as the crystallisation kinetics of sucrose are much slower than that of water, there is generally not sufficient time during the freezing process for sucrose crystallisation to occur. As the rest of the freeze drying process and subsequent storage take place in the glassy state, there is no further opportunity for sucrose to crystallise, and for this reason freeze drying is a popular method of producing food stuffs in the amorphous state

Freeze drying

Once the solution has been maximally frozen, the freeze drying process can begin by exposing the sample to a low vapour pressure headspace. This results in the sublimation of the pure ice crystals (known as primary drying) and desorption of water from the glassy phase (secondary drying) via exposed surfaces of the matrix. If the freeze concentrated solution is kept belowthe glass transition temperature then the sublimation of ice crystals leaves behind pores within the rigid structure, which increases the surface area for secondary drying. As the freeze concentrated phase undergoes secondary drying it is able to rise to a higher temperature without collapse occurring as the glass transition temperature rises. Therefore a trajectory such as from 'c' to 'd' can be followed. The sublimation process requires heat for the sample to maintain its temperature. Heat transfer to the sample is thus an important aspect of freeze dryer design.

Importance of the freezing step

The crystallisation ofwater to form pure ice crystals is a two-step process, requiring crystals to first nucleate and then grow. Both nucleation and growth processes require the solution to be supercooled belowthe equilibrium melting temperature of the aqueous solution by typically at least a couple of degrees Celsius. The rate of nucleation (the rate of formation of new crystals per unit volume) generally increases exponentially with the degree of supercooling, whereas the growth of crystals (the rate of increase in size) tends to increase in a less dramatic, linear fashion. Thus, as the temperature falls and the degree of supercooling increases, the nucleation rate increases more rapidly than the growth rate. Therefore slowcooling rates (which produces low supercooling) tend to favour growth and results in a small number of large crystals. On the other hand high cooling rates (equals high supercooling) tend to favour nucleation, which produces a larger number of smaller crystals. When cooling any object, however, the fastest rates of cooling invariably occur at the surface and the slowest rates in the centre. Thus, smaller crystals are generally found at the surface and larger crystals in the interior. The freezing stage, being the first stage, is critical to the overall success of the freeze drying process, for the following reasons:

(i) The sizes, shapes and distribution of crystals within the food as it freezes, translate directly into the sizes, shapes and distribution of pores in the final product. This not only affects the rehydration behaviour and appearance of the freeze dried product, but also the density.

(ii) Achievement of a connected network of crystals greatly assists the freeze drying process, as this results in a relatively easy path for water molecules to escape from the inside of the food through the pore network that takes its place. Achieving of a connected network of crystals generally requires a high water content in the initial feed (of around 80%). Thus, paradoxically, it can be faster to freeze-dry a product where the liquid feed has a higher initial moisture content (and is able to form a pore network) than one with a lower moisture content (where a network is not formed) and water is forced, in part, to diffuse through the food matrix. For a given material it is usually also found that slower cooling leading to larger crystals is more conducive to a connected network and faster freeze drying.

(iii) As mentioned earlier, small crystals must be produced if cellular material is to be freeze dried, to avoid rupture of cell walls. This overrides drying rate considerations for such foods.

EQUIPMENT AND OPERATION

Introduction

The general principles of freezing are outlined in other chapters in this book and these also apply here. In most instances the food is frozen on trays, either by contacting the tray with a cooled support surface, contacting the food with a cryogenic liquid (such as liquid nitrogen), or by air-blast freezing. There is generally a conductive resistance within the food, which limits the transport of heat from the food. In some freeze drying processes the trays are ribbed or finned to increase heat transfer rates in both freezing and freeze drying stages. The rate of freezing is important in determining ice crystal size, shape and distribution, which has important ramifications for damage to cells and the pore structure of the freeze dried product.

Freeze drying of beverages is generally performed from a concentrated solution which is previously prepared either by vacuum evaporation or by freeze concentration. In the commercial freeze drying of coffee a concentrated solution of typically 40% solids is used for freeze drying. This results in a relatively small fraction of ice forming but porosity is instead achieved by incorporating carbon dioxide under pressure into the coffee solution which forms a foam when the pressure is released. The liquid is quickly frozen to produce a solid foam, which is mechanically broken up into small nuggets (as seen in a typical jar of freeze dried coffee). The freeze drying time is much reduced as a result of carbon dioxide incorporation. The precise method of foaming has a large impact on the porous structure, which also influences the lightness or darkness of colour of the freeze dried product. The porous structure is just discernible in Fig. 25.2a.

Freeze drying

As mentioned in the introduction the main elements of a freeze dryer are:

(i) A vacuum tight chamber.

(ii) A means of removing air and other non-condensable gases, usually a vacuum pump.

(iii) A condenser to remove water and maintain a low partial pressure of water vapour in the freeze drying chamber.

(iv) Some means of supplying heat.

Freeze dryers are either designed for small-scale laboratory use or for large-scale food production.

Laboratory-scale equipment

Laboratory-scale freeze drier are either flask based or tray based. In the flask type (see Fig. 25.4) the material is placed in a glass flask, which is connected via a manifold to a condenser and vacuum pump. The use of a manifold allows more than one flask to be freeze dried at the same time. Heat is supplied by convection from the surrounding ambient air through the wall of the flask. This is essentially an uncontrolled method of heating, and the freeze dried material will establish its own temperature. This method is thus not suitable for materials with very low collapse temperatures. When loading the material should be applied in a thin layer around the flask wall. For solutions this is most easily achieved by freezing the solution in situ by rotating the flask containing the solution in a cold bath to freeze the solution in a thin layer on the flask wall. If drying more than one flask at a time it is particularly important to freeze dry nominally identical samples in each of the flasks. If samples show differential rates of drying then problems can arise as the fast drying material provides a rapid source of water vapour, which raises the overall vapour pressure of water in the chamber. This slows down the rate of sublimation of the slower drying materials, which is cooled less and so will rise to a higher temperature than if dried on its own. The possibility of collapse is thus increased.

Tray-type freeze driers come in various levels of sophistication. Some have controlled shelf temperatures (see Fig. 25.5), while others are free-standing shelves within a glassdomed chamber. Where there is more than one free-standing shelf it is also important to freeze dry nominally identical samples on each of the trays for the same reasons as given above for flask drying.

Laboratory freeze driers generally have condensers in the form of a cooled wall. This design allows a considerable quantity of water to be removed in a small space. Much of the Fig. 25.4 Flask style laboratory freeze dryer, with stainless steel manifold for multiple flask drying (although only one is attached in the picture). The condenser lies in the main (white coloured) body of the apparatus and is connected to the flask through the manifold. To the left is the vacuum pump with oil mist filter attached. cost of laboratory freeze dryers is due to the refrigeration apparatus that is required. A small vacuum pump (5 m^3 h^{-1}) is all that is required in these installations to evacuate air.

Industrial-scale equipment

Industrial-scale freeze driers are almost exclusively of the tray type (see Figs. 25.6 and 25.7). The trays can be flat, with a raised edge to contain liquid feeds if necessary, or can also be ribbed with metal slats protruding from the floor of the tray. Both batch and continuous dryers are used. In the case of continuous dryers, air locks need to be provided at each end for

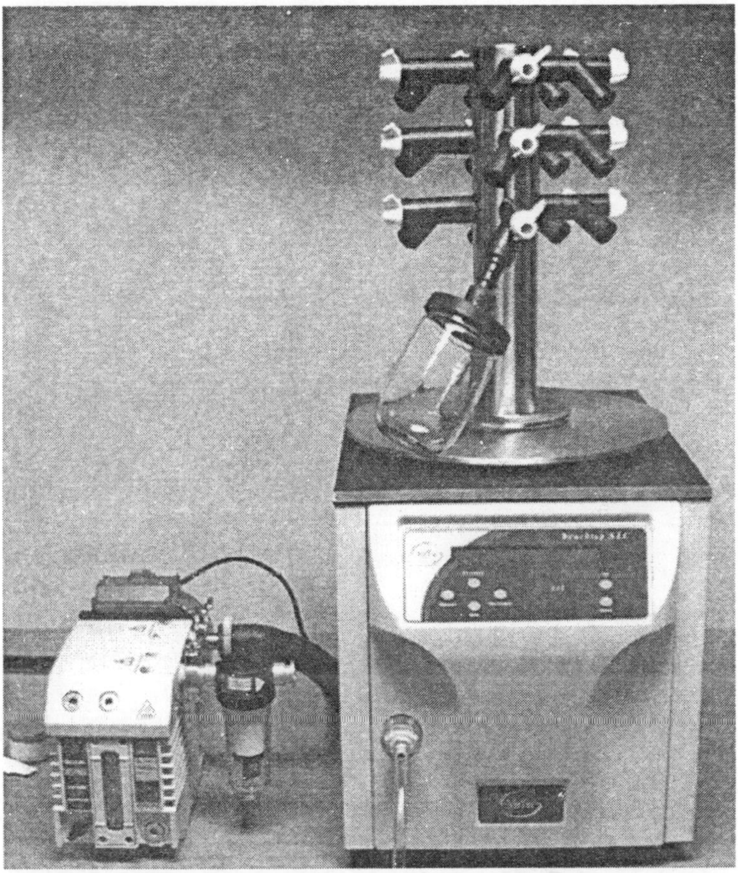

Fig. 25.4 Flask style laboratory freeze dryer, with stainless steel manifold for multiple flask drying (although only one is attached in the picture). The condenser lies in the main (white coloured) body of the apparatus and is connected to the flask through the manifold. To the left is the vacuum pump with oil mist filter attached.

trays to enter and leave without compromising the vacuum within the main chamber. Although many freeze driers share similar features there are many variations in how they are laid out. This is in contrast to freezing processes where equipment is much more standardised. Heating is provided either by conduction through the supporting shelf (with the shelf heated electrically or by circulating fluid) or by radiant heating from above each shelf.

Fig. 25.5 Larger laboratory shelf-style freeze dryer. The shelves are temperature controlled and are located in the upper part of the equipment behind the glass window. The condenser lies in the lower half (behind the black circle

In some installations a dry inert gas is also periodically fed into the chamber to provide heat for sublimation and to aid heat transfer from the heating surfaces to the material. Condensers can either be within the main chamber itself (see lower section of chamber in Fig. 25.6) or positioned in a separate chamber, which is isolated

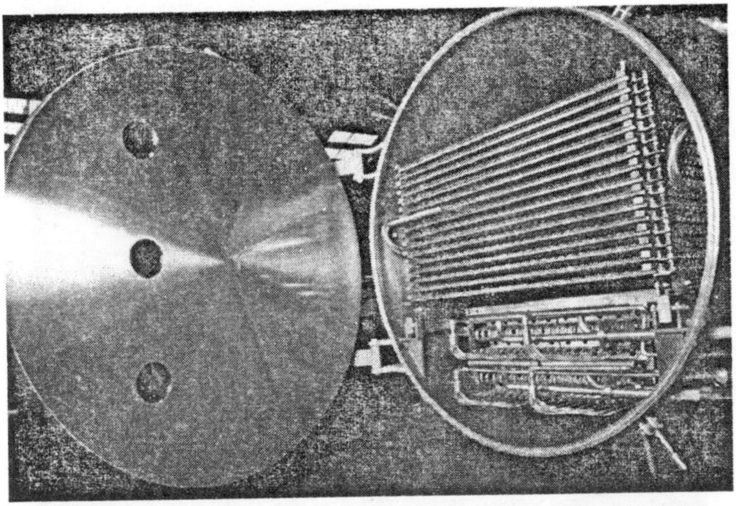

Fig. 25.6 Production-scale batch freeze dryer showing temperature-controlled product shelves (upper section) and condenser coils (lower section).

Fig.25.7 An example of production-scale freeze equipment. (a) and (b) inside of chamber showing shelves which are heated by circulating water, (c) trays loaded with frozen strawberries awaiting freeze drying, (d) the trays are mounted on carriers which are hung from overhead rails, which enables them to be easily moved around the factory and glide into the dryer between the heated shelves (in this case the trays are radiantly heated from both above and below).

by a valve – this allows 'pressure rise' measurements to be made. The distance between the drying chamber and the condenser should be as short as possible for the condenser to be as effective as possible in reducing the partial pressure in the chamber. The water molecules can typically travel at speeds of over 100 ms^{-1} between the drying shelves and the condenser coils. The condenser coils are generally tubular in nature, and build up an ice deposit of typically 1 cm thickness. A refrigerant passes through the coils, which is cooled in turn by a refrigeration unit. It is crucial that the temperature of the coils is uniform (less than 1 K variation). If parts of the condenser are warmer than others then sublimation will occur from these warmer parts to the cooler parts and the effective area of the condenser is much reduced. In large installations the condenser tubes are divided into sections, each having their own inlet refrigerant supplied in parallel.

Vacuum pumps are usually of the rotary vane type. They remove a fixed volume of air from the chamber per rotation, and so the volumetric rate of removal is constant. The mass of gas per unit volume depends on the pressure by the ideal gas lawand so the highest rate of ejection on a mass basis occurs when the chamber is at atmospheric pressure at the commencement of pumping down. The pump is connected to the drying chamber by a valve, which is used to control the chamber pressure. At steady state the vacuum pump needs to overcome the rate of ingress of air into the chamber via leaks or gases which have been desorbed from the food and water vapour.

An alternative means of providing a vacuum is by the use of steam ejectors. These use a jet of high-temperature steam passing through a section of the chamber to entrain gas molecules from the chamber. The steam subsequently passes through aVenturi to a condenser and is able to be simply pumped away as a liquid. Typically a two-stage (cascade) ejector arrangement is used whereby the second ejector entrains the steam and entrained gases from the first ejector. This method of pressure reduction is extremely rapid and allows operational pressures to be achieved in 6 minutes or so.

26

Process and Apparatus for Thawing Frozen Food

As the conventional thawing process, there can be mentioned (a) a process using hot air, (b) a process using microwaves, and (c) a heat radiation process. In the hot air process (a), if the temperature of hot air is too high, the surface portion of the frozen food is degenerated. Although it is considered that this disadvantage will be overcome if low-temperature air is used, a long time is required for the thawing in this case and the process is not applicable when rapid assortment or cooking is required. In the microwave process (b), the frequency that can be used at present is suitable for rotational vibration of the dipole moment of water, but this frequency is not optimal for ice and thus heat converges on the portion of water produced by thawing and the treatment effect becomes uneven. Namely, the central portion of the food remains frozen while the surface portion is boiled. In the heat radiation process (c), the thawing is effected by heat radiation from a surrounding heating plate, and far infrared radiation is especially effective. Nevertheless, this process has a problem in that the surface portion is readily deteriorated, the freshness is lost, and discoloration occurs, and a long time is required for completion of the thawing treatment.

Of the above-mentioned conventional thawing processes, the far infrared ray irradiation process is regarded as most advantageous, in that the efficiency of absorption of the far infrared ray energy is high and the energy is directly transferred to the interior of the food from the surface by heat radiation. But this process involves the problem of a loss of freshness and the long time required for completion of the thawing treatment.

The microwave process is effective for elevating the temperature of a frozen food, for example, from -30°C. to about -3°C. if a frequency suitable for ice can be adopted. But if the surface of the food becomes wet, a conduction electric current flows to weaken the electric field in the interior, and the surface portion is boiled because of a temperature difference between the surface portion and the interior. Therefore, it is difficult to uniformly and efficiently elevate the temperature from the frozen state at about -3°C. to the thawed state above 0°C. As a means for overcoming this disadvantage, a process is adopted in which a frozen food is irradiated with microwaves while cooling the surface portion of the food. But since the specific heat of the cooling air is low and the cooling capacity of the cooling air is readily lost by elevation of the temperature by heat received from the frozen material, it is necessary in this process to at a level lower than -10°C., and heat of the entire frozen food is taken by this cooling air, resulting in a reduction of the thawing efficiency. Therefore, the size of the apparatus must be increased, and accordingly, the cost is increased, and thus this process is practically worked only as a large-scale thawing machine for industrial purposes.

The primary object of the present method is to provide a process and apparatus by which thawing is accomplished in a shorter time than in the conventional techniques while preventing or minimizing any reduction of the quality of a food at the thawing step.

More specifically, in accordance with the present method, there is provided a process for thawing a frozen food, which comprises irradiating the frozen food with far infrared rays while supplying cold air to the frozen food to maintain the surface of the frozen food at a temperature not higher than 10°C.

Prior to the irradiation with far infrared rays, the frozen food can be irradiated with microwaves until the surface temperature of the frozen food is elevated to -5° to 0°C.

Furthermore, in accordance with the present method, there is provided an apparatus for thawing a frozen food, which comprises a thawing chamber for containing the frozen food therein, a far infrared ray heater for emitting an irradiation energy, which is disposed in the upper portion or side portion of the thawing chamber, and a cold air supply device for supplying cold air maintained at a desired temperature of at least -30°C. to the surface of the frozen food.

A microwave irradiation device can be equipped together with the far infrared heater so that the frozen food is first irradiated with microwaves and then with far infrared rays.

To increase the energy transfer during the irradiation with far infrared rays, it is sufficient to elevate the surface temperature of a far infrared ray radiator. In this case, the temperature-elevating rate in a food to be irradiated is increased, but the surface temperature of the food is elevated and thus an undesirable change in the food occurs. For this reason, in the usual thawing process, the surface temperature of the far infrared ray radiator (heater) is restricted.

In the present method, to prevent an elevation of the surface temperature of a food to be irradiated, cold air is applied to the food. As explained hereinbefore with respect to the irradiation with microwaves, it has heretofore been considered that the far infrared ray energy is wastefully consumed by the cold air and the irradiated surface portion cooled by the cold air, and therefore, a supply of the cold air is not significant from the viewpoint of thermal efficiency.

Contrary to this expectation, according to the research made by the present author it has been found that, if the surface temperature is maintained at a low level by cold air, according to the principle of radiation, the driving force to a high-temperature zone from a low-temperature zone is increased to increase the inflow rate of heat, i.e., the quantity of heat transferred per unit area and unit time, and desirably, the temperature on the high-temperature side (i.e., heater side) is further elevated and the heat inflow efficiency is proportionally increased. Accordingly, it is possible and preferable to elevate the far infrared ray energy

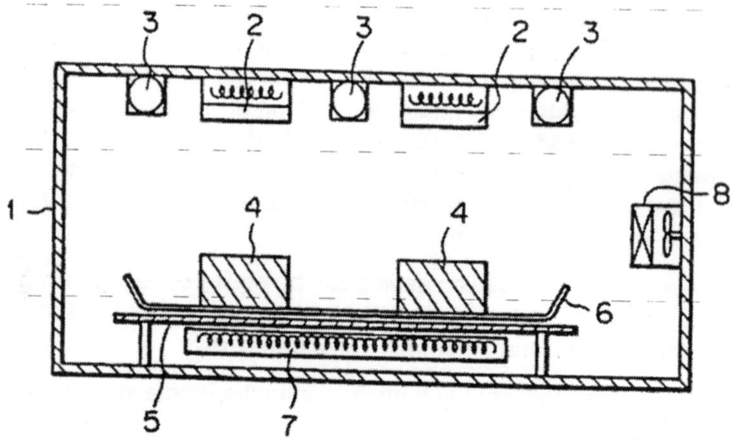

FIG. 26.1: Schematic diagram illustrating the thawing apparatus of the present method

to at least 0.5 W, especially at least 0.7 W, per gram of a food to be thawed.

In the present method, to prevent a reduction of freshness and deterioration such as discoloration of a frozen food when irradiated, the surface temperature of the frozen food is maintained at a level not higher than 10°C, preferably not higher than 6°C, by cold air. To maintain this surface temperature, preferably cold air having a temperature of -30° to 5°C is used.

In the present method, the frozen food can be irradiated with microwaves prior to the irradiation with far infrared rays. As pointed out hereinbefore, the irradiation with microwaves is effective before the frozen food is melted and becomes wet. Accordingly, the irradiation with microwaves can be applied prior to the irradiation with far infrared rays. At this step of the irradiation with microwaves, a supply of cold air is not absolutely necessary, but if a high uniformity is required, cold air must be supplied. The temperature at the switching point is -5° to 0°C., preferably about -3°C. Namely, the sensible heat, for example, spanning from -30°C. to -3°C. is dealt with by microwaves and the latent heat for melting the ice to water is then dealt with by far infrared rays. In the case of frozen foods, freezing is generally effected at a temperature lower than -30°C. When thawing of these frozen foods is carried out by heating, it is especially important that the foods are passed through the temperature range of from -10°C. to 3°C. as smoothly as possible. From this viewpoint, the combined application of the irradiation with microwaves and the irradiation with far infrared rays is preferred.

The apparatus of the present method will now be described with reference to the accompanying drawing. FIG. 26.1 is a schematic diagram illustrating an embodiment of the thawing apparatus, which comprises a thawing chamber 1, far infrared ray heaters 2, and microwave radiator devices 3 which are used in combination with the far infrared ray heaters 2 according to need. Frozen foods 4 to be thawed are placed on a plate 6 located on a bottom plate 5. A lower heater 7 may be disposed on the lower side of the bottom plate 5. A cold air device 8 is arranged in the thawing chamber 1. Preferably the temperature of cold air from the cold air device is varied from -30°C. to 5°C. Where microwaves are applied in combination with far infrared rays, the irradiation with microwaves is switched to the irradiation with far infrared rays at a cold air temperature of, for example, about -5°C. Since thawing times of frozen foods can be empirically known according to the kinds of frozen foods, this changeover can be performed by an automatic timer. Cold air from the cold air device is caused to flow in one direction or can be circulated.

Method

Frozen tuna slices maintained at -20°C. were used as the food to be thawed. Since the change of the quality in frozen tuna slices by thawing is more conspicuous than in other frozen foods, frozen tuna slices are very useful for evaluating the superiority or inferiority of the thawing process. Note, the frozen tuna slices used had a weight of about 250 g and a thickness of about 20 mm.

For the thawing operation, the frozen tuna slices were placed in the thawing chamber 1 shown in Fig. 26.1, but the microwave radiator device was not operated. The far infrared heater 2 was a ceramic-plasma-sprayed plate-shaped far infrared ray heater having a size of 200 mm×300 mm, and the surface temperature of the heater was controlled to 200°C. at an average electric

Table 26.1

		Example			Comparative Example		
Elapsing time	(min)	0	15	30	0	15	30
Cold air temperature	(°C.)	–18	–3	5	—	—	—
Top side surface temperature	(°C.)	–18.5	1.2	6.3	–6.0	10.3	16.2
Center portion temperature	(°C.)	–19.1	–5.0	–0.8	–14.7	–2.8	–0.9
		—	Hard as a whole	Easily cut, good hue	—	Icy as a whole and difficult to cut by kitchen knife	Deformed and peripheral portion blackened
Upper far-infrared ray heater							
Temperature	(°C.)		290			150	
Load	(W)		200			130	
Lower heater load	(W)		30			30	

power of 290 W. The frozen tuna slices were placed on the plate 6 and heated from below by the electric heating wire heater 7 at 30 W. To control the surface temperature of the frozen tuna slices, the temperature of cold air from the cold air device 8 was adjusted to a level shown in Table 26.1. The surface temperature and interior temperature of the tuna slices were measured, and the results are shown in Table 26.1.

27

Frozen food Masticating Machine

People are becoming increasingly preoccupied with the effects of diet on their health and overall wellbeing. For this reason, a growing number of Indians seek to reduce their intake of preservatives and food additives, reduce their consumption of fats and cholesterol, and lower their intake of processed sugar. In addition, a growing segment of the population needs to exclude all dairy products from their diet due to allergy. For all of the aforementioned people there is a need for a machine that can produce healthful desserts and frozen foods that will allow them to exclude the above named non-desired food ingredients from their diets.

Various devices have been suggested over the years for forming frozen products, such as dessert products like ice cream. None of these patents disclose a simple to use machine that produces pure masticated frozen foodstuffs with a creamy texture with no air or other ingredients added.

Therefore, there is a need for an apparatus for forming such frozen foodstuffs. Such an apparatus should be simple to use, economical and relatively easy to manufacture.

It is an object therefore of this method to provide an apparatus that creates a creamy textured frozen food product that utilizes as its only ingredient frozen fruits, vegetables, or other foodstuffs.

It is another object of this method to provide an apparatus to produce a frozen dessert that can be made without the addition of food additives and preservatives.

It is yet another object to provide a frozen dessert that can be made substantially fat free.

The present method relates to an apparatus to create a frozen confection which has properties such as taste and mouth feel similar to soft serve ice cream.

The method differs from all of the products which start with a liquid which is a mixture of some or all of the following; dairy products, water, fruit concentrates, sugar, emulsifiers, stabilizers, colors, and fats derived from vegetable, and/or animal sources. Typically the liquid is cooled and frozen while being whipped. The whipping action is what gives the products its overrun which is the entrainment of air therein. The percent of overrun is an expression of the amount of air that is frozen in said dessert. This entrainment of air is what usually gives the whipped frozen foodstuffs its creamy texture. This apparatus creates the creamy texture desired without any addition of emulsifiers and the like and without any overrun.

Most machines of this nature have been designed to separate, crush or extract. In the apparatus disclosed in this application whatever goes into the apparatus is ground so fine that no traces of small seeds or fiber are visible. All combinations of fruit or vegetables are completely mixed to create new flavors and taste stimulation. This is done while the foodstuffs are still frozen so there is no need for an additional refrigerating means within the apparatus. Dairy products are not needed for body or flavor. The finished product holds its shape long after thawing occurs. The masticating chamber and masticating element described below are designed to move a complete product with minimal waste of product hung up in the masticating chamber or on the masticating element.

This apparatus also is self-cleaning, with no need to disassemble the machine to clean the masticating element or masticating chamber. This is, of course, a significant safety feature because the masticating element is never exposed. Although not shown in the drawings those skilled in the art could easily add a water spray attachment to spray cleaning water through the hopper in into the masticating chamber to further facilitate the ease of cleaning. The masticating element is self-cleaning because the cutting grooves on the masticating portion of the masticating element releases product as it is used. This is possible because in the preferred embodiment the angle of attack of the cutting grooves is approximately 90 degrees. This allows the foodstuff to have a longitudinal movement towards the product delivery spout of the masticating chamber. Too great of a forward rake in the cutting grooves would trap foodstuffs and cause clogging, thus preventing a natural flow of product to the exit hole. To large of a backward rake would throw product perpendicular to the desired direction of product flow. In the preferred embodiment of the invention a semi-cylindrical shaped cutting groove is used although other shapes could be used as long as the angle of attack is 90 plus or minus 20 degrees.

Because of the need to not generate too much heat during the mastication process the number of cuts per revolution is key to the successful operation of the apparatus. The frozen food product is cut up to 8 more times per revolution than conventional crushing and juicing machines when operating. This is achieved by maintaining a low motor RPM, approximately 1,500 to 2,000 RPM, but having the masticating threads placed on the masticating portion of the masticating element in a threaded configuration. The preferred embodiment of the invention uses a fixed speed motor that operates at a speed of 1750 RPM but variable speed motors could be used as is well known by those skilled in the art. By using threaded style masticating threads a bonus is achieved. The threads also help to move the product along towards the product delivery spout. Frozen product has no natural flow and tends to bond with a surface of lesser temperature and thus the threaded nature of the masticating threads overcomes this problem. Also located on the masticating portion of the masticating element are the cutting grooves. These cutting grooves are longitudinally aligned grooves in parallel with the axis of rotation of the masticating element. They are semi-cylindrical in shape, and have a forward angle of attack, or cutting surface in the preferred embodiment, of 90 degrees to the inside of the masticating chamber when viewed against the rotational direction of the masticating element.

The frozen foodstuffs stay in the masticating portion of the masticating element described above long enough for a complete mastication. After it is ground it then needs to be mixed completely and moved out of the masticating chamber so a transferring portion is located on the masticating element after the foodstuffs pass the masticating portion. This transferring portion of the masticating element has multiple moving shoots trailing from the direction of rotation at a variable angle in order to create the pressure required to force the product out the product delivery spout of the masticating chamber. Variations of moving shoot angles in transferring portion of the masticating element create varying results in terms of mixing and exiting the foodstuff, all of which are considered disclosed by this application. If the angle is too great too much back pressure would develop and blow out could occur. If the angle is too little there is not enough pressure to force a frozen foodstuff out the product delivery spout.

The downward slope of the product delivery spout also creates enough pressure to uniform the product. This slope and shape also inhibits entry of inquisitive fingers. The angle of the product delivery spout provides a clean flow of product without collection of waste and provides for easy cleaning without removal of the masticating element. If the masticating chamber were at a 90 degree angle, as is commonly used, the spinning motion of the masticating element would sling the product out of the inlet hopper. With the down-sloped angle of the masticating chamber the product is thrown against the front wall of the inlet hopper and pushed back into the masticating chamber by the piston. In the preferred embodiment triangular shaped threads are used in the masticating and transferring portions of the masticating element because the triangle shaped threads results in the longest cutting edge when product travel and no clogging is desired, but those skilled in the art will envision other thread shapes, all of which are considered included in this disclosure. It should be recognized that additional rotational speed would also increase travel speed, but additional speed creates heat and would not preserve the original temperature of the frozen foodstuffs, which is an important part of this invention since no additional refrigeration is required to produce the creamy textured frozen product.

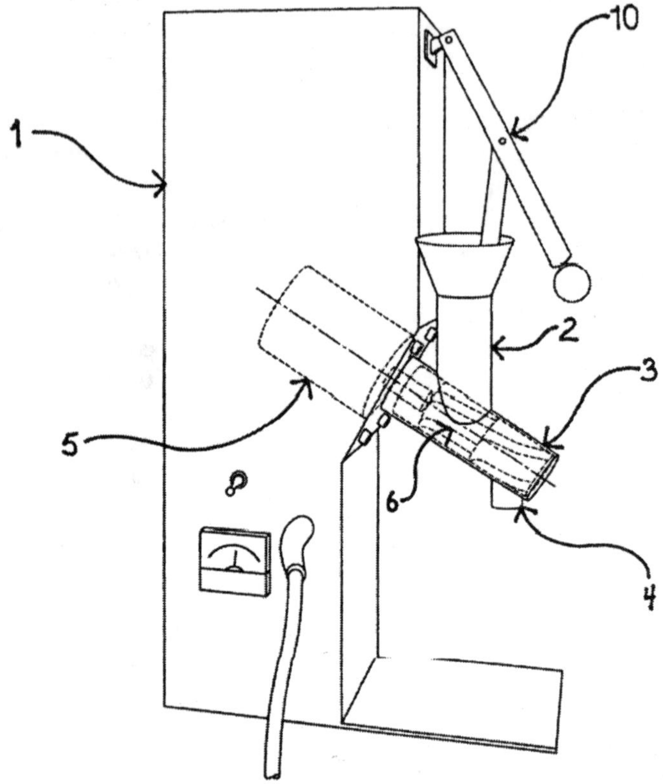

Fig. 27.1 Side view of the apparatus in accordance with the teachings of the method

Referring now to Figs. 27.1 and 27.2, the reader can readily see that the apparatus has a housing (**1**) with a motor (**5**) installed inside the housing (**1**) to turn the masticating element (**6**). An inlet hopper (**2**) for introducing foodstuffs therein is connected to the masticating chamber (**3**) at a greater than 90 degree angle such that the foodstuffs easily flow out of the masticating chamber (**3**). A plunger mechanism (**10**) is rotatably attached to the housing (**1**) such that a piston (**13**)is inserted into the inlet hopper (**2**) and the plunger mechanism (**10**) can be rotated such that it easily moves the piston through the inlet hopper (**2**) towards the masticating chamber (**3**) to move the frozen foodstuffs into the masticating chamber (**3**) with sufficient pressure to hold the frozen foodstuffs against the masticating element (**6**). The piston (**13**) has a cylindrically shaped portion that is conformably fitted to said masticating element on the end approaching the masticating element when said plunging mechanism (**10**) is operated and the piston (**13**) presses the frozen foodstuffs into the masticating chamber (**3**) against the masticating element (**6**). Alternatively, as shown in Fig. 27.2, the plunger mechanism (**10**) could be an actuator or other mechanical movement device that is electrically or hydraulically operated using methods well known to those skilled in the art.

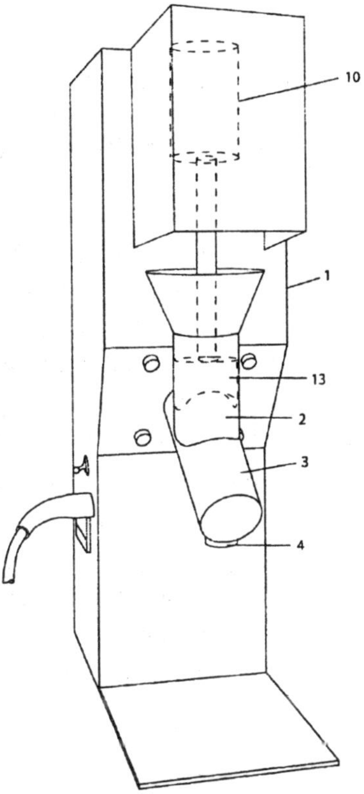

Fig. 27.2 Front view of an alternative embodiment of the apparatus in accordance with the teachings of the method

As disclosed in Fig. 27.3 the internal masticating element (**6**) is contained within the masticating chamber (**3**). In the preferred embodiment the tolerance between the masticating element (**6**) and the masticating chamber (**3**) is approximately 0.0060 inches. The masticating element (**6**) is directly connected to the motor (**5**) in the preferred embodiment but could be coupled to the motor (**5**) through gears, disconnects, and braking mechanisms (not shown) well known to those skilled in the art. The masticating element (**6**) could also be attached at the distal end of the masticating chamber (**3**) using a rotating axle and bearing mechanism (not shown) in order to add additional strength to the complete masticating structure as is well known to those skilled in the art. This internal masticating element (**6**) is formed with a masticating portion (**7**) having a, a plurality of

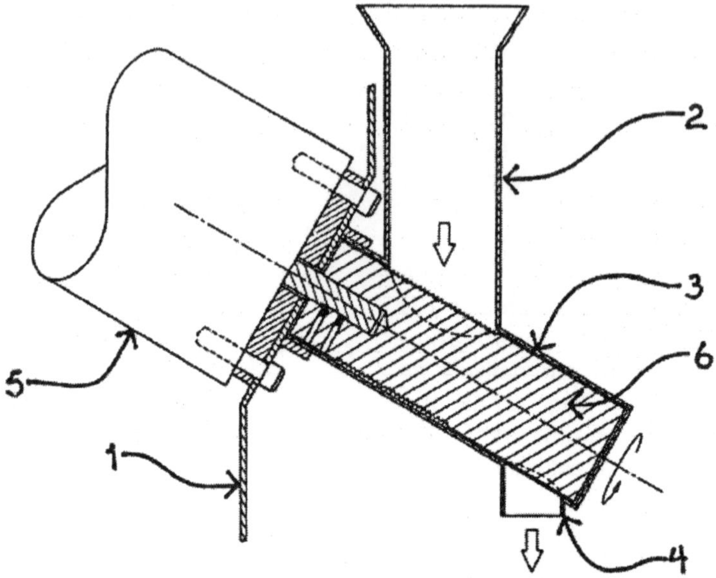

Fig. 27.3 A Cut away side view of the inlet hopper, mastication chamber, and product delivery spout

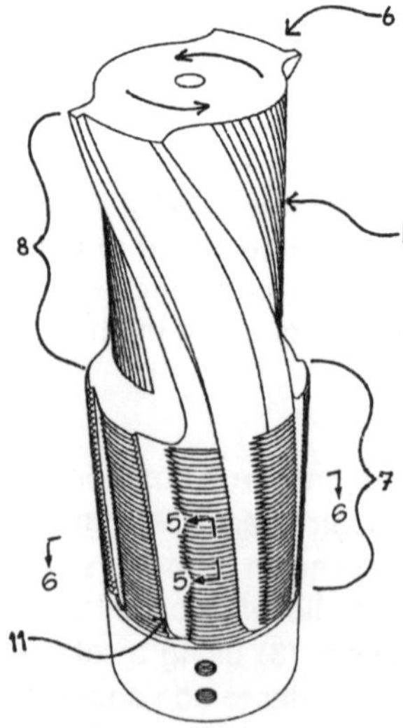

Fig. 27.4 A view of the masticating element

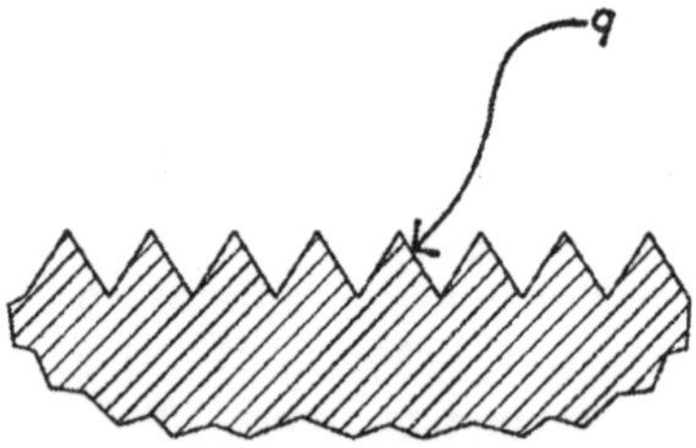

Fig. 27.5 A cut away view of the masticating element showing the masticating threads on the masticating portion of the masticating element

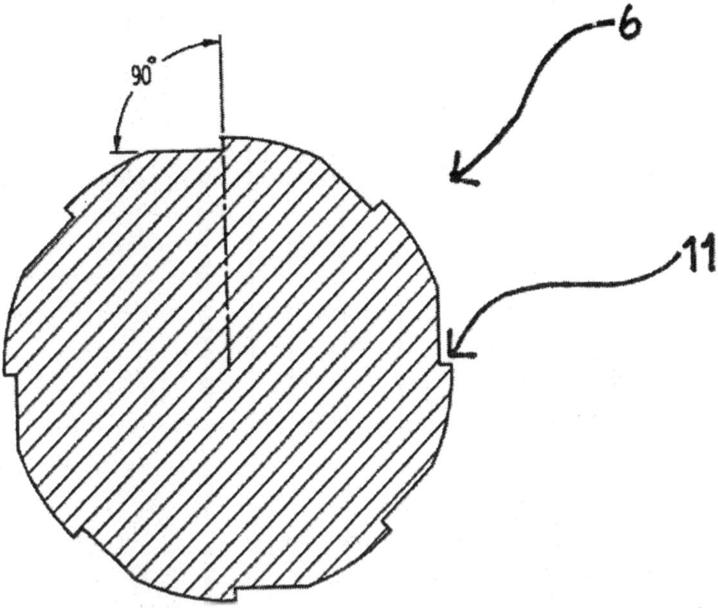

Fig. 27.6 A cut away view of the masticating element showing the attack profile of the cutting grooves on the masticating portion of the masticating element.

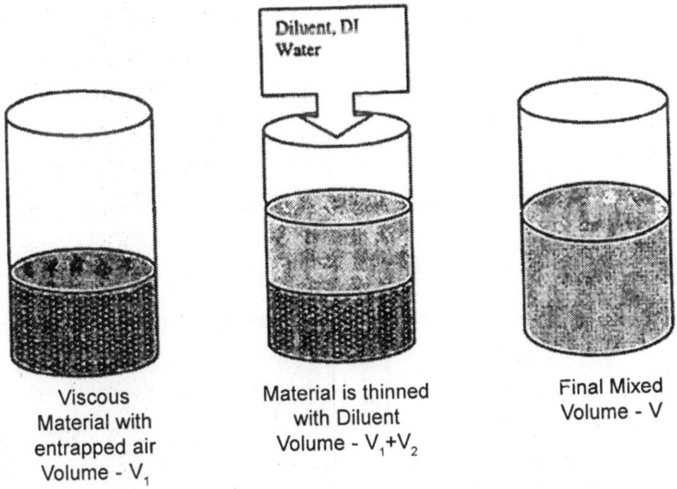

Fig. 27.7 A depiction of the test procedure

Trial No.	Machine Type	Fruit/Blend	Est. density g/cc	% Overrun
Trial 1	Disclosed apparatus	Banana	N/A	–4.46%
Trial 2	Disclosed apparatus	Banana	0.9594	–0.73%
Trial 3	Disclosed apparatus	Banana/Strawberry	0.7438	0.57%
Trial 4	Disclosed apparatus	Papaya	1.4980	–1.04%
Trial 5	Disclosed apparatus	Mango	1.1418	–1.64%
Trial 6	Disclosed apparatus	Mango	0.8303	–1.32%
Trial 7	Disclosed apparatus	Mango, Banana, Pineapple	1.0092	–1.29%

Fig. 27.8 A chart showing the resultant densities and overrun of the tested material.

threads (**9**) and a plurality of cutting grooves (**11**), as disclosed in FIGS. 27.4, 27.5, and 27.6 for masticating the frozen foodstuffs into the desired creamy texture. The cutting grooves (**11**) are semi-cylindrical in shape and form a 90 ± 20 degree angle of attack against the inside surface of the masticating chamber (**3**) when the masticating element (**6**) is rotating. The masticating element (**6**) also has a transferring portion (**8**) with moving shoots (**12**) as described above to move the masticated product out of the machine. The frozen fruits, vegetables, or other foodstuffs are easily loaded, masticated, and cleanly removed from the apparatus. When using frozen fruits this results in a non-dairy frozen dessert comprised of quick frozen fruit composite which has been masticated to achieve a desired creamy texture. The creamy texture is unique because it is the result of the sheering nature of the masticating element and not from added emulsifiers or overrun as shown in the test described below. Fruit, vegetables, or other frozen foodstuffs may be used alone or in combination with other flavoring agents such as vanilla extract, oils such as mint and powders or liquors such as chocolate and carob.

28

Apparatus for Defreezing Frozen Foods

Heretofore, in conjunction with the defrosting (or defreezing) of frozen foods, there have been proposed numerous types of defrosting apparatuses having various structures and configurations. Figures 28.6 and 28.7 of the attached drawings show schematically a typical structure of a hitherto known defrosting apparatus. In these figures, a reference numeral 1 generally denotes a box-like housing of a thermally insulated structure. Mounted on the top surface of this housing 1 are a compressor 3, a condenser 4 and a fan motor 5 which constitute major parts of a refrigerating unit 2. Also, a vaporizer or evaporator 6 also constituting a part of the refrigerating unit 2 is disposed at an upper position within the housing 1. A heating device 7 constituted by an electrical heater or the like is disposed beneath the evaporator 6 with a ventilating fan or blower 8 being mounted to the left of the evaporator 6 and the heater 7.

In the interior of the housing 1, a storage space for storing or accommodating therein frozen foods is defined by a horizontal shield plate 9 disposed below the heating device 7 and a pair of shelf receiving members 10 disposed vertically in opposition to each other and in laterally spaced relationship with the inner side walls of the housing 1. Each of the shelf receiving members 10 is provided with a plurality vertically spaced, L-shaped supporting fixtures 13, and shelves 14 are disposed between the paired shelf receiving members 10 while being supported on the respective supporting fixtures 13. The frozen foods 15 are placed on the shelves 14. A transverse air inlet port 11 is provided between one end of the shield late 9 and one end of the topmost shelf plate 14, while a transverse air outlet port 12 is provided between the other end of the shield plate 9 and the topmost shelf plate 14. Furthermore, openings corresponding to the inlet ports 11 and the outlet ports 12 are also formed in the shelf receiving members 10 between the adjacent shelves 14, these openings being denoted by the same reference numerals as the ports mentioned above, as will be seen in Fig. 28.7 (in which only the inlet ports or openings 11 are visible). The frozen foods 15 on the shelf plates 14 can be taken out from the housing 1 by opening a door(s) 16 mounted pivotally on the housing.

In operation, when the heating device 7 is activated simultaneously with the ventilating fan 8, the air within the housing 1 is first heated by the heating device 7, and the hot air resulting from the heating is forced to flow along paths indicated by arrows A, C, E and G through operation of the ventilating fan 8. More specifically, the hot air flows into the storage space through the air inlet ports or openings 11 mentioned above, and heat exchange takes place between the hot air and the frozen foods 15 on shelves 14 within the storage space. Thereafter, the air is expelled from the storage space through the outlet ports 12 as indicated by arrows B, D, F and H to be fed back toward the ventilating fan 8 for subsequent recirculation within the housing 1 in the manner described above.

In the prior art defrosting apparatus of the type described above, results of actually performed measurement of the hot-air temperature at the positions corresponding to the individual air inlet ports or openings 11 show that the temperature of the hot air becomes higher the higher the air inlet port is positioned, because high temperature air naturally exhibits a tendency to rise higher than low temperature air. Consequently, a longer time is required for defrosting the frozen foods placed on the lower shelves when compared with those positioned on the higher shelves, resulting in remarkable non-uniformity in the degree of defrosting among the foods to be defrozen. Under these circumstances, it was either necessary to put up with such non-uniformity in the defrosted state among the foods or alternatively to extend duration of the defrosting operation until the frozen foods placed on the lowermost shelf have been defrosted.

The defrosting apparatus can be operated as a cooling or refrigerating apparatus by causing a liquid coolant to flow through the evaporator 6 after the completion of the defrosting operation. In this case, when the defrosting period is extended for the reason mentioned above, the foods placed on the shelf of high level or position which are naturally defrosted earlier than those placed on the lower shelves would be rid of moisture, allowing surface fading or discoloration just about the time the foods on the lower shelf have been completely defrosted. It goes without saying that such faded or discolored foods are significantly reduced in commercial values.

Further, in the case where a relatively small amount of food is stored in the housing 1, there may be regions on the shelfs located along the flow path of the circulating hot air in which there are no foods to be defrosted. In that case, the hot air is fed back to the ventilating fan 8 through the associated outlet port 12 without undergoing heat exchange, which brings about the following. Namely, some defrosting apparatuses of the type described above are equipped with a temperature sensor on the air-intake side of the ventilating fan 8 for the purpose of determining the point in time at which the defrosting operation is to be terminated. When a predetermined temperature is detected by the sensor, a defrosting operation terminating signal is generated. Accordingly, when the situation mentioned above takes place in this type of defrosting apparatus, the sensor may detect the temperature of the hot air which has not undergone heat exchange with any foods, whereby a defrost inhibit signal would be produced to trigger the succeeding cooling or refrigerating operation notwithstanding the the fact that the frozen foods have not yet been satisfactorily defrosted. This means that a great difficulty is encountered in performing the automatic defrosting operation for a small amount of frozen foods.

Accordingly, it is an object of the present method to provide a defrosting apparatus in which frozen foods on all the shelves can be brought into contact with hot air of essentially uniform temperature so that all the foods can be defrozen satisfactorily within a substantially constant time.

Another object of the present method is to provide a defrosting apparatus capable of defrosting all frozen foods within a substantially constant time even when there is only a small amount of foods to be defrosted.

According to one aspect of the present method , an apparatus for defrosting frozen foods is provided, which comprises a housing constituted by an enclosing wall structure and defining inside of the wall structure a storage space for storing therein the frozen foods, the storage space including an access opening for allowing the foods to be put in and taken out of the storage space, a plurality of hot air inlet ports and a plurality of hot air outlet ports, the housing having a door for opening and closing the access opening, and further comprises heater means disposed at an upper position within the storage space for heating the air within the housing, ventilating means disposed within the housing for circulating the hot air resulting from the heating by the heater means throughout the storage space, inlet passage defining means which, along with the wall structure of the housing, define a hot-air inlet passage for introducing the hot air supplied from the ventilating means to the hot-air inlet ports, outlet passage defining means which cooperates with the wall structure of the case to define a hot-air outlet passage for introducing the air discharged through the outlet ports to the heater means, wherein the inlet passage defining means includes a guide plate disposed between the storage space and the wall structure of the housing and having an upper end secured to the storage space in a substantially hermetic manner, the guide plate having a communication aperture provided at a lower end thereof, a down-draft passage for the hot air defined between the guide plate and the housing for allowing the hot air fed from the ventilating means to flow therethrough, and an up-draft passage for the hot air defined between the guide plate and the storage space and communicated with the down-draft passage through the communication aperture, whereby the hot air is caused to flow into the storage space through the plurality of the hot-air inlet ports successively while being introduced through the upper-draft passage.

According to another aspect of the present method , there is provided an apparatus for defrosting frozen foods, which comprises a housing constituted by an enclosing wall structure and defining inside of the wall structure a storage space for storing therein the frozen foods, the storage space including an access opening for allowing the foods to be put in and taken out of the storage space, a plurality of hot air inlet ports and a plurality of hot air outlet ports, the housing having a door for opening and closing the access opening, and further comprises heater means disposed at an upper position in the storage space for heating the air within the housing, ventilating means disposed within the housing for circulating the hot air resulting from the heating by the heater means throughout the storage space, inlet passage defining means which, along with the wall structure of the housing, define a hot-air inlet passage for introducing the hot air supplied from the ventilating means to the hot-air inlet ports, outlet passage defining means which cooperates with the wall structure of the housing to define a hot-air outlet passage for introducing the hot air discharged through the outlet ports to the heater means, wherein the inlet port defining means includes a first guide plate disposed between the storage space and the wall structure of the housing and having a free upper end and a lower end provided with a communication aperture, a partition wall mounted between the first guide plate and the storage space in a hermetical manner for partitioning a vertical space between the first guide plate and the storage space into upper and lower passage sections, and a second guide plate disposed vertically within the upper passage section being coupled in a fluidtight manner to the storage space at an upper end and having a lower end provided with a second communication aperture, whereby a down-draft passage is defined between the first guide plate and the housing, while an up-draft passage for the hot air is defined below the partitioning plate between the first guide plate and the storage space and communicated with the down-draft passage through the first communication aperture, and wherein an upper down-draft passage portion is defined above the partitioning plate between the first and second guide plates with an upper up-draft passage portion being defined above the partitioning plate between the second guide plate and the storage space, the upper down-draft passage portion and the upper up-draft passage portion being communicated with each other through the second communication aperture, whereby the hot air is caused to flow along the up-draft passage and/or the upper up-draft passage portion separately while being introduced into the storage space through the plurality of hot-air inlet ports successively.

By the arrangement in which the hot air can be introduced into the storage space separately along the up-draft passage and/or upper up-draft passage portion, even a small amount of frozen foods can be satisfactorily defrosted by simply placing them in a region of the storage space which is associated with the up-draft passage or the upper up-draft passage portion and supplying the hot air only to that region.

For a better understanding of the present method , reference may be had to the accompanying drawings (Figures 28.1 to 28.7).

Referring to Figs. 28.1, 28.1A and 28.2, there is shown a first exemplary embodiment of the defrosting apparatus according to the present invention, wherein a reference numeral 1 generally denotes a housing of a thermally insulated box-like structure having a top surface on which mounted are mounted a compressor 3, a condenser 4 and a fan motor 5 which constitute major parts of a refrigerating unit denoted generally by a reference numeral 2. Further, a vaporizer or evaporator 6 constituting the refrigerating unit 2 in cooperation with the abovementioned components 3, 4 and 5 is disposed within the housing 1 at a top portion thereof. A heater unit 7 which may be an electrical heater or the like is mounted at a location beneath the evaporator 6. Furthermore, in the housing of the illustrated embodiment, three ventilating fans 8 are disposed on the left side of the evaporator 6 and the heater unit 7.

A storage space for storing or accommodating therein frozen foods is defined within the housing 1 by a shield plate 9, disposed substantially horizontally below the heater unit 7, in cooperation with a pair of shelf receiving members 10a and 10b which are vertically disposed in opposition to each other at a distance from respective side walls 1a of the housing 1 and extend downwardly to a bottom wall 1b thereof, and a rear wall 1c of the housing 1. Each of the shelf receiving members 10a and 10b is provided with a plurality of L-shaped supporting fixtures 13 with an appropriate distance therebetween, as will be best seen in Fig. 28.1A. Each of shelf plates 14 is adapted to be supported in a horizontal orientation on the associated pair of supporting fixtures

13 between the shelf receiving members 10a and 10b. In this manner, the storage space is divided in the vertical direction into a number of compartments which define, respectively, defrosting chambers of a small volume, wherein the frozen foods 15 are placed on the shelf plate 14 within each of the defrosting compartments. The shelf receiving member 10a located on the air inlet side of the storage space is provided with a transverse air inlet port 11 which extends transversely between one end of the shield plate 9 and that of the uppermost shelf plate 14, while the shelf receiving member 10b located on the air exit side is provided with a transverse air outlet port 12 which extends transversely between the other end of the shield plate 9 and that of the uppermost shelf plate 14. Furthermore, openings corresponding to the air inlet port 11 and the air outlet port 12 mentioned above are formed in the shelf receiving members 10a and 10b at positions between the adjacent shelf plates 14, respectively, as will be best seen in Fig. 28.2 in which the openings corresponding to the air entrance port 11 are shown representatively, being designated by the same reference numeral 11. In the case of the illustrated embodiment, two doors, i.e. upper and lower doors generally denoted by a numeral 16 are pivotally mounted on the housing 1 so that the food 15 resting on the shelf plates 14 can be removed from the housing 1 opening the corresponding door 16.

Further, mounted between the shelf receiving member 10a located on the air entrance side and the adjacent side wall 1a of the housing 1 is a solid guide plate 17 which extends downwardly from the one end of the shield plate 9 substantially in the vertical direction, wherein the guide plate 17 serves to define an air down-draft passage or duct 19a and an air up-draft passage or duct 19b between the shelf receiving member 10a and the adjacent side or lateral wall 1a of the housing 1, respectively. The guide plate 17 has a top end portion 17a which is connected in an airtight manner to the shield plate 9 at one end thereof, while the bottom end portion of the guide plate 17 is not connected to the bottom wall 1b of the housing 1 but spaced therefrom to form an air communication aperture so that both the ducts or passages 19a and 19b are in fluid communication with each other through an air flow reversing section 20 defined by the abovementioned air communication aperture.

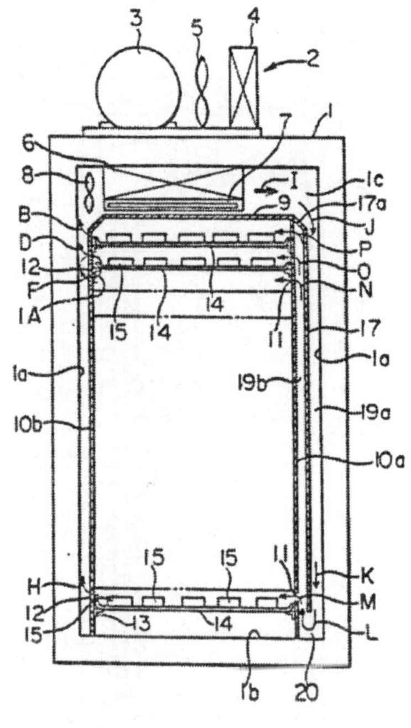

Fig. 28.1 Front view showing partially in section a defrosting apparatus according to an exemplary embodiment of the method with the doors being removed

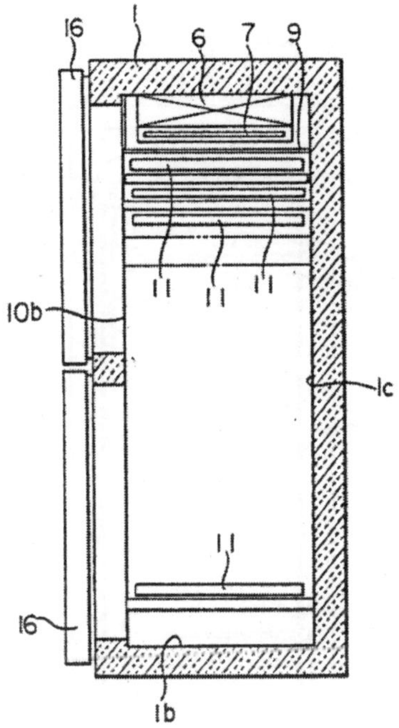

Fig. 28.2 Vertical sectional view showing schematically the defrosting apparatus shown in Fig. 48.1

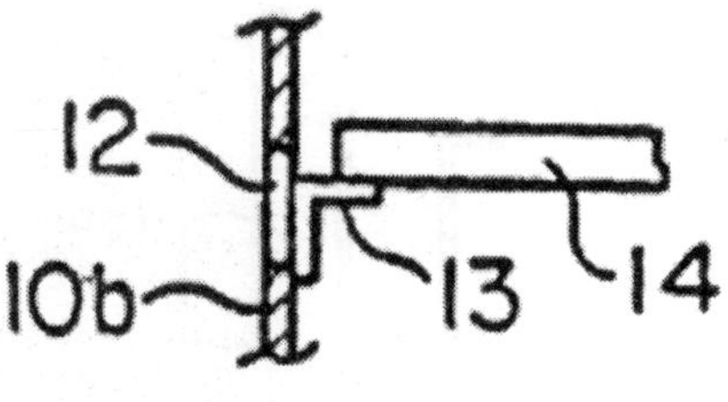

Fig. 28.1A An enlarged sectional view of a region 1A encircled by a broken line in Fig. 28.1

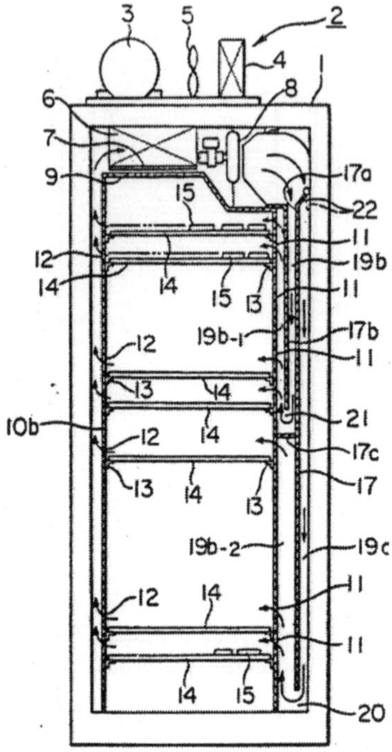

Fig. 28.3 A front view showing a defrosting apparatus according to another embodiment of the present method

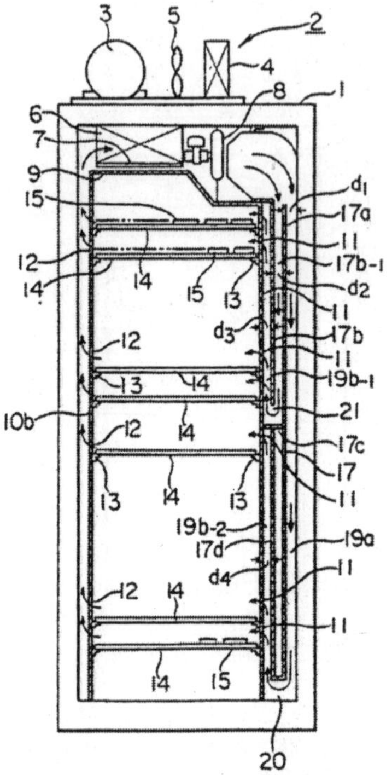

Fig. 28.4 A front view showing defrosting apparatus according to still another embodiment of the method

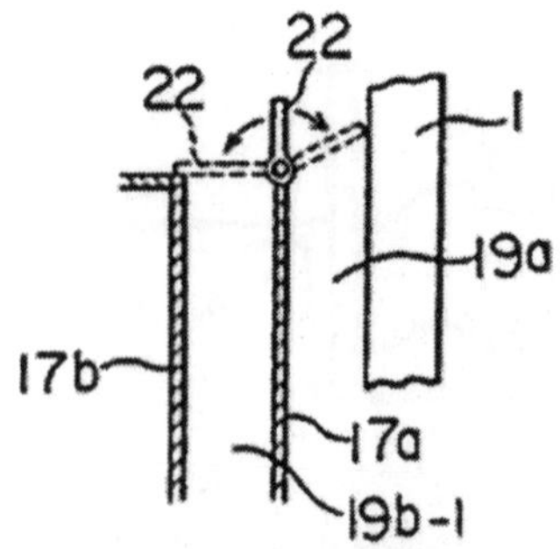

Fig. 28.3A A partially enlarged sectional view illustrating another mode for mounting the shutter plate in the defrosting apparatus shown in Fig. 28.3

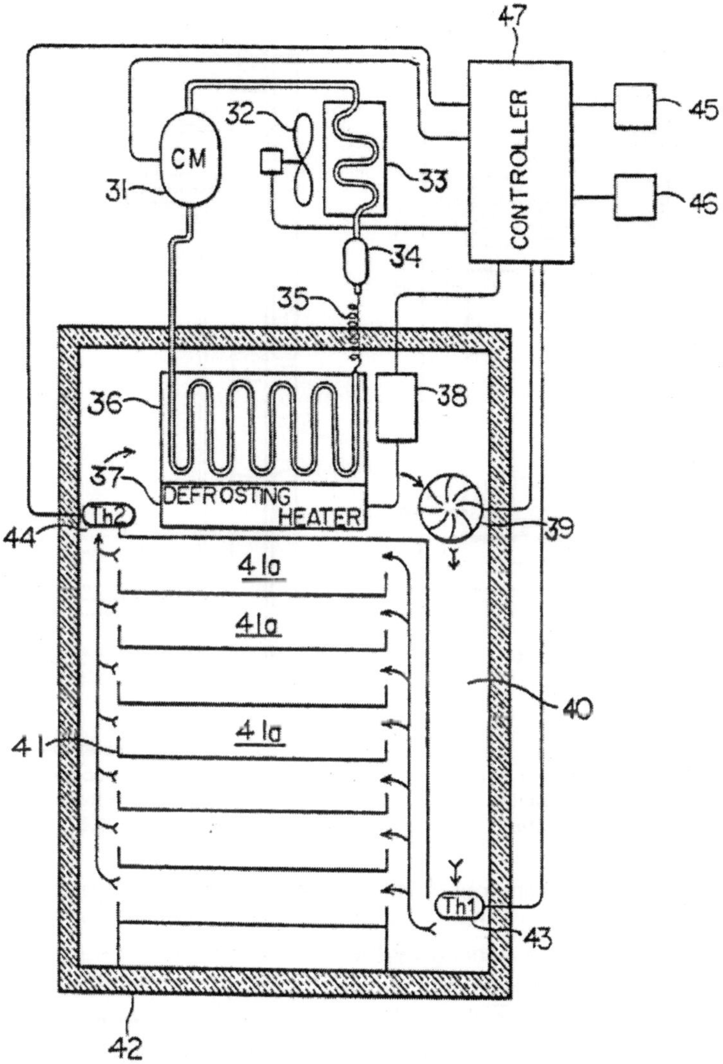

Fig. 28.5 A somewhat schematic front view, partially in cross section, showing a defrosting apparatus according to a still further embodiment of the method

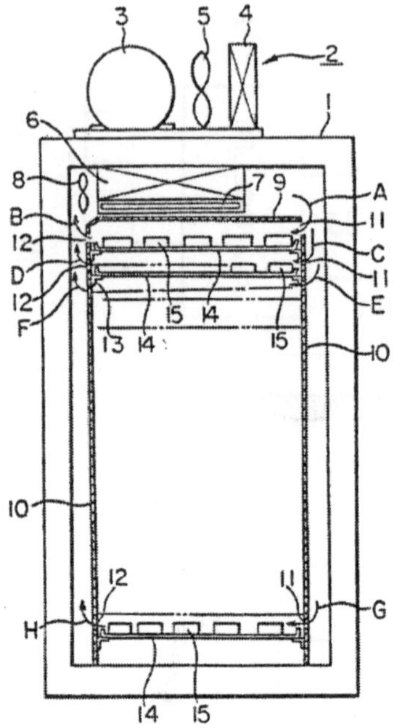

prior art

Fig. 28.6 is a front view similar to Fig. 28.1 and shows a structure of a prior art defrosting apparatus

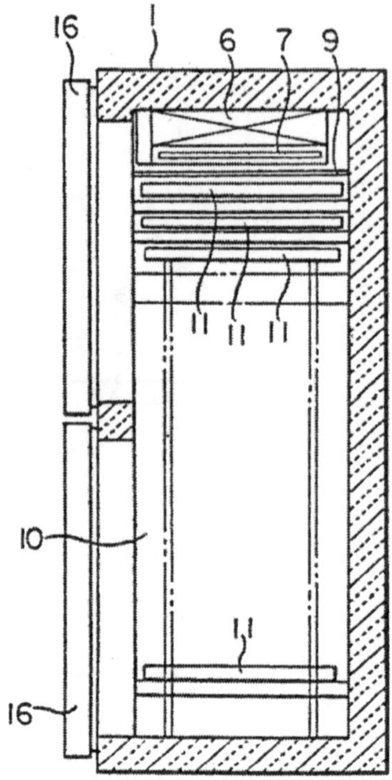

prior art

Fig. 28.7 is a schematic view showing in a vertical section the prior art defrosting apparatus shown in Fig. 28.6

In the defrosting operation, the heater unit 7 is activated with the ventilating fan 8 being simultaneously actuated. The hot air resulting from the heating by the heater unit 7 is forced to flow in the direction indicated by arrows I and J by the ventilating fan or blower 8 to pass through the passage 19a downwardly, as indicated by an arrow K toward the air flow reversing section 20, whereupon the flowing direction of hot air is changed over to the upward direction through the passage 19b. In the course of flowing upwardly through the passage 19b, the hot air flow branches into streams entering the defrosting compartments through the air inlet ports 11 successively starting from the lowermost one, as indicated by arrows M, N, O and P, resulting in that the frozen articles 15 disposed on the shelf plates 14 within the defrosting compartments are defrosted through heat-exchange with the hot air streams. After having undergone the heat-exchange process, the air is discharged through the air outlet ports or openings 12, as indicated by arrows B, D, F and H to flow back to the ventilating fan or blower 8 to be circulated repeatedly within the housing 1 in the manner described above.

As will be readily understood, the hot air stream entering a given one of the compartments has a higher temperature as that given compartment is located lower within the storage space. However, since the hot air within the passage 19b naturally has a tendency to rise up, balance is established between the temperature of the hot air and the flow of circulation. Thus, when the hot air circulating operation described above has been continued for a predetermined time, substantially uniform temperature distribution can be established among the food articles 15 on all the shelf plates, whereby all the foods can be defrosted substantially uniformly within an essentially identical defrosting period.

In connection with the detection of the completely defrosted state, it should be mentioned that the time determined empirically for defrosting the frozen foods may be set by a timer, wherein upon lapse of the set time the defrosting operation may be regarded as having been completed, because all the frozen articles can be defrosted within substantially the same time according to the present invention, as described above. Alternatively, the temperature prevailing on the intake side of the blower fan may be utilized for detecting of determining the completely defrosted state of all the articles. After the defrosting operation, the foods can of course be stored as chilled foods in a refrigerating environment by starting the operation of the refrigerating unit.

Fig. 28.3 shows a defrosting apparatus according to a second embodiment of the present method which differs from the preceding embodiment in that the ventilating fan 8 is so disposed as to suck the air from the side facing the evaporator 6 and discharges the air into the duct or passage 19b and in that the passage 19b is partitioned into an upper passage section 19b-1 and a lower passage section 19b-2 by a transverse partition wall or plate 17c. The upper passage section 19b-1 is further divided into two sub-passage portions by a second vertical guide plate 17b, which has an upper end portion connected in a fluidtight manner to the shield plate 9 of an offset configuration at one end thereof and the lower end is spaced from the transverse partition plate 17c. Furthermore, the first guide plate 17 has an upper end 17a which is not connected to the shield plate 9 and is adapted to cooperate with a shutter blade or plate 22 mounted pivotally on the lateral side wall 1a of the housing 1 in such a manner that when the shutter blade member 22 is at a position indicated by a broken line in Fig. 28.3, the hot air discharged from the ventilating fan 8 is introduced into both passages 19a and 19b while the hot air is forced into only the passage section 19b-1 when the shutter blade member 22 assumes the position indicated by a solid line in Fig. 28.3.

Referring to Fig. 28.3A, the shutter blade member 22 may be alternatively mounted pivotally on the first guide plate 17 at the top end 17a rather than the side wall of the housing 1. In this case, when the shutter blade member 22 is at a position indicated by a solid line in Fig. 28.3A, the hot air from the ventilating fan 8 is guided into both passages 19a and 19b. On the other hand, when the shutter blade 22 is rotated clockwise or alternatively counterclockwise, the hot air is introduced into only the passage section 19b-1 or alternatively into both the passage 19a and the passage portion 19b-2.

Parenthetically, it will be noted that when the shutter blade member 22 is at the broken-line position shown in Fig. 28.3 or at the solid-line position shown in Fig. 28.3A, the hot air is fed to all the passages. As will be readily appreciated, this situation corresponds to the case where there is no shutter blade member 22.

In operation of the defrosting apparatus shown in Fig. 28.3, the hot air flows into all the passages when the shutter blade member 22 is at the broken-line position. The hot air fed into the passage 19a flows downwardly therethrough and is reversed in the flow direction at the bottom section 20, continuing to flow upwardly through the passage section 19b-2 up to the partition plate 17c to enter the storage space through the inlet ports 11 formed in the shelf receiving member 10a, whereby the frozen foods 15 located in the lower region of the storage space are defrosted. On the other hand, the hot air fed into the upper passage section 19b-1 flows downwardly through the outer sub-passage to reach the flow direction reversing port 21, where the flow direction is reversed. The hot air then continues to flow upwardly through the inner sub-passage portion, finally entering the storage space through the hot air inlet ports 11 to defrost the frozen food articles 15 located in the upper region thereof. By the arrangement in which the hot air is supplied to the different regions within the storage space of the housing 1 through the separate passages in the manner described above, the temperatures at the various regions within the storage space can be made more satisfactorily uniform as compared with the preceding embodiment, whereby more uniform defrosting can be accomplished for all of the frozen foods placed on all the shelf plates 14 as a whole.

When the shutter blade member 22 is changed over to the solid-line position shown in Fig. 28.3 or alternatively to the phantom-line position shown in Fig. 28.3A, the hot air can be supplied only to the passage section 19b-1 or alternatively 19b-2. Accordingly, when a relatively small amount of frozen food is to be defrosted, the defrosting operation can be accomplished reliably within a short time by plating collectively the frozon articles in the upper or lower region of the storage space within the housing 1 and manipulating the shutter blade member 22 so that the hot air can be supplied only to the selected region where the frozen food articles are present.

Figure 28.4 shows a third embodiment of the defrosting apparatus according to the present method , which embodiment differs from the second one in that the shutter blade member 22 is not incorporated and that a spacer 17d is provided for the lower passage section 19b-2 between the shelf receiving member 10a and the lower portion of the first guide plate 17. In the case of this illustrated embodiment, the spacer 17d is in the form of an L-shape plate having an upper end and a lower end secured integrally to the lower end of the first guide plate 17 and the partition plate 17c. Due to the provision of this spacer 17d, the transverse dimensions d_1, d_2, d_3 and d_4 of the passage portions can be made substantially equal to one another, whereby the temperature distribution brought about by the hot air supplied to the lower and upper regions in the storage space from the lower and upper passage sections can be much more uniform, whereby a more uniform defrosting can be realized.

Referring to Fig. 28.5 there is shown schematically a fourth embodiment of the combined defrosting and refrigerating apparatus embodying the method , wherein reference numeral 42 denotes a box-like housing essentially made of a heat insulating material. A defrosting heater 37 and an intra-box air circulation fan 39 (i.e. fan circulating the air within the box-like housing) are provided within the box-like housing 42. Upon operation of the intra-box air circulation fan 39, the latter causes an air flow to be created through a duct 40 and spaces 41a defined between shelves 41 and which circulates as indicated by arrows. Disposed at an appropriate location (hereinafter referred to as an outlet port) within the duct 40 located on the discharge side of the air circulation fan 39 is a temperature sensor (Th1) 43 for detecting the air temperature at the outlet port, while there is disposed on the air exit side of the space 41a and preferably above the uppermost shelf 41, i.e. on the suction side of the air circulation fan 39 (hereinafter referred to as the inlet port) a temperature sensor (Th2) 44 for detecting the air temperature in the inlet port, wherein both of the temperature sensors 43 and 44 are electrically connected to a control circuit 47 also referred to as a controller.

Mounted fixedly in a conventional manner above the topmost shelf within the box-like housing 42 is an evaporator 36 which is connected to a compressor 31, a condenser 33, a dryer 34 and a capillary tube 35 in the manner shown in Fig. 28.5 to thereby constitute a cooling system of a known arrangement. Reference numeral 32 denotes a cooling fan for the condenser 33. The aforementioned defrosting heater 37 is disposed between the evaporator 36 and the uppermost shelf 41 and is connected to a thermostat 38 provided for the purpose of protecting the defrosting heater 37. The compressor 31, the defrosting heater 37 and the protecting thermostat 38 mentioned above are also connected electrically to the controller 47.

Further connected to the controller 47 are a defrosting start switch 45 serving for changing back and forth between the refrigerating mode and the defrosting mode as will be described hereinafter and a defrosting mode indicator lamp 46 which is lit during the defrosting operation mode. The control circuit or controller 47 is so arranged as to respond to the signals supplied from the outlet air temperature sensor 43 and the inlet air temperature sensor 44 for controlling the defrosting and refrigerating operations by supplying appropriate control signals to the compressor 31, cooling fan 32, defrosting heater 37, the intra-box air circulation fan 39 and others.

In the case of the illustrated fourth embodiment, the defrosting start switch 45 is constituted by a momentary type push-button switch which can be closed by being depressed by a user while opened when the switch is released. It should however be noted that the controller 47 remains in the defrosting operation mode once the defrosting start switch 45 is pushed even when the switch is subsequently released. Thus, the defrosting mode indicator lamp 46 continues to be lit, indicating that the apparatus is in the defrosting mode. At the end of the defrosting operation, the control circuit 47 is automatically changed over to the refrigerating mode.

Next, operation of the apparatus will be described in detail with reference to Fig. 28.5. In the refrigerating operation mode, the combined defrosting and refrigerating apparatus shown in Fig. 28.5 operates as a refrigerator while operating as a defroster or thawing machine in the defrosting operation mode. In the refrigerating operation mode, the air cooled down through heat exchange with the evaporator 36 of the cooling system is discharged from the intra-box circulation fan 39 into the interior space within the housing though the duct 40 to cool foods and the like disposed on the shelves 41 and then fed back to the evaporator 36 through the inlet port. In this refrigerating operation mode, the controller 47 responds to the signal supplied from the temperature sensor 44 mounted at the inlet port for turning on and off the compressor 31 and the cooling fan 32 so that the interior temperature within the housing can be maintained at a temperature level within a predetermined range of temperature.

According to the present method , the defrosting heater 37 is proportionally controlled during the defrosting operation so that the outlet air temperature detected by the temperature sensor 43 mounted at the discharge port of the air circulation fan 39 is maintained to be constant for defrosting the articles disposed on the shelves within the housing, as described hereinbefore. For having a better understanding of this control operation, the control performed for maintaining the outlet air temperature to be constant is described comparatively with the hitherto known apparatus in which such control is not carried out,

29

Machine for Cutting Frozen Foods

Frozen meat and fish constitute the bulk of the frozen food items which are the subject of the present method . Generally, the meat or fish is first formed into a block which is frozen to about 0°F. or lower. The low temperature is necessary for storage and subsequent processing of the block. Typically in such subsequent processing, the blocks are cut into slabs of various sizes, depending upon the desired final product. A frozen fish slab, by way of example, may be from three to four inches in width, from 16 to 20 inches in length, and from 1/4 to 3/4 inch in thickness. These slabs are then cut into frozen cut-up pieces which are battered, breaded and packaged for marketing.

The cutting step conventionally is carried out with a machine provided with a gang of meat saws or knives arranged in a cutting zone in a side-by-side array across the zone to cut the slabs simultaneously into a plurality of pieces of predetermined size. The frozen food slabs are carried on a table or support through which the saws or knives extend, and are stabilized during the cutting operation by stationary holddown means comprising essentially a metal plate positioned over the table from which it is spaced a distance sufficient to allow movement of the slabs along the table. Alternatively, the holddown plate is slotted to accommodate the saw blades. The slabs are fed onto the table from hoppers or feeders equipped with feed-regulating or reciprocating means. Preferably, a pusher means is provided to advance the slabs into the cutting zone, although the sequential feeding of the slabs can provide a self-pushing arrangement.

The aforementioned French Cut shape is obtained by employing a sloping table on which the frozen slabs travel. The saws protrude through slots in the table at an angle of about 45° with regard to the sloping surface of the table. In addition, the saws which are arranged in a line across the table are mounted on a single arbor so that the cuts through the fish slab are made simultaneously.

A number of difficulties have been encountered, particularly in making French Cuts in frozen fish slabs, primarily because of the coarser and more fragile texture of the fish. The sloping table with its parallel holddown plate was thought desirable because it facilitates to the downward movement of the slabs. However, such movement often is uncontrolled giving rise to misaligned positions of the slabs. Also, the simultaneous cutting action by the multiple saws exerts a substantial torque on the slab, which can result in further displacement or misalignment of the slab with regard to its direction of movement As a result, the final cut-up pieces may be irregular in shape.

Another disadvantage experienced with conventional machines is the difficulty of servicing and replacing the saws. Often, the malfunction of a saw blade can require the removal of all the saws and the arbor on which they are mounted. In addition, conventional machines have lacked versatility in the preparation of cut-up pieces of different shapes. Even adjustments to accommodate slabs of different thicknesses have been time consuming.

These and other disadvantages are overcome in accordance with the concepts of the present method by providing a machine with a horizontal table having an elongated surface which defines the path or line of travel of the frozen slabs and cut-up pieces resulting therefrom. A plurality of elongated slots is spaced and arranged in a staggered array diagonally across the table. A like plurality of circular saw blades protrudes through said spaced slots in the table, said blades defining an elongated and diagonal cutting zone. The blades rotate in planes angled with regard to the surface of the table, for instance, about 45°, to provide the desired French Cut.

As with the prior art, the frozen food slabs are fed onto the support from a feeder or hopper in a timed sequence. A plurality of pusher and holddown bars, driven by a pair of endless belts, engage the frozen food slabs in timed sequence with the feeder or hopper and move longitudinally above the machine support. The pusher and holddown means are slotted to accommodate the rotating saw blades.

In accordance with the method , the saw blades are arranged in gangs positioned in the diagonal line which extends across the surface of the support, each gang being offset laterally and longitudinally in the cutting zone with regard to an adjacent gang. In a preferred embodiment each gang is made up of a pair of saw blades. A typical machine can have five such pairs, each successive pair being spaced somewhat further from the receiving end of the machine and each such pair being mounted on a separate arbor. Thus, a slab is submitted to only two cuts at a time reducing the torque to which the slab is subjected. Further, the method with pusher and holddown bars obviates any tendency for the slabs to slide sideways or to otherwise move in a manner which would result in irregular shaped cuts. In addition, the invention facilitates repair and maintenance of the machine.

The accompanying drawings (Figures 29.1 to 29.9) are provided herein to better illustrate the method.

Now referring to Fig. 29.1, there is shown a machine for cutting frozen food slabs in accordance with the concepts of the present mathod . The machine comprises a table or support 10 which defines an elongated path of travel including the diagonal cutting zone A-E. The table has a receiving end 14 adjacent to which a feeder 16 is positioned. A plurality of pusher holddown bars 18 each engages frozen food slab 22 dispensed from the feeder 16 to move said slab 20 from the receiving end 14 through the cutting zone 12 to a dispensing end 22. In the embodiment illustrated, the pusher-holddown bars 18 are carried by a pair of endless roller chains 25-26 positioned above the table or support 10 parallel with the longitudinal side of the table or support.

In accordance with the concepts of the present method , the table or support 10 is provided with a horizontal surface which may be of metal or other materials of construction. The surface is provided with a plurality of elongated and parallel slots 28, 30; 32, 34; 36, 38; 40, 42; and 44, 46, arranged in pairs at five different cutting sites A, B, C, D, E. The sites are oriented in a diagonal array across the table from one end of the cutting zone 14 to the other, each cutting site being offset laterally and longitudinally from the adjacent site. Thus, each successive pair of slots is positioned further from the receiving end 14 of the machine than the preceding pair.

Referring to both Figs. 29.1 and 29.2, the machine is provided with a plurality of circular saws designated 28', 30'; 32', 34'; 36', 38'; 40', 42'; and 44', 46', the blades of which protrude through their corresponding slots which are dimensioned to allow free rotation of the saw blades. Each pair of saw blades, e.g., 28', 30' is mounted on an individual arbor 29, there being five arbors for the five pairs of circular saws or cutting sites. For convenience, circular saws 11 inches and 13½ inches, in diameter, have been found satisfactory. Only arbor 29 is shown. The saw blades are inclined at an angle between about 40° and 60° with respect to the surface 48 of the table 10, for instance, at an angle of about 45°. The blades protrude from the slots to a height slightly above the thickness of the frozen fish slab 20, generally three-fourths of an inch or less. The arbors are suitably driven by a drive means (not shown) in a clockwise direction so that the saw blades are cut in a direction opposite to the direction of advance of the slabs. Advantageously, the saw blades are easily removable from the arbors; and the arbors are individually removable from the cutting machine so that one or more pairs of saw blades can be removed for maintenance and repair or for accommodating slabs of smaller size without dismantling the entire machine.

The pusher-holddown assembly 18, which includes the pusher and holddown bars, and endless chain mechanism 24-26, are best illustrated in Figs. 29.1, 29.2 and 29.3. The endless chains are carried on two pairs of sprockets positioned on opposite sides of the machine at the receiving and dispensing ends 14 and 22, respectively, so that the chains travel in vertical planes parallel to the longitudinal sides of the table or support 10. Only two sprockets 52 and 54 for roller chain 26 are shown. A plurality of the pusher-holddown bars 18 are carried by the opposed endless chains at spaced intervals on the chains. This is accomplished in the embodiment shown by the use of specially shaped link members 56 interposed in the chain at spaced intervals. The link members are provided with a flange or pin 58 which engages opposite ends of the pusher-holddown bars assembly 18.

The pusher-holddown bars assembly 18 is generally U-shaped in cross-section with a downwardly extending pusher portion 60 in the form of a flap plate which extends almost to the surface of the table 10 when the pusher or holddown bars are on the lower run of endless chains 24-26. On the leading side of the pusher portion 60, there is provided a holddown portion 62. This is a portion which extends downwardly, in the form of a flap plate, but which is flanged with a forwardly extending horizontal flange portion 64, at an elevation spaced from the surface of the table 10 a distance essentially the same as the thickness of the slabs being cut.

As illustrated in Fig. 29.3, the end view of the holddown bar 64 is slotted to accommodate the saw blades which protrude above the table slots. Here, only the last two saw blades 44' and 46' are shown. The pusher and holddown bar slots are relatively wide since the saw blades are angled with respect to the table surface.

Attachment of the pusher and holddown bars assembly 18 to the endless chains is accomplished by employing a circular bar 66 which extends between the flange portions of link members 56. This circular bar in turn supports an intermediate elongated connector block 68 to which the pusher and holddown portions are attached. Shown in Fig. 29.1, the bar is angled at opposite ends so that it attaches to the link member 56 at right angles but extends across the table surface in an angled direction. The purpose of this is to help orient the food slab (i.e., frozen fish slabs) at an angle with regard to the direction of travel of the slabs in the machine. This can be varied depending upon the nature of the cuts desired.

In operation, the feeder 16 also referred to as hopper at the receiving end of the table 10 is positioned at the desired angle above the table, housing from 10 to 15 slabs of frozen food. A reciprocating plate (not shown) at the bottom of the feeder ejects the lowermost slab onto the table 10 and into position for engagement with an incoming pusher and holddown bars assembly. The movement of the endless belt carrying the assembly and the action of reciprocating plate are synchronized in such a manner that soon after the slab 20 is ejected pusher-holddown bars assembly arrives to engage said slab. Thus, the time at engagement lags slightly behind the time of slab ejection. Alternatively, the feeder can be positioned to deposit the slabs in the desired place by gravitational force with the help of guides (not shown). Also, if desired, the feeder can be positioned below the surface of the table 10 so that the top slab is ejected onto the table for engagement with the pusher-holddown bars assembly. In practice employing the depicted preferred embodiment, the frozen slabs move at the rate of approximately 90 slabs per minute. As the fish slab advances across the table it is cut by the first pair of saw blades 28', 30' and then by successive pairs in sequence. Throughout the path of travel on the table 10, the slabs are held firmly and experience no lateral movement. After the slabs are cut by the five pairs of saw blades, the cut-up pieces produced therefrom are moved from the dispensing end 22 of the machine for additional processing, such as battering, breading and packaging.

Fig. 29.4 depicts an isometric view of a frozen fish slab (3½ × 18 × ½ inch) oriented to the cutting position. The diagonal lines shown on the slab represent the cut edges to be made by the five pairs of saw blades.

Fig. 29.5 illustrates the final shapes of the cut-up pieces, piece C with parallelopiped shape representing the desired shape known as "French Cut." The longitudinal edge 70 and the hidden edge 72 of piece C are angled with regard to its surfaces due to the orientation of the saw blades, the angle being 45°. Piece B with its trapezoidal shape is known as a "tip cut" and piece A with a triangular shape is known as an "end cut." Advantageously, the cutting machine of the present invention has made possible the consistent production of seven, substantially identical French Cut pieces out of each frozen fish slab as shown in Fig. 29.4. Conventional machines were not capable of doing so.

Figure 29.6 is a schematic end view of a machine as described in Figure 29.1, 29.2 and 29.3 except for the pusher-holddown

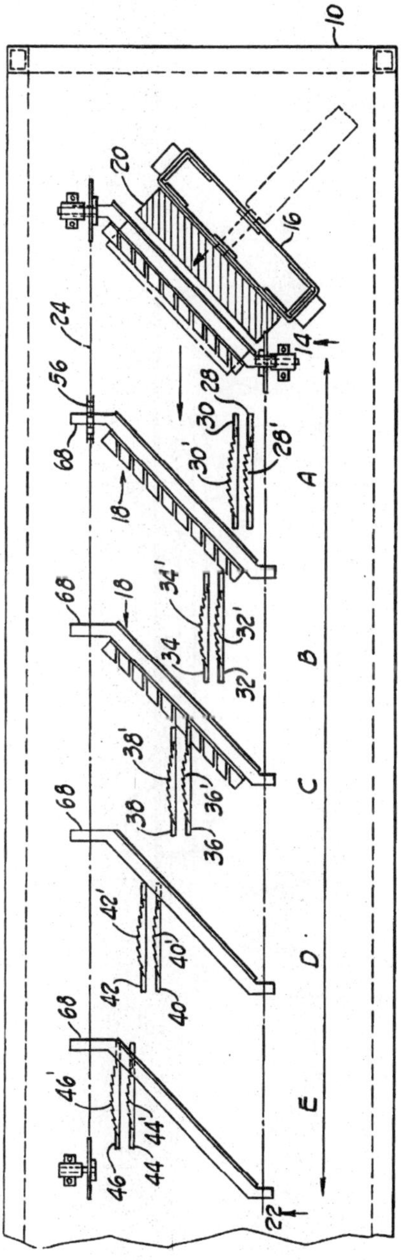

Fig. 29.1 A plan view of a substantial portion of a cutting machine in accordance with a preferred embodiment of the method

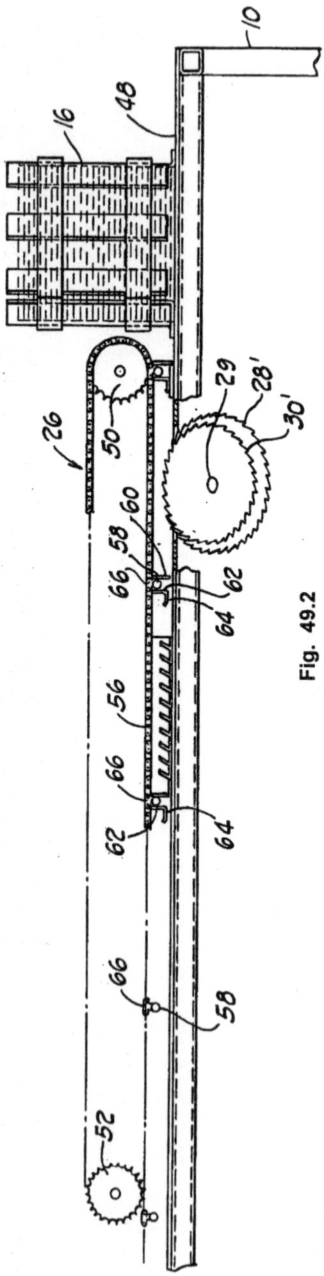

Fig. 49.2

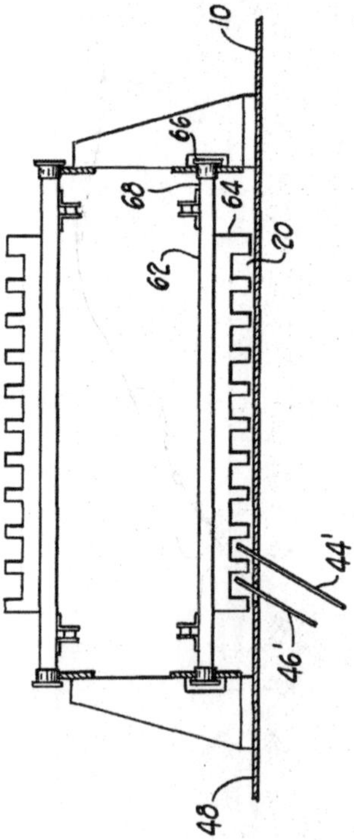

Fig. 49.3

Fig. 29.2 and 29.3 Elevation side view and end view, respectively, of the embodiment shown in Fig. 29.1

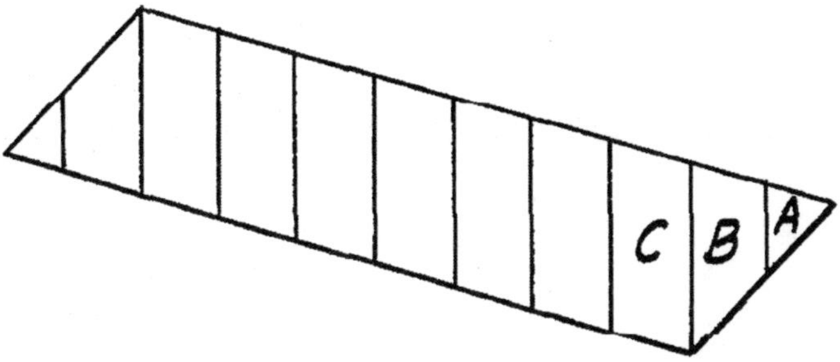

Fig. 29.4 An isometric view of a frozen fish slab

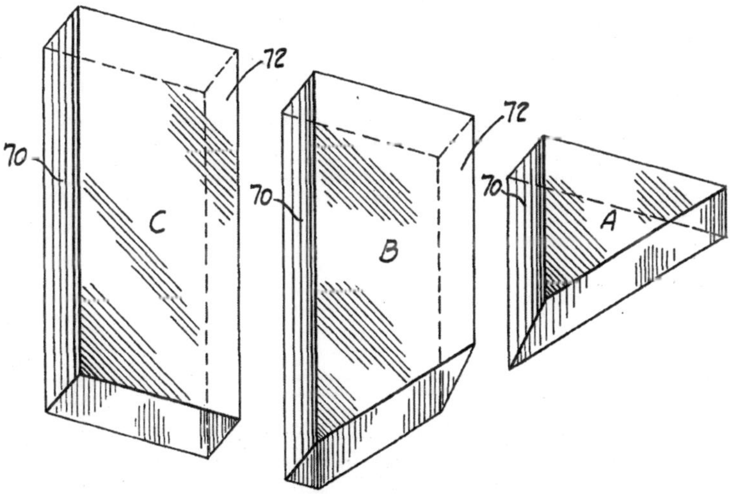

Fig. 29.5 An exploded view of cut-up pieces of the slab

bars assembly. Here, the same pusher bar 62 is connected to the endless belt through the same type of connector block 68, links 66 and roller chains 24-26. The holddown bar, however, is now a slotted plate 74 positioned above the table 10. Slotted plate 74 is parallel to the table's surface 48 with which it defines a space for the slab to move through said space being adjustable with the thickness of the slab. The slotted plate 74 conventionally is stationary. However, it can be movable as a part of a conveyor

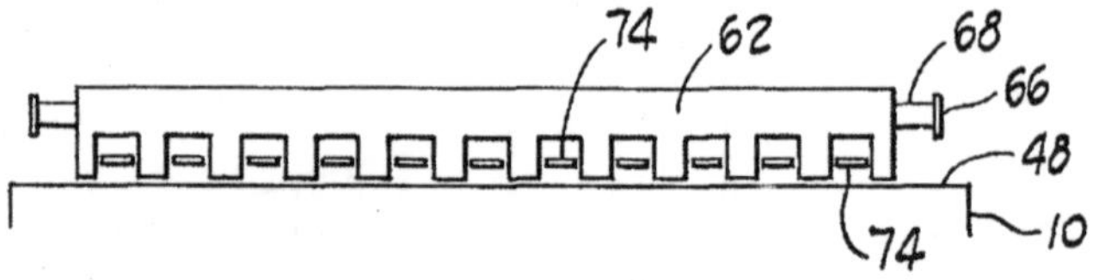

Fig. 29.6

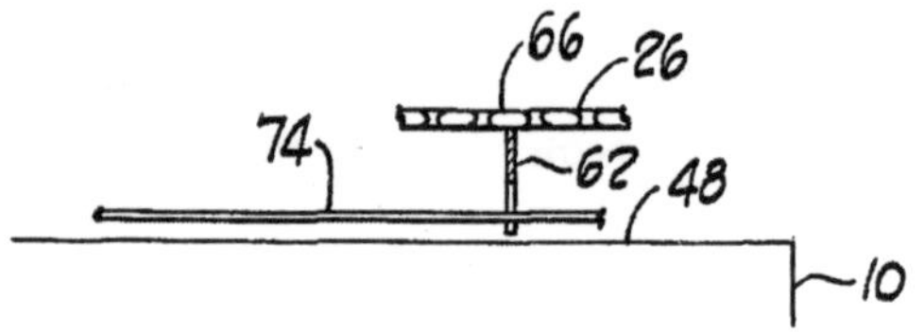

Fig. 29.7

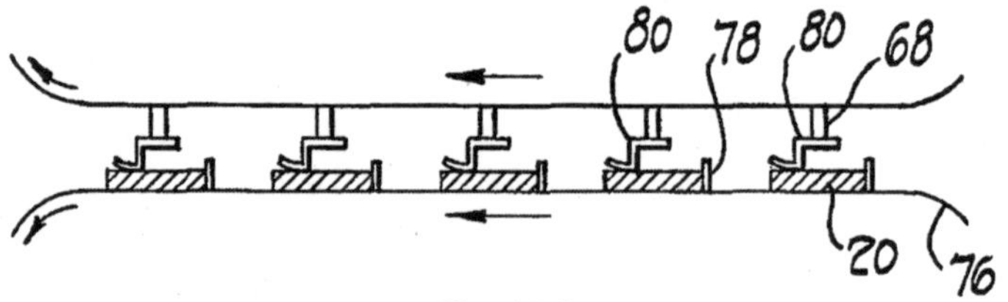

Fig. 29.8

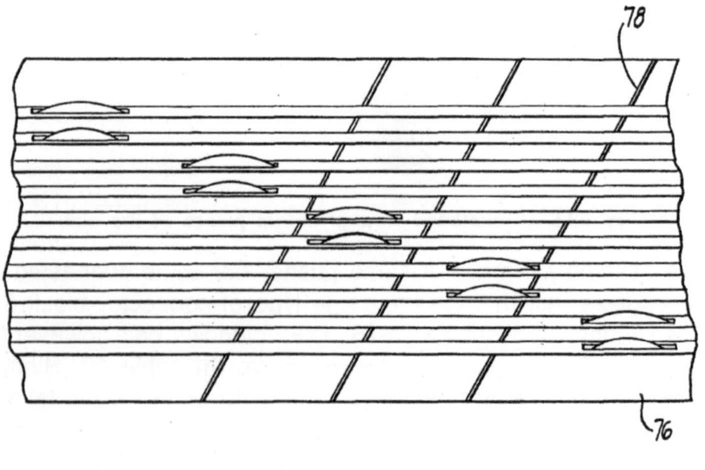

Figs. 29.6, 29.7, 29.8, and 29.9: Show modified embodiments of the support, holddown, and pusher means of the method

means (not shown) independent of the one moving the pusher bar 62.

Figure 29.7 is a schematic side view of the embodiment of Fig. 29.6, wherein the vertical bar 62 represents the pusher bar means which, in turn, is connected to the overhead conveyor means (not shown), through link 66. Holddown plate 74 is positioned parallel to support 10 with the area in between being adjustable to allow passage of the slab 20. In FIG. 29.7 the holddown plate 74 should not be construed only as a stationary fixed plate. As stated earlier, the plate can be movable and the movement in the direction of the path of travel can be effected by another independent conveyor means (not shown).

Figurs 29.8 and 29.9, respectively, show a side view and a plan view of another embodiment in accordance with the present invention. These embodiments are directed to movable support and pusher means. Thus the holddown means 80 depicted here is substantially the same as that described in FIGS. 29.1, 29.2, and 29.3. The pusher means, however, is now part of the movable support 76 in the form of vertical projection 78. Movable support 76 is, in effect, a part of an independent conveyor means (not shown), moving in the same direction as the conveyor overhead carrying the holddown bars, said support being slotted or divided, for example, into a plurality of belts to accommodate the various saw blades as detailed in Fig. 29.9. For efficiency and economy the movements of the two conveyors are timed in such a manner that the slab 20 is ejected onto the movable support 76 before the on-coming pusher projection 78. The holddown means 80 restrains the upward movement of slab 20 as well as its misalignment because slab is held tightly against the pusher projection and the support. Again, considering Figs. 29.7, 29.8 and 29.9 only one driven conveyor means is needed for movable support 76 having thereon the follower projections to advance the slabs which are contained by the slotted plate 74.

It should be noted that with the aforementioned embodiments the saw blades are maintained in the same position described earlier, i.e., inclined at an angle between 40° and 60°, to effect the desired French Cut. It is preferred that the saw blades are circular in shape.

30

Electrically Heated Frozen Food Server

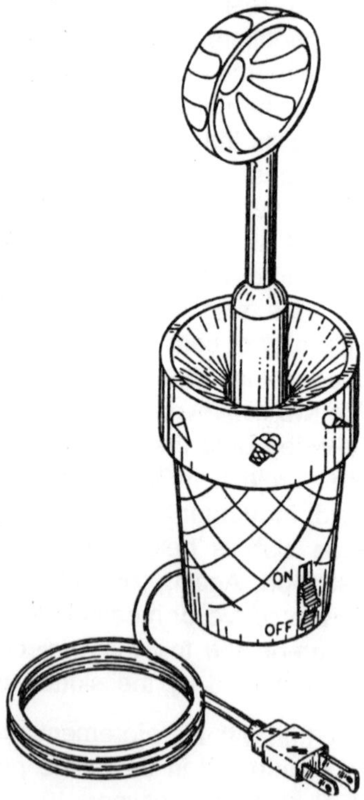

Fig. 30.1 A perspective view of an electrically heated frozen food server showing my new design;

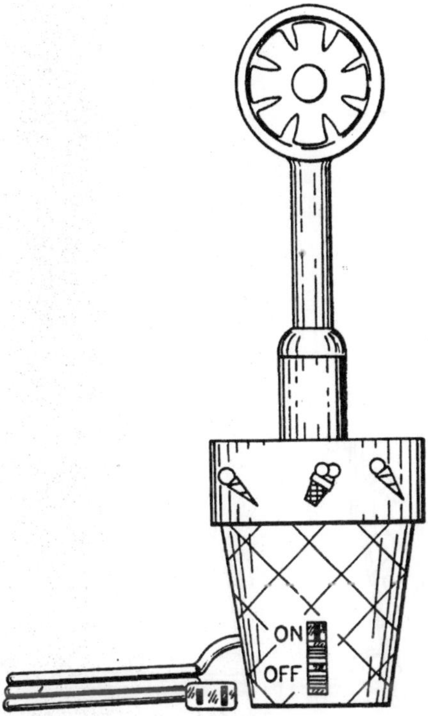

Fig. 30.2 Front elevational view thereof

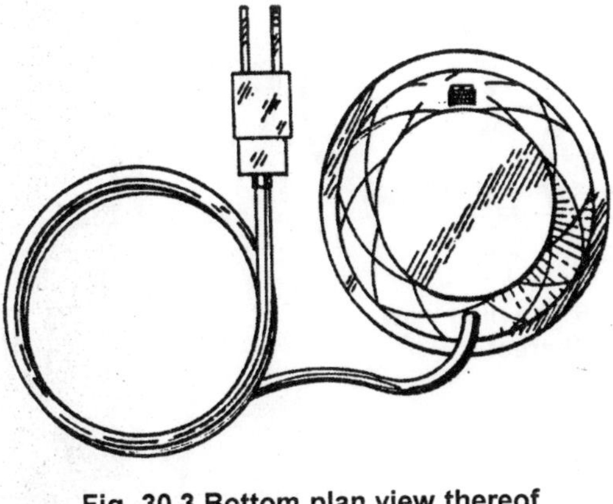

Fig. 30.3 Bottom plan view thereof

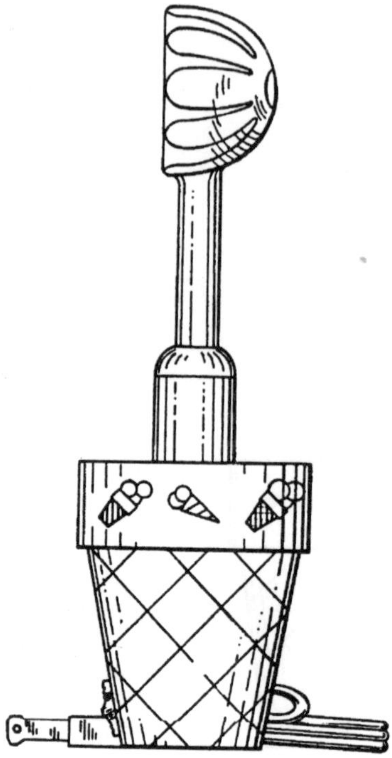

Fig. 30.4 Right side elevational view thereof

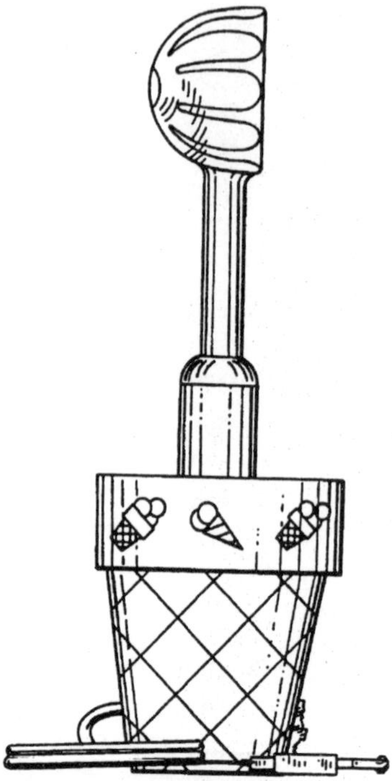

Fig. 30.5 Left side elevational view thereof

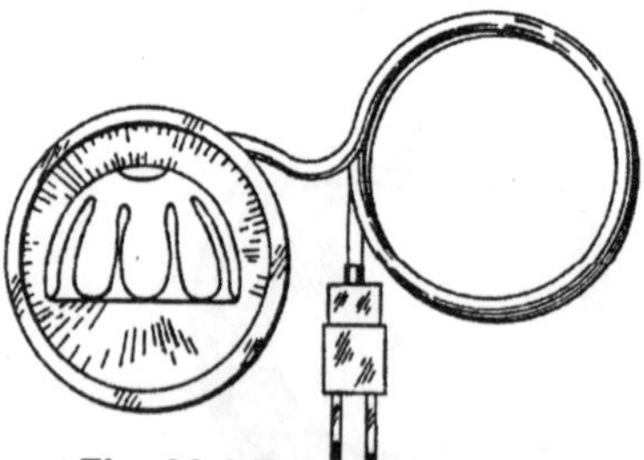

Fig. 30.6 Top plan view thereof

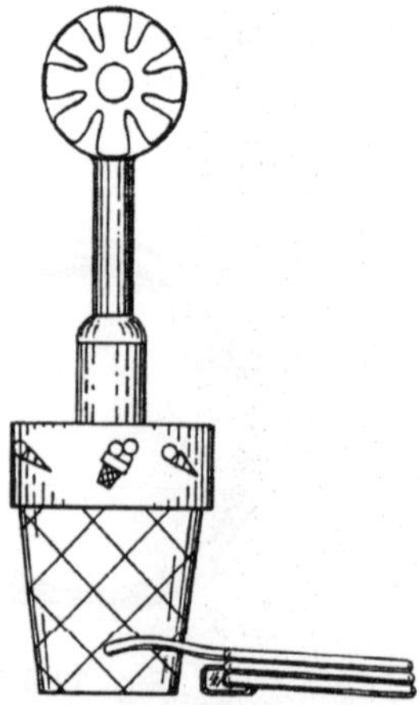

Fig. 30.7Rear elevational view thereof

31

Household Appliance for Making Frozen Food Products

Ice cream, frozen yogurt and other frozen food and confection products are available in packaged form in supermarkets and in other retail outlets. Yet in many households, a strong preference exists for such frozen products in homemade form. The reason behind this preference, say, in the case of ice cream, is that one can make ice cream with fresh cream, genuine fruit flavors and other natural ingredients of high quality that are free of chemical preservatives and other synthetic additives normally found in commercial products. The modern trend in our nutritionally conscious society is to avoid, if possible, all additives in otherwise natural food products.

Moreover, the cost of a homemade ice cream of high quality is usually well below that of a comparable commercially-produced product. Similarly, in the case of frozen yogurt, one can start with a home cultured yogurt of better quality than is available commercially in packaged form, for this yogurt is devoid of all objectionable additives.

Household ice cream makers are known which make use of a container or vessel in which the ingredients required to produce an ice cream of a desired flavor are stirred and homogenized. The vessel is surrounded by a freezing compartment which by heat transfer serves to chill the resultant mixture while it is being continually stirred. This freezing compartment may be of a type adapted to contain ice cubes or other forms of refrigeration.

The use of a manually-operated dasher in a household ice cream maker is a throwback to the farm days when ice cream was made by turning a crank handle. This type of operation is time consuming and difficult to carry out, and is therefore unacceptable to the modern householder. When, however, the ice cream appliance is motor driven, as in the Cristante patent, the appliance which incorporates this motor is then relatively expensive and bulky.

In view of the foregoing, the main object of this method is to provide a household appliance for making ice cream and other frozen food products in which motive power therefor is supplied by the existing power base unit of a standard household blender.

STRUCTURE OF APPLIANCE

Referring now to Figs. 31.1 and 31.2, there is shown a household appliance for making frozen food products such as milk shakes, ice cream and frozen yogurt. This appliance is constituted by a bowl assembly 10 in accordance with the invention which cooperates with the power base unit 11 of a standard household blender.

The case of unit 11 is provided with a top platform 12 having mounted thereon at equi-spaced circumferential positions adjacent the periphery four equi-spaced posts 13A, 13B, 13C and 13D. These define a cage or socket within which one normally places the bowl of the blender. However, in the present invention, nested in this socket is the bottom adapter ring 14 of bowl assembly 10 to maintain the assembly at a proper upright position on the platform. The cage or socket shown is by way of example, for various household blenders on the market have different forms of sockets or cages to accommodate the blender bowl.

As shown schematically in Fig. 31.4, housed within power base unit 11 is a motor 15 which is connected through a motor control circuit 16 to a cable 17 terminating in a plug 18 for insertion in an a-c power outlet (110 VAC). Motor control circuit 16 is

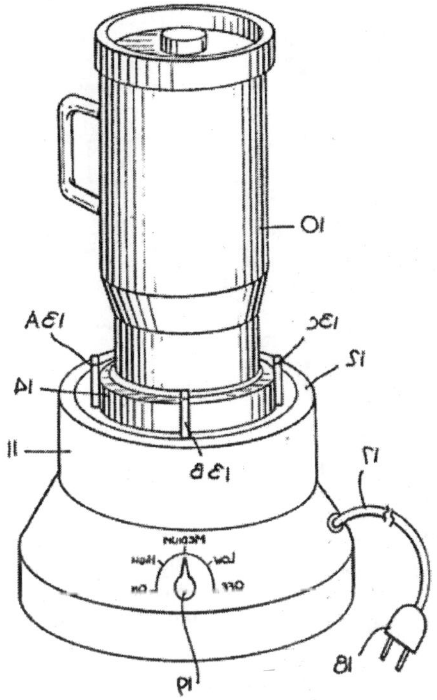

Fig. 31.1 Perspective view of a household appliance for making cold food products, the appliance being constituted by a bowl assembly in accordance with the method adapted to cooperate with the power base unit of a standard blender

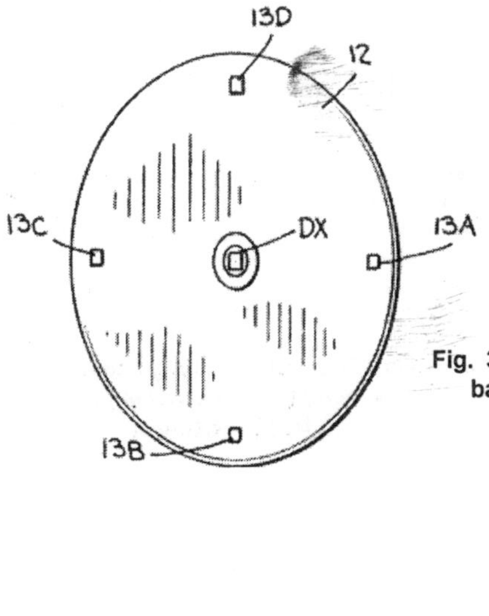

Fig. 31.2 Plan view of the power base unit showing the top platform thereof

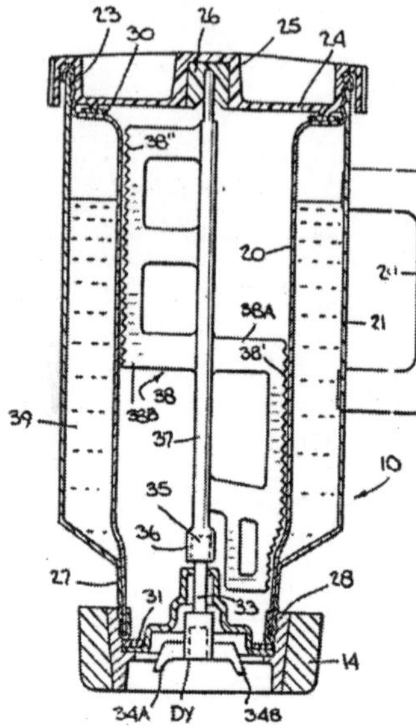

Fig. 31.3 Longitudinal section taken through the bowl assembly

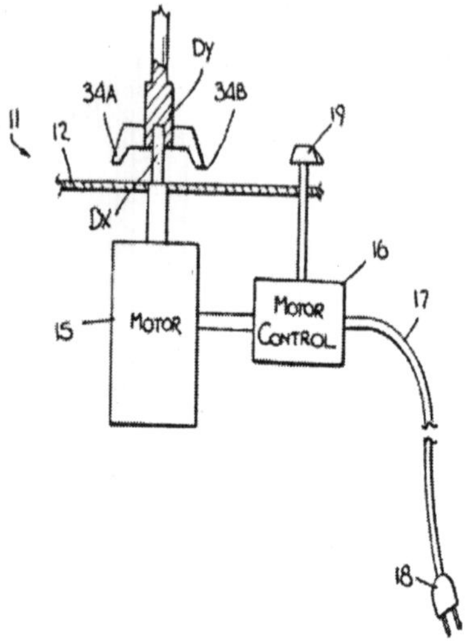

Fig. 31.4 Detail showing how the drive coupler of the unit engages the driven coupler of the assembly

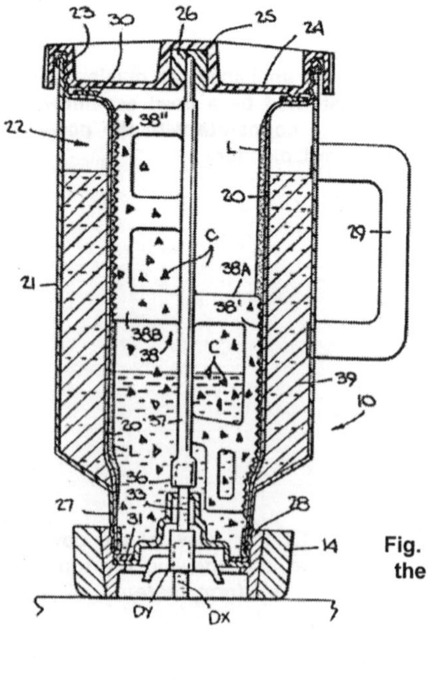

Fig. 31.5 Schematically illustrates the action of the dasher of the bowl assembly.

operated by a knob 19 which, as shown in Fig. 31.1, has an "off" setting as well as low, medium and high speed "on" settings to vary the motor's rotary speed accordingly.

Motor 15 is provided with a shaft that extends upwardly through top platform 12 and terminates in a drive coupler DX which in the form shown is a square shaft section of the type found in the power base unit of a Waring type blender. However, in other commercial household blenders, the drive coupler of the unit takes other forms to complement the driven coupler on the bowl. Thus, the couplers may have a star or toothed formation.

Referring now to Fig. 31.3, it will be seen that bowl assembly 10 comprises a cylindrical inner cannister 20 and a cylindrical outer shell 21, both preferably fabricated of aluminum. These are shaped to define a double-walled jacket 22 having an internal cavity. The upper end portions of inner cannister 20 and outer shell 21 are joined together to form an upper rim section 23. The wall of cannister 20 in rim section 23 is formed to create an internal threading for screwing a screw-on lid 24, preferably of clear plastic. Lid 24 is provided with a central hub 25 having seated thereon a bearing 26 of Teflon (PTFE) or other low friction material suitable for bearings, such as nylon.

The lower end portions of inner cannister 20 and shell 21 are joined together to form the cylindrical bottom section 27 of the bowl assembly. The wall of shell 21 is shaped to define external threading to receive a screw-on bottom ring 28 which has a tapered cross section. Fitting onto ring 28 is the adapter ring 14 which effectively enlarges the diameter of ring 28 so that it can nest snugly within cage posts 13A to 13D on platform 12 of the power base unit.

With other commercially available power base units, different ring diameters may be required. Thus, in some instances one may dispense with adapter ring 14 and place bottom ring 28 directly within the cage of the unit, and in other instances it may be necessary to use an adapter ring 14 whose diameter is different from that shown.

Attached to outer shell 21 is a handle 29. Seated on top of jacket 22 is an annular gasket 30 which is engaged by lid 24 to prevent leakage of fluid when the appliance is in operation.

A gasket 31 is also provided below the bottom section 27 of the assembly to prevent leakage in this region.

The re-entrant bottom wall 32 of the assembly which has a corrugated dome formation is adapted to support for rotation a short axle 33 which extends through the center of this wall. The lower end of axle 32 terminates in an external driven coupler DY having a square socket therein which is dimensioned, as shown in Fig. 31.4, to receive the square drive coupler DX of the unit when the bowl assembly is placed on platform 12 of the power base unit.

Driven coupler DY is also provided with opposing wings 34A and 34B which are adapted to fit within the teeth of a gear or star type drive coupler. Thus, driven coupler DY acts as a universal coupler for use in conjunction with various types of power base unit drive couplers.

The upper end of short axle 33 terminates in a shaft coupler 35 which is received within the complementary lower end socket 36 of the shaft 37 of a rotatable dasher 38. The upper end of dasher shaft 37 is received within bearing 26 on the removable lid 24. Thus, after the lid is removed from the bowl assembly, one can then remove dasher 38 for cleaning or replacement.

Dasher 38 is formed by a lower blade 38A secured to shaft 37 and a diametrically-opposed upper blade 38B, both blades being formed of flexible material and having large apertures therein. The edges 38' and 38" of blades 38A and 38B are in a serrated form and act to scrape off any ice build-up on the inner wall of cannister 20.

The internal cavity of the double walled jacket 22 is almost fully filled with a freezing agent 39 having a high heat capacity so that once frozen, it remains in this state for a prolonged period, even though it is in heat exchange relationship with a warmer, non-frozen body. This agent may be of the type disclosed in the Uesaka et al. patent 4,488,817 in which added to a water base are organic or inorganic salts such as glycol, ethyl glycol, polypropylene glycol, urea or NaCl. Or the freezing agent may be of the type disclosed in the Held et al. patent 4,357,809 in which use is made of a gel including cornstarch and borax. Or the gel may be of the type disclosed in the Spencer patent

3,885,403 formulated from water and a freezing point depressant, glycerine and propylene glycol with a thickening agent. The present invention encompasses any known freezing agent having a high heat capacity.

OPERATION OF APPLIANCE

Let us assume the appliance is to be used for a simple task; that is, to produce a chilled mixed drink whose components are various fruit juices and vodka or some other alcoholic beverage.

The bowl assembly 10 must be held in storage in a household freezer or in the freezer compartment of a household refrigerator for a period sufficient to thoroughly freeze the freezing agent. When the bowl assembly is to be put to use to produce the above-noted mixed drink, it is taken out of the freezer and placed on the platform of whatever power base unit is available in the household. Lid 24 is unscrewed from the assembly, and the various liquid ingredients are poured into cannister 20. Then the motor of the power base unit is turned on at the lowest speed to thoroughly intermingle the ingredients for a brief period, after which the motor is turned off to allow for heat transfer from the jacket having the frozen agent therein for a period sufficient to form a thin layer L of the frozen mixture on the inner surface of the cannister, as shown in Fig. 31.5.

The motor is then turned on again at low speed so that the serrated eges of blades 38A and 38B, which have sharp teeth, act to scrape the surface of frozen layer L to form fine ice chips C which, as indicated by the arrows, pass through the openings in the blades and are dispersed throughout the liquid mixture. Then the motor speed is increased to cause the mixture to froth, as a result of which air bubbles are intermingled therewith. This action is continued to permit further heat transfer between the liquid and the frozen jacket until the liquid mixture is very cold and ready to be served. At this point the motor is turned off, and the mixture is poured from the bowl assembly into glasses.

The same procedure can be used to make frozen daiquiries and similar alcoholic or non-alcoholic drinks such as milk shakes. The appliance is also usable in the making of ice cream, in which event fresh cream, flavoring and other ingredients are poured into the bowl and intermingled therein while being chilled to the desired consistency.

And instead of a dasher, use may be made of a rotating comminuting blade of the type used in a conventional blender, so that the appliance can be used in the same fashion as a conventional blender to grind up and mix ingredients, the difference being that the resultant mixture is chilled.

Because the dasher is removable from the bowl assembly, this makes it possible to withdraw the dasher after the ingredients are thoroughly mixed and before it has a consistency so viscous as to make removal difficult. Thus, in the case of ice cream and frozen yogurt, the dasher may be removed at an intermediate stage in the operation, then permitting heat transfer to continue until the product has the desired final consistency. Also, the fact that the dasher is removable makes it possible to separately clean this component as well as the bowl and lid therefor.

32

Frozen Food Transport

TRANSPORT AND STORAGE

Storage conditions should be maintained during transport. Transport vehicles are essentially cold stores on wheels but are more difficult to maintain at the correct storage temperature than large cold stores due to several factors:

(a) supplementary heat is introduced during loading and unloading the vehicle;

(b) defrosting has a more severe effect on foods compared to refrigerated stores (more restricted space for the coils, more humid air inlet);

(c) possible close contact between the foods and the lateral walls, through loading and displacements of the cargo, connected to the forces that the road circulation generates in the cargo (centrifugal forces).

Regarding (a), two aspects are important: the first is the time that is required for the loading/ unloading operation (the time must be the lowest possible) and the second is the level of protection of the cargo during these operations (Fig. 32.1).

Regarding (c), the problem can be severe when the vehicle is not operating and the sun is irradiating the roof and a lateral wall. In this case the external surface temperature can reach values close to 90°C and the internal surface temperature can be increased as a function of the proximity of the cargo to the wall (Fig. 32.2).

MODES OF TRANSPORT

The essential component of any system to transport frozen food is an insulated container. International transport vehicles have to comply with the ATP and ISO rules, where an overall coefficient of heat transfer (*K* coefficient) is defined and must be lower than $0.4 Wm^{-2} K^{-1}$ (ISO, 1996) The overall coefficient of heat transfer, which represents the insulating capacityof the equipment, is defined by the following formula:

$$K = WS^{-1}T^{-1}$$

where *W* is the thermal capacity required in a body of mean surface area *S* to maintain the absolute difference *T* between the mean inside temperature *Ti* and the mean outside temperature *Te*, during continuous operation, when the mean outside temperature *Te* is constant. The second main component is a refrigerating unit or a system to store energy at a temperature lower than that prescribed for the transport.

In some European countries (France, Germany, Italy, Portugal, etc.) national standards are very similar to ATP or ATP is adopted as national law. Also Australian standards have strong connections with ATP. In USA, a lot of voluntary standards are present, but no single standard is universally accepted.

The insulation

The main problem of the insulated container is that the insulating materials that can now be used have thermal conductivity coefficients that are too high and consequently the measured *K* values in the containers are very close to the limit values. The *K* values can be improved by enlarging the lateral wall thicknesses, but this then reduces the internal loading area available for storage. In Europe most cargo is palletised. A double pallet is 2.4 m wide whereas the width of European ATP vehicles are 2.6 m. Consequently, the wall thickness cannot be greater than 0.1 m and this is insufficient to provide enough space for pallets and the insulation thickness that is necessary for a low *K* value. Some

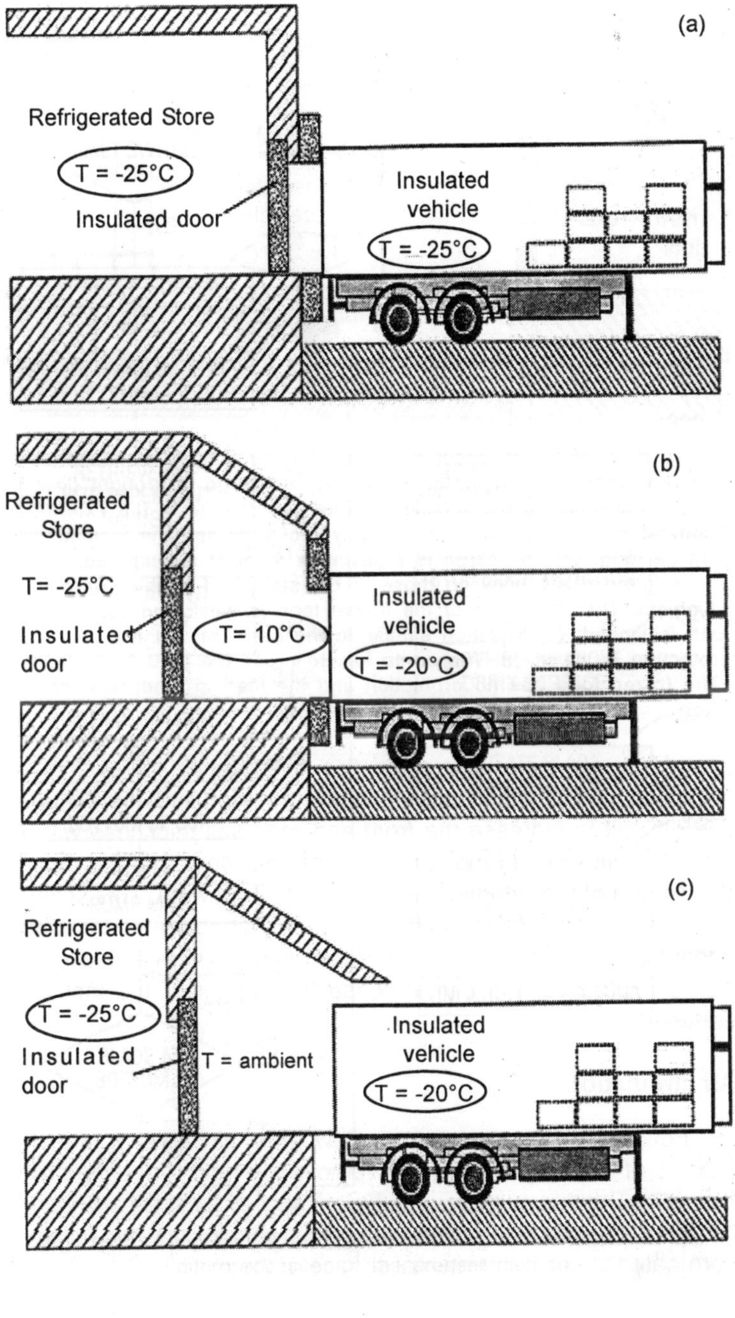
(a)
Refrigerated Store
T = -25°C
Insulated door
Insulated vehicle
T = -25°C
(b)
Refrigerated Store
T= -25°C
Insulated door
T= 10°C
Insulated vehicle
T = -20°C
(c)
Refrigerated Store
T = -25°C
Insulated door
T = ambient
Insulated vehicle
T = -20°C

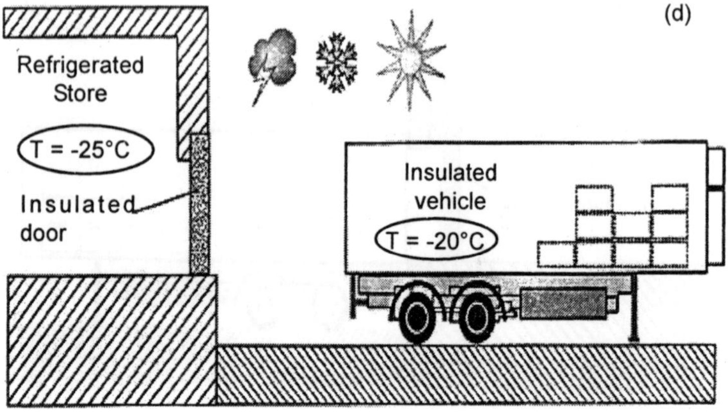

Fig. 32.1: Different layout situations for the loading of insulated vehicles from the refrigerated store: (a) The cargo is brought directly from the store to the vehicle, without any change in the external temperature. The frozen food is highly protected and the loading time can be long; (b) The cargo is crossing a room at a temperature that is intermediate between those of the store and of the external ambient. The protection of the frozen food is weak and the time to load is limited; (c) Situation similar to the case (b), but the degree of protection is lower: (d) The cargo has to cross the yard to be loaded. The frozen food has no protection and the loading time must be as short as possible.

manufacturers try to overcome this difficulty by increasing the thickness of the other walls (mainly the roof and the floor, as it is difficult to increase the front and rear wall thickness without affecting the ease of movement of the rear door and the correct positioning of the refrigerating unit on the front wall). This solution can reduce the *K* value; it also has an influence on the insulation ageing (the ageing is a function of the average thermal thickness), but is expansive and can increase the weight of the insulated container.

Air circulation

For a frozen cargo, the air flow must circulate around the volume of the cargo, in order to remove the heat that enters from the walls. For this purpose, a sufficient air gap must be maintained between the cargo and the walls (this can be created using a corrugated sheet in the internal surface of the vehicle or positioning

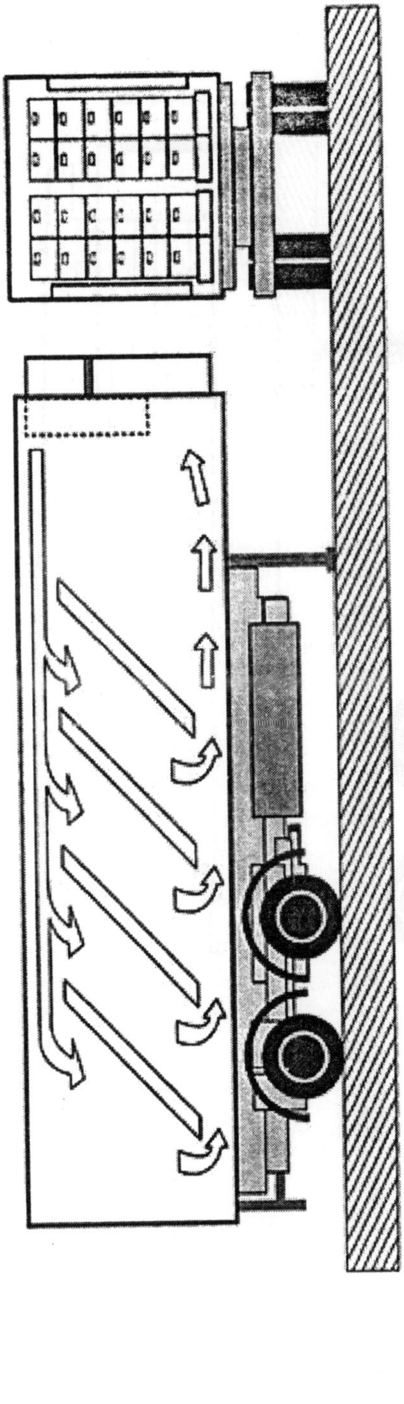

Fig. 32.2: Schematic drawing of the slowing bars between the internal walls surface and the frozen food cargo, in order to create some channels for the refrigerated air circulation. The return channels are made by the free spaces in the pallets.

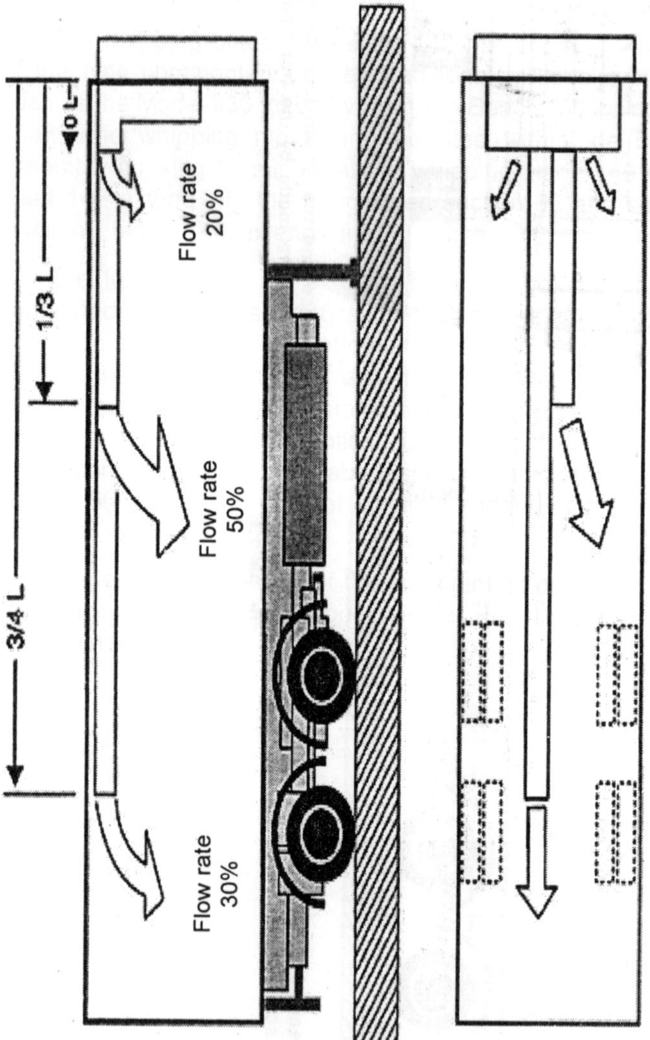

Fig. 32.3: Schematic drawing of the air ducts in the roof of a refrigerated vehicle.

some thick stowing bars between the cargo and the wall (Fig. 32.2). The use of roof ducts is fundamental: these ducts are normally manufactured from textile material and have different lengths: the shorter one should be open at one-third of the length of the roof, and the longer one at threefourths of the length of the vehicle (Fig. 32.3). The air flow rate is therefore sub-divided into a direct flow from the refrigerating unit immediately after the fans of the evaporator, and into a secondary flow that is directed from the ducts. The direct flow should be about the 20% of the total flow, the shorter duct will provide approximately 50% of the flow and the longer duct the residual 30%.

Refrigerating power

The most widely used system to refrigerate the inlet of the vehicle is a vapour compression mechanical system. Several configurations are possible, as shown in Table 32.1 For many years R12 was used as the refrigerant in these systems. R502 was an alternative choice, mainly for frozen containers. These refrigerants were banned by the Montreal Protocol and subsequently were replaced by R404A for higher capacities (large containers) and R134a and for lower capacities (small containers) and marine containers. Occasionally other gases are used as refrigerants but these are rare.

Several alternative refrigerants are currently undergoing development and may have potential in the future. These include:

(a) CO_2 in a transcritical cycle;

(b) air cycle;

(c) propane or other flammable refrigerants

CO_2, in a very limited number of examples, is also used in a direct form where it is directly expanded into an evaporator in the inlet of the vehicle from a tank of liquid CO_2.

Energy storage

Energy storage systems that maintain a low temperature below that required by the cargo are often used in transport vehicles.

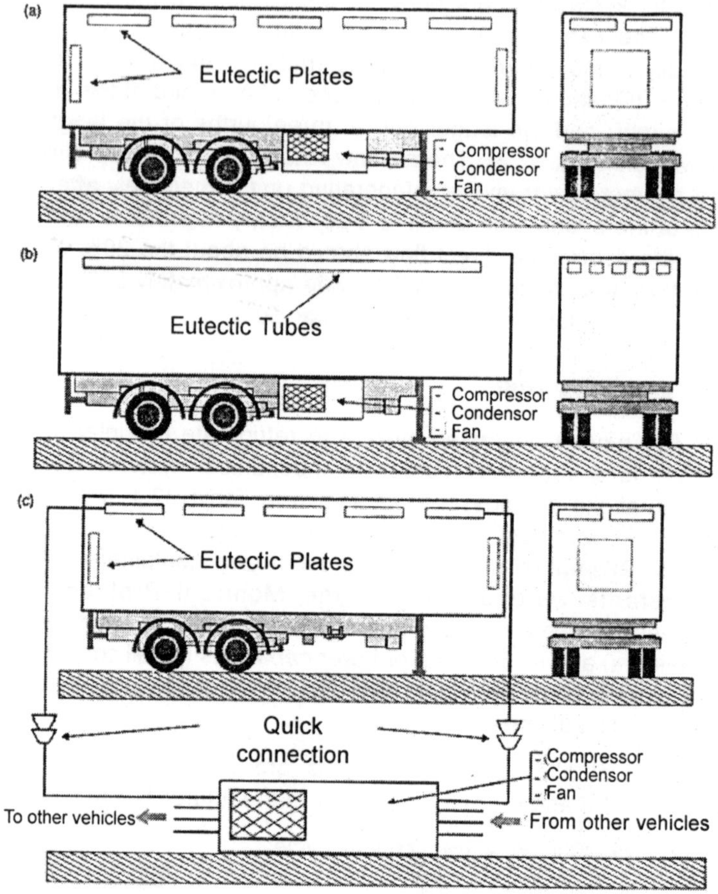

Fig. 32.4: Eutectic systems. (a) Layout of the plates. Normally the plates are placed under the roof. If a further plate is necessary, it can be placed in the rear or front wall, that are normally without doors (dotted plates). (b) Like (a), but with tubes in the place of the plates; (c) Eutectic plates whose compressor and condenser are not on board (like (a) and (b)) but separate. The separate refrigerating unit can feed more vehicles in the same time.

Normally these consist of a eutectic solution that changes phase at a low temperature. The solution is contained in a series of plates placed in the roof of the vehicle. Alternatively, the solution can be introduced in plastic tubes (Fig. 32.4). These systems have the following three advantages compared to direct expansion compression refrigeration cycles:

(a) no noise during food distribution (noise reduction is required by some regulations, mainly in the town centres);

(b) the ability to quickly restore the ambient temperature when the doors are opened for the charge or discharge of cargo;

(c) a high reliability: as the energy is stored in a passive system where mechanical breakdowns cannot prevent energy release.

In addition, these are also two peculiar problems:

(a) the higher weight and a lower stability of the vehicle, as the eutectic systems (plates or tubes are joined at the roof: the centre of gravity of the vehicle is shifted upwards);

(b) the limited operational time (when the whole solution has changed its phase, a stop is necessary to refreeze the solution).

The refreezing can be achieved by a vapour compression unit on board, that can work only when fed by mains electricity or can be a separate refrigeration system that can refreeze one or more vehicle in the same time. The vapour compression system can work with the standard refrigerants, or with newer refrigerants such as CO_2.

Multi-compartment vehicles

Multi-compartment vehicles can transport frozen and/or fresh products by operating more than one evaporator at different (or if needed the same) evaporating temperatures. The advantage of these vehicles is that the different compartments can be charged or discharged separately in such a way that the opened compartment does not influence the other compartments that remain closed (Fig. 32.5).

THERMAL LOADS

The thermal loads in a frozen food transport vehicle are caused by:

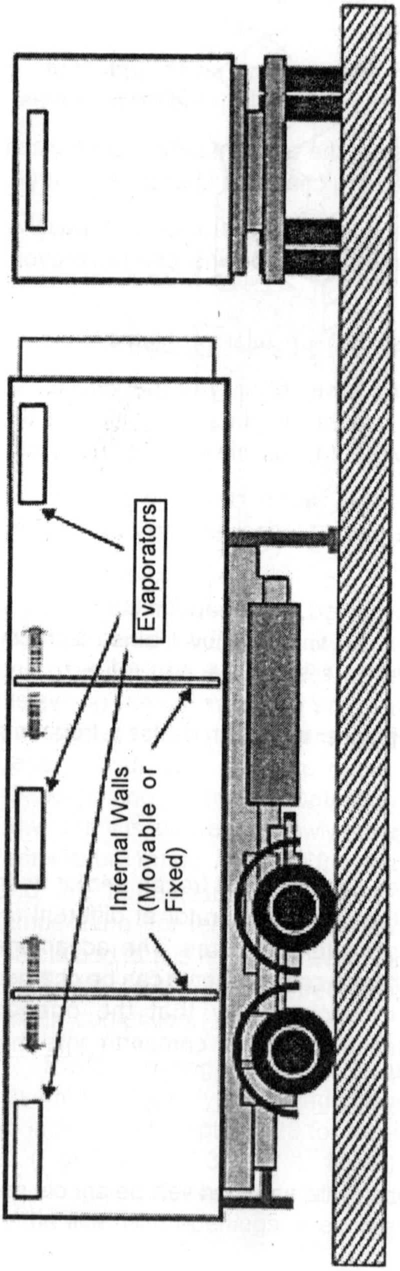

Fig. 32.5: Schema of a multi-temperature or multi-compartment vehicle.

(a) the temperature difference between the outside and inside of the vehicle. To compensate for this temperature difference, a low *K* value is required, that will in turn help the refrigerating unit maintain a stable energy consumption;

(b) the actual thermal load on a vehicle is very different from the thermal load used in the standard tests: not only the external temperature can be higher than +30°C used in the tests, but also solar radiation is not part of a standard test. The solar radiation can be direct or indirect (from surrounding walls and the ground). The influence of radiation is especially high when the vehicle is stopped and the external air velocity is low: when the vehicle is moving, the high surface heat transfer coefficient reduces the radiative effect on the vehicle;

(c) the air speed outside and inside the container can change the actual *K* value compared to the tested value, often increasing the value. The air speed during the standard tests is 1–2 m s^{-1}, while the external air speed on the road may be 20/30 ms^{-1};

(d) external warm air can enter the vehicle during operation due to differences in pressure between the inside and outside of the vehicle (this difference is due to the reduced pressure of the air at low temperature but more to the aerodynamic effects of the air all around the vehicle). An additional effect is the so-called 'pumping' of the lateral walls that are not absolutely rigid and inflect and deflect owing to the alternate eddies that are formed along the lateral walls during operation. This effect 'pumps' the cold air out and the warm air in (this effect is obviously greater in long vehicles)

(e) when the doors are opened, an exchange from external and internal air occurs, generating a supplementary infiltration heat load for the vehicle. This effect is more important for smaller vehicles that are dedicated to local delivery and is quite negligible for the longdistance transport vehicles that are normally closed at the beginning of the journey and only opened at arrival.

AGEING

Insulated containers

The importance of the *K* value has been highlighted previously. The change in the *K* value with time and 'ageing' of the insulation are important factors that cannot be underestimated. It is impossible to forecast the real ageing of a vehicle as the experimental data vary dramatically and only an average curve can be obtained to explain the basic physical phenomena of ageing An important factor affecting ageing is the average temperature of service of the vehicle and therefore, the aging in frozen food transport is the most severe. Another factor is the distance travelled per year by the vehicle. The physical phenomena of the ageing process are:

(a) migration of the air outside into the cells of the foam of the insulator material;

(b) migration of the blowing gas from the cells:

(c) condensation of water in the cells;

(d) damage to the cells that transform the closed cells in open cells

In the case of (a) and (b) probably only the first phenomenon is important in vehicles that are built by the sandwich technique: the second one is too slow to have any significant effect values of the experimental values per each year: these points are quite well fitted by the average curve.

Sandwich panels consist of strong skins (fibreglass-reinforced epoxidic resin or metal sheet) bonded to a core of insulating material (polyurethane foam, polystyrene foam). In the case of water condensation in the cells, Fig. 32.8 demonstrates that not only the thermal conductivity of the foam is affected by the condensation, but also the slope of the curve of the thermal conductivity versus the temperature (the phenomenon is correlated with the characteristic slope of the curve for the solid materials, in this specific case, the ice).

Refrigerating units

In practice, the performance of refrigerating units deteriorates over time and can be attributed primarily to a lack of maintenance of the units, a situation that is reversible. Only a small percentage of the deterioration is due to the real irreversible ageing of the units (Fig. 32.9). In all cases, if a good maintenance program is carried out, ageing of the refrigeration units would be just a fraction of the ageing of the insulation (Fig. 32.10)

COMPARISON BETWEEN FRESH AND FROZEN PRODUCT TRANSPORT

The main difference between fresh and frozen product is that the fresh product (fruits, vegetables, not completely ripened cheese) often has a metabolic charge (this charge is increasing with increasing temperature) while frozen foods have no supplementary charge. Consequently, a fresh cargo must be ventilated in such a way as to allow ventilation to every part of the cargo so that the temperature will not be increased in any position. On the contrary, a frozen cargo must be as compact as possible and air circulation is only required to the external surface of the compact cargo. The thermal inertia of the frozen cargo is large and therefore the ventilated air inside the vehicle only has to remove the heat transferred across the insulation from outside the vehicle.

Test standards require the temperature of transport vehicles to be not higher than –20°C. If the transport vehicle were to maintain the same conditions as many refrigerated stores, the transport temperature would be –25°C to –30°C. This situation implies that the *K* value should be lower than prescribed by the standards, and that, the loss of performance of the refrigerating unit at lower temperature must be considered (Fig. 32.11 shows a typical curve of the power and COP of a unit).

STANDARDS AND CLASSIFICATION

The most used standard is ISO 1492 'Thermal containers' that provides, together with data about the mechanical properties of the containers, thermal characteristics such as the *K* value of the container and its air leakage rate. The level of the air leakage rate is used to correct the *K* value. This standard is the basis for many certification and testing registers.

The ATP (Agreement on the international carriage of perishable foodstuff and on the special equipment to be used for such carriage) is an international agreement. The treaty has currently been signed by the following European countries: Albania, Austria, Belarus, Belgium, Bosnia and Herzegovina, Bulgaria, Croatia, Czech Republic, Denmark, Estonia, Finland, France, Georgia, Germany, Greece, Hungary, Ireland, Italy, Latvia, Lithuania, Luxembourg, Monaco, Montenegro, the Netherlands, Norway, Poland, Portugal, Romania, Russian Federation, Serbia, Slovakia, Slovenia, Spain, Sweden, the former Yugoslav Republic of Macedonia and the United Kingdom. The following non-European countries have also signed the ATP: Azerbaijan, Kazakhstan, Morocco, Tunisia, United States, Moldova and Uzbekistan. Switzerland signed the Agreement but has not ratified it. In Europe, Iceland, Malta, Cyprus and Ukraine have not signed the Agreement so far.

The text is deposited at the United Nations in NewYork and changes are discussed annually at an international conference in Geneva. Although ATP is mandatory only for the countries that have signed the Agreement, it is becoming a standard *de facto* and many national rules are derived from the basic text. The ATP prescribes steady state measurements of the *K* value and of the refrigerating power of the refrigerating units, and also particular procedures to maintain in service older vehicles.

After the approval in the EU in 1992, of two new directives, the main part of these directives was introduced into the ATP text. However, the philosophies of the ATP and of the EU directives are different; the ATP concentrates on physical characteristics of transport vehicles whereas the directives takes into consideration only the temperature of the food during transport and the systems used to measure them.

The ATP classifications for frozen foods are:

SYSTEMS OF TRANSPORT

A frozen cargo can be transported by road, rail, water or air. There can be specific systems or intermodal systems. In the first case we can have trucks,wagons, ships etc.; in the second case, we have different types of containers.

Road transport

The different types of trucks can be divided into (DIN 8959, 2000):

(a) short-distance delivery transport,

(b) medium-distance transport

(c) long-distance transport.

In case (a), this transport is characterised by short vehicles that are devoted to the transport from the last refrigerated store to the display cabinets in the supermarkets and food shops or directly to home. For many foods that are stored at low temperature, the eutectic plates system is often used. In case (b), medium-length vehicles are normally chosen (e.g. 6–8 m) and these vehicles transport foods from producer to store or from store to store. Mechanical compression refrigeration systems are mainly used in this type of transport. In case (c), the semi-trailer is the preferred vehicle and can carry up to 33 pallets. The possibility to overcome this limit does not seem realistic unless the maximum dimensions of the trucks are changed dramatically. The semi-trailer is a trailer without a front axle.Alarge proportion of its weight is supported by a road tractor. A semi-trailer is equipped with legs that can be lowered to support it when it is unhooked from the tractor. The maximum standard length for the insulated container is 13.60 m (together with the refrigeration unit).

This type of transport can act over long or medium distances and can often partially charge or discharge its cargo at stages during the journey. Often the journey is optimised from a logistic point of view by means of a communication system such as GSM or similar or a satellite communication system.

Rail transport

The main differences between road and rail transport are shown in Table 32.2. For rail transport the wagons are refrigerated by either mechanical or stored energy. Mechanical refrigeration for each single wagon is the predominant technology. In the past, systems that fed power to single refrigerating units in each wagon from a central wagon, used diesel as fuel. Another old system was based on iced water (stored in the two compartments at the extremities of the wagon).

It had several advantages:

(a) greater liability;

(b) lower maintenance;

(c) absolute interchangeability;

(d) the possibility to be fed by solid CO_2, becoming, without any change, a vehicle for frozen foods.

Water transport

A distinction is made between transport on internal waterways (rivers, channels, lakes) and the sea.

The most usual form of water transport is sea transport. In this case ships can be insulated and refrigerated (and was the case for the first refrigerated transport in the world) or can be container ships. A curious system is in use in Venice, where all the transport is carried out by water. The boats that carry frozen foods have an insulated (in some case also refrigerated) box that is built with the same technology as road vehicles. The box is not the usual parallelepiped shape (the roof is formed by two inclined planes) and the doors are in the roof.

Container ships can have two different layouts:

(a) self-refrigerated containers, each with its own refrigerating unit. In this case, the greatest problem is the space between each unit that must be sufficient to allow fresh air to be fed to each condenser, and in the lower decks the ventilation must be sufficient to remove the thermal energy released by the condensers;

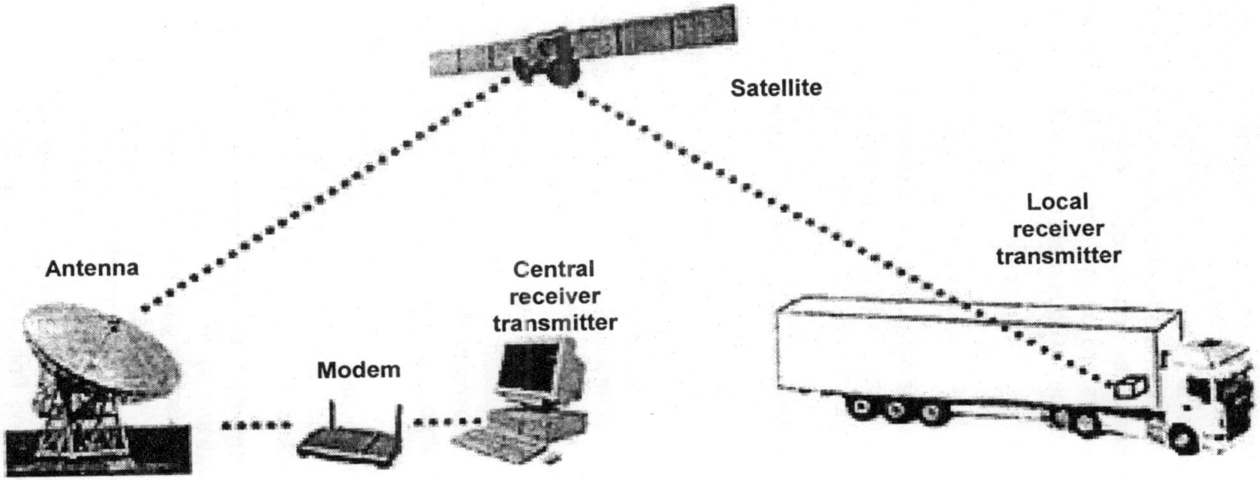

Fig. 32.6: Scheme of continuous contact between the vehicles and its headquarters by satellite. The system was devised as anti-theft device and was used for the information exchange in order to let the vehicle load and discharge the cargo partly, without coming back to the headquarter. In the future, the system could be used also for recording the data of the cargo (temperature, humidity,.....).

(b) insulated containers, specifically designed for ship transport. Each container has two circular holes in the upper and lower side of the front wall. These circular holes are connected with two flexible tubes that can supply cold air to the container and evacuate the exhaust air. Whilst the containers are on the docks, the containers can be attached to special equipment to achieve the same function.

Intermodal transport

Intermodal transport can be carried out using standard vehicles that can be carried on rail wagons (e.g. the piggyback system) or ships; however, these systems are heavy and not easy to use. However, most intermodal transport uses insulated boxes that can be transferred easily from ships to the rail wagons to road vehicles.

Case (a): the dimensions are standard for width and height (8) and the length is a multiple of 10 (to a maximum of 40). The thermal characteristic required by ISO 1942 is perfectly compatible with ATP. They can be attached to the frame of the vehicles by four corner fittings and can be stacked in a row of six containers.

Case (b): they are normally not parallelepiped as are adapted to the airplane shape. Insulation is poor (or absent) and the refrigeration can in some cases be solid CO_2. The main thermal problems concern the airport as during the flight the external temperature is very low.

Case (c): they are movable boxes that can be transferred from railways frames to road frames by mechanical forks or lifts, but they cannot be stacked.

Case (d): they are containers whose maximal dimension does not exceed 2 m, without any system for moving and blocking. They can be insulated but also refrigerated (mechanical systems, Peltier systems, and CO_2 systems). Roll containers are not standardised and there is some doubt that they can be considered ATP vehicles; a proposal to introduce the roll container into the ATP is under discussion. Their structure can be similar to that of road vehicles (assembling from sandwich panels) or can be made by a 'rotomoulding system'. The typical characteristic of this system is the construction of an external shell for the insulating foam by moulding polyethylene in big boxes that by rotating, can generate a cave shell in a monolithic system. The shell can be filled by polyurethane, expanded *in situ*, while the walls are contained in a rigid system to avoid deformations during the expansion.

Case (e): they are similar to the roll containers but cannot be defined as vehicles. The issue of where to put .the border between a real transport systems and simple packaging systems is subject of an ongoing debate. This problem impacts on the standard tests for these boxes. ATP standards can be used or specific standards such as EN 12571. The philosophies of the two standards are completely different. While ATP requires steady state measurements of the global heat transfer coefficient, EN 12571 requires only transient tests concerning the time that a certain quantity of a specific material can be maintained at a temperature higher (or lower) than a specific value. The main advantage of the use of mini containers is that the container can be filled directly in the cold store and opened directly at the end destination, without any break in the cold chain. The disadvantage is the high tare of the system and the necessity to return the empty containers to source.

The possibility to use containers with a *K* value greater than 0.4 W m^{-2} K^{-1} in a vehicle with a similar *K* value (the combined *K* value would be lower than 0.4 W m^{-2} K^{-1}) for the transport of the frozen foods is currently under discussion.

ENERGY LABELLING

The energy labelling system is widely used for domestic appliances and is mandatory in several countries, including the EU. Using as a basis an energy labelling scheme for refrigerated display cabinets, a labelling scheme for transport vehicles was studied and adopted. The basic value for the labelling was the *K* value with the results from the air-tightness test added. The basic philosophy was that no expensive measurement should be required. Only a very simple measure of the absorption coefficient of the external surface was proposed. All the other parameters

These containers can be sub-divided as shown in Table 32.3.

Table 32.3. Classification of the vehicles for the forzen foods transport, as prescribed by ATP

Type of container	Use	Standard (dimensions)	Standard (Thermal characteristics)
(a) ISO thermal containers	Road, rail, water	Yes (ISO 1942)	Yes (ISO 1492)
(b) IATA containers	Air, road	Yes (but adapted to each place)	No
(c) Swap bodies	Rail, road	Yes (UIC)	Yes (ATP)
(d) Roll containers	Road to road	No	Yes (ATP)
(e) Mini containers	Road to road	No	Yes (EN 12571)

were derived from geometrical considerations and from the presence or absence of some installations (e.g. bulk head, air ducts). The transport vehiclewas classified using two different and separate labels: one connected to the insulation and the other to the refrigerating unit.. The largest problem was the effect of ageing which could not be predicted: the energy consumption of a refrigerated vehicle is mostly dependent on the aged *K* coefficient, but this value cannot be forecast for a new vehicle, at least at the actual stage of the technology. This issue is currently being studied by a number of organisations and countries (German Government, Germanischer Lloyds, Transfrigoroute International, International Institute of Refrigeration).

LIMIT VALUES

Global heat transfer coefficients

The recommended *K* values for frozen and fresh foods are 0.4 and 0.7 W m^{-2} K^{-1}, respectively. Much discussion is on (especially regarding the *K* value for frozen foods) the difficulties in obtaining these *K* values using normal lateral wall thicknesses and the almost practical impossibility of maintaining these values after 6 years of service (the ATP prescribes the first check of in-service vehicles after 6 yr). Theoretically, these *K* values should be justified by some physical reason connected with the physical and biological changes during the transport of foodstuffs. However, the values appear to be based on the fact that historically pallets were not widely used and 100 mm of cork was the main form of insulation. Plotting the *K* values that are possible in these conditions we find the values are very close to the standard limits. Although *K* values are based on what was physically achievable with early vehicles rather than on any physiological changes in the food there are good reasons to maintain low *K* values. These include:

(a) the possibility of contact between frozen foods and walls;

(b) being able to maintain food temperature during any breakdowns or increased heat loads on the vehicle;

(c) reduced heat gain from ambient and consequently reduced refrigerating power and energy consumption.

Safety coefficient

The refrigeration unit safety coefficient is currently 1.75 (the refrigerating power must be higher than 1.75 *KST*), and 1.35 for an efficiency test. The value 1.35 was an empirical evaluation of the contribution to the thermal load on a vehicle due to solar radiation and by ageing of the insulation. No reason is reported for the value 1.75 . A larger value is sometimes requested in order to increase safety but can result in greater energy consumption.

THE FUTURE OF MATERIALS USED IN REFRIGERATED TRANSPORT

The Montreal Protocol and its successive modifications banned many of the insulation blowing agents used in the past. Many replacement blowing agents produce insulation with higher thermal conductivities and consequently *K* values have increased (Fig. 32.17). In the near future substances that have high global warming potential may be banned. Consequently, it is possible that only hydrocarbons, air, water, and CO_2 will be available as blowing agents for insulating panels in the future. This situation will probably lead to a further increase in the global heat transfer coefficient with all the problems. For a better understanding of this situation it is important to point out that the low thermal conductivity of expanded foam is caused mainly by the thermal conductivity of the blowing fluid in the gas phase. An empirical law states that the thermal conductivity of a gas is a function of its molecular weight. In these figures it is evident that there is no possibility of finding gases better than R11, at reasonable cost. Consequently, different insulation technologies should be explored. These include:

(a) vacuum insulation (some experiments have been carried out in the transport without appreciable success);

(b) aerogels (if the mechanical properties of these materials could be highly increased);

(c) reduction of the insulation cell dimensions (if the cell diameter in the insulating foam could be reduced by a factor of 100, the thermal conductivity of this hypothetical foam should be the same of a vacuum foam, and the blowing agent should have no importance, also ageing should be reduced for these materials)

Refrigeration system refrigerants

The refrigerants used in the refrigerating units of vehicles have also been affected by the Montreal Protocol but the replacement fluids have had little practical effect on the performances of the vehicles. CO_2 is already used in some vehicles and is forecast to be used more widely in the future. CO_2 has some important advantages:

(a) the dimensions of the heat exchangers and all the parts of the refrigerating unit can be reduced (the reduced volume is a very important factor in the transport technology);

(b) CO_2 is important in transport as it is a fire extinguisher;

(c) CO_2 is very cheap.

In addition, in the futurc particular attention will be paid to the performances of refrigeration units in warm climates where the COP of the units will change due to the hot ambient conditions. The global energy balance of a refrigerated vehicle should be rearranged in these more severe conditions, either from the point of view of the choice of the refrigerant or from that of the ratio between the refrigerating capacity and the heat gain through the insulation.

ALL FOLLOWING PROJECT REPORTS ARE READILY AVAILABLE

- Steel Furnitures And Electrical Appliances
- Steel Furniture And Fire Fighting Equipments
- Steel Furniture And Room Cooler
- Steel Wire Drawing And Galvanizing
- Steel Wire/Rod
- Steel Wool
- Ston Scrusher And Screening Plant
- Submerged Arc Welded Pipes
- Submersible Pump Manufacturing
- Super Enamelled Copper Wire
- Super Enamelled Copper Wire (From Copper Cathode Rod)
- Three Wheelers
- Tie-Rod Ends
- Tin Containers
- Toolroom And Sheet Metal Products
- Trolley (Shopping) For Carrying Of Stores At Super Market And Ware Houses
- Tractor Trailers
- Transmission Power Fitting
- Tubular Poles
- Tyre Retreading By Cold Process
- Super Enamelled Copper Wires
- Trolley (Shopping) For Carrying Of Stores At Super Market & Ware Houses
- Tmt Bars
- Tubular Poles For Electrical Transmission (By Fabrication Process)
- Tubular Poles Of M.S. & High Tensile Steel
- V- Belt
- Vacuum Cleaners
- Vacuum Flask (Stainless Steel)
- Valves For Refrigeration And Air-Condition
- Vehicle Welding & Painting
- Venetion Blind
- Washing Machines (Automatic & Computerised)
- Water Controller (Automatic)
- Watch Straps/Chains/ Bracelets/Belt Brass & Stainless Steel
- Water Coolers
- Welded Wire Mesh
- Welding Electrodes
- Wheel Barrow
- Wick Stoves
- Wind Mill Window Frame (Ferrous & Non-Ferrous)
- Wrist Watch

CHEMICALS (ORGANIC & INORGANIC) WITH PETROLEUM PRODUCTS

- Acetic Anhydride
- Acetic Acid (Glacial)
- Acetic Acid From Ethanol
- Acetone
- Acetylene Black
- Acetyl Chloride
- Acetylene Gas
- Acetylene Gas & Oxygen Gas (Integrated Unit)
- Acid Black Dye
- Acid Slurry
- Activated Alumina
- Activated Bleaching Earth (Activated Fullers Earth)
- Activated Carbon From Cashewnut Shell
- Activated Carbon From Rice Husk
- Activated Carbon From Rice Husk, Coconut Shell & Coconut Powder
- Activated Carbon From Wood
- Activated Carbon Powder & Granules From Coconut Shell
- Activated Carbon & Sodium Silicate From Paddy & Rice Husk
- Alcohol From Broken Rice
- Alum For Water Treatment
- Adhesive (Fevicol Type)
- Aerosol Insecticides Spray (Baygon, Hit, Mortein Type)
- Agarbatti Synthetic Perfumery Compounds
- Alcohol From Potato
- Alcohol From Rice Grains
- Alcohol From Rice Husk
- Alcohol From Molasses
- Alcohol, Beer, Starch, Liquid Glucose, Dextrose, Sorbitol, Vitamin-C,
- Alcoholic Beverages And Vinegar From Coconut Water
- Germ Oil, Cattle Feed Etc. From Maize
- Alkyd Resin
- Alkylated Phenol Likenonyl Phenol, Dodecyl Phenol
- Alum (Non Ferric)
- Alum (Ferric)
- Aluminium Chloride From Aluminium Ore
- Alum Cake
- Alum From Aluminium Hydrate
- Aluminium Ingot By Bauxite
- Aluminium Phosphide
- Aluminium Phosphate
- Aluminium Sulphate (Non Ferric Alum) 17% - 18% Alumina Content In Granules (2 Mm To 4 Mm) And Flakes
- Amines & Allied Products
- Amino Acid
- Ammonia Gas
- Ammonia Gas Bottling
- Ammonia Liquor
- Ammonium Nitrate
- Ammonium Chloride (Pure & Technical)
- Ammonium Sulphate
- Annato Seed Extraction And Processing
- Anti Corrosion Chemicals
- Anthranilic Acid From Phthalic Anhydride
- Anesthesia (All Types) Used In Hospitals
- Aniline
- Argon Gas
- Ariel Type Detergent Powder
- Anthraquinone
- Antimony Trioxide
- Atenolol
- Auramine "O"
- Azodicarbonamide
- Baking Soda From Ash
- Barium Carbonate
- Barium Compounds
- Barium Nitrate
- Barium Peroxide
- Barium-Thio-Sulphate Banzene
- Baryte Powder
- Bar Soap (All Varieties) Using Soap Noodles
- Beer Plant
- Belt Paste
- Beneficiation Of Chromite Ore Processing Charge Chrome
- Benzyl Acetate, Benzyl Benzoate, Benzyl Alcohol
- Beta Naphthol
- Bentonite Powder
- Benzoic Acid
- Benzidine
- Biofertiliser From Mother Culture
- Bio Oil For Power Generation From Coffee Husk
- Bio Gas Plant
- Bio Gas Filling In Cylinder
- Bio Tech Unit
- Bi-Chromate Of Sodium, Potassium & Ammonium
- Bi-Functional Black Mfgr.Reactive Dye (Dye From Cotton Yarn Dyeing)
- Bio-Fuel (Jatropha Cultivation And Extraction)
- Bituminous Roademulsion
- Black Phenyl
- Black Sulphur
- Bleaching Powder (Stable)
- Blue Detergent Powder
- Bone Crushing Plant
- Bone Meal (Calcined) Enrichment With Calcium & Phosphorus
- Boric Acid
- B.O.N. Acid
- Bromine Gas Plant
- Brandy
- Butanol
- Butyl Rubber For The Manufacture Of Tubes For Truck And Car Tyres
- 1,4, Butanediol
- Butyl Acetate
- Caffein From Tea Waste
- Calcined Lime (Dead Burnt Dolomite)

Market Survey Cum Detailed Techno Economic Feasibility Report on all Projects are available Contact.
"ENGINEERS INDIA RESEARCH INSTITUTE". 4449, Nai Sarak (D), Main Road, Delhi-110006 (India)
Ph. : 09811437895, 9811151047, 91-11-23918117, 23916431, 23947058, 64727385, 45120361
E-mail : eiriprojects@gmail.com, eiribooks@yahoo.com • website: www.eiri.in, www.eiriindia.org • www.eiribooksandprojectreports.com

VARIOUS PROJECT REPORTS IN CD-ROMS

100 NEW PLASTICS & ALLIED PROJECTS ₹ 25500/-

(Injection/blow moulding, acrylic, PVC/HDPE/PP/ABS/PET/BOPP/ based Project Reports)

LIST OF THE PROJECT REPORTS COVERED IN THIS CD

Acrylic sheet and moulded products, Audio cassettes parts by injection moulding, Audio cassette assembly & recording, Automobile injection moulded plastic components, ABS granules from abs scrap from (from old tv cabinets, White goods,etc., Air bubble packaging film, Ball pen manufacturing (automatic plant), bath tub (acrylic), Blow moulded plastic container, Blow moulding machine fabrication, B.O.P.P. film, B.O.P.P self adhesive tapes, Blister film P.V.C , Ball point pen, Refills & ink, Colour master batches for various plastics,Compact disk, dough moulding compound (dmc), Bulk moulding compound (bmc), Sheet moulding compound (smc), Disposable cups, Glasses etc., Disposable plastic syringes (sterilized), Discount/credit card, Electric switches, plugs, sockets, and other accessories, EVA (ethylene vinyl Acetate) sheet, Egg trays from plastics, EVA(ethylene vinyl acetate foot wear inject, Expanded cellular polyethylene sheet, fiber glass, Fibre glass sheets, FRP Products, H.D.P.E/P.P. Box strapings, HDPE/PP woven sacks (bags), HDPE fishing net, H.D.P.E. pipes , Helmet, H.D.P.E. and fitting pipes, Injection & blow moulded plastic products, Intravenous fluid plastic bottle, injection moulded plastic balls, Injection moulding for plactic componentc with tool room , lamination of co-extrusion multi layer film in roll form , lamination on hdpe woven clothes, Multi layer co-extrusion, 3 layer - film with lamination & printing, nylon granules from nylon waste, Nylon net for giving shade to tea plant in nursery, Pet bottles from pre-form (capsules), Pet granules (dana), Plastic injection moulding products, Plastic bangles by injection moulding, Plastic mat, Plastic moulded furniture, P.V.C. pipes and fittings, plastic films and sheets with printing (flexo and roto) ldpe/hdpe/pp/hm/pvc, Plastic collapsible tubes, Plastic granules, Plastic granules from fresh resin, Plastic (nylon) niwar, Plastic buttons by injection moulding methods, Plastic rope, Plastic corrugated sheet & boxes plastic tooth pick , P.V.C. films, poly-vinyl flooring pvc leather cloth, P.V.C. battery separator, polyurethane foam (p.u. foam), pvc foot wear, plastic tarpaulin, plastic milk crate and plastic fish crate, polythene bags, pouch making and gravure printing, Plasttic sutli or polypropylene sutli, Polymer pencil, plastic jerry cans, Pvc extrusion profiles (wiring channels), poly carbonate sheet, pvc/plastics (soft/rigid) films/sheet, polyster film, poly packs of polyethene film, P.V.C.flexible pipes, pvc resin from calcium carbide, pvc non-woven mat, plastic water storage tanks (hdpe) (sintex type), polymeric roofing felt, P.V.C. conduit pipes, polyster yarn from waste, Pet pre-form, pet bottles-cum-mineral water, pvc wires and cables, PVC cover & files (conference bags, folders, file covers, Diary covers etc.), polyester zip fasteners, Polypropylene & multifilament spinning yarn, plastic toys, plastic doors and windows, spoons (plastic), synthetic felt (plastic based) used in paper mill, Sport shoes (imported automatic plant) action, liberty etc. type, Thermocole based disposable glass, Cups & plates, Teflon - Coated - Electric cables, tooth brush, thermocole, unsaturated polyester resins 100. x-ray film.

6 AGARBATTI AND ALLIED PROJECTS # ₹ 15,000/-

Agarbatti, Agarbatti synthetic, Perfumery compounds (E.O.U.), Bamboo sticks for agarbatti, Mosquito coil agar batti (incense sticks), Mosquito coils and mats, Mosquito & flies repellant agarbatti (incense stick)

HAND BOOK OF PULP & PAPER, PAPER BOARD AND PAPER-BASED TECHNOLOGY

ISBN NO- 978-81-89765-09-5

₹ 1150/-

Pulpwood Technology, Alkaline Pulping Recovery units, Bleaching Chlorination Stage, Dyeing of Paper, Wet Strength in Paper and Paperboard, Paper Machine Forming Section, Paper Machine Press Sec., Paper Machine-Dryer Section, etc.

TECHNOLOGY OF HERBAL COSMETICS AND TOILETRIES PRODUCTS WITH FORMULAE

ISBN No. 978-81-89765-13-2

₹ 1100/-

The book Covers various Herbal Cosmetics, Skin Purification, Hair Conditioning, Regulatory provisions Relating to Manufacture of Cosmetics, Ultra Violet Protection Sunscreen Cream, Glow Pack (All Purpose Face Mask), Hair Oil with Vitamin-E, Lanolin & Protein, Herbal Cream (All Purpose), Jojoba Body Scrub, Face Wash, Liquid Bindi (Kum Kum) or Body Spot, Tooth Paste (Gel Type), Nail Polish Or Nail Enamel

HAND BOOK OF FLAVOURS & FOOD COLOURANTS TECHNOLOGY

ISBN NO- 978-81-89765-11-8 ₹ 1400/-

Flavours and Its Study, Changes in Food Flavour Due to Processing, Flavouring Materials Made by Processing, Production of Cocoa Powder, Imitation Meat Flavours, Cheese & Butter Flavours, Yogurt flavour, BioTechnology, Flavouring Materials etc.

PROFITABLE SOAPS & DETERGENTS PROJECTS IN CD

₹ 16000/- Or US$ 600/-

PROFITABLE COPPER & COPPER PROJECTS IN CD

₹ 20000/- Or US$ 600/-

PROFITABLE GINGER & GARLIC BASED PROJECTS IN CD

₹ 16000/- Or US$ 600/-

ENGINEERS INDIA RESEARCH INSTITUTE Mobile : 9811437895, 9811151047

4449, Nai Sarak, Main Road, Delhi - 110 006 (INDIA) Ph. 91-11- 23918117, 23916431, 23947058

BOOKS ON THINNER, PLASTIC FILMS, PLASTIC WASTE RECYCLING, ROTATIONAL MOULDING, MAIZE, INJECTION MOULDING, PLASTIC MATERIALS & POTATO

MANUFACTURING TECHNOLOGY & FORMULATIONS HAND BOOK ON THINNERS, PUTTY, WALL & INDUSTRIAL FINISHES AND SYNTHETIC RESINS

ISBN978-81-89765-32-3

₹ 900/- **Pages- 339**

The book covers Thinners, Inorganic Pigments, Titanium Dioxide Pigments, Organic Pigments, Extender Pigments, Putty, Glaxing, Compounds Caulking, Compounds and Sealants, Paint Driers, Paint Additives, Architectural Paints, Industrial Finishes etc.

ROTATIONAL MOULDING TECHNOLOGY HAND BOOK

ISBN- 978-81-89765-25-5

₹ 750/- Pages- 212

The book covers Innovative Rotomoulding, Technology of Rotational Moulding, Rotational Moulding Process, Roto moulding Technology Details, Materials that can be Roto moulded, Roto moulding Machines, Design Consideration for Roto mould Containers, Rotational Moulding Process Control, Rotational Moulding of Nylons, Moulds Fabrication for Roto moulding, Roto moulds for Cast Aluminium, Pin-holes and Bubbles in Roto moulded Products, Rotational Moulding of Liquid Polymers, Powdering Thermoplastic and Quality Consideration, Plastic Water Storage Tanks (HDPE), Sintex Type etc.

PLASTIC WASTE RECYCLING TECHNOLOGY

ISBN 978-81-89765-30-9

₹ 750 **Page No. 238**

The book covers Introduction, Details of Polymers, Types of Plastics, Identification of Plastics, Recycling of Plastic Waste, Recycling of Thermosets, Chemical Recycling, Recycling Commodities Plastics, Recovery of Chemicals from Plastic Waste, Factors Affecting Recycling Process, Automatic Scrap Recycling, Reclaiming Polyamide Spin Fibres, EPS-Recycling from Post-Consumer Expanded Polystyrene, New Patented Processes, Environmental Health and Future Prospects, Recycling Polyester Resins, Polyurethane Waste Recycling, Recycling and Government Policies, Identification of Plastics, Plastics and the Environment, Recycling An Industrial Approach etc.

INJECTION MOULDING OF PLASTICS

ISBN 978-81-89765-20-0

₹ 750/- Pages-319

The book covers Injection Moulding, Setting-up-Mould and Machine, Effect of Processing on Mechanical Properties, Mouldflow, Computer Controlled Automatic Injection Moulding Machine, Maintenance of Injection Moulding Machine, CAE and CAD Technology in Moulds Making, Injection Moulding process, Specialised Injection Moulding Process, Troubleshooting in Injection Moulding, Injection Moulding of Thermosets, Injection Moulding Machine, Design for Injection Moulds, Designing Moulds for Thermoset Processing, Injection Moulded Plastic Components, Plastic Moulded Toys, Plastic Injection Moulding Products, Plastic Injection Moulding Items etc.

HAND BOOK OF PLASTIC MATERIALS AND PROCESSING TECHNOLOGY

ISBN 978-81-89765-26-2

₹ 750/- Pages 231

The book covers Introduction of Plastic Materials, Polyethylene, Linear Low Density Polyethylene (LLDPE), Polypropylene, Copolymers of Ethylene, Polystyrene, Acrylic Plastics, Poly (Methyl Methacrylate), Acrylic Fibres, Poly (Vinyl Acetate), Poly (Vinyl Chloride), Polytetrafluoroethylene (PTFE), Coumarone-Indene Resins, Polyacetals and Polyethers (Acetal Resins), Polyamides, Polyimides, Polyesters, Polyurethanes, Polycarbonates, Epoxy Resins, Cellulose Plastics, Phenolic Resins, Amino Resins, Silicones, Additives for Plastics, Polybutylene Terephthalate, Polyethersulphone, Nylon, Polyvinylidene Fluride etc.

POTATO AND POTATO PROCESSING TECHNOLOGY

ISBN- 978-81-89765-29-3

₹ 750/- Pages-264

The book covers Introduction, Origin, Description of Plant and Flower Parts, Nutritive Value, Growth and Development, Agro-Techniques, Management of Water, Weed Management, Seed Production, Handling of Post Harvest Potato, Prospects for Potato Exports, Quality Parameters that influence Export Quality of Potatoes, Areas Suitable for Producing Seed Potatoes, Areas Suitable for Producing Processing Potatoes, Grading of Potatoes, Packing of Potatoes, Potato Storage, Quality Requirements, Potato processing, Dehydration of Vegetables, Potato Based Textured Snacks, Potato Chips/Wafers etc.

TECHNOLOGY OF PLASTIC FILMS

ISBN 978-81-89765-28-6

₹ 650/- Pages 165

The book covers Introduction, Theoritical Aspect of Die Design, Plastic Packaging Films, Oriented Packaging Films, Orientation Techniques, Technology of Commercial Shrink Films, Stretch Films and Laminates , Properties of Heat Shrinkable Films, Coextrusion, Different Types of Die, Detailed Drawings of 100 MM Mandrel Type Dies, Chilli Roll Casting of Film, Internal Cooling of Blow Films, Side Fed Co-Extrusion Film Dies, Materials of Construction for Dies, Temperature Control in Dies, Die Maintenance & Care, Production of Blow Films, Polythylene Film Manufacture and Control, Water cooled Polypropylene Film, Orientation of Film, L.L.D.P.E. Film Extrusion, Coextrusion Dies for Manufacturing Flat Films etc.

TECHNOLOGY OF MAIZE AND ALLIED CORN PRODUCTS

ISBN 978-81-89765-17-0

₹ 650/- Pages-258

The book covers Corn, Types of Corn, Botany of Corn, Cultivation Practices, Carbohydrates and Related Compounds, Quality Factors, Traditional Food Products from Corn, Corn Milling, Products and their Uses, Processing Ready-to- Eat Breakfast Cereals, Popcorn, Formulated Puffed Snacks, Manufacturing Corn Chips, Maize Products, Maize Starch, Sweet Corn, Baby Corn, Extruded Snacks, Corn Flakes, Liquid Glucose, Maize/Corn Oil, Malto Dextrin from Maize, Plant Economics of Non Roasted Corn Flakes (POHA), Starch from Maize, Snack Food, Yeast Dry Powder from Maize, Suppliers of Maize/Corn Processing Machineries, Present Manufacturers/Exporters/Suppliers of Maize and Maize Products.

ENGINEERS INDIA RESEARCH INSTITUTE Mobile : 9811437895, 9811151047
4449, Nai Sarak, Main Road, Delhi - 110 006 (INDIA) Ph. 91-11- 23918117, 23916431, 23947058

ALL FOLLOWING PROJECT REPORTS ARE READILY AVAILABLE

- Condenser For Motor Using Mpp Film
- Control Panel Board
- Cooling Coil For Air Conditioners
- Copper Strip Coil From Scrap
- Cordless Telephones
- Cyber Cafe
- Cyberkiosk
- Data Processing Centre
- D.C. Micro Motors
- D.G.Sets
- Display Systems (Led Type)
- Dish Antenna And Cable T.V. Network Equipment
- Distribution Transformers & Repairs
- Domestic Electrical Appliances-Room Cooler, Washing Machine, Water Heater, Electric Room Heater
- E-Commerce/Business
- Electric Energy Meter
- Electric Fans
- Electric Horn For Automobile
- Electric Lamp/Gls (Incandescent Lamp)
- Electric Mixer
- Electric Motors Up To 10 Hp. Rewinding Of All Types Of Motors Water Pumps
- Electric Motor Winding (For Fan, Mixies, Etc.)
- Electric Steam Iron
- Electrical Appliances
- Electrical Fixtures
- Electrical Stamping
- Electrolytic Capacitors
- Electromagnetic Relay
- Electronic Balast/Chok
- Electrical Choke
- Electronic Digital Watches
- Electronic Digital Weighing Machine
- Electronic Fire Alarm
- Electronic Gas Stove Lighters
- Electronic Phones, Dry Battery Packs And Chargers/Adapters
- Electronic Pressure Indicators, Electricals, Electronic Liquid Level Indicators, Electronic Temperature Indicator, Digital Tachometer
- Electronic Telephone Instruments
- Electronic Toys
- Electronic Watches & Clocks
- Fax Machines
- F.H.P Motors
- Floppy Diskettes
- Fluorescent Lamp Starter
- Fluorescent Tubular Lamps With Introduction To Mercury Vapour Lamp
- Franchisee Computer Education Centre (Rs. 10000)
- Gas Detector (L.P.G)
- Generator Set & Pump Sets
- Generator (Battery Operated)
- Gis Service Centre (Geographical Information Systems)
- Hardware Fitting For Transmission Line (Overhead Line Material
- Headers For Transistor Ics Semi Conductor
- H.T & L.T Insulators
- H.T & M.V Industrial Cubical Switch Board
- Information Moving Display (L.E.D Type)
- Insurance Claim Processing Centre (Eou) (Rs. 10000/-)
- Integrated Circuits
- Internet Based Stock Trading (Rs. 10000/-)
- Internet Service Provider (I.S.P.)
- Jelly Filled Telephone Cables
- Lap Top Computers
- Lead Acid Batteries
- Lead Acid Battery Plates And Assembling Of Battery
- Legal Transcription & Secretarial Services Center (Eou)(Rs. 15000/-)
- Light Emitting Diodes (L.E.D)
- Linear Ics Trainer Kit
- Loud Speaker
- L.T Transformer Repairing
- Medical Transcription Centre
- Metal Film Resistors
- Metallised Polypropylene, Polyester Film Capacitor
- Mica Base Electronic Components
- Mica Paper Waste Paper From Mica Waste
- Micro Processors Trainer Kits Based On Micro Processors
- Mini Computer (Personal Computer)
- Miniature Circuit Breaker (M.C.B)
- Miniature Watch Batteries (Button Cell)
- Mixer/Grinder (Mixi)
- Mono Chrome Computer Monitor
- Motor Start Electrolytic Capacitor
- Multi Layer P.C.B
- Multiple Relay For Low Voltage
- Neon Indicator
- Neon Sign Manufacture
- Optical Fibre Cables
- On Line Shopping Mall (Rs. 10000/-)
- Opto Mechanical & Electrical Equipments
- Photo Colour Lab
- Picture Tube (B/W)
- Plain Paper Copier
- Plastic Film Capacitors
- Polyester Capacitors
- Portable Generator Set
- Portal
- Portable Television(Tv)
- Power Capacitors

- Power Inverters
- Power Plant (Gas Based)
- Power Plant (Hydro Based)
- Power Transformers Up To 600 Kva
- Printed Circuit Board
- Pvc Wires & Cables
- Pvc Pipe And Fitting
- Re-Conditioning Of Picture Tube
- Resin Cast Ct & Pt (1 Kv)
- Semi Conductor Device
- Semi Conductors For Transistors & Diodes
- Setting Up Of A Video Studio
- Smoke Detectors
- Solar Cells
- Solar Modules
- Solar Power Plant (Energy)
- Solar Photo Voltaic System
- Solder Fluxes
- Solar Water Heating Panels
- Steel Furniture & Electrical Appliances
- Stereo Amplifiers
- Stereo Cassette Recorders/Players
- Street Light Fittings Surge Suppressor
- Tantalum Capacitors
- Teflon Coated Electric Cable
- Telemedicine (Distance Health Care) (Rs. 10000/-)
- Telephone Cord/Cable
- Telephone (Push Button Type)
- Telephone (Push Button & Cordless)
- Television (Ctv & B/W)
- Television (3-D)
- Television Deflection Components
- Television Signal Boosters
- Television Tuners
- Traction Batteries
- Training Institute Of Medical Transcription
- Transformer For B/W Tv
- Transformer For Voltage Stabilizer & E.H.T
- Transmission Power Line Fitting
- Transmission Tower Fitting
- T.V. News Channel
- Tv Audio Equipment Cabinets & Their Assembling Unit
- Un-Interrupted Power Supply (U.P.S)
- Variable Frequency
- Variable Voltage A.C. Drive
- Video Cassettes (Complete Manufacturing & Assembling)
- Video Cassettes Recorder (V.C.R)
- Video Film Studio
- Voltage Regulator For Automobiles
- Voltage Stabilizers
- Voltage Stablizer & T.V. Gain Booster
- Wax And Chemical Coated, Braided Tinsel Wire
- Website Design & E-Mail Registering
- Welding Electrodes
- Wind Energy Power Project (10 Mw)
- Wire Wound Potentiometers
- Wire Wound Resistance

Market Survey Cum Detailed Techno Economic Feasibility Report on all Projects are available Contact.
"ENGINEERS INDIA RESEARCH INSTITUTE". 4449, Nai Sarak (D), Main Road, Delhi-110006 (India)
Ph. : 09811437895, 9811151047, 91-11-23918117, 23916431, 23947058, 64727385, 45120361
E-mail : eiriprojects@gmail.com, eiribooks@yahoo.com • website: www.eiri.in, www.eiriindia.org • www.eiribooksandprojectreports.com